Race
and the Politics of
Welfare Reform

Race

AND THE POLITICS OF

Welfare Reform

Edited by
Sanford F. Schram, Joe Soss,
and *Richard C. Fording*

THE UNIVERSITY OF MICHIGAN PRESS
Ann Arbor

2006   2005   2004   2003   4   3   2   1

A CIP catalog record for this book is available from the British Library.

Library of Congress Cataloging-in-Publication Data

Race and the politics of welfare reform : edited by Sanford F. Schram,
    Joe Soss, and Richard C. Fording.
      p.   cm.
    Includes bibliographical references and index.
    ISBN 0-472-09831-4 (Cloth : alk. paper) — ISBN 0-472-06831-8
(Paper : alk. paper)
    1. Public welfare—United States.   2. Welfare recipients—
Government policy—United States.   3. Social service and race
relations—United States.   4. Racism—United States.   I. Schram,
Sanford F.   II. Soss, Joe, 1967–   III. Fording, Richard C., 1964–

HV95 .R33   2003
361.6'8'0973—dc21   2002015 8189

Acknowledgments

This volume involved the good efforts of many people—contributors, editors, publishers, reviewers, others. The editors thank each other for making this project such a congenial one. We also thank the contributors for submitting their chapters in a timely way and for dedicating themselves to producing quality scholarship. Thanks also go to Wesley Bryant for his excellent assistance during the final stages of editing. Thanks as well to Jeremy Shine at the University of Michigan Press for shepherding this book to completion. And lastly, thanks to our families for supporting our efforts on this project.

Chapter 4 in this volume by Martin Gilens builds on his book *Why Americans Hate Welfare: Race, Media, and the Politics of Antipoverty Policy* (Chicago: University of Chicago Press, 1999).

Chapter 7 is based on research supported by a grant from the Center for American Women and Politics (CAWP), New Brunswick, N.J., and appeared as a CAWP report.

Chapter 8 is a shortened and revised version of chapter 6 from Sanford F. Schram, *Praxis for the Poor: Piven and Cloward and the Future of Social Science in Social Welfare* (New York: New York University Press, 2002).

Chapter 9 includes revised material from Joe Soss, Sanford F. Schram, Thomas P. Vartanian, and Erin O'Brien, "Setting the Terms of Relief: Explaining State Policy Choices in the Devolution Revolution," *American Journal of Political Science* 45 (April 2001): 378–95.

Chapter 10 is a revised and expanded version of Susan T. Gooden, "All Things Not Being Equal: Difference in Caseworker Support toward Black and White Welfare Clients," *Harvard Journal of African American Public Policy* 4 (1999): 23–33.

Contents

Introduction

JOE SOSS, SANFORD F. SCHRAM, AND
RICHARD C. FORDING

Imagine what it would take for welfare politics in the United States to be unaffected by race. The social problems addressed by the welfare system—poverty, health, life skills, and the like—would need to be equally distributed across racial groups. The composition of welfare recipients, both in fact and in the public mind, would have to reflect the population as a whole. The term *welfare* itself would be stripped of racial connotations, and mass media and public officials would have to find ways to discuss the poor without an invidious racial subtext. To be unaffected by race, the political present would need to be shaken free of its past, so that the welfare system's legacy of racial bias would not limit the possibilities or define the problems for contemporary political action. The formation of political coalitions would need to be liberated from the divisive effects of racial prejudice and residential segregation. Political representation, policy implementation, and the power to influence them would all have to be made innocent of color.

The farther one takes this thought experiment, the clearer it becomes that welfare politics in the United States remains entwined with race. It also grows harder to imagine how people in this country could discuss welfare without taking race into account. Yet today, in a remarkable number of political venues, this is precisely what happens. Like the proverbial pink elephant at a cocktail party (the one that no guest will be first to mention), the "problem of the color line" is usually a subject of delicate avoidance when the conversation turns to poverty.[1] Some political elites and policy experts do pay close attention to the ways poverty-related outcomes vary across racial categories. But even in this company, the discourse tends to stay within a narrow range; race is usually treated as a self-evident basis for classifying people and social outcomes. Rather than delving more deeply into the construction or consequences of racial categories, a wide array of actors in welfare politics find it useful to assert that race has limited relevance. Conservatives dismiss the idea that durable racial disadvantages explain patterns of welfare usage. Liberals are equally quick to reject images of welfare as a program directed primarily at people of color. Few public voices suggest that racial subordination (past and present) plays a fundamental role in the ways Americans understand and practice welfare provision.

This book is about race in the United States and its distinctive effects on contemporary welfare politics. Over the past three decades, despite the lack of public attention to this issue, an impressive body of scholarship has grown up around the subject of race and welfare provision. Racial dynamics, in one form or another, played a key analytic role in a number of the classic works on welfare published between the 1960s and 1980s, such as Winifred Bell's *Aid to Families with Dependent Children* (1965), Frances Fox Piven and Richard Cloward's *Regulating the Poor* (1971), and Michael Katz's *The Undeserving Poor* (1989). More recently, scholars have focused direct attention on the racial dimensions of welfare politics in a series of landmark books, including Jill Quadagno's *The Color of Welfare* (1994), Robert Lieberman's *Shifting the Color Line* (1998), Michael Brown's *Race, Money, and the American Welfare State* (1999), Martin Gilens's *Why Americans Hate Welfare* (1999), and Kenneth Neubeck and Noel Cazenave's *Welfare Racism* (2001).

Through these works, as well as a large number of important publications in scholarly journals, evidence and explanation have become more sophisticated, and the interplay of race and poverty politics has come into sharper focus. To assemble the relevant literature, however, one must fish in separate disciplinary streams. Some questions have become specialized topics for historians; political theorists claim others. Much of the empirical research emphasizes field-specific debates about the dynamics of public opinion, policy implementation, or some other dimension of political life. This division of labor offers some advantages, but it also discourages an integrated understanding of how race has shaped the past and present of U.S. social policy. A major goal of the present volume is to counter this tendency toward balkanization. By bringing together diverse scholars with overlapping substantive concerns, we hope to encourage a richer dialogue centered on the role of race in U.S. welfare politics.

The need for such a dialogue, however pressing it may be for scholars, is more urgent for the public at large. During the past three decades, as the various streams of scholarship on race and welfare have flourished, public discussion of this issue has waned. Where in welfare politics today does one find candid talk of race and its impact on social policy? Who speaks openly of racial equality and justice? The contributors to this volume differ in their fields of interest, research methods, and theoretical orientations. But their work converges on a basic message for citizens and public officials: race matters for U.S. social policy. We hope readers will come away from this book recognizing what is lost when discussions of welfare proceed as if race were irrelevant. Whether the venue is Congress or a casual conversation, race should have a place in our deliberations about how the welfare system works, what it does, and what it might become in the future.

Our purpose in this volume, however, is not simply to make a case for race. The assertion that "race matters" in welfare politics is only helpful to the extent that it leads to more searching questions. Which aspects of race matter? How and for whom do they matter? In which arenas and under what conditions? Such questions lie at the heart of explanatory political analysis. They are also a prerequisite for the constructive political action needed to achieve a racially just welfare state. The contributors to this volume aim to illuminate the structural conditions, social processes, and causal mechanisms that account for the significance of race in welfare politics. Their work addresses the political contingencies that determine the scope, magnitude, and form of racial effects in a given place and time.

How, then, does race fit into the contemporary politics of welfare provision? Surely it does not matter now in the same ways it did in the first half of the twentieth century. People of color in the United States have gained political and civil rights (Klinkner and Smith 1999), and significant numbers now enjoy middle-class status (Hochschild 1995). The racial and ethnic composition of the population has become far more diverse, as Hispanic, Asian, and other groups have grown in number (Cohn and Fears 2001). Rather than being shut out of public assistance programs, people of color now make up a majority of public aid recipients (Schram, this volume). The white population now overwhelmingly opposes de jure discrimination (Schuman et al. 1997). The black population is now less concentrated in the South but more concentrated by residential segregation (Massey and Denton 1993). The U.S. population has diversified in ways that make racial and ethnic politics less and less of a "black and white" matter (Wu 2001; Suro 1999). The list could go on, but the key point should be clear. Race may be an enduring "American dilemma," but its role in welfare politics changes over time. The chapters that make up this volume are, each in their own way, designed to advance a historically specific understanding of welfare politics in the United States—a map of its racial dimensions in our time.

Our desire to present explanatory research that has practical relevance for welfare politics today reflects the dramatic changes that recently have taken place in U.S. social policy. In 1996, President Bill Clinton signed the Personal Responsibility and Work Opportunity Reconciliation Act (PRWORA), passed by the 104th Congress. The new law abolished the 61-year-old entitlement program, Aid to Families with Dependent Children (AFDC), that was the primary source of cash assistance for poor women with children. In its place, the 1996 legislation created a program organized around block grants to state governments, Temporary Assistance for Needy Families (TANF). Under the new system, states have gained more discretion over program rules; poor families have confronted new time limits on the receipt of aid, rules and benefits designed to promote work, tougher requirements for program participation, and penalties for noncompliance.

The new system, in conjunction with a strong economy and other changes in public policy, produced a stunning decline in the national welfare caseload. The number of welfare recipients in the U.S. fell from 12.2 million in August 1996 to 5.8 million in June 2000. Evaluations of the reforms appeared in droves, offering a diversity of claims regarding their effects on poor, single women and their children. But even as the 1996 legislation came up for evaluation and reauthorization in 2002, the racial dimensions of reform continued to be ignored by policymakers. What role did race play in the public deliberations and expressions of public support that gave rise to welfare reform? How has race influenced the ways state policymakers and local administrators have used their newfound discretion? How have different racial groups fared under welfare devolution and the new policies it has engendered? By addressing these and other questions, the essays in this volume challenge us to rethink contemporary welfare politics and provide resources needed to understand the role of race in welfare reform.

To provide an overview of the book as a whole, the remainder of this chapter offers a preliminary sketch of the ways race and welfare policy come together in specific arenas of the political process. At the outset, however, two points about the focus of this volume merit some elaboration. First, we emphasize race in this book because we place it among the most crucial forces in U.S. welfare politics, not because we consider it to be "more important" than gender, class, or other aspects of social stratification. Pitting these categories against one another as alternatives is far less productive than identifying the contributions of each and the distinctive characteristics of their intersection in a given place and time. Second, although this book is nominally about race (broadly defined), most of the chapters focus on European and African Americans; other racialized groups receive only intermittent attention. This emphasis is not accidental. It is partly a reflection of the current state of scholarship; it is equally a response to the unique significance that black-white relations and the cultural categories of black and white have had for the development of the U.S. welfare system. Race in the United States is rapidly changing in ways that force scholars to rethink the prevailing emphasis on dichotomous "black and white" analysis. As the scholarship in this volume demonstrates, however, African Americans continue to hold a distinctively prominent and disadvantaged position in U.S. poverty politics.

Historical Process and Institutional Development

"The instinctive attitude of a great many," Marc Bloch (1953, 38) once wrote, is to experience the present as if it stood outside the flow of history—to "consider the epoch in which we live as separated from its predecessors by contrasts so clear as to be self-explanatory." Today, such an "instinctive attitude" toward history remains a stumbling block to understanding the politics of welfare reform. Many efforts to explain the present make only passing reference to earlier sequences of events. In some cases, the past is used simply to "sketch in the historical background" before turning to a snapshot analysis of contemporary reform. Little effort is made to confront the legacies of racial subordination in the United States or the ways in which race has shaped institutional development in this country. In other cases, analysts briefly address racial aspects of U.S. history but do so only to contrast the present era with earlier periods of racial prejudice and discrimination. In these linear accounts of racial progress, one finds the mirror image of sweeping claims that U.S. welfare provision has been unremittingly racist. The past is treated only as a point of contrast, not as a source of contemporary politics; the present is identified as an era in which race matters "less," not an era in which race matters in new ways. As Theda Skocpol (1995a, 129) has argued, such all-or-nothing accounts of race and U.S. social policy cannot help but distort the historical record and its implications for contemporary politics.

> African Americans have not invariably been excluded from U.S. public social benefits, nor have they always been stigmatized when they did receive them. The overall dynamic since the Civil War has not been a linear evolution, moving from the exclusion or stigmatization of African Americans toward their (however partial) inclusion and honorable acceptance within mainstream U.S. politics and policies. There have been more ups and downs, more ironies and reversals, in the history of African American relationships to U.S. social policies across major historical eras.

In each period of reformation in U.S. welfare history, the relationship between race and social provision has taken on complex and distinctive forms. When Civil War pensions were created in the late nineteenth century (an era of overt white supremacy in most U.S. institutions), over 180,000 black Union veterans received the same eligibility for federal benefits as their white counterparts (Skocpol 1992, 138). By contrast, the state-run mothers' pensions that developed in the early twentieth century generally excluded women of color, a pattern that emerged from the discriminatory use of local discretion and also functioned to reinforce the prestige of the program as aid for "good mothers" (Bell 1965; Gooden, this volume). The Social Security Act of 1935 established a broad national system of provision, but its passage hinged on support from southern representatives of white cotton interests. The result was a bifurcated system that, by excluding domestic and agricultural workers from social insurance coverage, effectively denied African Americans access to the more generous channel of federally controlled resources (Lieberman 1998; Brown 1999). By the next great era of reform, the 1960s, race had taken on a new but no less central role in the political process. Northern migration nationalized race relations as a political issue; the civil rights movement and urban unrest brought these relations to a higher place in the public consciousness. Great Society efforts found much of their inspiration and ultimately some of their political frustration in the demands people of color were making for full inclusion as rights-bearing, democratic citizens (Piven and Cloward 1993; Quadagno 1994).

Close inspection of these historical twists and turns is an essential step in the process of understanding how race and welfare reform relate in our present era. This is so for two reasons. First, historical comparisons make it possible to bring the particular features of our current situation into dialogue with more general theoretical accounts. They help us see what is distinctive, and what is not, about race in contemporary welfare politics. They direct our attention to processes and locales that may seem obscure to current observers but nevertheless have racial consequences. They suggest which types of developments one should expect to enhance or diminish racial distortion.

Second, beyond the merits of comparative analysis, the relevance of historical analysis derives from the fact that political events can never be wholly separated as discrete cases. The sequence of events matters in political life (Pierson 2000). Policy outcomes in one era can generate political contradictions that must be resolved in the next (Quadagno 1994). They can influence which political conflicts emerge and which political arenas serve as their eventual site of resolution (Skocpol 1992). They can shape popular understandings of social problems, perceptions of social groups, and orientations toward political demand making (Schneider and Ingram 1997). Some political choices create "path dependencies," self-reinforcing dynamics in which once-imaginable alternatives come to be seen as too costly, obscure, or inconsistent with current practice to merit serious consideration (Pierson 2000). Other political choices generate negative feedback: cultural backlash, countermovements, or a conventional belief that we must avoid repeating some "mistake" of an earlier period. For these and other reasons, efforts to understand contemporary welfare politics must seek out and illuminate the presence of the past.

Accordingly, the first section of this volume focuses on historical processes and patterns of institutional development in U.S. welfare politics, giving special attention to their racial origins and implications. In chapter 1, Robert Lieberman presents a cross-national analysis of how racial divisions have contributed to welfare state development in the United States, Great Britain, and France. His chapter not only highlights how racial politics has shaped the structure of the U.S. welfare system; it also clarifies the mechanisms that account for such racial effects. Specifically, Lieberman directs our attention to the ways different racial formations may encourage or impede the development of pro-welfare political coalitions. His analysis elucidates the distinctive features of race in U.S. politics as well as the racialized nature of institutional arrangements that remain at the heart of recent struggles over welfare reform.

In chapter 2, Michael Brown offers a historical perspective on race and its intersection with federalism and localism in the U.S. political system. His analysis illuminates the historical and racial roots of policy devolution, a defining feature of the block grant system that structures the TANF program. Equally important, Brown uses historical and contemporary examples to demonstrate the profound fiscal constraints and racial distortions that can emerge when control over social policy is decentralized. The focus of this chapter is fiscal federalism, but Brown uses this concept as the starting point for a broad analysis of race as a dimension of culture and political economy in the current era of reform.

In chapter 3, Richard Fording illuminates the recent historical context of welfare reform by examining the policy choices states made under AFDC waivers during the five years that led up to federal action in 1996. Fording's analysis demonstrates that the historical legacy of race and welfare continued to be evident in the ways states undertook welfare experimentation in the 1990s. Three findings stand out. First, Fording shows that the racial composition of a state is strongly related to ways white people stereotype African Americans and estimate the black share of the poverty population—two key predictors of individual-level support for welfare. Second, state policy choices during the AFDC waiver period were significantly related to the racial composition of welfare rolls. Third, state policy choices also depended significantly on the racial composition of political representatives in government. This last point bears particular attention. Fording's analysis underscores that African Americans are not just passive actors in welfare politics, limited to the role of targets for the actions of white actors. African American agency is, in its own right, also an important factor affecting welfare policy. When African Americans are better represented in government, welfare policies are more likely to respond to the needs of welfare recipients (who are disproportionately black).

Taken together, the chapters by Lieberman, Brown, and Fording invite us to construct a more precise, historically grounded understanding of race and welfare politics in our time. They underscore how historically racialized patterns of exclusion and agency remain an important part of the context for understanding welfare policy today.

Mass Media and Public Opinion

The second section of this book turns our attention more directly to the ways race and welfare come together in mass communication and public sentiment. Popular images and attitudes play a variety of roles in welfare politics. Aggregate public opinion may rarely be decisive in the policy process (Noble 1997), but it almost always plays a contributing role in the process that shapes policy outcomes in the United States (Sharp 1999; Stimson, Mackuen, and Erikson 1995; Wright, Erikson, and McIver 1987). In addition to its direct impact on representatives who must anticipate electoral accountability (Arnold 1990), majority opinion also provides elite advocates with a crucial political resource—the presumption that democratic governments should "give the people what they want" (see, e.g., Mead 1992). Moreover, the importance of media portrayals and mass attitudes extends beyond the governmental components of welfare politics. Negative images of welfare have the power to stigmatize and to deprive groups of full and equal status in the citizenry. They can operate as mechanisms of informal social control, deter demands on public programs, and divide the poor against one another (Piven and Cloward 1993; Schneider and Ingram 1997).

The past decade has produced a growing body of research showing racial distortions in the ways media stories portray poverty and welfare issues (Williams 1995; Gilens 1999; Clawson and Trice 2000). Between 1967 and 1992, black people accounted for an average of 57 percent of the people pictured in major newsmagazine poverty stories—a figure that was about twice the true proportion of black people among the nation's poor during this time (Gilens 1999, 114). In addition, pictures of white people were significantly more likely to accompany positive stories; pictures of African Americans predominated in periods of hostility toward welfare, in stories that took a more negative view of the poor, and in stories that focused on more stigmatized subgroups of the poor (Gilens 1999). As Clawson and Trice (2000) have shown, these particular patterns of distortion in media coverage continued throughout the most recent period of welfare reform. From 1993 to 1998, media images of the poor continued to emphasize black people; welfare recipients tended to be portrayed as undeserving; and black faces predominated in poverty stories that adopted a negative tone or emphasized unsympathetic traits.

In this context, it is hardly surprising that public responses to poverty and welfare exhibit strong racial patterns. African Americans are far more likely than their white counterparts to favor generous social programs (Shapiro and Young 1989; Kinder and Winter 2001). White Americans tend to substantially overestimate the black percentage of the poor and, partly as a result, view the plight of the poor through the lens of antiblack stereotypes (Gilens 1999). Among white Americans, black people are more likely to be seen as lazy (Gilens 1999); if poor, they are more likely than whites to be judged personally responsible for their poverty (Iyengar 1990) and less likely to be seen as deserving public assistance (Peffley, Hurwitz, and Sniderman 1997; Gilens 1995, 1996a). The impact of racial attitudes on white support for welfare tends to vary depending on the nature of immediate racial cues (Peffley, Hurwitz, and Sniderman 1997). But in the main, the evidence suggests that antiblack stereotypes enhance the likelihood that white Americans will view welfare recipients as undeserving, withdraw support from welfare spending, and prefer get-tough approaches to benefit provision (Gilens 1999).

Among public opinion researchers, there continue to be heated debates about the nature of white racial attitudes and their impact on policy preferences (Sears, Sidanius, and Bobo 2000). Most agree that "old-fashioned" racism, with its overt endorsement of biological hierarchy and legal segregation, has declined substantially since the 1940s (Schuman et al. 1997; Sniderman and Piazza 1993; Page and Shapiro 1992). The controversy focuses on what kinds of policy-relevant attitudes have replaced the old racism. One influential thesis argues that a new, less overt form of "symbolic racism" or "racial resentment" has emerged among white Americans—a blend of socialized antipathy toward blacks; perceptions that black people violate cherished values related to work, self-restraint, and respect for authority; and resentment toward black people for allegedly receiving special government treatment they do not deserve (Sears 1998; Sears et al. 1997; Kinder and Sanders 1996). A second group of scholars has offered a more structural theory of "laissez-faire racism" emphasizing group position and racialized competition over status, power, and resources (Bobo, Kleugel, and Smith 1997). A third group treats racial subordination as the product of a more general tendency toward "social dominance" in public attitudes and group relations (Sidanius and Pratto 1999). A fourth group, which has been sharply critical of the symbolic racism thesis (Sniderman and Tetlock 1986), now attributes a relatively small role to race per se, emphasizing instead the varying ways in which political principles get applied to race-related policy agendas (Sniderman and Piazza 1993).

The differences among these schools are complex and, in some respects, probably cannot be settled on the basis of survey or experimental evidence (Hochschild 2000). Regardless, our purpose in this book is not to resolve such broad theoretical disputes, or even to ask how research on race and welfare opinion might illuminate them. Our theoretical interests lie more directly with the question of how mass media and public opinion fit into the collection of forces that link race and welfare politics in the United States. With this in mind, the second section of our book offers perspectives from leading public opinion scholars on mass media, mass attitudes, and the racial dimensions of welfare politics.

In chapter 4, Martin Gilens examines media responses to the social and political events of the 1960s in an effort to explain how the American public came to view poverty and welfare as racial issues. In his previous work, Gilens (1999) has suggested that the racial basis of poverty reporting shifted dramatically in the 1960s and that an increased media emphasis on African Americans went hand in hand with declining mass support for welfare over the ensuing decades. Here, he returns to the tumultuous years of the 1960s to show how a potent tie between race and poverty was forged against a backdrop of black northern migration, increased welfare participation, a civil rights movement demanding economic equality, and the turbulence of urban unrest. Examining 40 years of news coverage, he helps us understand "how the poor became black" and "welfare" became a target of public animosity.

In chapter 5, James Avery and Mark Peffley add greater precision to our understanding of how racial patterns in news reporting can influence public assessments of welfare. Employing an experimental approach, they demonstrate that the race of a pictured recipient is an important factor affecting the ways individuals' interpret stories on welfare reform. Specifically, they find that when news stories present images of black recipients, they are more likely to be interpreted in a negative manner. Building on Gilens's chapter, which describes the parallel growth of racialized news coverage and public hostility toward welfare, this chapter provides more direct evidence of a connection between media imagery and public evaluations.

In chapter 6, Martin Johnson adds significant evidence regarding the impact of white racial attitudes on welfare policy outcomes in the states. Using opinion data drawn from the National Opinion Research Council's General Social Survey (1974–98), Johnson examines how white perceptions of African Americans have related to patterns of state benefit provision over time. Unlike past studies, which have focused on a single level of analysis, Johnson's work shows that individual-level attitudes aggregate in ways that have direct effects on state policy outcomes. White racial attitudes, he concludes, are a major factor shaping patterns of state welfare generosity.

Public Discourse

The three chapters on mass opinion raise questions of public discourse, but do not entirely resolve them. Public discourse on welfare has many facets, some of which cannot be captured in quantitative studies of media coverage and mass attitudes. To understand these aspects of discourse, we must ask critical questions about race and welfare such as the following. How and why do racial categories get construed in particular ways at particular times in U.S. welfare politics? Whose voices get heard in public deliberation and with what authority? What does "race" mean to the actors involved, and why are particular issues understood in racial terms? How do racial categories get used when they are discussed explicitly in welfare talk, and how do such categories function as an implicit aspect of coded language and veiled imagery? In what ways does race constitute an object of dispute in welfare discourse, and in what ways does it define terms of debate that are shared by the primary disputants?

The contemporary era of welfare reform is marked by a racial discourse that is truncated and skewed in a number of politically consequential ways. With the "old-fashioned" brand of racism now largely discredited, we inhabit a discursive moment defined by a mixture of corrosive racial resentments, fears of being labeled "racist," and uncertainties about whether it is wise to speak of race at all. Too often, race now operates by stealth, embedded in ostensibly neutral language (Williams 1997; Ansell 1997). Many conversations take on a "we all know what we're talking about" feel, trading on race-coded euphemisms regarding "urban" and "inner city" problems, "cultural backgrounds," the need for "personal responsibility," the troubles of the "underclass," and so on. As George Orwell noted many years ago (1954), such euphemistic language nourishes political ideas that cannot bear the cold light of direct analysis; it protects the existing social order at the expense of clear thought and open deliberation.

When elites invoke race explicitly in public discussions of social policy, it is usually to describe group differences in particular traits, social behaviors, or economic outcomes. Such descriptions of group differences can be informative, but, taken alone, they provide a very thin and politically domesticated mode of race-based analysis. Too often, they create an illusion that racial questions are being squarely addressed, when in fact pivotal questions are being evaded. Facts are often presented with little discussion of what race means or how (in observers' understandings) it actually contributes to group difference in outcomes. In addition, some racial disparities seem to merit close attention while others remain obscure. It is now standard for policy briefs and public hearings to compare white and black rates of poverty, single motherhood, and the like. By contrast, it is rare to find public discussion of the disparities in treatment and benefits that these groups receive in various sectors of the welfare system. Many elites talk about race, but few talk about which groups get what from government or *why* skin color continues to be so consequential for life outcomes and positioning in the social structure.

In recent years, it has become increasingly common to view race as a social construction. People who share particular characteristics, such as Jewish or Irish people, may be understood as a distinctive racial group in one time and place but not in another (Brodkin 1998; Ignatiev 1995). Racial classifications can be structured as multiple categories of difference but are often a binary contrast of "pure" and "tainted" opposites (Fredrickson 1997, 77–97). Two constructive processes merit special attention. The first, racial formation, refers to the processes by which social, economic, and political forces shape the content, meaning, and importance of racial categories in a particular societal domain (Omi and Winant 1994). The second, racialization, refers to processes that extend racial meaning to relationships, practices, groups, or social issues that have previously not been subject to racial classification (Omi and Winant 1994). From this perspective, race-based analysis must not be limited to studies of group behaviors and attitudes; critical questions must be asked about why (and with what consequence) specific racial formations and racialized understandings predominate in particular eras of welfare politics. Accordingly, the third section of this volume explores race as a malleable element of welfare discourse that is constituted through structural processes, displayed for strategic purposes, and enacted in public debate.

In chapter 7, Holloway Sparks explores the discursive practices employed in deliberations over welfare reform in the 1990s. Specifically, she shows how racial categories and meanings interacted with gender and class to undermine the legitimacy of welfare recipients' perspectives. Sparks argues that in this discursive context, recipients were only able to find voice in the welfare reform deliberations when they identified themselves as "success stories" who showed they could leave welfare for work and behave in a manner consistent with white, middle-class values. The terms of this "participation" in the 1996 welfare reform deliberations silenced critical perspectives on the legislation that could have highlighted race, gender, and class biases as well as the experienced needs of welfare recipients. Her essay suggests how the seemingly neutral discursive practices associated with welfare reform worked to reinscribe racial disadvantage.

In chapter 8, Sanford Schram explores the politics of racial representation in welfare discourse more generally in ways that suggest difficult issues in the period after welfare reform. On one side, Schram's analysis points to the risks associated with a history of race talk that demonizes persons of color, especially African Americans. Schram argues that the dominant idiom in welfare discourse reifies racial categories in ways that can suggest blacks are inferior to whites in terms of ability and effort. Accordingly, there may be good reasons for advocates of a racially fair welfare system to avoid invoking race or highlighting the disproportionate presence of black recipients on the welfare rolls. On the other side, however, Schram suggests that such a strategy risks participating in the silence that surrounds racial inequity in the United States; it fails to name or challenge the social and economic processes that make persons of color more likely to need public assistance. With the welfare population becoming increasingly composed of nonwhites under welfare reform, Schram emphasizes that we need to discuss race and welfare in ways that attend to the risks of reifying race and demonizing the racialized "other."

Policy Choice and Implementation

Welfare provision in the United States has always reflected its political setting in a system that emphasizes federalism, localism, and a relatively weak and fragmented national government (Noble 1997). Unlike many European states, the United States never developed a uniform national system of public assistance; the amount and form of aid for the poor has always depended on action in state and local political arenas (Skocpol 1996). Legislative changes and court rulings in the 1960s produced a more stringent set of national standards regulating state governments' welfare efforts (Davis 1993; Melnick 1994). Interstate variation, however, remained a defining characteristic of the AFDC program, and over time the pendulum began to swing back toward greater state control (Peterson and Rom 1990; Weaver 2000). At first, this shift was expressed through a growing number of federal waivers that permitted state officials to deviate from national rules under the AFDC program (Lieberman and Shaw 2000). Eventually, with the enactment of welfare reform in 1996, states gained more authority over eligibility rules and administrative procedures than they had enjoyed for three decades (Mettler 2000).

The fourth section of this volume explores the implications of devolution for policy choice and implementation under welfare reform. Since the mid-1960s, scores of studies in political science have employed the cross-state variation as a kind of laboratory for studying the policy process. The early literature in this area focused primarily on the ways state political institutions affected state welfare policies. Much of this work suggested that features of the political environment, such as party competition and party control, had little or no effect on state policies (Dawson and Robinson 1963; Dye 1966; Fry and Winters 1970; Hofferbert 1966). Rather, state welfare policies appeared to be almost entirely driven by state economic capacity.

Eventually, improvements in measurement and statistical techniques began to uncover significant effects for a number of political variables including state ideology (Wright, Erikson, and McIver 1987), party competition (Holbrook and Van Dunk 1993), and party control (Brown 1995; Jennings 1979). Consequently, state politics scholars have turned their attention to other types of possible influences on welfare policies. In recent years, this has included the degree of class bias in the electorate (Hill, Leighley, and Hinton-Andersson 1995), mass insurgency (e.g., Fording 2001; Schram and Turbett 1983), interstate competition (Peterson and Rom 1989; Rom, Peterson, and Scheve 1998), and labor organization (Radcliff and Saiz 1998).

Despite its many important insights, the literature on state politics has rarely paid sufficient attention to the role of race in welfare policy-making. Almost without exception, researchers in the 1960s and 1970s ignored race as an influence on state welfare policies. With the publication of Gerald Wright's influential analysis of AFDC benefits in 1976, however, this began to change. Wright (1976) demonstrated that benefit levels were related to both the racial composition of the state population and the degree of racial liberalism, as represented by the progressiveness of a state's civil rights laws. Even after these findings, however, few studies of welfare policy published over the next two decades focused on race as an explanatory factor. Of those studies that did examine race, nearly all treated it as a "control variable" rather than as the primary focus of attention. In the last few years, this pattern has begun to change as researchers have brought race into the foreground of the state policy-making process.

In chapter 9 Joe Soss, Sanford Schram, Thomas Vartanian, and Erin O'Brien explore the racial underpinnings of the tough new rules and penalties that proliferated in state welfare programs under welfare reform. The first part of the chapter investigates which states were most likely to adopt stringent welfare policies. The analysis reveals that states with more people of color in their welfare caseloads were significantly more likely to adopt strict policies, but, equally important, the strength of this relationship varies across specific types of program rules. The second part of this chapter presents an individual-level analysis designed to illuminate public support for these tough new program rules as it stood at the time of federal action in 1996. The results suggest that whites are far more likely to support get-tough welfare reforms than blacks. Moreover, the racial divide on support for get-tough policies seems to derive, in part, from the impact of racial attitudes. A variety of attitudes drove white support for new time limits and work requirements; but even after accounting for these factors, negative beliefs about people of color emerge as a primary influence.

Public support and state policy formation take us part of the way toward understanding the new policy environment that has emerged under welfare reform. Welfare policy-making, however, goes beyond the choice of which policies to adopt; it is equally important to ask how such policies get implemented. A major portion of the "governmental actions that shape the quality of people's lives appear in the decisions we classify as 'implementation'" (Edelman 1983, 134). Such actions are rarely visible to the public but can be decisive both for individuals and aggregate policy outcomes. By writing procedural rules and interpreting these rules in specific cases, administrators determine how general laws actually get applied to citizens' lives (Meier 1993; Kerwin 1994). People who work in welfare agencies almost inevitably find that they have some discretion in dealing with applicants and clients. Such discretion may be used to provide more personalized or equitable services (Goodsell 1981). But it can also be used in ways that discriminate against particular categories of people or deflect demands for benefits (Lipsky 1984; Hasenfeld 1987). For all these reasons, implementation processes are now widely viewed as a continuation of "policy-making by other means" (Lineberry 1977, 71). For the poor, who tend to be marginalized at other points in the political process, welfare agencies are especially significant sites of politics (Piven and Cloward 1993). Welfare participation offers poor people a rare opportunity to influence public allocations; it also brings them into direct contact with the state's power to monitor, control, and punish the citizenry (Soss 2000).

Throughout U.S. history, the politics of implementation has played a key role in frustrating the goals of racial justice. Hard-won voting rights have been undercut by discrimination at the ballot box; civil rights have turned to dust at the courthouse and police station; social rights have come undone at local hospitals, schoolhouses, and welfare agencies. Through much of the twentieth century, welfare administration for poor families was shot through with racial bias. State governments were free to define program eligibility rules, and local caseworkers were given a wide berth to enforce the rules as they saw fit. African Americans, concentrated in the South, often had no access to benefits or found that access varied according to the labor needs of local cotton growers (Piven and Cloward 1993). In many states, caseworkers could use "man in the house" and "suitable home" rules to deny benefits to women who allegedly lived with an unrelated male or violated some other norm regarding domestic arrangements. To obtain evidence of such violations, caseworkers could enter and inspect recipients' homes at any time, sometimes during unannounced "midnight raids." Such practices were often aimed selectively at "undeserving" black recipients; they constituted a form of intimidation that kept the welfare rolls down, regulated domestic behavior, and controlled local race relations (Piven and Cloward 1993).

In the 1960s, political mobilization produced a string of legal victories and administrative reforms that limited the scope of caseworker discretion and brought greater equity to eligibility decisions. State and local officials continued to control access to AFDC benefits, and in many respects clients were still subject to the discretionary actions of caseworkers (Prottas 1979; Handler 1992; Soss 2000). But such activities were constrained by the federal government in ways they had not been in the past. Predictably, the new arrangements produced a sustained increase in the welfare caseload and brought African Americans onto the rolls in far greater numbers (Mink 1994). Welfare reform in the 1990s was, among other things, a concerted effort to cut back the federal limits on state and local administration (Weaver 2000). The new logic of implementation created by these reforms is partly a "return to the past," but it proceeds under a very different configuration of policy mandates, program rules, and societal conditions. Under TANF, agency workers have an expanded scope of discretion that includes when to divert would-be applicants, whether to grant exemptions from program rules, whom to sanction for what kinds of infractions, and which clients to inform about which available benefits and services.

The racial implications of the new discretion are complex and only now beginning to emerge. To begin with, white families have left the welfare rolls faster than nonwhites, increasing the proportion of recipients who are African American and Latino. Between 1997 and 1999, the percentage of TANF families that identified themselves as white dropped from 42 to 33 percent, while percentage that reported their race as black rose from 34 to 46 percent (Zedlewski and Alderson 2001). In addition, the consequences of strict new welfare rules appear to be falling disproportionately on nonwhites. For example, while 63.7 percent of black TANF families participated in state programs that employed a full-family sanction in 1999, only 53.7 percent of white families did the same.[2] Moreover, available state-level studies "which examined reason for exit found that minorities were generally more likely than Whites to have their cases closed due to sanctions rather than earnings (according to administrative data)" (Lower-Basch 2000). Similarly, a recent analysis estimated that African Americans will make up over two-thirds of all families that will be forced off the rolls due to the federal five-year time limit on program usage (Duncan, Harris, and Boisjoly 2000).

In chapter 10, Susan Gooden explores the TANF implementation process, seeking out its racial dynamics and consequences. Her work highlights the ways in which administrative outcomes emerge out of the interactions of a variety of participants, including agency managers, street-level workers, clients, and community members. In taking up these interactions, Gooden shows how the racial logic of TANF implementation relates to the development of welfare administration over the past century. Drawing on her own research, Gooden explains why and how racial bias influences the ways caseworkers treat TANF recipients. Especially important, Gooden concludes with concrete proposals for establishing racial fairness as a measure of performance for caseworker action and welfare administration more generally.

Welfare in Context: Race and Social Policy in the States

In contemporary political rhetoric, "welfare" is often addressed as if it were a unique program, wholly unrelated to the broader system of social policies pursued by federal, state, and local governments. In some respects, the politics of "welfare" may very well be distinctive; but in truth, welfare provision in the United States consists of many social policies that relate to one another in complex ways. As a result, one major challenge for students of welfare politics is to understand how developments in one policy area affect changes in other policy areas. A second and related challenge is to understand which political patterns in a given policy domain are distinctive, and which reflect more general tendencies in U.S. social provision. Just as historical comparisons are essential for an adequate understanding of contemporary welfare politics, so too are comparisons across related policy domains.

Accordingly, the fifth section of this volume consists of two chapters designed to locate welfare politics within the broader context of social policy choice in the states. In chapter 11, Caroline Tolbert extends the scope of our analysis to consider the relationship between race and health care policy. Specifically, Tolbert employs survey data to analyze racial and ethnic voting patterns in California's failed 1994 ballot initiative to adopt a universal health care system. In doing so, Tolbert makes two important contributions to the volume. First, following up on the chapters by Fording and Sparks (as well as Soss, Schram, Vartanian, and O'Brien's discussion of the racial divide in opinion), Tolbert's analysis underscores the need to address people of color as active and distinctive agents in social welfare politics. Second, Tolbert shifts our attention away from the actions of legislators to the direct efforts of citizens to shape public policy. Today, most research on welfare policy formation focuses on legislative action. Over the last two decades, however, direct referenda have become critical for social welfare outcomes—often with major implications for disadvantaged minorities. Tolbert's analysis offers sorely needed insight into the ways racial and ethnic groups behave when they are given a chance to exercise direct control over social policy.

In chapter 12, Rodney Hero broadens the analysis further to illuminate a number of general theoretical and methodological issues related to the study of race and social policy. In addition to offering a general framework for analyzing racial composition and social policy, Hero demonstrates that the racial composition of a state's population influences a wide variety of social policy outcomes. Equally important, his analysis shows that racial factors affect different domains of social policy in different ways. In doing so, Hero suggests that race is a fundamental but highly variable force shaping U.S. social policy.

Ending a Book, Continuing a Dialogue

Because the central goal of this volume is to expand and sharpen our dialogue on race and welfare in the United States, we have chosen not to end with a summary conclusion by the editors. Instead, we have invited a major scholar of welfare politics to reflect on the material presented by our contributors. Frances Fox Piven's commentary offers her own perspective on race and welfare politics. Her critique of racialized practice in the U.S. welfare system places contemporary welfare politics in a historical perspective that highlights the interplay of race and political economy. In so doing, Piven offers a provocative response to this volume's open invitation to rethink the problems and possibilities of race in U.S. welfare politics. We hope that readers will be inspired to follow suit, developing their own responses and beginning the hard work of confronting the enduring relationship between race and welfare in the United States.

NOTES

1. For an elaboration of this metaphor, see comments by Janet Robideau, cited in Neubeck and Cazenave 2001.

2. If the percentage of black families participating under this policy were made equal to the percentage for white families (53.7 percent), the number of African American families at risk for a full-family sanctions would be reduced by about 102,000 families. These calculations were made by the authors based on 1999 caseload data from the Administration for Children and Families' Third Annual Report to Congress (August 2000, table 10:6) and sanction policy information gathered by the State Policy Documentation Project.

History

CHAPTER 1

Race and the Limits of Solidarity

American Welfare State Development in Comparative Perspective

ROBERT C. LIEBERMAN

The 1990s was not the first era of American welfare reform in the twentieth century. Three times before—during the Progressive Era, the New Deal, and the Great Society—Americans dramatically reshaped welfare policies, creating the familiar complex of programs that was reformed yet again in 1996. Perhaps the dominant theme of this history has been the deepening and increasingly troubling link between race and the politics of American social policy. The relationship between African Americans and the American welfare state has been a varied and changing one. Largely excluded from Progressive and New Deal policies of social provision, African Americans increasingly claimed rights to social benefits, culminating in the War on Poverty and the expansion of welfare rights in the 1960s. Far from excluding African Americans and other minorities, these developments explicitly targeted attention and resources on problems of minority poverty and exclusion.

In each of these episodes of reform, the status of African Americans in national politics has been crucial in shaping policy outcomes (Skocpol 1995a). In the Progressive Era, most African Americans lived in the South, where they were denied civil and political rights under the violent repression of Jim Crow segregation. Thus they were almost universally excluded from state-level Progressive social policies such as mothers' pensions. The New Deal represented a major breakthrough both for national social policy and for the political status of African Americans. The Social Security Act of 1935 created the first permanent national welfare policies, and northern African Americans began to switch their political allegiance to the newly dominant Democratic party. But the major partner in the New Deal coalition was the white South, whose disproportionate power limited the New Deal's capacity to include African Americans in social provision on equal terms. In the generation after the New Deal, however, African Americans both moved north in large numbers and mobilized a national social movement to demand the civil and political rights long promised but not yet fulfilled. As that movement bore fruit in the 1960s, African Americans were able to use their new-found political status to demand greater access to existing welfare benefits and new policies to promote equal opportunity. But the cruel irony of the Great Society is that these very policies fueled growing racial resentment and widened a burgeoning split in American welfare politics that divided white from black, middle- and working-class Americans from the poor, and cities from suburbs, leaving African Americans increasingly isolated—politically, socially, economically, and geographically—from the main currents of the American political economy.

The pattern of twentieth-century reform suggests that a crucial question in understanding the fate of African Americans in the American welfare state is whether they have been part of the broad national political coalitions that are always necessary to achieve lasting policy reform. The terms on which African Americans participate in these coalitions have shaped welfare policies, particularly by shaping the boundaries of inclusion and exclusion that those policies embody. These boundaries, in turn, affect the prospects for minority incorporation into social provision, whether as honorable beneficiaries or as marginal clients. These considerations, moreover, are not mere remnants of the past. The racial divide was at the very center of the politics of welfare reform in the 1990s, because of racialized perceptions and misperceptions of Aid to Families with Dependent Children (AFDC) and other policies, racially divided opinions about the proper direction of the welfare system and the federal government's role in social provision, and the shifting place of African Americans in electoral and party politics (Gilens 1999; Bobo and Smith 1994; Williams 1998). Thus in order to understand the politics of welfare reform in American politics in the 1990s and the prospects for minorities in the new American welfare regime, it is essential to understand the historical dynamics of race and the politics of welfare policy coalitions.

Race is often held up as the essence of American exceptionalism, the single feature of American society and politics that, more than anything else, distinguishes the United States from other countries. Ira Katznelson (1981), for example, argues in *City Trenches* that racial (and ethnic) divisions inscribed in the urban landscape of the late nineteenth century account for the distinctive pattern of American working-class formation. Others point to racial and ethnic heterogeneity to explain the peculiarities of American welfare-state development (Lieberman 1998; Smith 1997; Quadagno 1994; Brown 1999). The United States, however, is not the only Western industrial democracy with a multiracial society. Great Britain and France, as well as other European countries, increasingly have significant populations of non-European origin that are identified as racially distinct from their society's dominant group—Africans in France, for example, and South Asians and West Indians in England. These racial encounters are transforming European politics, introducing a new and complex layer of social, economic, and political conflict into these societies and spawning a grimly familiar litany of problems: racism, discrimination, inequality, isolation, political powerlessness, and even racial violence. In Europe, too, racial division is becoming an increasingly vexing issue in welfare politics, as minority groups seek to claim welfare rights and right-wing politicians draw a link between race and welfare as part of their racist and xenophobic appeals. At the same time, however, different societies conceive of and cope with racial difference in dramatically different ways.

A comparative approach, then, can help us to understand how and why race has been so important to American welfare politics. By isolating critical similarities and differences—both the common elements of racial conflict in different countries and the variations in racial politics in different political settings—comparison can point the way toward a more general, causal explanation for the existence and form of racialized political conflict and its consequences for welfare politics. In this chapter I place the formation of the American welfare state in comparative context in order to expose more clearly the mechanisms by which racial politics helped shape the structure of the American welfare state. I begin with an account of how race can shape the formation of policy coalitions, and in particular the ways in which race might induce or inhibit the formation of the cross-class coalitions necessary for the adoption of welfare policies. I then reexamine the familiar history of the enactment of New Deal social policies, setting it alongside social developments in Great Britain and France, to suggest that racially structured coalitions were central to the development of the American welfare state.

Racial Rule and the Limits of Solidarity

A focus on the building of solidaristic national coalitions for welfare policy means a focus on the institutional roots of the American welfare state and the connections among race, political institutions, and policy in American history. It is a common observation that the American welfare state is more fragmented and less universal than the welfare states of most other developed democratic nations—prone to division between generous social insurance policies for workers and stingy and punitive public assistance benefits for the poor; variable from state to state because of the federal structure of American politics; and lacking policies that most other countries provide, such as universal health insurance, family allowances, child-care (Esping-Andersen 1990).

Scholars have offered a variety of explanations for this pattern of development (see Skocpol 1992, 11–40). Some explanations focus on the American national values of liberal individualism, belief in self-reliance, and skepticism toward government (Hartz 1955). But these accounts cannot fully explain why some national welfare policies have been strikingly successful in the United States or why other liberal societies, such as Britain, have opted for more expansive social policies than the United States. Others emphasize the strength of business and the weakness of organized labor in the United States, both of which helped to close off the social democratic route to the welfare state that prevailed in much of Europe. But these explanations, which give great weight to class conflict, fail to account for the cross-class nature of the coalitions that underlie welfare policy-making, both in the United States and elsewhere (Baldwin 1990). A perspective that is to explain the emergence and sustenance of these coalitions must consider the political settings in which both values and interests—rooted not only in class but also in race, gender, and other social relations—are formed and mobilized and in which conflicts among competing values and interests are fought out and resolved, resulting in the enactment of policies. These considerations suggest the critical importance of the national political institutions that play a particularly important role in advancing or inhibiting such coalitions—above all legislatures and executives, political parties, bureaucracies, and federalism—in shaping the development of national welfare states.

A number of prominent scholars of American and comparative politics and history have also placed race at the center of the formation of governing coalitions in multiracial societies. From the very beginnings of colonial American politics, as Edmund Morgan (1975) demonstrates, a racial hierarchy that distinguished slaves from free men and women helped unify whites across class distinctions around an emerging American ideology of freedom and equality. In his classic *Southern Politics in State and Nation*, V. O. Key (1949) argues that the imperatives of segregation and white supremacy emanating from the Black Belt—the swath of the American South where African Americans were most heavily concentrated, so named because of the dark, rich topsoil that made it ideal for growing cotton—constricted the formation of class-based politics. Rather than uniting "have-nots" of both races and pitting them against the white "haves," as the ill-fated Populist movement had intimated, southern politics under Jim Crow revolved around racial fear and resentment (Woodward 1974; Goodwyn 1976). Whites often (but not always) came together across class lines to form a broad political alliance that shaped not only southern but national politics as well—through Democratic dominance in the South, the structure of the Democratic party, and the organization of Congress, which gave white southerners disproportionate influence over national politics and policy for much of the twentieth century (Key 1949; Potter 1972; Bensel 1984, 147–74).

As Katznelson, Geiger, and Kryder (1993) have shown, the South was the pivotal player in the formation of policy coalitions in Congress in the middle of the century. Southern Democrats generally voted with other Democrats, except on civil rights and labor issues, when they routinely combined with Republicans to form a conservative coalition. This voting pattern, combined with southern control of key congressional committees through the ironclad seniority rule in Congress and the perpetual reelection of Democrats from the one-party South, gave white Southerners extensive power to shape policy. At the very least, southern representatives were able to block legislative initiatives that threatened their regional political economy that linked white supremacy and labor-repressive agriculture with local control of the apparatus of the state, or to modify policy initiatives to make them "safe" for the South (Moore 1966; James 1988; Lieberman 1998). In this way, race was central to the development of many of the core domestic policies of the twentieth century.

More broadly, Anthony Marx (1998) compares the process of state building and racial formation in the United States, South Africa, and Brazil, countries that share histories of colonization and slavery. He argues that the creation of legal structures of racial subordination in the United States and South Africa resulted from whites' need to overcome divisions of class, region, and the like in order to consolidate their hold on developing state power in the wake of emancipation and decolonization. In Brazil, where such imperatives were absent from the state-building process, the same sort of legally imposed apartheid did not result. These studies suggest that race might, under certain conditions and over certain issues, be central to the political dynamics of state and nation building, the construction of essential political institutions that define patterns of governance and political inclusion over the long run. In particular, they highlight the role that race might have played in either creating or inhibiting the cross-class coalitions that have historically been necessary for the formation of national welfare states, developments that have both state- and nation-building implications. Finally, they suggest the value of examining American political development in comparative perspective, the better to isolate the ways in which race shapes the formation of welfare state coalitions.

For the United States, then, the question is to what extent race was an essential ingredient in the construction of social policy coalitions at the critical formative moment of the American national welfare state, the New Deal. It is important to note that this is a different question from the presence or absence of racism in policy deliberations or in society at large, which is the starting point for many analyses of the impact of race on American politics and public policy (Bell 1992; Hacker 1992; Kinder and Sanders 1996). The question is not one of simply searching for evidence of racist intent on the part of the framers of the Social Security Act of 1935, as some analysts have intimated, and concluding from its relative absence (relative, that is, to other policy debates of the same era) that racial exclusion from the act's policies was simply an incidental effect that followed from nonracial causes (Davies and Derthick 1997). Rather, the question is whether the particular configuration of American race politics ruled out certain coalitions—and hence certain policies—and made other coalitions and policies possible. But this question poses serious problems of explanation and inference if we look at the United States alone: how can we know what might have happened in the absence of racial division in American society? One way around this problem is to trace very carefully and precisely the mechanisms and processes by which racial considerations might have affected decision making and coalition building in social policy enactments. Several works that follow this approach have found strong evidence that race was, in fact, causally central to the American story, although others have argued that policy effects that appear to be racial in origin could just as plausibly result from other causes (Lieberman 1998; Brown 1999; Davies and Derthick 1997).

An alternative approach is to compare the United States to other countries that share certain political and social characteristics in order to see how countries with differently organized racial politics confronted similar problems of welfare state development and whether particular racial configurations are associated with particular social policy coalitions. In the United States, the centrality of race, usually taken as an exceptional feature of American politics, arises from the history of African slavery in North America that reaches back almost as far as permanent European settlement of the continent (Berlin 1998; see also Tannenbaum 1946; Elkins 1959). But slavery was only one form of rule based on racial distinctions. More generally, the processes by which racially defined rule shapes political institutions and strategic political circumstances may apply in a variety of contexts (Davis 1966). Other systems in which rule is based on racial categories include apartheid (including Jim Crow in the American South), certain brands of nationalism (including nationalism's totalitarian variants), and, most relevant for the present comparison, imperialism and colonialism.

"Two new devices for political organization and rule over foreign peoples were discovered during the first decades of imperialism," wrote Hannah Arendt (1968, 185). "One was race as a principle of the body politic, and the other was bureaucracy as a principle of foreign domination." Like slavery and segregation, imperialism in the nineteenth and twentieth centuries constituted rule by "whites" of European descent over "blacks," conducted through a set of formal institutions and social arrangements supported by an ideology of racial superiority. All of these forms of rule were also justified and explained by other means—economic, political, diplomatic—and a complete explanation of slavery, segregation, or imperialism would surely involve all of these (see Baumgart 1982). But underlying these explanations, or at least deeply intertwined with them, is what W. E. B. Du Bois (1986, 16) called the color line, "the relation of the darker to the lighter races of men in Africa and Asia, in America and the islands of the sea." Similarly, imperialism and colonialism, no matter how extensively they involved other factors, constituted irreducible structures of racial rule.

The high point of imperialism and colonialism in Europe in the late nineteenth and early twentieth centuries also coincided with the formative period of European welfare states. The welfare state traces its origins to a political moment in which imperial conquest and colonial rule were at the center of political life. Both enterprises were part of the process by which European states negotiated the transition toward mass politics and democracy, which required new means for securing the allegiance of the working class and creating an "imagined community" among citizens (Hobsbawm 1987, 101–7; Anderson 1991). Thus the politics of welfare state building, the construction of a means of social solidarity at home, was connected to the process of drawing race-based distinctions between national citizens and colonial subjects across national boundaries. Seen in this light, the welfare state is potentially an agent of the political construction of race-based national solidarity. By linking social groups to each other and to the state through a network of social rights, welfare state institutions created in this context were thus instrumental in defining the rights of differently situated racially defined groups of citizens and subjects to what T. H. Marshall (1964) described as full membership in society, and to state protection against what Franklin Roosevelt (1938, 3:291) called "the hazards and vicissitudes of life."

Racial Legacies and the Formation of Welfare Coalitions

The welfare state is a particularly useful focus for the comparative study of race relations. It is, among other things, a mechanism of social solidarity, a means of linking citizens to the state through a set of social rights and to each other by ties of interdependence (Marshall 1964; Baldwin 1990). Of course, welfare states are at once inclusive and exclusive mechanisms. On the one hand, they embody these solidaristic ties among a community of citizens. On the other hand, they define a boundary between the community and outsiders, depending on who is eligible for assistance on what terms, and in so doing they can also construct and reconstruct lines of inequality and social division within societies along lines not only of class but also of gender, citizenship, and race (Esping-Andersen 1990; Freeman 1986; Orloff 1993; Lieberman 1998). Thus the welfare state is one of the key defining structures of social and political inclusion and exclusion in the modern nation-state. But welfare states differ in the balance they strike between their inclusive and exclusive imperatives, and so the welfare state is critical to understanding the capacities of states to incorporate racial minorities.

Thus variations in the nature of imperialism and colonialism (or patterns of racial rule more generally) were potentially of critical importance in shaping welfare state formation. In particular, the domestic politics of imperial rule—the extent to which clear racial boundaries between home citizens and colonial subjects underlay the power and democratic legitimacy of metropolitan political elites in imperial powers—had important effects on the politics of social solidarity. To the extent that imperial politics demanded a hard and fast racial line between citizens at home and subjects abroad, social welfare policies were more free to insist on a high level of social solidarity among their beneficiaries. In other words, the presumption of racial homogeneity at home allowed for the construction of welfare systems with more forceful and authoritative means of connecting individual citizens to the state. There were both positive and negative reasons for this outcome. On the positive side, the challenge of imperial rule demanded an "imperial race," which placed a burden on the state to ensure the health and welfare of its own citizens. On the negative side, the hermetic racial division between home and abroad meant that a strong, centralized, and deeply penetrating welfare state did not pose an unacceptable challenge to a racial hierarchy that ordered political life within the home country. But where the boundaries of imperial and racial citizenship were more permeable, the possibilities for social policy were restricted by the possibility of racial inclusion. The presence of racial diversity *within* rather than *across* national boundaries changed the solidaristic imperatives of social politics, making the creation of centralized national welfare states rather more politically dangerous. In such countries, the problem of distinguishing between those who were and were not entitled to consideration as members of the solidaristic national community was a more complicated political and administrative enterprise, since one could not simply presume that social and national boundaries coincided. Rather, welfare states in these countries were more likely to take complex institutional forms, involving decentralized decision making and administration rather then constructing direct links between citizens and the state.

This argument about the connection between forms and patterns of racial rule allows for a comparison of the role of race in welfare state formation in the United States, Britain, and France. In the late nineteenth and early twentieth centuries, all three countries ruled over far-flung territories with racially diverse populations with states that institutionalized racial rule in some form. Although the United States, among these three countries, would conventionally be considered the most multiracial, many more people 'of non-European descent were ruled from London or Paris than Washington. In the early twentieth century, both the British and French empires had majority nonwhite populations by a wide margin, while the nonwhite population of the United States hovered at around 10 percent (Lieberman 1997). The principal difference in the form of racial rule was whether racial minorities were located inside or outside national boundaries. In the United States, the racial minority population was located entirely within the country's home borders, and the immediate proximity of African Americans posed a particular set of political challenges for American whites, especially in the post–Civil War South (Key 1949). In Britain and France, by contrast, almost all nonwhites lived in the colonies and not in the home country (although in France, as we shall see, national and racial boundaries remained more politically porous than in Britain), producing a very different set of political challenges for white elites at home.

But the geographical and political proximity of blacks and whites did not alone determine the impact of racial rule on the welfare state. Equally important was the centrality of race to the process of building political coalitions around social reform, particularly whether or not race emerged as a significant or even dominant line of political cleavage that altered or even trumped other potential cleavages—primarily class (Lipset and Rokkan 1967). Internal racial distinctions were not a necessary condition for the formation of race-based social reform coalitions. In both the United States and Britain race helped overcome class-based political conflict and was one of the central axes around which the politics of welfare revolved; the political construction of racial distinctions was critical in the creation of cross-class coalitions for welfare policy in each country. But the difference between internal racial conflict in the United States and the appearance of internal racial homogeneity in Britain proved critical in pushing the two countries toward different approaches to constructing welfare institutions. In Britain in the years before World War I, social reform and imperial fervor were the twin pillars behind a political coalition that created inclusive national welfare policies as a means of unifying Britons across class and against a racially defined threat from outside. In the United States the coalition behind the welfare state in the 1930s also depended on the protection of racial rule, but there the imperative of uniting whites against blacks produced an approach to welfare policy that was necessarily exclusionary and decentralizing rather than inclusionary and national.

Race was hardly absent from French politics in the late nineteenth and early twentieth centuries, but it did not come to trump or displace other more fundamental cleavages in French social politics. Like Britain, France did not confront black-white racial diversity within its national borders, but it was consumed in the early twentieth century with intense conflicts over anti-Semitism in society and politics, conflicts in which Jews were routinely portrayed as an alien race (Sternhell 1986; Birnbaum 1993). At the same time, the process of French nation-building in the Third Republic had been one of continual assimilation of non-French populations within France itself, many of whom were seen as racially distinct, even equivalent to France's African subjects. Eugen Weber (1976, 485) even goes so far as to suggest that "the famous hexagon [a traditional name for the territory of France because of its six-sided shape] can itself be seen as a colonial empire shaped over centuries." Thus the prospect of racial diversity in interwar France, both metropolitan and overseas, was an opportunity as well as a threat to political elites, and French imperialism was less consumed with constructing racial distinctions across national boundaries. French social reform in the interwar years did not mobilize racial antagonisms to overcome class divisions, whether to inclusionary or exclusionary effect, resulting in the perpetuation of the Third Republic's corporatist pattern of social provision, based on civil society attachments.

Coalition Building in Three Countries

The United States

In the United States, it was not only the presence of African Americans within national boundaries but also their status as presumptive citizens (at least under the original intent of the Thirteenth, Fourteenth, and Fifteenth Amendments to the Constitution) that posed the fundamental conundrum of social politics: how to produce welfare policy without running afoul of the South. The historical connection between race and the politics of the welfare state arose primarily because of the particular configuration of political institutions by which whites ruled over blacks, not only in the southern states but also in the national government. The segregated, white supremacist South of the first half of the twentieth century set up an elaborate set of mechanisms to disenfranchise African

Americans and to undermine the rights that the Constitution seemed to protect. Although Reconstruction, the postwar military occupation of the South, ended formally in 1877, northern Republicans continued to try to use federal power to enforce black voting rights in the South until the 1890s (Valelly 1995). Consequently southern politicians developed a very strong interest in protecting state- and local-level political autonomy from national incursions. The South was a one-party region and elected only Democrats to Congress (with very rare exceptions). Once in Washington, southern Democrats, who won essentially perpetual reelection, climbed the rigid seniority ladder in Congress so that when Democrats controlled Congress, southerners chaired committees, in an era in which congressional rules gave committee chairmen tremendous power over policy-making. Although twentieth-century southern Democrats were more heterogeneous than is commonly recognized, they were reliably unified (and often allied with Republicans against their fellow Democrats) on civil rights and labor issues, and they used their pivotal legislative position to challenge (and usually to defeat or amend) any policy provision that they regarded as a challenge to the southern system of racial supremacy and labor-repressive agrarian peonage (Key 1949; Katznelson, Geiger, and Kryder 1993).

Until the New Deal, social reform at the national level was almost nonexistent, for a number of reasons. As Theda Skocpol (1992) has shown, the structure of American political institutions—separated powers; a locally representative Congress; decentralized, patronage-based, nonprogrammatic political parties; a weak bureaucracy; federalism—militated against national social insurance and other European-style welfare policies, as did the lack of national mobilization behind such policies. Moreover, the Supreme Court routinely blocked attempts at social and economic reform until the middle of the 1930s. Some reforms were possible, especially maternalist policies such as mothers' pensions, maternal and child health assistance, and protective labor regulations for women, but very few workingmen's social policies succeeded until the 1930s. The localized structure of most maternalist social policies, especially mothers' pensions, meant that they largely excluded African Americans. Several southern states had no mothers' pensions at all; those that did declined to operate them in heavily black counties and used discretionary administrative tactics to direct benefits to white families (Howard 1992; Ward 2000).

Franklin Roosevelt's New Deal, abetted by the Supreme Court's timely about-face, brought the national government into the business of social reform. Like other countries' old-age insurance schemes, Social Security was adopted by a coalition that wedded industrial interests and landed interests who practiced labor-repressive agriculture. Roosevelt's reform coalition, which combined northern urban workers, midwestern farmers, and southern whites, was in many respects similar to the industrial-agrarian coalitions that produced social reform in many European countries, and it pursued a familiar reform agenda: social insurance, labor rights, and economic regulation (Baldwin 1990). The essential elements of the New Deal coalition were the urban workers of the North and the Bourbon planters of the South. Neither bloc could make policy without the other, and in particular the committee structure of the House and minority protections in the Senate gave southern members of Congress inordinate power to shape policy. It is little surprise, then, that the Social Security Act, like most other New Deal enactments, benefited these groups. In this respect, the American case closely resembles comparative cases such as Germany and Austria, where similar coalitions adopted social insurance schemes in the late nineteenth and early twentieth centuries (Köhler and Zacher 1982; Rueschemeyer, Stephens, and Stephens 1992).

But whereas these European coalitions were conservative, even authoritarian, coalitions of upper classes who proffered social insurance to workers as a defense against socialist agitation, the New Deal coalition was a cross-class coalition that wedded the social democratic impulses of southern workers with the often reactionary demands of the white southern elite (Ritter 1983; Baldwin 1990; Heclo 1986; Skocpol 1991). The American coalition was built on racial rather than class hierarchy, and the southern planter class used its strategic control of fragmented state institutions to perpetuate racial exclusion and reproduce the racial order of the southern states (Marx 1998). The exclusion of agricultural workers from Old-Age Insurance served the interests of this coalition for different reasons. For the white South, it prevented African Americans from entering into a direct relationship with the national government unmediated by local structures of white power and ensured the perpetuation of their status not just as low-wage workers but as political and social inferiors; for southern Democrats, it allowed the adoption of one pillar of an ambitious agenda for industrial economic security.

The resulting policy settlement, the Social Security Act of 1935, took the form of a race-laden institutional bargain between the southern and northern wings of the Democratic party over the terms and mechanisms of inclusion in the welfare state—that is, over the boundaries of social solidarity. The Roosevelt administration proposed a widely inclusive set of social policies under national control, combining fully national social insurance for all workers with financial support for state public assistance policies such as mothers' pensions, under terms that would give the federal government substantial administrative and political leverage (Lieberman 1998). This package—inclusive, national social policy—proved unacceptable to southern congressional leaders because it threatened to create direct links between southern African American workers and the national state, effectively mobilizing a class coalition against racial hegemony. The responsible congressional committees, both chaired by southerners, altered Roosevelt's proposal by eliminating agricultural and domestic workers from eligibility for national social insurance on the one hand and removing federal controls over state public assistance on the other. Occupational exclusions eliminated more than three-fifths of the African American workforce from the protection of social insurance; radically decentralized public assistance allowed wide areas of discretion to local elites in setting benefit levels and requirements. The result was a structurally limited, decentralized, and bifurcated welfare system that perpetuated African American dependence on local political and economic elites for their livelihoods (Skocpol 1988). Thus at the founding moment of the American welfare state, the particular institutional configuration of racial rule effectively blocked the formation of a more fully reformist coalition, joining classes across racial lines in support of more a more broadly solidaristic welfare state. Instead, even though African Americans were nominal partners in the New Deal coalition (although not solidly until 1936 or even after), the imperatives of racial dominance outweighed conventional class position in defining interests and cleavages in the social politics of the 1930s (Weiss 1983; Carmines and Stimson 1989; Katznelson 1981).

The welfare system that emerged from the New Deal moved on two tracks. Social insurance policies—Old-Age Insurance (Social Security) and Unemployment Insurance—were national policies that paid benefits linked to workers' contributions as a matter of right. Although it weathered considerable uncertainty through the 1940s, Social Security was politically unassailable by the early 1950s, largely because of its contributory structure but also because of equitable professional administration and skillful political management (Derthick 1979). As a result, it not only included African Americans fairly and without discrimination, it also expanded to include previously excluded occupations, including farm work and domestic labor, effectively bringing many African American workers into the national welfare state on the same terms as whites. By contrast, public assistance policies (especially AFDC, the program most commonly called "welfare"), which disproportionately targeted African Americans, were decentralized and parochial, placing near-complete authority in the hands of local political elites. The result was widespread discrimination against African Americans in AFDC administration, not only in the South but in southern cities as well, especially cities dominated by traditional party organizations (machines), another setting in which African Americans were dependent on white elites for their access to benefits (Lieberman and Lapinski 2001; Katznelson 1976). While regular workers gained nationally protected social rights through an expanding social insurance regime, African Americans were disproportionately relegated to weaker, partial, and fragmented links with the welfare state through public assistance. Thus entering the post–World War II era, the United States had a two-track welfare state with a strong racial valence essentially built into its institutional structure, the legacy of the configuration of racial rule that structured social politics in the 1930s.

There are alternative interpretations of the evidence about racial exclusion from Social Security. Gareth Davies and Martha Derthick (1997, 221–24) also make a comparative argument, although one that is more of an exercise in taxonomy than serious causal reasoning about the process of building a social policy coalition in the 1930s. Many other countries already had old-age insurance systems in place as the United States was contemplating one, and as they stood in 1935 most of those systems covered agricultural workers, suggesting that feasibility was not an insurmountable problem for the coverage of farm employees. This fact was well known to the Roosevelt administration appointees and staff, whose original draft of the Social Security Act also included agricultural workers (Lieberman 1998, 42–43; U.S. Social Security Board 1937, 183). However, Davies and Derthick correctly point out that in many of these countries, agricultural workers had initially been excluded and were brought under the social insurance umbrella only later. They use this observation to bolster their argument that by excluding farmworkers at the outset the United States was merely following the lead of more experienced nations and attempting to create a workable system. As they also point out, many proponents of Old-Age Insurance, including the secretary of the treasury, worried about the feasibility of covering agricultural workers and recommended deferring such coverage. Many others, however, argued on the other side that feasibility was not a problem and offered concrete proposals to facilitate coverage of agricultural, domestic, and casual labor (Lieberman 1998, 41–42). In this superficial reading, the comparative evidence about feasibility can, it would seem, support either reading of the evidence.

This version of the comparative argument, however, does not help to resolve the causal question about the roots of exclusion in the American case because it does not identify the political mechanisms or processes that made exclusion a compelling part of a coalition-building strategy for Social Security's advocates. What is worth comparing is not only the outcomes of the legislative processes of welfare state development but also, and most centrally, the processes themselves. The pertinent question is not what kind of overseas models were available to American policy-makers but rather what were the implications of agricultural inclusion or exclusion for the possibility of forming a winning coalition in Congress for what was, after all, a bold and controversial policy initiative. To the extent that welfare state building entailed constructing mechanisms of social solidarity, broadly inclusive coalitions should form. Patterns of exclusion, by contrast, are particularly revealing about the social and political bases of the welfare state, and in the United States the systematic exclusion of African Americans from national social provision suggests further comparative examination of the way race affected the shape of solidaristic, cross-class coalitions.

France and Britain also built welfare states in the early twentieth century in political contexts that were highly charged by racial antagonisms. Social reformers in all three countries faced similar problems of coalition-building for policies of social provision, the challenge of devising policies that would knit disparate social groups together across class lines under common ties of solidarity and social citizenship while at the same time drawing clear boundaries between full citizens and outsiders. Race was an important boundary condition in each case, although it played different political roles in shaping social policy coalitions in each country. Brief, suggestive sketches of the role race played in the politics of welfare state development in each country can throw important light on the American experience by zeroing in on the institutional mechanisms that made race especially important in the American case.

Great Britain

In imperial Britain, in contrast to the United States, race politics was not defined by proximity but by distance. For the most part, the racial divide in the British Empire was a geographical one, with whites living at the center, in the British Isles, and nonwhites at the periphery, in overseas colonies and dominions. But the politics of racial rule, in the form of imperial politics, was at the center of British politics in the late nineteenth and early twentieth centuries. The last third of the nineteenth century was an uncertain and unsettled period in British politics. Reform acts in 1867 and 1884 quadrupled the size of the British electorate, marking the transition to mass democracy and upending the elite patterns of British party politics (Hobsbawm 1987, 85). The relatively stable Liberal-Conservative partisan alignment of the generation after the first Reform Act shifted to one of Conservative dominance after the Liberals split over Irish Home Rule in the 1880s; meanwhile the new Labour party began to gather strength among recently enfranchised workers. But although Tory hegemony meant that liberal social reform lay mostly dormant, social politics remained alive because of the key figure in the new Conservative majority, Joseph Chamberlain, a renegade Liberal and an advocate of social reform who became colonial secretary in a Conservative-Unionist government in 1895.

What linked these elite factions and made the Conservative-Unionist alliance cohere was imperialism, support for the maintenance and strengthening of the empire. But in the new world of mass politics, empire was not an easy political sell. The Conservative-Unionists could not easily mobilize popular support for traditional imperial aims of glory and commerce; Liberals tended toward humanitarian sympathy for oppressed colonial peoples, while Labour was coming to oppose what it saw as the economic and political exploitation inherent in imperial rule (Clarke 1996, 20). In response, Chamberlain began to shift the focus of British imperialism away from the Indian Raj and toward other colonies and dominions peopled and governed by emigrating white Britons—especially Canada, Australia, New Zealand, and South Africa—knit together by national ties and racial affinity, economic ties, and democracy. Essential to this political stance was a conception of Britain's racial mission to lead the colonial world for both the enrichment of Britain and the betterment of imperial subjects. The notion of an "imperial race," distinguishing white Britons from nonwhite colonial peoples, was central to the politics of imperialism at the turn of the century (Semmel 1960).

The centerpiece of Chamberlain's imperial policy was tariff reform, a system of free trade within the empire and protection from outside goods, especially a tax on foreign grain. In order to sell tariff reform to the working class, which traditionally supported free trade because it kept food prices low, Chamberlain linked tariffs with social reform—old-age and unemployment pensions, and labor exchanges. Social reform appealed to imperialist politicians for a number of reasons. For Chamberlain and others, imperial strength was essential to Britain's continued prosperity and economic dominance, and hence to the welfare of the working class. For others, such as the Fabian socialists and Liberal reformers, the proposition was the reverse: the welfare of the working class and the breeding of a healthy and robust "imperial race" were essential to the success of the empire. Like imperialism, social reform constituted a long-standing project that was by itself too weak to sustain a majority coalition. By reframing social reform as an imperial policy, reformers made both policy courses possible where neither would have been sustainable by itself (Semmel 1960).

The fight over tariffs divided old-line Conservatives, while the defense of free trade galvanized Liberals, and although Chamberlain's tariff-reform proposals were defeated, the link between imperialism and social reform opened new political possibilities. The Liberal government formed in 1905 was dominated by a group of so-called Liberal Imperialists for whom the goals of imperialism and social reform were inseparable. Behind Prime Minister Herbert Henry Asquith, they pursued an ambitious social reform agenda that formed the basis of the British welfare state, along with an expensive naval buildup for the defense of the empire (Kennedy 1976, 205–37; Clarke 1996, 53–56). Under the leadership of Chancellor of the Exchequer David Lloyd George and president of the Board of Trade Winston Churchill, the Liberal government enacted a series of social reforms that undermined the locally operated Poor Law system that had prevailed in England for more than three centuries (Polanyi 1944). Legislation in 1908 created a national system of labor exchanges to help the unemployed find work; the Old Age Pension Act of the same year enacted noncontributory, means-tested pensions. Finally, in 1911 the National Insurance Act created a system of compulsory, contributory national unemployment and health insurance (Baldwin 1990, 99–102; Ogus 1982, 173–87; King 1995).

Together, these policies took an important step toward centralizing the British welfare state, creating direct and unmediated links between nearly all workers in Britain (and their families) and the state by providing benefits as a matter of right (Marshall 1964). These policies thus constituted an important mechanism of social solidarity underpinned by a broad coalition that brought together middle- and working-class concerns. Such national solidarity, constructed by social policies aimed partly at unifying an "imperial race," served as a counterweight against the class warfare that seemed to be tearing continental Europe apart. British social imperialists on the right and the left alike believed that the amelioration of working-class conditions was necessary to prevent fore-stall "divisive" socialism that would foment class conflict and undermine the empire (Semmel 1960; Hobsbawm 1987, 101–4). Like American wel-fare policies, then, the coalition behind these policies was built on a foun-dation of racial rule that served to unify Britons across classes in favor of moderate social reform. But unlike American race politics, which differ-entiated Americans from each other along internal, institutionally and politically constructed racial lines, British race politics constructed a national racial community against others abroad and thus identified a national interest in welfare policy that began to unify British citizens in a network of social solidarity through the welfare state and the mecha-nisms of social citizenship.

France

In France, as in Britain, the politics of race was primarily a matter of the distinction between the colonies and the metropole. And as in Britain, imperialism and social reform mingled in French politics in the late nine-teenth and early twentieth centuries, suggesting at least the possibility of a similar cross-class social-imperial coalition that might have linked race-based imperial rule with domestic social solidarity in the form of welfare policies. In fact, some social reformers in France explicitly invoked the importance of racial distinctions and imperial rule in support of soli-daristic policies (Elwitt 1986, 82–84). But political differences between France and Britain—in both the character of race politics and the struc-ture of national political institutions—prevented this coalition from forming, resulting in a more decentralized welfare state rooted more directly in civil society than Britain's. Thus race politics in France did not provide the impetus to overcome the mediated and indirect structures of social provision that had developed in the nineteenth century.

One important difference was the status of social imperialism in the French intellectual and political universe. Unlike the British theorists and practitioners of the politics of social imperialism, French social imperial-ists tended to be opponents (or at least skeptics) of democracy (Semmel 1960, 237–38; Baumgart 1982; Renouvin 1983). In the early years of the Third Republic monarchism remained a potent force in French politics (Nord 1995, 3, 59–61, 134–35; Cobban 1965, 3:15–23). It was antidemo-cratic politicians and intellectuals such as Maurice Barrès, Léon Daudet, and Charles Maurras who most directly advocated links between social reform and racially inflected notions of national unity. Moreover, Maurras along with other more respectable conservative social reformers supported decentralized social policy, which would place power in the hands of local elites and corporate bodies, reminiscent of feudalism, rather than the state. Thus French social imperialism was not poised to produce a coalition for national, centralized social reform as a vehicle for cementing national unity.

A second important difference was that internal differences were more salient in French national and colonial politics than in British politics. French nationalism was aimed largely at domestic enemies, particularly Jews. Antisemitism, particularly during and after the Dreyfus affair, was a critical focal point of mass politics and a vehicle for national political mobilization and cross-class political alliances (Sternhell 1986, 44–48; Birnbaum 2000; see also Cobban 1965, 3:90). At the same time, France was continuing inside the hexagon its process of internal assimilation of regional and linguistic minorities, who were commonly compared in official discourse to racially distinct Africans and other external colonial subjects (Weber 1976, 485–88). Finally, French colonialism was more focused on the prospect of the assimilation of colonial subjects into the French nation, in keeping with the nineteenth-century pattern of internal assimilation of both natives and immigrants. In both metropolitan and overseas France, policies aimed at assimilation between Europeans and non-Europeans was fiercely controversial, and these controversies often had explicitly racial grounds (Lebovics 1992; Cobban 1965, 3:91–93; Elwitt 1986, 83–84; see also Cooper 1996). Thus French politics struggled with both internal diversity and the possibility of external association, making the formation of a racially constructed, cross-class coalition for social reform unlikely and, by the same token, rendering social reform problematic as a vehicle for pursuing national unity.

The structure of French political institutions was a further barrier to the construction of a stable coalition for national unity through social reform. The Third Republic was dominated by a parliament with neither a strong executive nor a robust party system, so that despite mass suffrage the representation of social interests beyond the republican bourgeoisie was limited (Hoffmann 1963, 12–18). Thus even when a broad coalition that included the more moderate representatives of labor came to power in 1899, it proved to be short-lived and disinclined to move toward serious national social reform (Hobsbawm 1987, 102; Elwitt 1986, 293–95; Cobban 1965, 3:56–60). Thus to the extent that the raw materials existed for a coalition in favor of social reform as an agent of national social solidarity as a response to the imperatives of racial rule, French political institutions were ill equipped to sustain such a coalition.

The consequence of these forces for French social reform was that welfare policies developed not through the construction of national, state-led policies but by the accretion of decentralized, corporatist welfare schemes that were neither state-administered nor state-financed (Chapman 1995, 293–95; Baldwin 1990, 102–5; Ashford 1991). These policies had their roots in the nineteenth-century flourishing of *mutualité*, mutual societies organized around occupational, fraternal, or other local attachments. A series of French welfare policies took this form, from workmen's compensation to old-age pensions to family allowances (Saint-Jours 1982, 107–19; Pedersen 1993, 224–91; Weintrob 1996). Unlike Britain, France did not create centralized, state-led welfare before World War II, although not for lack of trying—a serious attempt to create national, compulsory, contributory old-age pensions failed in 1910. When national social insurance did pass in 1930, followed by family allowances in 1932, they left in place the *mutualité*-based structure of earlier welfare policies, so that attachments to the French welfare state remained mediated by civil-society attachments and contributed only weakly, if at all, to the construction of social solidarity before World War II.

Conclusions

The contours of racial rule in the United States, Great Britain, and France contributed to the construction of differently configured welfare states in which citizens and groups of citizens were connected to the state through different institutional mechanisms. In Britain and the United States welfare state institutions were the product of coalitions that united whites across class to provide racially exclusionary social benefits; the difference between the two lay in the difference between internal and external patterns of racial rule, which led similarly drawn coalitions to embrace very different prescriptions for social reform. In France, by contrast, the imperative of racial solidarity did not produce a coalition for nationalizing social reform because of differences both in colonial relations and in political institutions. Only in the United States did these early welfare state developments have immediate and direct implications for racial minorities—African Americans—who were widely excluded from social benefits in the wake of the New Deal through deliberately fragmented institutions. But each system created a set of institutional terms by which groups could form attachments to the welfare state and acquire rights to social provision, and it was these institutions that would structure the later incorporation of racial minorities into welfare systems. These institutions were far from innocent of the historical legacies of racial rule that structured the politics of their creation, and none of these countries would have to wait long to see how these policy systems would respond to the challenge of increasingly multiracial societies.

Above all, these comparative patterns puncture the mythology of American racial exceptionalism by undermining the supposition that the American welfare state was uniquely stunted or thwarted by racial division. Other countries, too, faced broadly similar political tasks in building national welfare states in the face of race-based challenges to national solidarity that stemmed from racial rule in the form of slavery or colonialism. Thus simply to say that race or racism impeded the growth of a national, inclusive welfare state in the United States begs important questions of definition and causation. What precise characteristics of America's racial-political complex shaped welfare policy-making? How were racial classifications filtered through different political and institutional contexts to produce different outcomes? And what social and political mechanisms made race relevant to welfare state building in particular ways at particular historical moments?

Much of what we thought we knew about American racial exceptionalism turns out, on comparative examination, to be not exceptional but relatively universal among Western countries seeking to build solidaristic national welfare states—racialized definitions of nationhood, attempts to define the contours of social citizenship and welfare rights along racial lines, dilemmas surrounding the legitimacy of multiculturalism, and even more particular technocratic problems of localism and policy design (Favell 1998; Lieberman 1999). But at the same time, the comparison also helps to refine, if not exactly to reinforce, our sense of American racial exceptionalism by focusing attention on what, precisely, is exceptional about American race politics, on what stands out from the more general patterns that emerge from comparative analysis. It is not race per se that is exceptional in American political history, but the particular way it is arrayed across American political institutions, practices, and beliefs that has made it especially powerful in shaping policy—the ways race interacts with regionalism and federalism, the structure of

Congress and political parties, and the peculiar dynamics of coalition formation in American national politics.

The comparison also suggests further directions and possibilities for research on racial influences on national politics and policy-making. Viewing the United States in comparative perspective helps to uncover broad-brush patterns of linkage among race, national political institutions, and the possibilities for coalition building for solidaristic policies of social provision. But these large-scale patterns still leave unanswered fundamental causal questions about the mechanisms of racial influence on policy, the ways in which racial classifications in national politics can act in both overt and covert ways to shape political institutions and practices as well as policy outcomes. Only more fine-grained historical research coupled with careful theorizing can unpack these problems.

But this is a crucial task if students of American welfare policy (and of American politics and public policy more generally) are to understand some of the profound paradoxes and dilemmas of our time. Although America is much less segregated and much less outwardly racist than it was a half-century ago, race remains one of the deepest and most intractable dividing lines of contemporary American politics. Despite dramatic advances in civil and political rights for American minorities, they remain, in many ways, poorly integrated into the welfare state and into American national life (Schuman et al. 1997; Bobo and Smith 1994; Gilens 1999; Lieberman 1998, 1999). In order to understand these curious patterns of our own day, it is essential that we begin to explore not simply how America's peculiar and distinctive racial culture affects our politics but how patterns of historical embeddedness have shaped the possibilities of politics—how race is "built into" American political institutions and practices in both visible and invisible ways.

In the 1990s, as Americans turned once again to welfare reform, the place of African Americans in the political system was once again of critical importance in shaping social policy. While they remained overwhelmingly Democratic voters, African Americans were no longer at the center of the Democratic party's national agenda. Touting his credentials as a "new Democrat," Bill Clinton promised to move his party away from its focus on issues of civil rights and poverty and toward issues that would woo back the white working- and middle-class constituencies that had abandoned the party in the wake of the 1960s. At the same time, Republicans "mastered a politics permeated by race-coded messages that played on the anxieties of white Americans" in order to retain the loyalty of those same constituencies (Williams 1998). With African Americans increasingly marginal to the political strategies of both parties, increasingly isolated from the center of American politics, and increasingly linked in the public mind with the pathologies associated with welfare, the conditions were bleak for African American participation in a broad, solidaristic welfare policy coalition. It was these structural conditions that set the stage for the Personal Responsibility and Work Opportunity Reconciliation Act of 1996. Armed with a historical and comparative account of the linked roles of race and welfare in American politics, we can better understand how this reform came to pass and what it might mean for the fate of America's minorities under the new welfare regime and for the future of American race politics.

CHAPTER 2

Ghettos, Fiscal Federalism, and Welfare Reform

MICHAEL K. BROWN

Welfare reform in 1996 had little to do with poverty; it had a lot to do with racialized politics of poverty. Conservatives declared that anything was better than the old welfare system for poor women and that their plans for tough work requirements and time-limited benefits was a policy of hope. What they were really interested in was politically exploiting the issue and painting the Democrats as defenders of "amoral" black women in ghettos. Liberals rationalized welfare reform as necessary, but they also understood it to be a way of banishing race, and racialized poverty, from the political lexicon. For the Democrats welfare reform was as much about solving their frayed relationship with disgruntled, irate middle-class white voters as it was about poverty. Now many liberals think that replacing the cash entitlement of Aid to Families with Dependent Children (AFDC) with a work-based safety net precludes racial stigmatization of social benefits and ensures political legitimacy for antipoverty policies. Rather than suppressing the debate about race and poverty that began with Lyndon Johnson's War on Poverty and Daniel Patrick Moynihan's famous report, welfare reform will reopen it.

Opponents of the 1996 welfare reform legislation feared that repealing AFDC's cash entitlement would lead to untold misery. In a scathing editorial, the *Washington Post* called the Personal Responsibility and Work Opportunity Reconciliation Act (PRWORA) "reckless because it could endanger the well being of the poorest children in society in the

47

name of a series of untested theories about how people *may* respond to some new incentives." Others worried that welfare reform would unleash a "race to the bottom" as states competed to lower benefits and keep migrating poor people out. Today any lingering concern that poor children will be plunged into misery is quickly forgotten amid cheers over plummeting caseloads. Yet the euphoria over the so-called success in replacing welfare payments with paychecks masks the real dilemma underlying welfare reform—a conflict between the fiscal incentives embedded in the Temporary Assistance for Needy Families (TANF) program and racialized poverty concentrated in big-city ghettos.

Changes in the racial composition of poor women remaining on the rolls expose the political trap at the heart of the new welfare policy. In many states whites have left the rolls faster than blacks. The proportion of white families in TANF sharply dropped to 31 percent of all cases; racial minorities now account for over two-thirds. Meanwhile, states have amassed financial windfalls due to the rapid decline in caseloads and fixed federal financing. Most states are either hoarding this money or passing it on to white middle-class voters in the form of tax cuts and other subsidies. Whether this surplus will be used to help the African American and Latina mothers remaining on the rolls is an open question.

Policymakers assumed that PRWORA's work requirements and time limits would be cushioned by public investments in education, job training, child-care, and other services for poor women. Yet states are encouraged by the financial incentives of the act to push welfare recipients into any available jobs or workfare, and the fiscal structure of the law provides no guarantees that financial windfalls will be used to help those most in need. When it converted the AFDC entitlement to cash benefits into a block grant administered by states, Congress reduced the money states were required to contribute to welfare and gave them considerable freedom in allocating federal dollars. Other than a frail hope that governors and state legislators could do better, there is little to prevent the money from being used for white middle-class constituencies rather than poor African American women and Latinas living in urban ghettos.

Race and devolution have been antagonistic features of federal social policy since the 1930s. Title IV of the Social Security Act gave states control of AFDC benefits and eligibility and led to pervasive racial discrimination in both the North and the South. Supreme Court decisions and civil rights laws curtailed these abuses in the 1960s by diminishing state authority over eligibility and by ordering states to provide due process of law to poor women who lost their benefits. These policy changes partially centralized AFDC. The 1996 welfare reform law unwinds the welfare system once again and grants states enormous authority over poor women and their children (Mink 1998, 44–64). Before the 1960s the antimony between race and devolution was based on southern efforts to exclude eligible African Americans from welfare in order to uphold Jim Crow and northern ambivalence toward black migration from the South. Today it turns on the antagonism between race and fiscal federalism. It is conflict between the changing racial composition of the TANF rolls and state control of how federal funds are allocated, not the so-called race to the bottom in which states compete to lower benefits, that will determine whether this social experiment succeeds or fails.

Political conflict between Democrats and Republicans over fiscal federalism and social welfare that goes back to the 1930s produced the antinomy between race and fiscal federalism embedded in the welfare reform law. PRWORA's fiscal structure and incentives are the result of state governments' attempt to shift all the costs of federal social policy to the national government and Republicans' strategy of using block grants to limit growth of the welfare state. This fiscal structure is not easily reconciled with the urban concentration of racialized poverty, and, in fact, it is a consequence of the racial politics of welfare—opponents of federal social policy using race as a political weapon to undermine support for the welfare state.

Why Liberals Should Hate Block Grants

The contradiction between fiscal federalism and race was the unspoken corollary to the debate over race and poverty that preceded passage of the 1996 law. The debate assumed that the persistence of racialized poverty (African American and Latino poverty rates three times those of whites) was rooted in individual failure by and large—the failure of poor blacks to accept work when it was available, a failure to stay in school, or a refusal to get married. Conservatives demanded work requirements and individual responsibility of poor women as way of reforming "ghetto culture." Forcing poor African American mothers to work would change their values and "break the culture of poverty," according to Mickey Kaus (1992, 127). Liberals accepted the need for work and self-discipline; they merely sought to soften the program with a plan for guaranteed jobs. Although many liberals acknowledged that the massive decline in good jobs in big cities was the main cause of urban poverty, they nonetheless believed the so-called pathological behavior of the poor was just as relevant. Thus, they were willing to accept time limits on benefits and to allow states to make moral improvement a condition of aid.

This debate misconstrues the problems facing poor women and their children and fails to explain why racialized poverty endures. Growth in the number of female-headed families among African Americans has less to do with persistent poverty than the loss of jobs in inner cities, declining demand for unskilled labor, and racially segregated neighborhoods.[1] Equally important to these well-known causes of racialized poverty is one that often goes unstated: public disinvestment in ghetto communities. The problem with governmental policy is not that it has been too generous or that it contributes to the bad behavior of poor women. Rather, it has always been insufficient. Neoliberal welfare reformers recognized these realities and assumed that any policy predicated on eliminating the AFDC entitlement and forcing poor women into the labor market would require substantial public investment in day care, employment training and education, health services, and a variety of social services. This was the premise underlying their hopes for the 1988 Family Support Act, which was supposed to provide new resources for poor women and their families. And it was the basis of the Faustian bargain neoliberals made when they agreed to the 1996 welfare reform bill.

TANF appealed to many "new Democrats" because it held out the possibility of fashioning a race-neutral, work-conditioned safety net that could address inner-city poverty. Whites, particularly white Democrats, strongly prefer race-neutral policies (Sniderman and Carmines 1997, 104–10). Neoliberal welfare reformers also assumed that TANF was a way of reconciling the mantra of individual responsibility that is the ideology of welfare reform with the economic realities of low-wage labor markets. The challenge facing policymakers, they assume, is how to make a work-conditioned safety net function in an hourglass economy where demand for unskilled labor has dramatically declined and economic growth is less effective in reducing poverty. It was obvious during the long debate over welfare reform that any work-conditioned policy would be very expensive. Yet liberal welfare reformers lost their wager when they agreed to block grants. TANF's fiscal structure undermines any possibility of building a viable work-conditioned safety net: it gives states powerful financial incentives to reduce caseloads and few incentives to reduce concentrated poverty in inner cities.

Under TANF federal funding no longer oscillates with changes in caseloads, as it did under AFDC. The AFDC entitlement was based on an open-ended grant-in-aid in which the federal government matched state expenditures on a sliding scale that provided proportionally more resources to poor states. Regardless of the number of cases, the federal government paid from 50 to 80 percent of the statewide average cost of the caseload. Congress replaced this open-ended grant with a block grant and capped spending at $16.5 billion annually. The money is allocated to the states based on their 1994–95 caseloads. TANF is a far more rigid program than AFDC. From the vantage point of the federal budget, an "uncontrollable" entitlement program is now a fixed appropriation where Congress will determine the volume of spending. From the vantage point of states, caseload reductions yield a financial windfall. Since federal funding no longer fluctuates with the size of the caseload, states are allowed to keep any unexpended federal dollars.

States lost open-ended federal funding but acquired more freedom to choose how to spend federal money. Under the law states may shift up to 30 percent of TANF funds to either the Child Care Development Fund (CCDF) or the Social Services Block Grant (SSBG).[2] States can also reallocate federal welfare dollars. The law requires that state funds be spent for former AFDC programs or programs for TANF recipients, but no such restriction applies to federal dollars. Conceivably states could use federal dollars to pay for other state social welfare programs and reduce the amount of state spending. By substituting federal for state dollars, governors and legislatures free up state money for tax cuts or other programs.[3] Executives and legislators can also reallocate TANF dollars geographically, and they will undoubtedly succumb to the temptation to do so—at least if experience with previous block grants at the city and county level is any guide.

Capped funding, substitution of federal for state dollars, and geographical dispersion of TANF funds potentially vitiate any work-based safety net. So far, though, the anticipated fiscal crunch has failed to materialize. Total spending is down due to the mandated reduction in the state contribution, but because caseloads have declined so far so fast and funding is based on the higher 1994–95 caseloads, states have reaped a financial windfall. According to the General Accounting Office, states received $4.7 billion more under TANF for their 1997 caseloads than they would have received under the "pre-reform cost structure."[4] Presumably, states will be able to increase spending for the remaining women and children, though there is no guarantee they will do so. What is clear is that TANF's fiscal incentives have driven states to adopt a "work first model."[5]

Some states have been very aggressive in using the law to push recipients into any available job. Caseloads in Wisconsin, Wyoming, Idaho, and Mississippi have dropped by 80 percent or more, and in 13 other states the decline exceeds 60 percent. Many states have transformed welfare offices into job centers. States have made the application process more difficult, and some states "divert" poor mothers from assistance by paying them to stay away. Needy and eligible individuals are deterred, as a consequence, from seeking cash assistance. What states have not done is provide alternatives to employment such as education or job training. Just 6 percent of the two million adults on the TANF rolls are in educational or work-training programs. However, many states have made it easier for single mothers to work and keep their benefits, and as a result about one-third of those women remaining on the TANF rolls combine work with welfare (U.S. Department of Health and Human Services 2000d, 1, 5).

The large decline in caseloads has not been matched by a comparable decline in poverty rates or increase in wages. One recent study found that the income of single mothers who had dropped out of high school rose by 7 percent under TANF, while their poverty rate declined by 2 percent. But TANF's work requirements have had no effect on personal earnings, suggesting that other sources of income such as friends, family, or transfer payments like the Earned Income Tax Credit (EITC), food stamps, and TANF have been more important in lowering poverty (Schoeni and Blank 2000, 21, 23). Single mothers who went to work did not gain much, and some women are clearly worse off. Disposable income increased by just $292 among the poorest 40 percent of single mothers between 1995 and 1999; those women in the bottom 20 percent saw their disposable income decline by 4 percent (Primus 2001). This is hardly surprising in the new world of welfare reform where cash benefits have been curtailed.

Sheldon Danziger worries that "we have in place a safety net that does very little to provide work opportunities for those who have trouble finding a job or working full-time full-year" (2000, 5). This may be true, but Danziger elides the question of race and TANF's fiscal incentives. The disproportionate number of black women and Latinas who remain on the TANF rolls face severe obstacles to stable employment in well-paying jobs. Black women remaining on TANF are more likely to lack education and job skills than white women, and most of the valuable jobs are located in the suburbs at considerable distance from public transportation and poor neighborhoods. And while employers *say* they are willing to hire poor single mothers, in fact they are often reluctant to do so. Besides the geographical barriers to employment, black and Latino welfare mothers, according to Harry Holzer and Michael Stoll, are "less likely to be hired in suburban and/or smaller establishments, and for blacks, in the retail trade industries" (2000, 16). The poor single mothers who would benefit from a program capable of meeting their needs for education, job training, transportation, and day care are mostly black and Latina.

We face the same question that vexed policymakers in the 1960s: how to get nonstigmatized aid to poor blacks and Latinos. Richard Titmuss, the doyen of British social policy, thought the solution was universalistic social policies. But the political will and support for such policies is lacking, and any effort to target resources to the inner-city poor may be undermined by the fiscal incentives of PRWORA.

What are the origins of this perverse policy? It was no accident. As Republicans clearly understand, a block grant with fixed funding is a form of budgetary control. According to one congressional aide involved in creating the program, block grants "are one of the best ways to cut the budget. The cuts are so ethereal. You don't have to specify what will really happen to people and programs. You just give the states less money and let them decide" (Conlan 1998, 237). Republicans initially introduced legislation converting 336 federal programs into eight block grants, and tried to eliminate the federal entitlement for welfare, Medicaid, and food stamps. They were hardly interested in improving governmental efficiency. Republican affection for block grants goes back to the 1960s and their efforts to derail the Great Society. In fact, there is a consistent theory of devolution and budget cutting that runs from Nixon to Newt Gingrich. TANF's paradoxical discrepancy between fiscal incentives and racialized poverty should be understood as the result of a partisan political struggle over financing of federal social policy that dates to the New Deal and the racial conflict defining the history of AFDC and the antipoverty programs of the Great Society.

The Political Economy of Devolution

Race and fiscal federalism have been antagonistically linked since the New Deal, when the federal government assumed greater responsibility for subsidizing the activities of state and local governments. From FDR on, national politicians chose to use state and local governments as conduits for national policies; they only differed in the latitude they granted to subnational governments. If federalism has been constitutive of the welfare state, it has also impeded the redistributive policies needed to either ameliorate or diminish poverty while permitting racial discrimination to flourish and reinforcing the hierarchy of white over black. African Americans have always understood that a decentralized welfare state would only sustain the color line. During the debate over the 1935 Social Security Act, Walter White of the NAACP warned Eleanor Roosevelt that "if the Federal Government continues to make lump grants to the States and leaves expenditures to the States it should not abandon all responsibility to see that Federal funds are not used to grind a section of its citizenry further into the dust" (Kifer 1961, 234).

Redistribution is a national function. Relying on the states to redistribute resources from wealthy citizens and places to impoverished citizens and communities is a dead end. Such a policy, Richard Musgrave observes, "can only operate within narrow limits" (1997, 67). States have few incentives to mount redistributive social programs and will seek, ordinarily, to shift the burden of spending to the national government. Tax revenues needed to fund governmental services depend on private investment and the willingness of taxpayers to pay up. Any government is an "economic parasite," Joseph Schumpeter memorably wrote, and it "must not demand from the people so much that they lose financial interest in production or at any rate cease to use their best energies for it" (1991, 112). Since capital and taxpayers are highly mobile, state governments must compete for economic resources just as nation-states compete in the global economy. High-tax states intent on redistribution may find themselves at a disadvantage in attracting new investment and retaining the support of taxpayers. These costs can be avoided by transferring the burden for social expenditures to higher levels of government, in effect shifting the burden and political responsibility for taxation upward.

The New Deal established shared fiscal responsibility for social policies, using federal grants-in-aid to subsidize state-run programs. Joint financing of categorical grants-in-aid is less a venture in cooperative federalism than an endless game waged by politicians to shift the responsibility for raising taxes to finance the welfare state. The allocation of tax burdens between the federal and state (or local) governments depends on whether states must match federal spending and how much they must pay. Matching grants, such as the federal subsidy for AFDC, lower the "price" to states of providing a good or service and thus affect state and local spending and taxation. The higher the federal contribution, the lower the price to states. What matters to states is what proportion of costs the federal government assumes and whether the federal contribution is capped, covering only a portion of total costs. States prefer high federal matches and seek to have most of the costs of the service covered. They will also try to shift the costs of existing state programs to the federal government. States often try to reclassify state activities so they are eligible for federal aid, and historically they have been quite inventive.

Federal policymakers seeking to limit spending (or taxation) prefer a low federal match or fixed spending limits, or both. National policymakers do not always seek to limit federal tax burdens. When they want to stimulate spending for services that states might not be inclined to undertake and they perceive constraints on taxation to be low, they will endorse, as they did in the 1960s, high federal contributions to grants-in-aid.

National grants-in-aid are imperfect tools of redistribution. They can be used to equalize the fiscal resources at the disposal of places, states for example. Since the 1930s, Congress has diverted proportionally more federal resources to southern states to compensate for the lack of fiscal capacity. But it is more difficult to use grants-in-aid to equalize the distribution of cash transfers or services to individuals. Redistribution to individuals is much easier through a national system of cash transfers where the federal government can control eligibility criteria and benefit levels. Once federal officials decide to use grants-in-aid to redistribute cash payments or services, they "must take into account the fact that states will further reallocate the resources at their command after the center has done its redistribution" (Dixit and Londgegan 1998, 178). State reallocation of federal resources may entail the diversion of money to constituencies or programs other than those specified by federal legislation; it may also result in discrimination.

Fiscal federalism is usually justified on grounds of efficiency—minimizing externalities in the provision of public goods and enhancing responsiveness to citizens' preferences for different bundles of basic services, taxes, and regulation. It is usually assumed as well that decentralization of public services promotes democracy and protects individual rights from overweening central authorities. Doubtless, federalism has promoted diverse responses to public problems, and it might even be seen as a bulwark against federal intrusion. Yet these conventional justifications for federalism evade its role in perpetuating inequalities. Decentralization to small units ignores, as Grant McConnell observed long ago, "questions of power within the unit of organization" (1966, 115). McConnell's point, of course, was that some individuals or groups gain by decentralization, while others may lose.

Depending on the limits imposed on subnational governments, fiscal federalism holds federal policy hostage to the potentially pernicious inclinations of local majorities and their official representatives. Historically, states have had wide latitude under the police powers, the reserved powers delegated to states by the Tenth Amendment to the Constitution, to "promote the health, safety, morals, and general welfare." These powers have been used to regulate any moral conduct deemed inappropriate by a majority—Sunday blue laws for example—and they did little for a long time to protect individual rights from arbitrary state laws (Lowi 1995, 28–29). Buoyed by the ideology of "states rights," state laws were used to uphold slavery and Jim Crow—*Plessy v. Ferguson* upheld segregation as a reasonable use of a state's police powers. Until the 1960s, the rights granted to African Americans by the Fourteenth and Fifteenth Amendments had little meaning in a society determined to defer to local (white) majorities. Federalism has been one of the chief bulwarks of racial domination in the United States.[6]

Franklin D. Roosevelt decided against creating an entirely national welfare state in the 1930s, and he refused to fund national standards for categorical public assistance. This ensured that federal welfare policies would be used as weapons of racial oppression. Many federal social policies were affected as a result, not just the categorical public assistance programs of the Social Security Act. Works Progress Administration (WPA) jobs were usually allocated with a preference for unemployed white workers in mind, and federal housing programs were implemented by local officials with an eye to maintaining residential segregation (Brown 1999, 82–85; Jackson 1985). Blacks have historically dissented from this notion of federalism, and from the 1930s to the present, they campaigned for national social policies (Hamilton and Hamilton 1997).

Whether fiscal federalism facilitates racial discrimination depends, in part, on the level of national control over states' decisions. Besides holding states accountable to constitutional standards of due process and equal protection, choices about the type of grant-in-aid used to distribute federal dollars determine whether fiscal federalism is permissive or nonpermissive. Categorical grants restrict state spending to legally defined programs and allow national officials to narrowly target resources to the needs of specific groups or individuals. Unless federal policymakers set standards for the distribution of resources, however, even categorical grants can be used as tools of discrimination. Broad-based grants are far more permissive. These grants give state and local officials wide authority to allocate resources among competing uses. Revenue sharing, for example, gives state and local officials substantial autonomy to spend federal dollars as they wish, and if there is no required state contribution or match, subnational governments can easily substitute national dollars for local dollars. Block grants are a hybrid; such grants restrict spending to specified policy issues—urban redevelopment for example—but grant state and local officials substantial autonomy in deciding how to address the issue. Unlike categorical grants, block grants lend themselves to the dispersion of funds across numerous and diverse constituencies. Indeed this is their chief virtue from the point of view of state and local politicians.

The Antinomies of Race and Fiscal Federalism since the 1930s

Cooperative federalism, as Democrats and Republicans have euphemistically referred to federal grants-in-aid since the 1930s, masks a political struggle over both the allocation of tax and spending burdens and the racial bias produced by white control over the distribution of benefits and resources at the local level. As the recent history of federal transfers for the poor and other antipoverty policies reveals, the antinomy between race and fiscal federalism has been indelibly shaped by partisan conflict over the financing of federal social policy and widening social divisions over, first, dismantling Jim Crow and, then, how to overcome the legacy of slavery and Jim Crow. TANF's discrepancy between needs and resources emerges from a 50-year struggle over race and money.

Although Roosevelt underwrote state welfare programs with federal subsidies, he chose to use fiscally constrained but permissive grants-in-aid. Lyndon Johnson's Great Society rectified the New Deal's permissive federalism by imposing limits on state authority while expanding federal financing of social policies. Conservatives responded by attempting to derail the Great Society through devolution and budget cutting. Block grants were the weapon of choice. Race amplified these partisan divisions over tax and spending burdens. Initially, southerners used their power over the distribution of federal grants to stave off an assault on Jim Crow and build a racially segregated welfare state; after the 1960s, Republicans used dissension over race and welfare to drive a wedge between Democratic constituencies.

FDR and Harry Hopkins, director of the Federal Emergency Relief Administration, were reluctant to assume the full cost of financing social programs. From the outset, they insisted that states share the obligation of financing relief during the depression and in the new welfare state. The

1935 Social Security Act established a permanent federal subsidy for state categorical public assistance programs. But FDR, intent on limiting the growth of federal spending and thus tax increases, expressly chose to impose a ceiling on federal payments. The federal ADC subsidy, for instance, applied only to first $18 for the first child (and $12 for the second child). If states made payments above this limit, they were on their own. Southern Democrats lobbied Roosevelt to raise the ceiling (some wanted full federal funding of public assistance), but he refused (Brown 1999, 44–45).

By the late 1930s southerners were advocating variable grants-in-aid, a scheme to shift much of the financing for public assistance in the South to the federal government. Roosevelt initially refused to back these proposals, but after 1945 northern Democrats reversed themselves and supported funding formulas that would increase the federal share of public assistance funding, mainly in the South. Faced with united opposition from a coalition of Republicans and southern Democrats to their plans for a national "cradle to grave" welfare state, this was one of the few ways northern Democrats could expand social welfare programs. Republicans invariably fought these legislative proposals, and in 1958 the Eisenhower administration tried, but failed, to reduce the federal share of public assistance costs to an average of 50 percent. Changing the funding formula had the desired effect: real welfare benefits rose dramatically, more than doubling between 1940 and 1965 (Moffitt 1988, 4–5). Aid to Dependent Children (ADC) benefits increased in the South as well as the rest of the nation (even with the rise in real benefits, welfare payments were still extraordinarily low).

Democratic success in raising welfare spending was costly. Southerners typically agreed vote for changes in public assistance formulas and other federal welfare programs so long as they retained control of the distribution of benefits. What this meant, as northern Democrats were well aware, is that federal policies would be wielded as tool to keep African Americans in their place. Adam Clayton Powell, then the lone African American in Congress, often attached antidiscrimination riders to social welfare bills, which northern Democrats then voted to remove. Democratic legislative victories, thus, depended on sacrificing any presumption of racial equality (Brown 1999, 132–33).

Southerners took full advantage of their power over the allocation of federal grants-in-aid to build a segregated welfare state and exclude blacks. Federal grant-in-aids for hospital construction authorized by the 1946 Hill-Burton Act were used to build segregated hospitals throughout the South (Smith 1999, 103). By the early 1950s, all southern states had severely restricted eligibility for ADC. Similar restrictions were enacted in some northern states, notably Michigan and Illinois, where growing case-loads were composed mainly of African American women. Discrimination was the order of the day: in the South eligible African Americans were denied aid; in the North they were admitted to the rolls but given lower benefits (Lieberman 1998, 126–40). In either case, needy African American families were denied aid, and many poor women were deterred from applying for the assistance they were legally entitled to receive.

White southerners' ferocious defense of their Jim Crow privileges, fueled by their virulent hostility to the stirrings of the civil rights movement, and a palpable fear and dislike of black immigrants in the North spurred the welfare purges of the 1950s. In both regions, politicians exploited white fears in elections and local welfare officials succumbed to the demands of white majorities or farmers and businessmen looking for low-wage labor. Roosevelt's permissive federalism also gave local officials control of federal urban renewal and public housing programs. Many cities used urban renewal money to forcibly displace African Americans living on prime downtown land and transformed public housing into a tool to maintain residential segregation (Hirsch 1983).

Great Society liberals repealed Roosevelt's permissive, fiscally constrained federalism. They began by raising federal contributions to grants-in-aid, enabling them to launch new programs and change the spending priorities of state and local governments. In 1965 Democrats succeeded in eliminating the federal ceiling originally imposed by Roosevelt on public assistance payments to states. Congress had removed the federal cap on individual grants in 1958 but still limited federal payments to the overall average individual benefit payment in a state. This average was initially set at $30 and raised to $32 in 1965. With a deft slight of hand, Congress also gave states the option seeking reimbursement for public assistance costs under the more liberal Medicaid formula. This policy effectively removed the ceiling on average payments, which meant that the federal government would henceforth pay a proportion of the total costs of AFDC. Not surprisingly, almost all states chose this financing option by the mid-1980s (Myers 1985, 723–24, 751–55). By then the federal contribution to AFDC averaged 60 percent of total welfare payments.

Hardly any programs were immune, however, as Democrats changed funding formulas in both old and new programs. The Manpower Development and Training Act's federal match was initially 50 percent, but in

1963 the Kennedy administration convinced Congress to raise it to 100 percent for one year, and then Congress renewed it each year thereafter. Similarly, in older programs like vocational rehabilitation, which the Johnson administration expanded and redirected toward a poor clientele, the match was raised from 50 to 75 percent. By raising the federal match, the Great Society stimulated spending by state and local governments and changed their spending priorities "to a greater extent than had been seen in the previous thirty years" (Reischauer 1986, 182–83).

Great Society liberals were willing to use federal resources to induce state and local spending; they were unwilling to give state officials much autonomy. Most Democrats understood that attacking African American exclusion from federal programs and curtailing abuses required centralization. Title VI of the 1964 Civil Rights Act was perhaps the single most important step taken to limit state abuses of federal grants-in-aid. Federal officials used this law, which banned discrimination in the distribution of federal funds, to undo segregated schools and hospitals in the South. Centralization was the impulse behind most of the new Great Society programs. Liberals insisted on project grants, thus tying recipient governments to federal requirements (Reischauer 1986, 183). They also centralized old programs. Beginning in 1967, Robert Weaver, secretary of the Department of Housing and Urban Development, imposed new rules on urban renewal, forcing local officials to adhere to national goals and curtailing their discretion. Urban renewal was a very different program after 1967 (Sanders 1980, 108, 112).

Although many of Lyndon Johnson's advisers wanted a national standard for AFDC benefits, the administration never proposed such a change to Congress. Rather, they tried to make food stamps into a national welfare program, believing that it would "supplement local welfare systems and . . . correct local welfare disparities" (Brown 1999, 300). Johnson refused to convert food stamps into a supplement for AFDC, but Nixon did, and by 1973 it was a national welfare program. It was the Supreme Court, not the president or Congress, that changed the administration of AFDC. In a series of important decisions, the Supreme Court sharply limited the authority of states to arbitrarily deny poor women benefits or make a woman's sexual behavior a condition of aid. The Court did not create a constitutional right to aid, but it did impose constitutional standards of due process on states' use of their police powers to regulate the lives of poor women. AFDC was a much different program thereafter.[7]

Lyndon Johnson succeeded in increasing public investment in education, job training, and neighborhood facilities in poor ghetto communities. As welfare rights protest and Supreme Court decisions opened up welfare, the number of poor women and children receiving aid rose from about 3 million in 1960 to almost 11 million by 1973. Yet the effort to raise benefits by supplementing AFDC with food stamps was stillborn. AFDC benefits declined dramatically over the 1970s, falling 25 percent in real terms; by 1984 the combined net AFDC/food stamp benefit was only 5 percent higher than the AFDC benefit in 1960. Ironically, when Congress made food stamps a national program, it gave states an incentive to substitute food stamp benefits for AFDC; many states saw no need over the 1970s to raise welfare benefits. All Congress did, Robert Moffitt ruefully observed, was "provide a large measure of budget relief to the states" (1988, 49). So while many more eligible women received food stamps and AFDC with less harassment, they lost ground.

After the 1960s conservatives waged a political campaign to unwind the Great Society and reestablish state authority over welfare (Mink 1998, 33–44, 50–57). Republicans were intent on rolling back Great Society programs where possible or limiting their growth. The 1996 welfare law is the culmination of conservatives' success in manipulating the backlash to the Great Society's centralization and expansion of social welfare during the 1960s, a campaign based on the political exploitation of the vulnerability of poor African American women, who became the scapegoats for the "failures" of the Great Society.

Republicans countered the Great Society's centralized, narrowly targeted grant-in-aid policy with a political strategy that combined revenue sharing or block grants with fixed limits on federal spending. They appropriated the idea of sharing federal revenues with state and local governments from the Democrats—revenue sharing was first introduced by a member of John F. Kennedy's Council on Economic Advisers—and turned it into a weapon against the Great Society. Republicans introduced some 50 revenue-sharing bills during the 89th Congress (1965–66). Some of these bills sought to consolidate categorical programs into block grants and were justified as a necessary administrative reform; most were designed as "substitution" bills in which revenue-sharing funds replaced existing grants-in-aid. Charles Goodell, a New York Republican, described revenue sharing and block grants as the alternative to the "philosophy of the Great Society." As such it was deeply attractive to conservative Republicans seeking to halt the progress of Lyndon Johnson's War on Poverty. Seventy-five percent of the Republicans who favored revenue sharing voted against new grants-in-aid more than 60 percent of the time.

In fact, the most conservative GOP members of Congress consistently supported revenue sharing (Dommel 1974, 65–67).

It was the Nixon administration that perfected the Republican strategy. Nixon and his advisers toyed with the idea of converting most grants-in-aid into revenue sharing but abandoned the idea because of anticipated political opposition. They then hit upon the idea of converting categorical matching grants to block grants, or special revenue sharing, as it was called. Nixon's advisers understood block grants as a way to limit federal spending and, ultimately, to limit the growth of government. The Revenue Sharing Working Group, set up in the fall of 1970 to plan the effort, identified the goal as "termination of categorical grant programs to cut [the] size and spending of the federal government." The administration preferred block grants with no maintenance of effort (MOE) requirement, or no state and local match, because it would allow state and local governments to substitute federal for local dollars and limit the growth of the public sector. An MOE requirement was inconsistent with their prime budgetary objective: reducing the size of government (Brown 1999, 317–18). Block grants were attractive to the Nixon administration for another reason. They presumed that block grants would diminish the power of national constituencies pushing to expand various categorical programs. Henceforth, local officials would decide how to allocate the limited funds available.

Nixon succeeded in creating only two block grants, but Ronald Reagan picked up where Nixon left off; only the scale of his ambitions differed. Upon taking office, Reagan proposed $14.1 billion for new and existing block grants, a reduction of 21 percent over fiscal year 1981 expenditures. In fact, two-thirds of Reagan's proposed 1981 budget cuts came out of federal aid to state and local governments, which made up only 17 percent of the federal budget (Conlan 1998, 113). The Reagan administration succeeded in creating nine new block grants and consolidating 77 programs and eliminating another 62. Republicans also cut some of the federal strings on block grants imposed by Democrats during the Carter years. Perversely, at the same time the Reagan administration saddled welfare and child nutrition programs with new eligibility requirements, they loosened the targeting requirements for the education block grant, giving local politicians more discretion in allocating funds. Reagan did not get every thing he asked for; still, spending for grants-in-aid declined by 10 percent in constant dollars between 1981 and 1987. Social programs were deeply cut.

Republicans prefer devolution for both ideological and political reasons. Conservatives have always believed that devolution leads to a smaller government, and they have plausible reasons for this assumption—tax competition limits the size of government at the state and local level or at the very least constrains redistribution. George Peterson believes that conservatives expect "governments directly accountable to local voters will choose to spend less than a central government where the voters' will is filtered through interest groups" (1984, 218). This is true enough, but it understates the Republicans' ideological animus toward the welfare state, and the Great Society in particular, an animus that has driven Republican budget cutting for three decades.

Devolution also yields political advantages. Republicans couch their case for devolution on its virtues. Local taxpayers, not federal bureaucrats, they say, should decide what are the important needs government should meet. Allowing local politicians more say-so in the allocation of federal funds usually means that Republican constituencies and middle-class taxpayers are more likely to get their share of federal dollars, something that Republican members of Congress are not likely to let their constituents forget.

Why congressional Republicans preferred block grants with spending caps during the welfare reform debate is plain enough. But why would the states go along with them? Governors scotched an attempt by the Reagan administration to shift the burden of welfare to states, mainly because funding would have been cut by 25 percent. In 1995, though, Republican governors (and eventually some Democratic governors) jumped on the bandwagon. Early on a few Republican governors forged an alliance with the new House leadership, and together they devised an audacious plan to eliminate the state match for AFDC and shift all responsibility for funding to the federal government. The Republicans' original bill capped funding for all low-income block grants and allowed states to shift money between TANF, food stamps, and Medicaid (Conlan 1998, 279, 280–82).

Governors lost their fight to eliminate the state match, but they gained considerable flexibility in running TANF and allocating resources. The final bill also minimized the risks to the states by allowing them to impose shorter time limits on benefits than the federal law required. Moreover, Republican governors, who were among the strongest supporters of converting entitlements to block grants, saw few political risks since they represented mostly nonurban, affluent constituencies (Weir 1999, 56–57). They were undoubtedly aware of the political benefits of distributing money saved from welfare to new groups of grateful voters.

The Republican formula of block grants and budget cuts may appeal to white suburban voters. What it has meant for poor African American women is much different. Together, states' decision to substitute food stamps for raising AFDC benefits and the advent of block grants denied poor women in inner-city communities needed aid at the same time they were stigmatized as the progenitors of a threatening underclass. This experience, not the pleas of reformers for a work-conditioned safety net, suggests the likely outcome of welfare reform.

The Color of Block Grants

It is usually assumed that welfare reform will lead to a "race to the bottom" because high-benefit states will attract ever-larger numbers of poor women who search for the most attractive benefit package. As costs escalate, states will seek to stem migration by reducing benefits; thus all states will have powerful incentives to keep benefits as low as possible. This is a plausible model of what might happen, but the evidence on its behalf is weak (Schram and Beer 1999). It is far more likely that the financial incentives of block grants will undermine the premises of the program and preclude allocation of resources where they are needed most

By converting AFDC to a block grant, Congress gave states incentives to reduce spending on TANF. Under open-ended matching grants, states paid 40 cents for an additional dollar of AFDC benefits; with block grants and a cap on federal spending, an additional dollar of TANF benefits now costs states $1. Moreover, once the cost of food stamps to states is taken into account, the real cost of increasing benefits by one dollar is $1.43. Even with a TANF subsidy that pays 40 percent of the cost of a dollar of increased benefits and federally funded food stamps, states would pay almost the full cost of the extra dollar of benefits.[8]

Lacking incentives to increase spending to meet needs, states will be tempted to substitute other federal programs for increases in welfare benefits, just as they substituted food stamps for increases in AFDC benefits in the 1970s. During the Reagan years, for example, states responded to the massive cuts in the Social Services Block Grant by shifting $112 billion from the low-income energy assistance block grant, where federal funding was increasing (U.S. General Accounting Office 1998, 35). But states may also be tempted to substitute federal dollars for state spending, and politicians may be reluctant to spend funds on selected but needy communities.

Whether the so-called work-conditioned safety net is shredded and whether impoverished ghetto communities receive needed resources depends on how states respond to fiscal shortfalls, to the temptation to substitute federal for state dollars, and to political pressure to geographically disperse TANF funds. There are powerful fiscal incentives for state officials to reallocate the resources needed to substantially diminish inner-city poverty to state welfare programs, which are designed to meet broad, statewide needs, or to disperse the funds to white beneficiaries in the suburbs or the rural hinterlands. There is no way to judge conclusively the outcome of the complicated social experiment that has just begun. We can derive some very suggestive answers, however, from the first three years of TANF and the history of block grants.

How have states responded to the financial windfalls, and is there any evidence of substitution? Total welfare spending actually declined in 21 states despite a substantial increase in available resources because of lower caseloads and a fixed federal subsidy based on the much higher 1994 caseloads. At the same time spending per recipient went up. The federal maintenance-of-effort requirement acted as a brake on state spending reductions, preventing states from reducing state expenditures to zero. This is a source of considerable frustration to many state budget officials, one of whom told the GAO that states "will no longer realize any budgetary savings from a declining case load because they must spend the same amount of state funds on their welfare program as they did in the previous year even if their case loads are lower" (U.S. General Accounting Office 1998, 11, 14).

States are reallocating resources from cash benefits to services of one kind or another. Between 1994 and 1999 expenditures for cash assistance under TANF declined by $10.6 billion. Rather than increase cash benefits, states have used federal money for job placement services (but not necessarily training), child-care, and related supportive services. One careful study of four states (California, Georgia, Missouri, and Wisconsin) found that spending for work-related services almost doubled between 1995 and 1999, even though overall these four states spent less on low-income services in 1998–99 than they did under the old policy regime, 1994–95. Spending on cash benefits in these four states declined dramatically. Simultaneously, there was a massive rise in spending for child-care and employment training, mainly because federal funding increased (in California child-care spending jumped by $998 million; in Wisconsin it was up almost $100 million) (Ellwood and Boyd 2000, 9, 12).

One reason states are funding social services for the working poor is that federal regulations have made it much easier to do so. TANF regulations allow states "to use their welfare block grant to pay for child care, transportation, and job retention services to help people who have left welfare stay off the rolls," and these payments are not subject to time limits (only direct cash payments to families are subject to time limits).[9] Yet all four states, according to Deborah Ellwood and Donald Boyd, were also reducing spending on programs for low-income families while adding resources to other welfare programs, including substance abuse programs, mental health, child welfare, and senior services. Even so, state spending declined in these programs, as well as in federally funded child-care and employment training, suggesting that all four states were substituting federal for state funds.[10]

States are already taking advantage of a loophole in the law that permits them to shift funds from TANF into the Child Development Fund or Social Services Block Grants. States transferred a total of $6 billion, or 13 percent of all TANF spending in the first three years of the program. There are undoubtedly good policy reasons for transferring TANF funds into a statewide child-care program. It allows states to evade the time limits on TANF funds and bolsters a statewide program. But it also allows states to reduce their own contributions to the two programs and then use money for other state services or tax cuts. Both Wisconsin and Connecticut, for example, shifted federal dollars into these programs and then reduced state spending.

In a variation on this strategy some states have replaced state spending on welfare with TANF funds. This is possible only because federal funding is higher than it otherwise would be (the windfall), and by law the MOE requirement is 20 percent lower. States basically reallocate the budgetary savings. Oregon is a prime example. Officials in that state reallocated $55.2 million of state funds, thereby increasing the federal share of the state's TANF program from 56 to 68 percent (U.S. General Accounting Office 1998, 15).

No one knows how widespread substitution is, but one can assume that many states are doing it or thinking about it. The GAO found that 11 states had shifted money; another recent study found 6 states—Connecticut, Kansas, Minnesota, New York, and Texas—had used TANF funds to pay for services previously funded with state monies and then used the savings for tax cuts among other gifts to the middle class. New York alone may have diverted as much as $1.3 billion from TANF to state programs that "freed up an unprecedented amount of state money that has been used to help pay for politically popular programs." One New York

Democrat told a reporter, "what the state is doing here is subsidizing other areas of government at the expense of welfare recipients."[11]

The reallocation of federal dollars to other state programs is not the whole story. Many states have simply failed to spend all allocated federal funds and have accumulated large unobligated balances. Federal law does not require that states spend all their federal money within a single fiscal year. These unobligated balances totaled $2.8 billion after the first three years of operation. The net effect of all this maneuvering is to substantially reallocate funds in a program that was once solely dedicated to helping poor women. Even though federal spending per family rose dramatically, actual spending increased more modestly. Consider Pennsylvania. In that state federal funding per welfare family rose by 56 percent between 1994 and 1998, but Pennsylvania officials reduced state spending by $109 million and have failed to spend $158 million of TANF dollars. So, in fact, actual spending per family rose just 23 percent.[12] And this money, if past experience is any guide, will be geographically dispersed.

American politicians face strong political incentives to spread the money across constituencies. Governors and legislators build political coalitions by distributing side payments to their allies, and in a system of territorial representation this means politicians will build support for their agendas and programs by spreading funds across legislative districts. It is very difficult to ensure that needed resources reach geographically isolated, poor communities. Both of the big block grant programs of the 1970s, the Community Development Block Grant (CDBG) and the Comprehensive Employment and Training Act (CETA) allowed mayors and members of the city council to spread funds throughout cities and thus reduced the share of benefits going to poor communities. CETA shifted funds from central cities to suburban jurisdictions, and CDBG reduced resources originally targeted on the poor in favor of middle-class constituencies. Only one-third of CDBG resources in Boston, Cleveland, and St. Louis ended up benefiting low- and moderate-income families. A study of CETA's implementation in Cleveland concluded that one-third of the program benefits went to "more affluent families . . . The most disadvantaged workers in the city have been under represented in the program" (Brown 1999, 330–32; Tompkins 1981, 42, 59).

Similarly, many states used the new Reagan era block grants to increase the number of beneficiaries by dispersing resources to suburban and rural cities and schools districts. According to one study, Illinois politicians decided to distribute 70 percent of education block grant funds according to enrollments, which led to a "clear redistribution of funds away from Chicago and other larger school systems with concentrations of lower income students." Michigan changed the funding formula for the Community Services Block Grant and reduced Detroit's share of CSBG money from 53 to 27 percent (Detroit sued the state and later settled for a 42 percent share) (Elling 1988, 72–73).

Both the Nixon and Reagan administrations combined block grants with cuts in federal funding for education, social services, and employment training, reducing federal spending for the remnants of the Great Society's service programs 40 percent in real dollars by 1988. Since much of this money was distributed through block grants, diminishing federal resources were spread out over a larger number of beneficiaries. Republicans succeeded in reversing the Great Society's policy of using categorical grants-in-aid to narrowly target federal resources. Even though states restored some of the money, federal grants to central cities were sharply cut. In cities with a population of 300,000 or more, federal aid as a percentage of city's general expenditures dropped from 22 percent in 1980 to 6 percent in 1989, mainly due to budget cuts and geographical dispersion of the remaining funds (Caraley 1992, 11).

TANF's experience so far is quite different because the financial windfall masks the underlying conflict between needs and resources. Incentives for states to substitute federal for state dollars and geographically disperse the remaining funds, juxtaposed with the changing racial composition of the TANF caseload, pose the obvious question: how will states respond to a caseload composed mostly of women of color who face severe obstacles to permanent, well-paying jobs as economic growth diminishes?

Given white electoral majorities, state and local politicians have few incentives to develop a work-related safety net for poor black and Latino communities. White Americans remain profoundly hostile to policies that appear to be distributing benefits by race, while generously supporting policies that help all the poor. One recent survey found that only 50 percent of least prejudiced whites expressed any support for race-specific policies but 80 percent said they would support race-neutral policies. Other surveys have produced similar results (Sniderman and Carmines 1997, 107; Quadagno 1974, 172–73). Yet the underlying structure of racial inequality in the United States—residential segregation, labor market discrimination, gaps in income and wealth—will inevitably undermine any pretensions to a so-called race-neutral safety net whether it is conditional on work or not. African American women and Latinas are not only a higher proportion of the TANF caseload today, they are geographically concentrated. Almost 60 percent of the TANF caseload is concentrated in the nation's 89 largest urban counties, where the large majority of poor black and Latino families live. The combination of perverse fiscal incentives and white hostility to any policy that appears to disproportionately benefit blacks may once again leave poor African American women and Latinas isolated and bereft of needed aid. Sharp reduction in funds for inner-city communities is unlikely. Instead, funds will be incrementally siphoned off from other programs and shifted away from urban jurisdictions and poor inner-city communities.

Race and Poverty: The Next Round

TANF is less a new experiment in federalism, as some have claimed, than a successful effort to put welfare policy in a straitjacket.[13] It is hard to imagine how policymakers could have designed a more perverse policy than if they had set out intentionally to do so. Claims that the new welfare policy will improve the well-being of most poor women are open to question so long as TANF's fiscal incentives are intact. A more honest claim, which some conservatives will admit to, is that TANF was intended to reduce caseloads and over time reduce spending on welfare. Editorial writers, pundits, and most policy analysts admitted that replacing the AFDC entitlement with a work program would be more expensive. To suppose, though, that a program emerging from protracted conflict between liberals and conservatives over social spending and the maneuvering of states to divest themselves of as much of the fiscal responsibility for social policy as possible would lead to a safety net for poor working women is a pious hope. There is no other way to read the historical evidence recounted in this chapter.

The current policy will intensify scrutiny of the women of color who remain on the TANF rolls. The success of the many, mostly white, women who have left welfare will call into question the motivation of those who remain. There is no reason to suppose that TANF will ever become as racially stigmatized as AFDC, but a welfare caseload composed largely of women of color is not likely to induce sympathy or an acknowledgment that addressing inner-city poverty requires something more than a call for individual responsibility.

There is only one other time when the racial composition of welfare caseloads changed so radically, the 1930s. In the midst of the Great Depression, black workers were much more likely than white workers to be on work relief or general relief, but as caseloads plummeted in the late 1930s, whites left the relief rolls at a faster rate than blacks. Thereafter, African American workers made up a sharply higher proportion of people on work relief in northern cities. This did little to call attention to the brutal labor market discrimination during the depression that denied black workers jobs and prolonged their need for relief. Instead, politicians pointed to the "large numbers of Negroes who, after having sampled the pleasures of relief, refused to work any more" (Brown 1999, 77–81, 90).

Historical parallels are inexact; the predicament of poor African American women and Latinas on TANF is very different from that of black workers in the 1930s. But the stereotype of black indolence persists and will form the subtext for any debate over the failures of TANF. This need not be the case. Instead of waving the flag of individual responsibility, Congress might reconsider the perverse fiscal incentives embedded in the welfare reform law. Congress could impose stiff requirements that federal dollars be allocated for poor inner-city communities. Congress could also expand the Earned Income Tax Credit, provide health insurance, and even consider a non-work-related entitlement for poor mothers. But that would require an admission that only national policies can address race and poverty.

NOTES

1. The President's Council of Economic Advisers recently estimated that if there had been no change in black family structure since 1967, the poverty and income gaps between blacks and whites would have declined by only one-fifth. "These are surprisingly modest effects," the CEA noted (Council of Economic Advisers 1998, 133).

2. However, only 10 percent of TANF funds can be transferred to SSBG, and it must be used for programs for families with incomes below 200 percent of the poverty line. See U.S. General Accounting Office 1998, 150. Transfer of TANF funds to SSBG will be limited to 4.25 percent of the block grant beginning FY 2001.

3. Deborah Ellwood and Donald Boyd (2000, 19) think that the leeway granted states by the legislation to substitute federal for state resources is inadvertent. This strikes me as unlikely.

4. U.S. General Accounting Office 1998, 11. Altogether, 46 states had more total resources under TANF than they would have had under the AFDC grant system (U.S. General Accounting Office 1998, 4).

5. Richard P. Nathan and Thomas Gais (1999, 16–17) attribute the work-first model to a change in the culture of welfare departments. What has changed is the fiscal incentives.

6. On one interpretation, however, federalism permitted African Americans to launch and sustain a successful attack on Jim Crow. See Young and Burstein 1995.

7. The major Supreme Court decisions were *King v. Smith,* 292 U.S. 309 (1968); *Goldberg v. Kelly,* 397 U.S. 254 (1970) ; and *Shapiro v. Thompson,* 394 U.S. 618 (1969). For a detailed discussion see Bussiere 1997.

8. This is because the federal government reduces the food stamp allocation for individual families by $.30 for every dollar of welfare benefits above a base income. As a result the real cost of raising benefits by one dollar is $1.43, of which the federal government will pay only 57 cents (45 percent of $1.43), leaving states to pick up the remaining 86 cents. See Chernick and Reschovsky 1999, 166–67.

9. U.S. Department of Health and Human Services, "HHS Fact Sheet: Clinton Administration Finalizes Welfare Regulations" (Washington D.C., April 9, 1999), cited in Ellwood and Boyd 2000, 4.

10. Total social services spending declined by 14 percent in Wisconsin and by 1 percent in Georgia; it rose in Missouri and California (Ellwood and Boyd 2000, 10, 18).

11. Raymond Hernandez, "Federal Welfare Overhaul Allows Albany to Shift Money Elsewhere," *New York Times,* April 23, 2000.

12. "Leftover Federal Welfare Money Either Baffles or Inspires States," *New York Times,* August 29, 1999, 20.

13. Robert Inman and Daniel L. Rubinfeld think welfare reform is an "experiment with an alternate paradigm of federalism" (1997, 60). They fail to address to the distributive problems of fiscal federalism; for a critique see Musgrave 1997.

CHAPTER 3

"Laboratories of Democracy" or Symbolic Politics?

The Racial Origins of Welfare Reform

RICHARD C. FORDING

In August 1996, President Clinton signed into law the Personal Responsibility Work Reconciliation Act (PRWORA), the most comprehensive and far-reaching collection of public assistance reforms seen in decades. While the legislation affected a number of federal programs, much of the discussion surrounding this legislation has been focused on the Aid to Families with Dependent Children (AFDC) program, the primary source of assistance for poor children and their parents at the time the legislation was passed. This attention is well justified. As is well known, PRWORA terminated AFDC, replacing it with the Temporary Assistance for Needy Families (TANF) program. Unlike its predecessor, the TANF program no longer represents a federal entitlement, leaving states wide discretion in determining eligibility. Although the federal government still shares the cost of the program with the states, a number of other changes have been implemented. The most important of these changes have included time limits on the receipt of aid, work requirements for able-bodied adult recipients, and a host of other requirements designed to force welfare recipients to act more "responsibly" while receiving aid.[1] Overall, PRWORA clearly represents a more punitive and restrictive approach to public assistance.

As sweeping as this legislation was, it was not unexpected. Indeed, upon achieving a majority in Congress in 1994, national Republican leaders placed it high on their list of legislative priorities. In addition, national Democratic leaders, and especially President Clinton, seemed to agree that drastic welfare reform was needed. Most importantly, however, state governments wanted reform. The most direct evidence of this fact can be seen by an examination of AFDC waivers received by state governments in the years immediately preceding PRWORA.[2] Between 1992 and 1996, state governments were granted a total of 171 waivers designed to affect the behavior of AFDC recipients in some way.[3] Thus, by 1996 comprehensive welfare reform was not only anticipated by observers, but to a significant degree had already been achieved.

In contrast to the relative unanimity of opinion surrounding the inevitability of welfare reform, there appears to be much less agreement concerning theoretical explanations to account for it. Many accounts of welfare policy-making in the 1990s have described the welfare reform movement as a creative attempt by government to address the shortcomings of the public assistance system of the Great Society, and in particular the AFDC program. According to this perspective, most important among these shortcomings were disincentives, which over time have contributed to a relatively permanent urban underclass characterized by welfare dependency, unemployment, and a general deterioration of moral and social responsibility (e.g., Murray 1984; Mead 1992). By the 1990s, these alleged consequences had led to widespread dissatisfaction with public assistance programs, sparking the welfare reform movement. Viewed in this light, welfare reform has often been characterized as "policy innovation," while state level reforms made possible by AFDC waivers have similarly been described as state "experimentation." Though states have taken different approaches to welfare reform, this perspective sees innovating states acting as "policy laboratories," with the common purpose of improving both the effectiveness and the efficiency of welfare.

Many critics of welfare reform argue that it is not welfare or the poor, but deteriorating urban environments that have led to the problems cited by many who have called for restrictive welfare reform. This being the case, it has often been alleged that the "problems" with welfare have been socially constructed and that welfare reform has instead been driven by other factors. Although a number of alternative explanations have been offered, social scientists and commentators alike have increasingly cited the importance of racial stereotypes and the so-called racialization of poverty as at least partly responsible for the success of welfare reform (e.g. Brown 1999; Gilens 1999; Handler 1995; Noble 1997). If true, this claim has enormous implications, not only for contemporary policy-making, but for theories of democratic governance as well.

Although many studies have addressed the relationship between race and welfare policy, a number of questions remain unresolved. Individual-level (survey-based) studies have consistently found a relationship between racial stereotypes and welfare attitudes, yet these findings do not necessarily imply that stereotypes actually affect public policy outcomes. Aggregate-level studies, on the other hand, have consistently found a significant relationship between the racial context in a state and welfare *benefit levels*, but this research fails to demonstrate if and how racial attitudes are related to racial context, or if racial context is related to welfare *reform*, which largely affects eligibility requirements.

In this chapter, I attempt to shed more light on these questions. In the first section, I review the history of the AFDC program and welfare reform efforts that preceded the passage of PRWORA. I then examine the social science literature that has addressed the relationship between race and welfare policy, arguing that relatively little evidence exists that directly links racial attitudes to welfare reform policies. In the third and fourth sections I provide some evidence that such a link does in fact exist by showing that (1) welfare reform efforts in the early 1990s were strongly related to the racial context in a state, and (2) that the racial context in a state is related to white stereotypes of African Americans. In the conclusion, I discuss the implications of this analysis for state policy research and the future of welfare reform.

Ending Welfare as We Knew It: A Recent History of Welfare Reform

Johnson's War on Poverty and the Expansion of AFDC

Throughout much of the history of the AFDC program, and at least through the late 1960s and early 1970s, efforts to reform AFDC often had the effect of expanding both the scope of coverage and the generosity of the program. When it was first implemented as part of the Social Security Act in 1936, the program (then known as Aid to Dependent Children, or ADC) provided benefits for poor *children* deprived of "parental support." As states were given broad powers to determine the definition of "support" and hence eligibility, receipt of aid was often denied to children if their mother was thought to be involved with a man, especially if a man was living in the house (Day 1997). In addition, many states denied assistance to children if they were the product of out-of-wedlock births or divorced parents, as these conditions were considered immoral (Katz 1996). Finally, ADC rolls were kept low due to the denial of assistance to African Americans by many states, especially in the South (Quadagno 1994).

By the early 1970s, the AFDC program had changed dramatically. In 1950, the program was expanded to include the adult caretaker, and in 1962 the name of the program was changed from ADC to AFDC to emphasize the family unit. The most significant period of expansion, however, occurred during the 1960s. Due to a number of social and political forces, including the acquisition of political power by African Americans, the massive waves of urban political violence, the welfare rights movement, and the liberal mood of the 1960s (Katz 1996; Fording 1997; Piven and Cloward 1971), AFDC benefits and caseloads reached unprecedented levels by the early 1970s. Between 1960 and 1974, the AFDC caseload more than tripled (Fording 1997). This dramatic increase was facilitated by a number of program reforms including the abolition of residency requirements, the elimination of "man in the house" and "suitable home" rules in determining eligibility, the eligibility of two-parent households, and the shifting of eligibility decisions from caseworkers to welfare bureaucrats who followed strict (and objective) application procedures. In addition, due to increases in AFDC benefit levels and the expansion of the food stamp and Medicaid programs (for which AFDC recipients were automatically eligible), the total value of benefits received by AFDC recipients rose dramatically as well.

The War on Welfare

As early as the mid-1960s, rising caseloads and benefit levels began to spark criticisms that the public assistance system, and especially AFDC, created work disincentives. In 1967, Congress addressed this concern by passing the first significant program designed to put AFDC recipients to work. Signed into law by Lyndon Johnson, the Work Incentive Program (WIN) sought to make the receipt of welfare contingent upon participation in some type of work-related activity. WIN required all qualified adult recipients to register and be referred to state agencies for training and employment services. Despite the promise of day care, upon implementation WIN proved to be a failure. Due in part to the large amount of discretion afforded local officials in granting exemptions, by 1971 only

24 percent of all WIN employment assessments were deemed "appropriate for referral," and only 118,000 adults were enrolled. Only 2 to 3 percent of the eligible recipients obtained jobs through WIN (Handler 1995).

In 1971, Congress passed tougher legislation, known as WIN II, which differed from its predecessor in that it placed more emphasis on immediate job placement. Though sanctions were strengthened and participation criteria liberalized, WIN II also proved to be less than effective at achieving its goals. The program did register more recipients, but by the end of the decade the total number registered still represented only 40 percent of AFDC recipients. Of those registered, only about half actually participated, and of those who participated only about 25 percent found jobs. Subsequent studies revealed that the vast majority of the participants who found jobs did so on their own, suggesting that "under the best scenario, WIN II removed less than 2% of the AFDC recipients from the rolls and reduced grants by an additional 2%" (Handler 1995, 60).

As Ronald Reagan began his first year in office in 1981, the welfare issue had reached the "crisis" level, sparking even tougher approaches to welfare reform. The "war on welfare," as Michael Katz has called it, continued to follow a two-pronged strategy. The first strategy, which had actually begun during the 1970s, consisted of benefit reductions for public assistance programs. AFDC was hit hardest, as maximum benefit levels decreased in real terms between 1981 and 1990. This was usually accomplished not by actual benefit cuts, but rather by states letting inflation take its toll. Efforts to reduce the attractiveness of welfare through program reforms at the national level also increased throughout the 1980s. Due to 1981 legislation crafted by the Reagan administration, the earnings disregard for AFDC recipients was drastically reduced, effectively reducing the income and eligibility of many AFDC recipients.

As an alternative strategy to reduce AFDC caseloads, the Reagan administration encouraged states to craft their own reforms through WIN demonstration projects permitted by 1981 legislation. Some of the more "successful" state initiatives were ultimately used as models in constructing the Job Opportunities and Basic Skills Training Program (JOBS), which took the place of WIN II in 1990. The last significant national-level attempt at welfare reform prior to PRWORA, JOBS differed from WIN II in its emphasis on education and training in addition to job search and placement. Like its predecessors, however, JOBS fell short of expectations, and by the early 1990s record increases in AFDC recipient rates had sparked a movement toward fundamental and comprehensive welfare reform.

The Proliferation of AFDC Waivers and State Welfare Reform

In 1962, amendments to the Social Security Act permitted states to obtain waivers, or exemptions from federal regulations in the implementation of AFDC. For many years, this provision was used to allow states to experiment with different methods of administering AFDC, and was not anticipated to be a means by which states could gain more control over eligibility decisions. Consequently, few states initially sought waivers, and less than a dozen significant exemptions were granted by 1977 (Hanson and Heaney 1997).

By the 1980s, due in large part to the encouragement of Ronald Reagan, a few states began to use waivers to implement their own brand of welfare reform, usually as pilot projects in just a handful of counties. Although states varied in their approaches to welfare reform, many of these "experiments" allowed states to implement tougher work requirements than allowed under WIN II. It was during this period in 1986 that Wisconsin, led by newly elected governor Tommy Thompson, became a leader in the reform movement. Under Thompson's leadership, Wisconsin obtained waivers for important programmatic changes, including new definitions of eligibility for AFDC.

The use of waivers by states increased significantly in 1992 after President Bush made the use of waivers an important part of his welfare reform agenda. After inviting states to apply for waivers in his State of the Union address, the Bush administration subsequently approved 13 waiver requests for ten states in 1992 (Hanson and Heaney 1997). The emphasis on waivers as a means to reform was continued by President Clinton in 1993. The Clinton administration further encouraged waiver applications by relaxing the cost neutrality rule imposed by the Reagan and Bush administrations, and in 1995, Clinton announced the use of a fast-track review process that encouraged even more applications. The impact was nothing short of a revolution in welfare policy. By the end of 1996, a total of 400 waivers had been requested by states (Hanson and Heaney 1997), and nearly all states were implementing their own brand of welfare reform to varying degrees. These waivers allowed states much greater flexibility in determining eligibility, and included reforms designed to encourage or require work, promote "responsibility," and in many cases to end welfare receipt altogether by imposing time limits. Many of these reforms adopted as state demonstration projects were included as mandatory requirements (or in some cases state options) in PRWORA.

Race and Welfare Reform: Assessing the Evidence

The Literature

Three bodies of literature address the relationship between race and welfare. Historical accounts of welfare policy-making clearly indicate that race was one of the primary influences in the construction of the U.S. welfare state during the passage of the New Deal (e.g. Brown 1999; Lieberman 1995b; Quadagno 1994). Southern congressmen were instrumental in excluding the vast majority of African Americans from Social Security coverage by excluding agricultural and domestic workers. This left poor African Americans with only Aid to Dependent Children and state and local General Assistance programs from which to seek relief, programs where state and local officials had almost complete discretion in making eligibility decisions. Though the politics and the administration of the AFDC program eventually evolved past such overt forms of discrimination, many social scientists have argued that the legacy of racial prejudice is one of the primary reasons why the U.S. welfare state is underdeveloped compared to other industrialized democracies.

Exactly how racial attitudes influence welfare policy today is addressed by a much different literature. An emerging body of evidence, based on survey and experimental research, has found a strong link between white attitudes concerning blacks and welfare. Several studies have demonstrated that white attitudes toward welfare policy are strongly related to white stereotypes of blacks (Gilens 1996a, 1999; Nelson 1999; Peffley, Hurwitz, and Sniderman 1997; Peffley and Hurwitz 1998). This research suggests that the most important stereotype is the belief that blacks lack a strong work ethic. In addition, survey experiments consistently find that the effects of stereotypes on welfare attitudes are stronger when respondents believe that the targets of the policy are black rather than white (Gilens 1996a; Peffley, Hurwitz, and Sniderman 1997). Thus, due to the "racialization" of poverty in the minds of whites (Gilens 1999; Kellstedt 1997), despite a decline in racial prejudice over the years, white attitudes toward blacks continue to have a significant impact on attitudes toward welfare today.

Finally, a third set of studies suggests that race is an important factor in welfare *policy-making*. Using state-level data, several studies have found AFDC benefits to be influenced by the racial context in a state. For example, even after controlling for several demographic and economic variables, Orr (1976) found AFDC benefits to be negatively related to the percentage of the AFDC caseload that is black. These findings have been supported by subsequent studies, even after controlling for partisan and ideological differences across states (Hero 1998; Howard 1999; Plotnick and Winters 1985). Other studies have examined the effect of the racial composition of the state population, finding similar results (Brown 1995; Wright 1976). Thus, as Gilens (1999) concludes, analyses of state welfare policy "that have included some measure of the racial mix of a state's poverty population have consistently found race to be a significant influence on state AFDC policy" (176).

Assessing the Evidence

All three types of studies—historical, individual-level, and state-level—provide important insights into the relationship between race and welfare. Although the historical research certainly contributes to our understanding of the role of race in the development and structure of the American welfare state, important policy and attitudinal changes over the last four decades prevent us from simply assuming that racial attitudes continue to play a role in contemporary policy-making. Thus, judgments concerning the relationship between race and welfare reform would seem to hinge on the evidence provided by the individual- and state-level studies.

The individual-level studies provide strong evidence that racial stereotypes are related to welfare attitudes, even as late as the 1990s. Yet despite the strength and consistency of this finding, it does not tell us much about the relationship between racial attitudes and welfare *policy outcomes*. Though we should expect public opinion to be related to public policy in a democracy in the long term, there are a number of reasons why this relationship may not hold in each and every case. Interest groups, electoral pressures, low voter turnout or strong-willed elected officials may all serve to weaken the linkage between mass opinion and policy for a particular policy issue. Given the important implications of a possible relationship between racial attitudes and welfare reform, the individual-level results can only be considered suggestive.

The state-level studies would seem to provide the connection to policy outcomes that the individual-level studies fail to offer. Upon closer examination, however, the state-level studies are limited as well, especially if one is interested in the relationship between race and welfare *reform*. The most fundamental issue concerns the fact that nearly all of these studies have relied on AFDC benefit data as the dependent variable.[4] The use of such data presents two related problems if we wish to extend these results to contemporary policy-making and welfare reform. First, AFDC benefit levels have been relatively stable throughout the recent history of the program, and therefore values for any given year are highly correlated with values from much earlier time periods. For example, the simple correlation between the AFDC maximum benefit level (for a family of four) in 1990 and the same variable in 1970 is .79.[5] This means that cross-sectional variation in benefits in 1990 still reflects the causal forces that were operating during earlier decades. As the racial context across states has not changed much since 1970, it is therefore difficult to determine from these studies if a relationship between race and welfare reflects contemporary or past racial attitudes.

A second, and perhaps more fundamental problem with studies using AFDC benefit data is that there is no compelling reason to believe that AFDC benefit levels are related to state welfare reform initiatives. Indeed, the simple correlation between the number of AFDC waivers adopted by a state and the AFDC benefit level in that state is close to o ($.08$, $p = .54$), suggesting that states with low benefits were just as likely to pursue welfare reform as states with high benefits.[6] Thus, even if we accepted the results of past empirical studies of the relationship between racial context and welfare policy, we have little reason to believe that the findings from these analyses can be generalized to welfare reform.

Even if we were to ignore the focus on benefits, however, the state-level studies are limited due to their lack of attention to the causal mechanisms linking the racial context in a state, which is most always used as the relevant independent variable representing a "race effect," to welfare policy. In most cases, the effect of racial context is somewhat ambiguously attributed to racial attitudes or prejudice, and the racial composition of the AFDC caseload (or simply the percentage of the population that is black) is used as a surrogate for "perceptions of recipients' deservingness" (Plotnick and Winters 1985, 466) or similarly, "the potential effects of a population's attitude toward welfare recipients" (Brown 1995, 29). Thus, the underlying assumption made by these studies would appear to be that as the percentage of the caseload that is black increases, due to racial prejudice or stereotypes white opposition to generous welfare policies increases as an increasing share of benefits is distributed to the black poor. For the most part, this rationale for including state racial context remains an empirical question that has rarely been addressed.[7]

In summary, despite a large and diverse literature on the relationship between race and welfare policy, this literature is of somewhat limited use in evaluating the effect of race and racial attitudes on welfare reform. Though individual-level studies find a strong link between racial stereotypes and welfare attitudes, this research is only suggestive in that it does not explicitly link these attitudes to policy outputs. The state-level studies do examine policy outputs, but they are equally limited in that nearly all have failed to examine welfare reform initiatives. In addition, state-level studies fail to adequately conceptualize the possible relationships between racial context, racial attitudes, and welfare policy. These issues are addressed in a series of analyses below.

Racial Context and Welfare Reform Initiatives in the States

As a first step in investigating the relationship between race and welfare reform, I examine the relationship between the racial context in a state—as measured by the percentage of AFDC families headed by an African American *(%AFDC black)*—and state AFDC waiver adoptions. While PRWORA was ultimately crafted and passed by national policymakers, as I detailed above, the impetus for reform originated from the states in the form of AFDC waiver adoptions. Given this fact, to examine the relationship between race and welfare reform, I examine patterns of adoption of three categories of AFDC waivers across states.

The first category of waivers sought to encourage welfare recipients to work through various work requirements. A second category of waivers attempted to instill a sense of moral, social, and parental responsibility among AFDC recipients and included such noted reforms as the family cap, school attendance requirements, strict child support enforcement, and teen parent supervision, among others. Finally, a third category of waivers reflected the most punitive of reforms—time limits on assistance.[8] Together, these reforms represent the restrictive nature of welfare reform, and many are now required of all states in administration of the TANF program.

The time period for the analysis is 1992–96. Although some states did receive waivers prior to 1992, these waivers were almost exclusively work related, and many were not implemented statewide. Most importantly, however, standards for approval were significantly loosened by President Bush in 1992, and even more so by President Clinton through 1996. This opened the floodgates for waiver requests along a variety of dimensions of reform, providing the momentum that ultimately resulted in the passage of PRWORA.

Additional Explanations for State Waiver Adoptions

In addition to the racial composition of the welfare caseload, welfare reform was undoubtedly spurred and facilitated by various additional forces, and it is critical to control for these potential alternative influences if we are to isolate the true effect of racial context. The sources of these explanations span both popular and academic literatures and include such factors as African American political mobilization, ideological and partisan forces, the alleged poor performance of traditional public assistance programs, state fiscal pressures, the "devolution revolution," and the effects of state labor markets. Each of these alternative explanations is briefly discussed in turn below.[9]

Race and representation.   Most of the research on state welfare policy has assumed that racial context influences welfare policy solely through its effect on white attitudes. The ultimate impact of race on welfare, however, is likely more complex than past studies reflect. In addition to its effect through racial attitudes, there is good reason to suspect that state racial context may also affect welfare policy through its relationship with black political power. Keech (1968) was among the first to recognize these two paths through which racial context might affect public policy in his study of black political power after the passage of the Voting Rights Act of 1965. Based on his findings, Keech concluded that policy responsiveness to blacks is ultimately a function of white hostility to blacks *and* black political power, both of which he claimed were positively related to black population size. Since Keech's initial work, several studies have found at least some evidence that areas with large black populations may in fact elicit greater levels of responsiveness to black interests (e.g. Bullock 1981; Button 1989; Hero 1998).

Although much of this research has examined policies with clear racial implications, there is good reason to believe that black political power may have a similar influence on state welfare policy. Since the New Deal, welfare policy has consistently been a high priority of mainstream civil rights organizations (Hamilton and Hamilton 1997). In addition, a handful of studies have found black representation to be positively related to various indicators of welfare generosity, including AFDC benefit levels (Mueller and Kreueger 2001), AFDC recipient rates (Fording 1997, 2001), and roll call votes concerning redistributive policies in state legislatures (Herring 1990). Consistent with this reasoning, I examine the effect of black political power on state welfare reform initiatives.

Although black political power could potentially be operationalized in a number of ways, I examine its impact through the level of African American political representation *(African American representation)*, which I measure as the percentage of all state elected officials that are black.

Ineffective public assistance programs. By the 1990s the rhetoric of both Democrats and Republicans had come to reflect a belief that AFDC was ineffective, and that the program actually exacerbated poverty by providing work disincentives and by promoting a generally irresponsible lifestyle. Perhaps the most common complaints about the performance of AFDC along these lines have been that (1) AFDC discourages work and therefore leads to "welfare dependency"; and (2) AFDC encourages out-of-wedlock births. To capture these potential influences on state reform efforts, I include two variables in the analysis. *AFDC dependency* is defined as the percentage of AFDC families that have been receiving AFDC for more than four years. *Out-of-wedlock births* is defined as the percentage of all births to single teen mothers in a state. Both variables are hypothesized to be positively related to AFDC waiver adoptions.

The cost of public assistance. A second source of motivation for welfare reform, it is alleged, has been the high costs of the public assistance system due to the expansion of the AFDC rolls in the late 1960s and 1970s. I account for state fiscal pressures in two ways. First, I include the variable *AFDC recipient rate,* which is defined as the number of AFDC families per 1,000 state population, and which is expected to be positively related to state waiver adoptions.[10] I also account for more general state fiscal pressures by including *State revenue,* a variable measuring per capita state revenues, adjusted for cost of living differences both over time and across states using the state deflator constructed by Berry, Fording, and Hanson (2002).

Welfare reform as policy innovation. Many studies of state policy innovation have found that larger states (measured by population) are more likely to innovate due to the greater availability of "slack resources" to devote to innovation (Gray 1994). Accordingly, I include *State population,* measured as total state population (in millions), as a measure of a state's propensity for policy innovation. In addition, we might expect that recent reform efforts in a state are related to past efforts at welfare policy innovation. In other words, we might expect that certain states are inherently more concerned about welfare and over time tend to be consistently among the leaders in welfare innovation. This possibility is explored by including a measure of *Propensity for welfare innovation* constructed by Gray (1973). As this measure is based on the order in which states adopted welfare innovations, and thus smaller values mean a greater propensity for innovation, we would expect this variable to be negatively related to waiver adoptions.

Ideological cleavages. Popular accounts of welfare reform have observed that the welfare reform movement has been played out amid ideological and partisan cleavages that have traditionally been formed (in part) over issues related to the scope and generosity of the welfare state. To capture the impact of this traditional left-right ideology, I include *State liberalism,* a measure of citizen ideology developed by Berry et al. (1998), which is hypothesized to be negatively related to state waiver adoptions.

Some have argued that the welfare reform debate reflects conflicts over moral values, rather than traditional disputes concerning the size of government. Although debates over welfare have always been closely tied to "traditional" values, some have argued that this emphasis has increased in recent decades due to the mobilization of the Christian Right (Weaver 2000), and the responsiveness of the Republican party to their agenda. To capture the influence of moral conservatism, I therefore include *Protestant fundamentalism,* a variable measuring the percentage of a state's population that belongs to a fundamentalist church.

Political parties. Many analysts have cited the political power of Republicans at the state level (especially Republican governors) as being an important force in spurring reform, particularly those reforms that are restrictive and punitive. To capture the effect of partisan forces I include *Republican governor,* a dummy variables measuring the presence of a Republican governor. I also include an interaction term—*Republican governor × Protestant fundamentalism*—to model the presumed dependence of Republicans on the Christian Right. Thus, while the presence of a Republican governor in a state is hypothesized to be positively related to punitive waiver adoptions, this effect is hypothesized to increase as the size of the Christian Right increases in a state.

In addition to partisan control, we might also expect that welfare reform is related to party competition (Key 1949; Lockard 1959). As it has been applied in the literature, the hypothesis predicts that in two-party, or competitive states, social welfare policies are likely to receive attention and support from political elites because "the process of competition between two organized and enduring political parties . . . forces the candidates and/or parties to appeal to the have-not groups for support" (Dawson and Robinson 1963, 283). I include a dynamic measure of *Party competition* based on the competitiveness of the most recent gubernatorial election and the margin of seats held by the majority parties in both chambers of the state legislature. This variable is hypothesized to be negatively related to restrictive waiver adoptions.

Welfare reform and labor markets. A number of different theorists have suggested that welfare reform efforts are in part designed to increase the competitiveness of low-wage labor markets, allowing businesses employing low-wage workers to keep labor costs low (Noble 1997; Piven and Cloward 1971). To the extent that this is the case, we might expect that in states where the relative number of businesses employing low-wage workers is high, ceteris paribus, the probability of waiver adoption is high as well. This influence is captured by including *Low-wage sector,* a variable measuring the number of retail trade sector jobs in a state (per 1,000 state residents). This occupational category includes workers in all types of retail and clerical jobs, most of which require few skills and are the most likely source of employment for welfare recipients.

Additional explanatory variables. We might expect that the probability of obtaining a waiver varies a function of the number of waivers already implemented by a state. This may be the case for at least two reasons. First, states that have successfully obtained waivers in the past may be more likely to apply for waivers in the future, as these states have already absorbed the costs of learning how to navigate through the waiver application process. Alternatively, the probability of applying for waivers may be a negative function of the number of past waivers. This might be expected if the number of possible reforms is considered to be relatively finite (within a particular waiver category), and therefore as states accumulate waivers they exhaust opportunities for reform. Given these possibilities, I include *Existing waivers,* which is measured as the cumulative number of waivers obtained by states in each category (beginning in 1992).

Finally, I include yearly dummy variables to account for the possibility that states became more inclined to obtain waivers as time passed due to both national diffusion processes and the fact that the Clinton administration encouraged state requests for waivers throughout the 1993–96 period by loosening administrative requirements.[11]

Estimation and Results

Although the three types of waivers share certain important features, they seek to accomplish their objectives in very different ways. Consequently, separate analyses may reveal interesting differences in the effects of the independent variables (and especially racial context) across waiver categories. I estimate each model for the five-year period 1992–96. For each state, the dependent variable takes on a value of 1 for each year that a waiver is approved, while all other years take on a value of 0.[12] Given the binary nature of the dependent variable, I estimate the model using logit analysis. The results for these models are presented in table 3.1. Although the theoretical focus of this paper is on the various effects of race and racial politics, the results offer many interesting findings. In discussing the results, I therefore begin by summarizing the findings con-

TABLE 3.1. Logit Estimates for State Waiver Adoption, by Waiver Category, 1992–96

Independent Variables	Work Req's Coeff.	SE	Time Limits Coeff.	SE	Responsibility Coeff.	SE
AFDC recipient rate	.092	.085	.019	.073	−.027	.067
AFDC dependency	−.005	.034	−.079	.035	−.003	.028
Out-of-wedlock births	−.086	.037	.028	.051	.005	.033
State population	−.012	.043	−.060	.069	.039	.047
Historical propensity for innovation	.002	.025	.022	.034	.013	.023
Republican governor	.056	.643	.901	.693	−.021	.564
Protestant fundamentalism	−.091*	.045	.017	.062	−.020	.033
Republican governor × Protestant fundamentalism	.136**	.044	−.023	.048	.071*	.033
Party competition	−.003	.026	.081*	.038	.014	.023
State ideology	.037	.026	.050	.029	.020	.024
%AFDC black	.036**	.013	.036**	.014	.041**	.014
Black representation	−.157*	.093	−.063	.108	−.221*	.097
Low-wage sector	.114**	.041	.118*	.050	.026	.035
State revenues	−.217	.228	−.777*	.447	−.388	.377
Existing waivers	−2.89**	.595	−2.68**	.818	−2.529**	.605
1993	.311	.811			−1.206	.872
1994	1.48*	.765	1.704*	.809	1.257*	.610
1995	3.230**	.820	3.527**	.887	1.956**	.699
1996	3.047**	.807	3.653**	.960	2.332**	.763
Constant	−8.70**	4.105	14.99**	6.809	−4.904	3.279
Log likelihood	−80.654		−64.763		−94.078	
Pseudo R^2	.27		.30		.22	
N	245		245		245	

*$p < .05$, one-tailed   **$p < .01$, one tailed

cerning the many hypotheses representing alternative explanations for welfare reform. I then turn my attention to the relationship between race and welfare.

Generally speaking, the results provide little support for the characterization of welfare reform as a response to the failures of the AFDC program. As is evident from the table, neither of the variables representing AFDC performance (*AFDC dependency, Out-of-wedlock births*) is significantly related to the adoption of waivers. Nor does waiver adoption appear to be related to variables measuring a state's general propensity for innovation (*State population, Historical propensity*). At the very least, this suggests that if welfare reform has indeed been driven by the motivation to "fix" AFDC, objective indicators of the problems cited by many proponents of welfare reform are uncorrelated with subjective perceptions.

In contrast to these results, several of the variables representing both political and economic explanations for welfare reform prove to be significant predictors of waiver adoptions. As for the effects of state political variables, Republican control of the executive appears to have been an important factor in state welfare reform efforts. As hypothesized, however, this relationship is only significant to the extent that the Christian Right has a strong presence in a state. This suggests that the battle over welfare reform has been to some extent a battle over moral values, and that the aggressiveness of the Republican party on this issue has perhaps been motivated by the mobilization of the Christian Right.

Moving to the effect of party competition on waiver adoptions, the results suggest that this variable did not have the anticipated negative effect. In fact, for the case of time limits, high levels of electoral competition actually served to increase the probability that states pursued welfare reform. While it is possible that the liberalizing effect of competition may be confounded by the presence of other forces that served to promote reform, these results suggest that there may be reason to question the liberalizing effect of competition in the context of welfare reform.

As for state economic conditions, the results provide some evidence that state fiscal pressures may have played a role in state reform efforts. This is evident by the fact that *State revenue* proves to be negatively related to the adoption of waivers imposing time limits. This finding is consistent with theory, as this is the category that is most punitive, and thus may be the most effective in reducing state costs. The effect of labor market demands is significant for both work requirements and time limits, and varies across waiver categories much as theory would predict.

The effect is strongest for time limits, undoubtedly the least costly strategy for pushing welfare recipients into low-wage labor markets, while its effect is weakest (and statistically insignificant) for waivers requiring responsibility.

The Impact of Race on Welfare Reform

Although welfare reform seems to have been driven by various aspects of state political and economic environments, perhaps the strongest and most consistent finding in these results is the effect of race. For each of the three waiver categories, the racial composition of the AFDC caseload is positively and significantly related to waiver adoption. As the coefficients in table 3.1 are not substantively interpretable, we can easily evaluate the magnitude of this relationship by examining figure 3.1, which displays predicted probabilities for state waiver adoptions by the percentage of the AFDC caseload that is black (with all other variables set at their mean values). These results tell a very disturbing, yet familiar story. For work requirements and responsibility waivers, in states where the relative number of black AFDC families was the largest (70–90 percent), the probability of adopting a waiver was five to six times greater than that of states where the AFDC population was predominantly white. A similar pattern is observed for waivers imposing time limits, although the effect is weaker.

Though a state's racial context appears to have spurred welfare retrenchment in the 1990s through its relationship with the racial composition of the welfare caseload, it may have also offered blacks a political remedy in the form of black representation. Based on the results in table 3.1, this appears to have been the case to some extent, as the level of black representation is *negatively* related to waiver adoption for work requirements and responsibility waivers. This suggests that for these two types of waivers, black representation may have served to help balance the effect of racial stereotypes.

Racial Context and Welfare Attitudes

The results in the previous section find that the racial composition of the AFDC caseload served to increase the probability that a state would adopt a restrictive waiver during the early 1990s. Yet, as I have argued in the earlier sections of this chapter, while this evidence is suggestive, it is

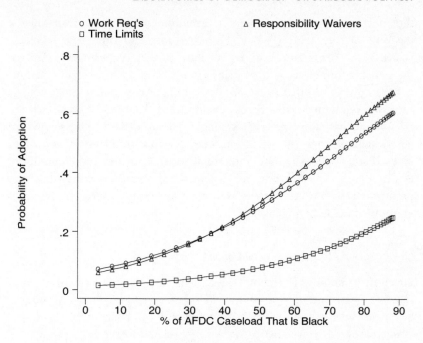

Fig. 3.1. Probability of waiver adoption, by racial composition of AFDC caseload

not exactly clear what this means about the effect of racial attitudes on welfare, and thus the relationship between race and welfare reform. On the one hand, these findings could in fact reflect the effect of white attitudes on policy outcomes. On the other hand, this finding could be spurious, meaning that the racial composition of the caseload is related to something else that has not been controlled for, and thus it is not white attitudes, but something else that is responsible for the observed effect. In either case, this suggests that further empirical analysis is necessary to provide some evidence that a state's racial context is in fact related to the relevant white attitudes concerning welfare.

At the individual level, several studies have found a strong relationship between racial attitudes and the degree to which welfare recipients are judged deserving (Gilens 1995, 1996a, 1999; Peffley, Hurwitz, and Sniderman 1997). Two specific types of racial variables appear to be most important. First, white perceptions of the work ethic among blacks are consistently found to be the most important predictors of welfare deservingness (Gilens 1995, 1999). Experimental studies, however, reveal that the effect of this racial stereotype is conditioned by a second variable—the race of the target (Peffley, Hurwitz, and Sniderman 1997; Gilens 1996a, 1999). For example, in the "welfare mother" experiment found in the 1991 National Race and Politics Survey (NRPS), whites were asked to make a number of judgments about a hypothetical welfare mother whose race was randomly varied across respondents. Analyses of these experiments find that stereotypes are strongly related to white assessments of deservingness when the welfare mother is explicitly identified as being black (Peffley, Hurwitz, and Sniderman 1997). Thus, the individual level evidence suggests that white stereotypes about blacks interact with white perceptions of the race of the welfare population to affect judgments about welfare deservingness.

Linking Racial Attitudes to Racial Context

Given these findings at the individual level, there are two possible ways that the racial composition of the AFDC rolls might be related to the relevant attitudes among whites. White stereotypes concerning the work ethic among African Americans could be related to the racial composition of the welfare caseload. We might expect this for at least two possible reasons. Given the predominant view among Americans that poverty is due to a lack of individual effort and that welfare receipt is unnecessary, one might expect that in areas where blacks comprise a large share of the welfare caseload, whites would come to believe that blacks choose not to work. Alternatively, several studies have found a strong relationship to exist between the size of the black population in a state and various measures of racial prejudice (Glaser 1994; Giles and Buckner 1993; Huckfeldt and Kohfeld 1989). Since stereotypes and prejudice are related, we may therefore expect to find a similar relationship between the black share of the welfare caseload (which is highly correlated with black population size) and stereotypes that blacks lack a strong work ethic.

Even if this is not the case, however, it is still possible that the racial composition of the AFDC caseload is related to white attitudes that are directly relevant in explaining welfare policy outcomes. This is due to the fact that the survey evidence suggests that it is not just stereotypes, but the combination (interaction) of stereotypes and the presence of black welfare recipients that influences attitudes toward welfare deservingness. Thus, even if there were no (or even random) variation in stereotypes across states, to the extent that whites are able to accurately estimate the relative size of the black recipient population in their state, we would expect support for restrictive welfare reform to be related to the racial composition of the AFDC population. While it seems straightforward to assume that whites are capable of accurately estimating the relative size of the black poor/welfare population in their state, survey data have shown that such perceptions are in fact quite distorted. As Gilens (1999) concludes, "despite the large state-by-state differences in the percentage of blacks among the poor, personal experience seems to have little impact on public perceptions of the racial composition of the poor" (137).

To determine if a state's racial context is in fact related to white racial attitudes, I examine the relationship between items taken from the 1991 NRPS and two measures of the racial composition of the target population for welfare—the percentage of the AFDC caseload that is black (*%AFDC black*) and the percentage of the poverty population that is black (*%Black poor*). First, I examine the hypothesis that white perceptions of the racial composition of the target population for welfare policies are related to objective measures of racial context in a state. As noted previously, using NRPS data, Gilens (1996b, 1999) found that white estimates of the black share of the poor population are, on average, inflated, and that they appear to be unrelated to the actual black share of the poor in a state. Two aspects of Gilens's analysis are worth noting. First, Gilens's conclusion that white perceptions are unrelated to state-level conditions is based on a casual inspection of white perceptions for only a handful of states. Thus, a more systematic analysis may be warranted. Second, the question that he examines asks individuals to estimate the percentage of the poor that are black *in the United States,* not just in their state. Thus, if it is found that state-level conditions are not related to national-level estimates, as Gilens reports, then this could mean one of two things. Either whites are insensitive to the racial context in their state, or alternatively, respondents simply understood the question and could easily distinguish between national- and state-level conditions. However, if state-level conditions *are* found to be to related to national-level estimates of the size of the black poor population, this would provide strong evidence that whites are sensitive to the racial context in their state and could make reasonable estimates of the size of this population in their state if they were asked.

I reexamine this question by regressing white estimates of the black share of the national poverty population (from the NRPS) on both measures of state racial context. The results from this analysis are summarized in table 3.2. Scanning the results in the first two rows in the second column of the table, we find mixed results. The racial composition of the

AFDC caseload is significantly related to white perceptions of the black share of the poor, while the actual black share of the poor in a state is unrelated to white estimates. Rows 3 and 4 of the table report estimates of the same relationships after taking the natural log of each of the independent variables. These relationships are significantly stronger and suggest that the racial context in a state has the greatest effect on white perceptions where the black population is relative small, and that this effect diminishes as the black population size increases. Given the fact that state-level conditions are even weakly related to national-level perceptions, however, this gives us some confidence that if we were able to examine white perceptions of the size of the black poor *in their state,* these estimates would be at least moderately correlated with reality.

I now examine the relationship between racial context and white perceptions that "blacks are lazy"—the stereotype found to be the most important determinant of white attitudes concerning welfare. To examine variation in this important stereotype, I regress white perceptions of the work ethic among blacks (agreement with the statement that "blacks are lazy") on both measures of racial context. These results are presented in the third column of table 3.2 and show that white stereotypes are strongly related to the size of the black poor/welfare population in a state. This finding is consistent with studies that find a relationship between racial prejudice and black population size at the state level, and together with the results presented in column 2 of table 3.2, suggests that measures of racial context in state-level studies of AFDC benefits are indeed reasonable surrogates for the relevant individual-level attitudes

TABLE 3.2. Relationship between Racial Attitudes and Alternative Measures of State Racial Context

	Individual-Level Variables	
State-Level Variables	White Estimate of Black Poor	White Belief That Blacks Are Lazy
%AFDC black	.042* / 1.87	.0010** / 4.85
%Black poor	.041 / 1.31	.0013** / 4.38
Log of %AFDC black	1.110* / 2.19	0.18** / 3.98
Log of %Black poor	.923* / 1.81	.018** / 3.88
N	1,831	1,852

Note: Cell entries are unstandardized slope coefficients and *t*-values. Individual-level data are taken from the National Race and Politics Survey, 1991. For measurement details, see appendix.

$*p < .05$, one tailed $**p < .01$, one-tailed

that drive white opinions about welfare policy. In addition, these results suggest that the strong effect of the racial composition of the AFDC case-load on restrictive waiver adoptions may in fact be rooted in white attitudes and their connection to state policy outcomes.

Conclusion

Several studies over the years have reported a significant relationship between the racial context in a state and the generosity of its welfare payments. This research is subject to two important limitations. First, by focusing exclusively on benefit data, these studies are limited in their ability to explain contemporary changes in welfare policy such as recent welfare reform. Second, past studies have failed to adequately conceptualize how the racial context in a state might be related to welfare. The results of the analyses reported in this chapter address each of these weaknesses in important ways.

While several state-level studies have found a relationship between welfare payments and racial context, none have looked at the effect of race on efforts to reform AFDC through the adoption of federal waivers. Based on the results of this analysis of state waiver adoptions, the percentage of the AFDC caseload that is black proves to be the strongest and most consistent predictor of the adoption of work requirements, time limits, and state efforts to regulate "irresponsible" behavior. These findings are relatively consistent with those found by Soss et al. (2001) in their study of state TANF plans, and together with their analysis provide strong evidence that welfare reform has been partly driven by racial attitudes. Based on this fact, this suggests that future analyses of state welfare policies cannot be considered complete without considering the effects of race.

In doing so, however, the results of this analysis also provide one important caveat. Although racial context appears to limit the generosity of state welfare policies through racial attitudes, past studies have ignored the possible ameliorative effects of racial context through its relationship with black political power. Indeed, my analysis of state waiver adoptions does find that black political representation has served to partly offset the impact of white racial attitudes on welfare policy-making. Whether this finding can be replicated in other policy-making environments (including current TANF policies) remains to be seen, but this finding is consistent with other studies that find that black political power to be related to welfare generosity (e.g. Fording 1997, 2001; Herring 1990; Mueller and Kreueger 2001). Thus, it appears that black representation may hold some promise as a possible remedy for the policy effects of racial stereotypes.

APPENDIX: DATA AND SOURCES

Individual-Level Variables (Source: National Race and Politics
Study, 1991)

Perception of welfare recipients as deserving: "Most people on welfare could get by without it if they really tried." o = Disagree strongly, .33 = Disagree somewhat, .67 = Agree somewhat, 1 = Agree strongly. "Most people on welfare would rather be working than taking money from the government." o = Disagree strongly, .33 = Disagree somewhat, .67 = Agree somewhat, 1 = Agree strongly. Scores from the first question are subtracted from the second question. The index is rescaled to range from o (most undeserving) to 1 (most deserving).

Perception of blacks as lazy: "Now I'll read a few words that people sometimes use to describe blacks. Of course, no word absolutely fits everybody, but, as I read each one, please tell me using a number from o to 10 how well you think it describes blacks as a group. If you think it's a very good description of most blacks, give it a 10. If you feel a word is a very inaccurate description of most blacks, give it a o." Respondents' scores for "hardworking" are subtracted from their scores for "lazy." The index is then rescaled to range from o (most hardworking) to 1 (most lazy).

Percentage of the poor who are black: "Just give me your best guess on this one—what percent of all the poor people in this country would you say are black?"

Age: Age in years, recoded to range from o to 1
Gender: o = Male, 1 = Female
Region: o = non-South, 1 = South
Education: "What is the highest grade or year of school you completed?"
o = Eighth grade or lower, 0.2 = Some high school, 0.4 = High school graduate, 0.6 = Some college, 0.8 = College graduate, 1.0 = Some graduate work or graduate degree
Marital Status: o = not currently married, 1 = currently married
Family income: Coded in 13 categories, from less than $10,000 (scored o) to more than $70,000 (scored 1)
Party identification: Seven-point measure ranging from strong Democrat (o) to strong Republican (1)
Ideology: Seven-point measure ranging from strong liberal (o) to strong conservative (1)
Individualism: "The government in Washington tries to do too many

things that should be left up to individuals and private businesses."
o = Disagree strongly, .33 = Disagree somewhat, .67 = Agree somewhat, 1 = Agree strongly

Waiver Categories and Examples of Waiver Provisions (Source: Ziliak et
al. 1997)

Waivers Requiring Work

Narrowing of criteria for exemptions from JOBS participation
Sanctions for failure to work or participate in a training program
Require community service work in exchange for benefits ("workfare)
Expand job search requirements
Expand case management services
Wage subsidies in private sector jobs
Employers contribute to special accounts for education and training
Public/private partnerships
Workplace mentoring

Time-Limited Assistance

Time limit on receiving benefits
Requirement to work or participate in training after a specified time
period
Develop/sign a self-sufficiency plan or agreement with goals and dead-
lines
Sanctions to enforce self-sufficiency agreements

Encourage Parental Responsibility and Child Support Enforcement

Expand child support enforcement programs
Increase child support pass-through
Minor parents required to live at home or in a supervised setting
Teen parents required to attend school
Children required to attend school, be immunized, get health check-ups
No increase in benefits if another child is born ("family cap")

State-Level Independent Variables

AFDC benefit level. Data obtained from the Department of Health and
Human Services and the Green Book.
AFDC dependency. Percentage of AFDC families that have been receiving
assistance for at least 48 months (continuously). Source: U.S. Department of Health and Human Services, *Characteristics and Financial
Circumstances of AFDC Recipients* (Washington, D.C.: U.S. Government Printing Office, various years).
AFDC recipient rate. Number of AFDC families per 1,000 state population. Source: U.S. Department of Health and Human Services, *Char-*

acteristics and Financial Circumstances of AFDC Recipients (Washington, D.C.: U.S. Government Printing Office, various years).

Out-of-wedlock births. Percentage of all births in a state to unwed mothers. Source: Urban Institute's state database (http://newfederalism .urban.org/nfdb/index.htm).

Historical propensity for welfare innovation. Measure of welfare policy innovation, based on order of adoption. Source: Gray 1973.

State population. State population in millions. Source: Statistical Abstract of the United States (Washington, D.C.: U.S. Government Printing Office).

Republican governor. Source: Statistical Abstract of the United States (Washington, D.C.: U.S. Government Printing Office).

Protestant fundamentalism. Percentage of state population belonging to a protestant fundamentalist church in 1990. Source: Meier and Haider-Markel 1996.

Party competition. Yearly measure of partisan competition, computed as follows. First, I obtained the average of the following three variables, which I term Average Majority Percentage: (1) percentage of vote obtained by incumbent governor in most recent election; (2) percentage of seats held by majority party in state senate; (3) percentage of seats held by majority party in state lower chamber. A scale of party competition was then computed as 100 Average Majority Percentage. Source: Statistical Abstract of the United States (Washington, D.C.: U.S. Government Printing Office).

State ideology. Yearly measure of state liberal ("citizen") ideology (0–100). Source: Berry et al. 1998.

%AFDC black. Percentage of AFDC families headed by an African American. Source: U.S. Department of Health and Human Services, Characteristics and Financial Circumstances of AFDC Recipients (Washington, D.C.: U.S. Government Printing Office, various years).

Black representation. Percentage of all elected officials in a state that are black. Source: Joint Center for Political Studies, Washington, D.C.

Low-wage sector. Number of retail trade workers per 1,000 state population. Source: Bureau of Labor Statistics, "Most Requested Series" (http://stats.bls.gov/top20.html).

State revenue. Total revenue per capita, in thousands of dollars. Adjusted for cost of living across states and over time using state CPI reported in Berry, Fording, and Hanson 2000. Source: Statistical Abstract of the United States (Washington, D.C.: U.S. Government Printing Office).

Existing waivers. Cumulative number of waivers received (total and by category). Source: Calculations by author.

NOTES

1. Examples of new state requirements (or in some cases state options) that are designed to promote responsibility include provisions affecting teen eligibil-

ity, restrictions on benefits for children born to AFDC mothers, school attendance requirements, and paternity establishment.

2. Federally granted AFDC waivers, which were permitted by Section 1115 of the Social Security Act, allowed states to deviate from federal guidelines in some way in the implementation of the program.

3. This figure accounts for waivers granted to implement (1) different types of time limits, (2) work requirements, (3) work incentives, or (4) measures to enhance "responsibility." See appendix for details.

4. A recent exception to this generalization is the study of state TANF policies by Soss et al. (2001), who find that the racial composition of the caseload was negatively related to program generosity.

5. See appendix for data sources.

6. Data for the number of waivers and for AFDC benefits are described in the appendix.

7. One exception in this literature is Johnson (2001), who uses aggregated survey data from the General Social Survey as a direct measure of racial attitudes. Johnson finds that racial tolerance is positively related to state benefit levels.

8. This category also includes waivers for time limits on work requirements, requirements to develop a self-sufficiency plan with goals and deadlines, and sanctions to enforce self-sufficiency agreements. The classification scheme, and as well the waiver data used in this paper, are taken from Ziliak et al. 1997. See the appendix for more details on these categories.

9. Data sources for all of the independent variables discussed in this section are given in the appendix.

10. I choose this variable over a measure of expenditures due to the fact that AFDC receipt automatically makes one eligible for a number of other programs and services including Medicaid and job training and education services, all of which require considerable state investment and which are not captured by an AFDC expenditure variable.

11. Additional independent variables were also examined, and included such variables as tax capacity, tax effort, AFDC benefit level, gubernatorial power, legislative professionalism, and the number of waivers adopted by a state's neighbors (where neighbors were defined as in Berry, Fording, and Hanson 2002). None of these variables proved to be significantly related to state waiver adoptions in any of the models. The finding that waiver adoptions do not appear to be influenced by waiver adoptions in neighboring states is particularly relevant for the debate concerning the possible existence of a "race to the bottom" in state welfare policy, and the possibility that welfare policy is driven by interstate competition (Peterson and Rom 1990; Rom, Peterson, and Scheve 1998). My results suggest that to the extent that welfare competition exists, it is limited to benefit levels.

12. Thus, the research design can be characterized as a discrete-time event history analysis (Box-Steffensmeier and Jones 1997). Unlike the typical event history setup, however, all states remain in the data set after the first adoption as they continue to be "at risk" to adopt additional waivers in the future.

*Mass Media &
Mass Attitudes*

CHAPTER 4

How the Poor Became Black

The Racialization of American Poverty in the Mass Media

MARTIN GILENS

Race and poverty are now so closely entwined that it is hard to believe there was a time when discussions of American poverty neglected blacks altogether. African Americans have always been disproportionately poor, but black poverty was ignored by white society throughout most of our history.

In the following pages, I analyze over 40 years of news media coverage of poverty in order to trace changes in racial images of the poor. I find that until the mid-1960s, poverty appeared overwhelmingly as a "white problem" in the national news media. But in a very brief period beginning in 1965, the media's portrayal of American poverty shifted dramatically. Although the true racial composition of the American poor remained stable, the face of poverty in the news media became markedly darker between 1965 and 1967.

The most obvious explanations for the news media's changing racial portrayal of the poor—the civil rights movement and the urban riots of the mid-1960s—played a role, but cannot account for the nature or timing of the shifts in media images. Nor is this change in the media's portrayal of poverty merely a reflection of the increasing visibility of African Americans in the news more broadly.

Instead, the changing racial images of the poor in the mass media are best understood as reflecting two very different processes that converged in the mid-1960s. First, the stage was set by a series of historical changes and events that made black poverty a less remote concern for white Americans. These included the migration of African Americans from the rural South to the urban North, the increasing representation of blacks among AFDC beneficiaries, the civil rights movement, and the riots of the mid-1960s. But these changes only created the environment in which racial portrayals of poverty were transformed. The proximate cause of that transformation was the shift in the moral tone of poverty coverage in the news. As news stories about the poor became less sympathetic, the images of poor blacks in the news swelled.

The association of African Americans with the "undeserving poor" is evident not only in the changing media coverage of poverty during the mid-1960s, but throughout the period studied. From the early 1950s through the early 1990s, images of poor blacks increased when the tone of poverty stories became more critical of the poor and decreased when coverage became more sympathetic. Similarly, images of African Americans were most numerous in news stories about the least sympathetic subgroups of the poor. As I discuss below, these differences in the racial portrayal of the poor cannot be accounted for by true changes in the racial composition of the poverty population or by racial differences across subgroups of the poor. Rather, the media's tendency to associate African Americans with the undeserving poor reflects—and reinforces—the centuries-old stereotype of blacks as lazy.

Real-world changes in social, economic, and political conditions combined with existing racial stereotypes to shape the media's coverage of welfare and poverty over the past decades. But this coverage has in turn shaped social, economic, and political conditions as states have dismantled and reformulated their welfare policies in response to the 1996 PRWORA reforms. American democracy is far from perfect. But public policies do reflect—if inconsistently and incompletely—the public's preferences (Monroe 1979; Page and Shapiro 1983; Wright, Erikson, and McIver 1987; Monroe and Gardner 1987; Shapiro and Jacobs 1989; Stimson, Mackuen, and Erikson 1995). In the case of welfare, however, citizens' preferences have been shaped by media portrayals that exaggerate the extent to which poverty is a "black problem" and that systematically associate African Americans with the least sympathetic subgroups of the poor. Other chapters in this volume ably document the many ways in which welfare reform has been infused with racial considerations and reflective of racial biases. In this chapter, I show how distorted news coverage of poverty has helped to generate a citizenry that views welfare and poverty through a racial lens.

African Americans: The Once-Invisible Poor

The American public now associates poverty and welfare with blacks. But this was not always the case. The "scientific" study of poverty in America began around the end of the nineteenth century. During this period social reformers and poverty experts made the first systematic efforts to describe and analyze America's poor (e.g., Warner 1894; Hapgood 1902; Lee 1902; Hunter 1904; Hollander 1914). Racial distinctions were common in these works, but such distinctions usually referred to the various white European "races" such as the Irish, Italians, and Poles; this early poverty literature had little or nothing to say about blacks.[1] The Great Depression, of course, brought the topic of poverty to the forefront of public attention. But as the American economy faltered and poverty and unemployment increased, white writers and commentators remained oblivious to the sufferings of the black poor.[2]

The economy grew dramatically after the war, and living standards rose quickly. In contrast with the depression, poverty seemed like a distant problem during the postwar years. Poverty was "rediscovered," however, in the 1960s. Stimulated by the publication of John Kenneth Galbraith's *The Affluent Society* (in 1958) and Michael Harrington's *The Other America* (in 1962), the American public and policymakers alike began once more to notice the poor. During the 1960 presidential campaign John Kennedy is said to have been shaken by the grinding poverty he saw in West Virginia, where a lack of both education and job opportunities had trapped generations of poor whites in the primitive conditions of rural poverty (Patterson 1994, 126). And early in his presidency Kennedy inaugurated a number of antipoverty programs focusing on juvenile delinquency, education and training programs for those lacking marketable skills, and federal assistance for depressed regions of the country. But the poverty programs of the early 1960s, and the popular images of the poor that went along with them, were just as pale in complexion as those of the turn of the century. Attention to poor blacks was still quite limited both in the mass media and, apparently, among Kennedy administration staffers.[3] If there was a dominant image of poverty at this time, it was the white rural poor of the Appalachian coalfields.

Background Conditions for the Racialization of Poverty

Popular images of poverty changed dramatically, however, in the mid-1960s. After centuries of obscurity, at least as far as white America was concerned, poor blacks came to dominate public thinking about poverty. Two decades-long changes helped to set the stage for the "racialization" of popular images of the poor. The first was the widespread migration of rural southern blacks to northern cities. At the turn of the twentieth century, over 90 percent of African Americans lived in the South, and three-quarters of all blacks resided in rural areas (Meier and Rudwick 1970, 213). Blacks had been leaving the South at a slow rate for decades, but black out-migration from the South grew tremendously during the 1940s and 1950s before tapering off during the 1960s. As a consequence of this migration, African Americans, who only accounted for 2 percent of all northerners in 1910, comprised 7 percent by 1960, and, perhaps more importantly, made up 12 percent of the population in urban areas (Turner 1993, 249, 251).

As we'll see below, the racialization of public images of the poor occurred fairly suddenly and dramatically between 1965 and 1967. Clearly there is no simple connection between the growth of African American communities in northern cities and public perceptions of the poor as black. Nevertheless, the growth of the black population in the North was one link in a chain of events that led to the dramatic changes in how Americans thought about poverty.

A second change that paved the way for the racialization of poverty images was the changing racial composition of AFDC, the nation's most conspicuous program to aid the poor. As established in 1935, the ADC program (as it was then called) allowed individual states considerable discretion to determine both the formal rules governing ADC eligibility and the application of those rules. As a result, African Americans were disproportionately excluded from ADC. In 1936, only 13.5 percent of ADC recipients were African American, despite blacks' much higher representation among poor single mothers (Turner 1993, 108). Over the next three decades, however, the proportion of blacks among ADC recipients rose steadily (fig. 4.1). This increase resulted from a variety of influences, both legislative and economic. For example, the establishment of Social Security Survivors' Benefits in 1939 removed proportionately more white than black widows from the ADC rolls, thereby increasing the percentage of blacks among those remaining.[4] In addition, an increase in the federal matching-grant contribution to the ADC program from one-third to one-

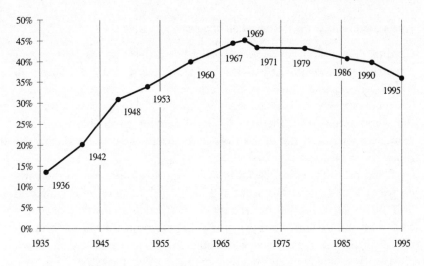

Fig. 4.1. The percentage of blacks among ADC/AFDC recipients, 1935–95

half of total state ADC expenditures encouraged some states to expand their coverage or to begin participating in the ADC program for the first time (Turner 1993).

As figure 4.1 shows, the percentage of African Americans among ADC/AFDC recipients increased steadily from about 14 percent in 1936 to about 45 percent in 1969, after which point the proportion of blacks declined slowly until it reached 36 percent in 1995.[5] During the middle to late 1960s, then, African Americans made up a very substantial minority of AFDC recipients. Consequently, as the welfare rolls expanded sharply in the late 1960s and early 1970s, the public's attention was drawn disproportionately to poor blacks. Yet the pattern of growth of African American welfare recipients shown in figure 4.1 also makes clear that the sudden shift in images of poverty during the 1960s cannot be attributed to any sudden change in the makeup of the welfare population. The proportion of blacks among AFDC participants had been growing steadily for decades. Like black migration to the North, the changing racial composition of the welfare rolls constituted a background condition that contributed to the changes in public perceptions of the poor, but it did not serve as a precipitating cause of those changes. After all, the proportion of blacks among welfare recipients was almost as high in 1960 as it was in 1967, yet public concern in 1960 was still focused on poor whites, in particular, the poor rural whites of Appalachia.

Proximate Events in the Racialization of Poverty

Gradual demographic changes in residential patterns and welfare receipt by African Americans helped lay the groundwork for the changes to come in how Americans viewed the poor. The more proximate events that contributed to these changes were a shift in focus within the civil rights movement from the fight for legal equality to the battle for economic equality, and the urban riots that rocked the country during the summers of 1964 through 1968.

Black protests against racial injustice had been sporadic in the early decades of the twentieth century and had largely died out during World War II. But in the mid-1950s, the modern civil rights movement began a concerted and sustained effort to force an end to the injustice and indignities of racial segregation. In December 1955 Rosa Parks was jailed for refusing to vacate her seat on a segregated bus. Ms. Parks's quiet protest began the Montgomery bus boycott, led by a previously unknown young black minister named Martin Luther King Jr. The eventual success of the yearlong bus boycott led to a decade of demonstrations, protests, and sit-ins, throughout the South, all pressing the demand for legal equality and an end to racial segregation.

The struggles of the early civil rights movement were for equal rights, black enfranchisement, and an end to legal segregation. These efforts produced their most significant successes with the passage of the 1964 Civil Rights Act and the 1965 Voting Rights Act. In the second half of the 1960s, civil rights leaders shifted their attention from legal inequality to economic inequality. Although the battle for black enfranchisement in the South had a long way to go, the first large urban uprisings during the summer of 1964, and the greater number of ghetto riots during the summers to follow, shifted both the geographical and programmatic focus of the struggle for racial equality.

Of course, racial economic inequality was hardly a new concern to civil rights leaders. In 1963, the National Urban League called for a "crash program of special effort to close the gap between the conditions of Negro and white citizens," and released a ten-point "Marshall Plan for the American Negro." In the same year, Martin Luther King issued a similarly conceived "G.I. Bill of Rights for the Disadvantaged" (Davies 1996, 56ff.). But these early efforts were almost wholly overshadowed by the struggle for basic civil rights in the South.

In 1966, however, Martin Luther King and the Southern Christian Leadership Conference (SCLC) focused their attention on the plight of the black urban poor of the northern ghettos. With help from the AFL-CIO and the United Auto Workers, King and the SCLC organized demonstrations and rent strikes in Chicago to dramatize the dire economic conditions facing so many urban blacks. King called for a variety of measures aimed at improving the lot of Chicago's black population: Integrating the de facto segregated public schools, reallocating public services to better serve minority populations, building low-rent public housing units, and removing public funds from banks that refused to make loans to blacks (Brooks 1974; Bloom 1987).

For all his efforts, King achieved little in Chicago. But the concern with northern urban blacks' economic problems exemplified by the Chicago Freedom Movement, and the 1968 Poor People's March on Washington helped to focus public attention on the problem of black poverty.

At least as important as the shifting focus of civil rights leaders were the ghetto riots themselves. Poor blacks, for so long invisible to most of white America, made their presence known in the most dramatic way possible. During the summer of 1964 riots broke out in Harlem, Rochester, Chicago, Philadelphia, and New Jersey. Five lives were lost and property damage was estimated at six million dollars (Brooks 1974, 239). Civil rights leaders attempted to respond to these disturbances, but much of their attention, and the rest of the country's as well, was still focused on the South. The Voting Rights Act had been passed, but much work remained in actually registering black voters. Mississippi, in particular, had been staunchly resisting blacks' efforts to vote.

To press for voting rights in Mississippi, the leading civil rights organizations united to mobilize local blacks and out-of-state volunteers for the Freedom Summer of 1964. Nine hundred volunteers, many of them white college students from the country's elite universities, joined the effort to register Mississippi's blacks. White Mississippi responded with violence. Twenty-seven black churches were burned that summer in Mississippi, and 30 blacks were murdered between January and August 1964 (Brooks 1974, 245). But the nation's attention was grabbed by the murder of three young civil rights workers, James Chaney, Andrew Goodman, and Michael Schwerner, the first a black Mississippian, the other two white New Yorkers. The three disappeared while returning from an investigation of the burned-out Mt. Zion Methodist Church in Neshoba County, Mississippi. Only after a six-week search by the FBI were their bodies found, buried in an earthen dam.

Despite the riots, news coverage of race relations during the summer of 1964 was dominated by the events in Mississippi. But in the next few years, ghetto uprisings and the militant voices of Malcolm X, Stokely Carmichael, and the Black Panthers would become increasingly central fixtures in the struggle for racial equality. In August 1965, the Los Angeles neighborhood of Watts exploded. A six-day riot left 34 people dead (all but 3 of them black), 900 injured, and nearly 4,000 arrested (Sitkoff 1993, 187). The Watts riots were followed that summer by more disturbances in Chicago, and in Springfield, Massachusetts. The summers of 1966 and 1967 saw even more rioting, as blacks took to the streets in literally dozens of American cities. In 1967 alone, rioting led to at least 90 deaths, more than 4,000 injuries, and nearly 17,000 arrests (Sitkoff 1993, 189).

Portrayals of Poverty in the News Media

It is clear that the black poor were ignored by white Americans through most of our history, including the first two-thirds of the twentieth century, and equally clear that blacks now figure prominently in public perceptions of the poor. Unfortunately, pollsters did not think to ask about perceptions of the racial composition of the poor until recently. But we can examine changes in the way the poor have been portrayed in the mass media. While we cannot assume that media portrayals necessarily reflect popular beliefs, changing images of the poor in the news can tell us both how news professionals thought about the poor during different time periods, and what sort of images of poverty the public was being exposed to through the mass media. Since we have good reason to think that media portrayals have a strong impact on public perceptions (see below), news images provide at least some evidence of how the American public viewed the poor. At the very least, media coverage will tell us something about the aspects of poverty (or the subgroups of the poor) that played a prominent role in public discussion of these issues during different periods.

To assess changes in news media portrayals of poverty, I examined three weekly newsmagazines: *Time, Newsweek,* and *U.S. News and World Report.* I chose these magazines because they are widely read, national in scope and distribution, and have been published continuously for many decades. They also contain large numbers of pictures, an especially important consideration in studying the *racial* portrayal of the poor. To the extent that our interest lies in the perceptions of the racial composition of the poor that magazine readers are likely to form, the pictures of poor people are far more influential than the textual information these magazines contain. First, the typical reader of these magazines looks at most, if not all, of the pictures, but reads far fewer of the stories. Thus, even a subscriber who does not bother to read a particular story on poverty is quite likely to see the pictures of poor people that it contains (Kenney 1992). Second, while specific information about the racial makeup of the poor is found periodically in these newsmagazines, such information is quite rare. Between 1960 and 1990, less than 5 percent of poverty-related stories had any concrete information on the racial composition of the poor, or any subgroups of the poor such as AFDC recipients or public housing tenants.[6] Finally, research on the impact of news stories and the process by which readers (or television viewers) assimilate information suggests that people are more likely to remember pictures than words, and more likely to form impressions based on examples of specific individuals than on abstract statistical information.[7]

To assess media portrayals of poverty, I first identified every poverty-related story in these three magazines published between 1950 and 1992. Using the *Readers' Guide to Periodical Literature,* a set of core topics, including "poor," "poverty," "welfare," and "relief," were developed. In each year, stories indexed under these topics as well as cross-references to related topics were collected. In all, 1,256 stories were found under 73 different index topics. (See Gilens 1999 for details of the topics and number of stories indexed under each.) It is important to note that the stories selected for this analysis were only those that focused directly on poverty or related topics. Many stories with a primary focus on race relations, civil rights, urban riots, or other racial topics also included discussions of poverty, but in these contexts readers would expect to find coverage of black poverty in particular, and might not draw conclusions about the nature of American poverty in general. By excluding race-related stories, however, this analysis provides a conservative estimate of the extent to which African Americans populate media images of the poor.

To determine the racial content of news magazine coverage of poverty, each poor person pictured in each of these stories was identified as black, nonblack, or undeterminable. In all, there were pictures of 6,117 individual poor people among the 1,256 poverty stories, and of these race could be determined for 4,388, or 72 percent (poor people for whom race could not be determined are excluded from the results reported below).[8] The percentage of blacks among pictures of the poor was similar at each magazine, ranging from a low of 52 percent at *U.S. News and World*

Report to a high of about 57 percent at *Time*.[9] Combining the coverage of poverty from the three magazines, over half (53.4 percent) of all poor people pictured during these four-and-a-half decades were African American. In reality, the average percentage of African Americans among the poor during this period was 29.3 percent.[10]

Magazine portrayals overrepresent African Americans in pictures of the poor, but the degree of overrepresentation of blacks was not constant throughout this period. The thick line in figure 4.2 shows the variation in the percentage of African Americans pictured in poverty stories in *Time, Newsweek* and *U.S. News and World Report* between 1950 and 1992. (Adjacent years with small numbers of poverty stories are combined to smooth out the random fluctuations that result when the percentage of blacks is calculated from a small number of pictures.) Images of poverty in these magazines changed quite dramatically in the mid-1960s. From the beginning of this study through 1964, poor people were portrayed as predominantly white. But starting in 1965 the complexion of the poor turned decidedly darker. From only 27 percent in 1964, the proportion of African Americans in pictures of the poor increased to 49 percent and 53 percent in 1965 and 1966, and then to 72 percent black in 1967. Nor did the portrayal of the poor return to its previous predominantly white orientation. Although there have been important declines and fluctuations in the extent to which blacks were overrepresented in pictures of poverty (which we'll explore shortly), African Americans have dominated news media images of the poor since the late 1960s. In the period between 1967 and 1992, blacks averaged 57 percent of the poor people pictured in these three magazines.

Early Newsmagazine Coverage of Poverty: 1950–64

The 1950s contained both few stories on poverty and few pictures of blacks in the stories that were published. Between 1950 and 1959, only 18 percent of the poor people pictured in these magazines were African American. The increased attention to poverty in the early 1960s was accompanied by some increase in the proportion of blacks among the poor, but this racialization of poverty images was quite modest compared with what was to come.

Newsmagazine coverage of poverty was generally rather sparse between 1960 and 1963. The poverty stories that did appear during this period were primarily in response to the Kennedy administration's antipoverty initiatives, which included a new housing bill, the revival of

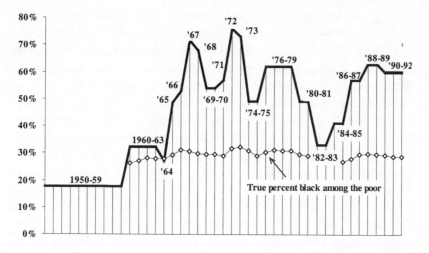

Fig. 4.2. Percentage African Americans in newsmagazine pictures of the poor, 1950–92, compared with true percentage

the depression-era food stamp program, and federal aid for distressed areas. These policy-focused stories were illustrated almost exclusively with pictures of poor whites.

A second theme in media coverage of poverty during 1960–63 was welfare abuse and efforts to reduce it. Some of these stories focused on Senator Robert Byrd's 1962 investigation into welfare fraud in Washington, D.C. Pictures of poor blacks and poor whites were both found in these strongly antiwelfare stories.

Newsmagazine coverage of poverty in the early 1960s presaged later coverage in two ways. First, stories on new policy initiatives tended to be both neutral in tone and dominated by images of whites, a pattern that was repeated in coverage of the Johnson administration's War on Poverty three years later. In contrast, the more critical stories about existing programs, such as reports on the Byrd committee's investigation of welfare abuse, were more likely to contain pictures of blacks. Once again, this pattern is repeated in the later 1960s as largely negative "field reports" from the War on Poverty programs start to appear in the media.

The quantity of poverty coverage in the news expanded dramatically beginning in 1964 and reached its height between 1965 and 1969. The impetus for this growth in coverage was the Johnson administration's War on Poverty, announced in January 1964. Almost four-fifths of all poverty-related stories published in 1964 dealt explicitly with the War on

Poverty, as did a majority of the poverty-related articles appearing in 1965 and 1966. By 1967, stories about urban problems and urban redevelopment became an important component of poverty coverage, but stories on welfare, jobs programs, and other aspects of the War on Poverty continued to account for most of the poverty-related news coverage.

For our purposes, the most significant feature of news stories on poverty in 1964 was the strong focus on the War on Poverty on the one hand, and the continued portrayal of the poor as predominantly white. A good example of this overall tendency is the most substantial poverty story of the year, a 12-page cover story called "Poverty, U.S.A." that *Newsweek* ran on February 17. The cover of the magazine showed a white girl, perhaps eight or ten years old, looking out at the reader from a rustic shack, her hair disheveled and her face covered with dirt. As this picture suggests, the story had a strong focus on Appalachia, but it profiled a variety of poor people from around the country. Of the 54 poor people pictured in this story, only 14 were black.[11]

This story was typical of War on Poverty coverage during 1964 in its substantial focus on rural poverty, in its emphasis on images of poor whites, and in its generally neutral tone. Like this story, most of the early coverage of the War on Poverty consisted of descriptions of its programs, profiles of Johnson's "poverty warriors," and accounts of poverty in America, most often illustrated with examples of individual poor people. Clearly, the expansion of news coverage that accompanied the War on Poverty did not coincide with the racialization of poverty images. At its inception at least, the War on Poverty was not portrayed by the news media as a program for blacks.

The Racialization of Poverty in the News: 1965–67

The year 1965 saw another large jump in media attention to poverty, and a clear turning point in the racialization of poverty images in the news. The percentage of blacks among pictures of the poor jumped from 27 percent in 1964 to 49 percent in 1965. One factor that clearly does *not* explain the racialization of poverty in the news during this period is true change in the proportion of blacks among the poor. As the thin line in figure 4.2 shows, the true percentage of blacks among the poor increased only marginally between the early and late 1960s (from 27 percent to 30 percent), while the percentage of blacks found in news magazine portrayals of the poor more than doubled during this period.

Nor can the dramatic change in the racial portrayal of poverty be attributed to a broader increase in the representation of African Americans in the news. It is true that the proportion of black faces in the major weekly newsmagazines increased steadily from only 1.3 percent in the 1950s to 7.2 percent in the 1980s (Lester and Smith 1990).[12] But a close look at the mid-1960s shows no evidence of a sudden shift in the overall racial mix of newsmagazine photographs. In fact, the overall proportion of African Americans among people pictured in *Time* and *Newsweek* actually declined slightly between 1964 and 1965.[13]

What did change dramatically between 1964 and 1965 was the evaluative tone of stories covering welfare and the War on Poverty. Whereas coverage in 1964 focused on the initiation of the War on Poverty and general descriptions of the American poor, stories in 1965 were much more critical examinations of the government's antipoverty efforts. Three lines of criticism were prominent: First, many stories questioned Sargent Shriver's leadership of the antipoverty effort, focusing on mismanagement, confusion, and waste in the Office of Economic Opportunity. Second, considerable attention was devoted to local disputes between city government and community groups over control of War on Poverty resources. Finally, substantial coverage focused on difficulties within the Job Corps program, one of the first War on Poverty programs to get off the ground. General stories on the War on Poverty and stories about problems in the Job Corps accounted for most of the poor people pictured in early 1965. Fifty percent of the poor pictured in War on Poverty stories during this period were black, as were 55 percent of those in stories on the Job Corps.

We saw above that media coverage from the early 1960s tended to use pictures of poor blacks to illustrate stories about waste, inefficiency or abuse of welfare, and pictures of poor whites in stories with more neutral descriptions of antipoverty programs. This pattern is repeated in 1964 and 1965, as coverage of the War on Poverty becomes more critical and portrayals of the poor become "more black." This association of African Americans with negative stories on poverty is clearest in coverage of the Job Corps. The most visible of the War on Poverty's numerous job training programs, the Job Corps consisted of dozens of residential centers in both urban and rural locations at which young men (and less often young women) were to learn discipline along with basic job skills.

News coverage of the Job Corps program focused on problems such as poor screening of participants, inadequate facilities, and high dropout rates. But the most sensational objections concerned the behavior of Job Corps members and the aversion to Job Corps centers by nearby towns.

For example, a long story in *U.S. News and World Report* published in July 1965 (and illustrated with about equal numbers of blacks and non-blacks) reported charges of "rowdyism" at Job Crops centers, including a dormitory riot in Tongue Point, Oregon, "in which lead pipes were hurled," and the expulsion of eight girls from a St. Petersburg, Florida, center for drinking. "Another worry," the story indicated, was the "antagonism between Corpsmen and nearby townsmen." People in Astoria, Oregon, for example, "complain about hearing obscene language at the movie theater," while residents of Marion, Illinois were upset about a disturbance at a roller skating rink that occurred when some Job Corps members showed up with liquor. Although these incidents were not explicitly linked to black Job Corps participants, the pictures of blacks in Job Corps stories (comprising 55 percent of all Job Corps members pictured) was much higher than the proportion of African Americans pictured in the more neutral stories about the War on Poverty from the previous year.

As we'll see, the pattern of associating negative poverty coverage with pictures of blacks persists over the years and is too widespread and consistent to be explained as the product of any particular antipoverty program or subgroup of the poor. But the sharp increase in the percentage of African Americans pictured in poverty stories in 1965 can also be attributed to the increasing involvement of civil rights leaders in the antipoverty effort. Neither civil rights leaders nor the civil rights movement was mentioned in any of the 32 poverty stories published in 1964, but during the first half of 1965 almost one-quarter (23 percent) of the poverty-related stories made some mention of black leaders. Most of these stories dealt with the battles for control over War on Poverty funds, especially, but not only, those channeled through the Community Action programs. Although the involvement of black community leaders was a minor element in news coverage of poverty from this period, it undoubtedly helped to shift the media's attention away from the previous years' focus on poor whites.

Coverage of poverty during the second half of 1965 was similar to that of early 1965 with two exceptions. First, the Watts riots, which began on August 11, intensified the growing awareness of black poverty in this country. Perhaps surprisingly, neither the Watts riots themselves, nor the problems of inner-city blacks, figured prominently in poverty coverage during the second half of 1965. Nevertheless, 26 percent of poverty stories from the latter half of 1965 did make at least a brief mention of the riots.

To more fully assess changes in media coverage of poverty during the

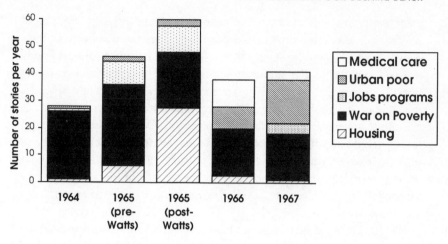

Fig. 4.3. Subject matter of newsmagazine poverty stories, 1964–67

crucial years of 1964 to 1967, figure 4.3 shows the main subject matter of newsmagazine poverty stories (with 1965 broken into two periods to compare pre-Watts and post-Watts coverage). In every year during the mid-1960s, the War on Poverty was the single most common poverty subject in these magazines, accounting for 45 percent of all poverty stories over these four years. As figure 4.3 shows, coverage of urban poverty did increase in 1966 and 1967 to the point where almost as many stories in 1967 were written on problems of the urban poor as on the War on Poverty.

Part of the racialization of poverty during this period clearly concerns the growing focus on America's cities. There is little evidence of an immediate change in media coverage of poverty after Watts. But coverage did change in response to the greater number of riots in the summers of 1966 and 1967. At least as important as the riots themselves was the reactions to those riots both in the greater focus on urban poverty among civil rights leaders and in government efforts to address the problems of the black ghettos, or at least to placate their residents. The percentage of poverty stories that mentioned ghetto riots or civil rights leaders increased from 26 percent in 1965, to 31 percent in 1966 and 38 percent in 1967.

How are we to understand the changing focus of poverty coverage over this four-year period and the concomitant racialization of poverty images? One possibility is that a series of events (e.g. riots, new government programs) led news organizations to focus on new aspects of poverty or new subgroups of the poor, and that these subgroups happened to be disproportionately black. This explanation is almost surely true to some degree. For example, pictures of the poor in stories on urban poverty in between 1964 and 1967 were 95 percent black. Consequently, the increase in urban poverty stories accounts for some part of the racialization of poverty coverage during this period. On the other hand, even if we exclude urban poverty stories, the percentage of blacks in pictures of the poor grew dramatically over these four years; of those stories that were not focused on urban poverty, the percentage of blacks among pictures of the poor more than doubled, growing from 27 percent in 1964 to 58 percent in 1967.

While growing attention to urban poverty did contribute to the changing racial portrayal of the poor between 1965 and 1967, it cannot explain the sharp increase in the percentage of blacks in poverty pictures between 1964 and 1965. Coverage during both of these years was dominated by stories on the War on Poverty with no particular emphasis on urban problems in either year. Furthermore, the jump in percentage black had already occurred before the Watts riots in August 1965; indeed, newsmagazine poverty stories included just as high a percentage of blacks in the first half of 1965 as they did in the months following Watts.

A second possibility is that the mainstream (white-dominated) news media were more likely to associate negative poverty stories with blacks and neutral or positive stories with whites. I have already suggested that this tendency can be observed in the coverage of poverty between 1960 and 1963, and this same phenomenon might explain the sharp increase in pictures of poor blacks between 1964 and the earlier (pre-Watts) months of 1965. Negative views of blacks were even more common in the 1960s than they are today (e.g., Schuman, Steeh, Bobo, and Krysan 1997), and it would be surprising if these attitudes were not shared, at least to some degree, by the white news professionals who shaped the coverage of poverty under examination. Notions about blacks' "cultural foreignness" especially with regard to the mainstream values of individual initiative and hard work might well have led newsmagazine writers, editors, and photographers to associate African Americans with negative coverage of poverty.

Of course, the racial patterns within poverty coverage in 1960–63 and 1964–65 are slender threads on which to hang so important a claim. A wealth of other evidence, however, points in this same direction. In particular, we can make use of the full breadth of newsmagazine coverage between 1950 and 1992 to examine, first, how racial images of the poor change over time as media coverage responds to changing social conditions, and second, the differences in the racial portrayals of different subgroups of the poor. In both cases, we'll find that positive coverage of poverty that focuses on either more sympathetic subgroups of the poor, or periods of time in which the poor as a whole were viewed more sympathetically, was more likely to include pictures of poor whites than the negative coverage of poverty associated with less sympathetic groups and less sympathetic times.

Changing Racial Portrayals of the Poor: 1968–92

Poverty took on a black face in newsmagazines during the tumultuous years of the mid-1960s. But as urban riots subsided and the country's attention turned elsewhere, the racial portrayal of the poor in news coverage did not return to the predominantly white images of the 1950s and early 1960s. Instead, as figure 4.2 shows, the racial representation of the poor in media images of poverty fluctuated considerably, with very high proportions of African Americans in 1972 and 1973, and dramatic "whitening" of poverty images during the economic recessions of 1974–75 and 1982–83. To understand variations over time in the racial portrayal of poverty, I next examine the two extremes in the racial images of the poor.

Images of Blacks and the "Welfare Mess": 1972–73. Coverage of poverty during 1972 and 1973 focused primarily on perceived problems with welfare and efforts at welfare reform. The percentage of all Americans receiving welfare increased dramatically from about 2 percent in the mid-1960s to about 6 percent in the mid-1970s. By the early 1970s, the expansion of welfare came to be viewed as an urgent national problem that demanded action. Newsmagazine stories during 1972 and 1973 almost invariably referred to this situation as the "welfare mess," and published story after story focused on mismanagement in state welfare bureaucracies and abuse of welfare by people who could be supporting themselves.

Welfare recipients were no more likely to be black during 1972–73 than they were a few years earlier. Nevertheless, this period of sustained negative coverage of welfare portrayed poor people and welfare recipients as black to the greatest extent of any point in the 43 years of coverage examined. Blacks comprised 70 percent of the poor people pictured in stories indexed under poverty and 75 percent of those pictured in stories on welfare during these two years. Nor was the heavy representation of blacks limited to stories on poverty and welfare per se. Virtually all poverty-related coverage during these two years—whatever the topic—was illustrated with pictures of blacks. During 1972 and 1973, African Americans composed 76 percent of the poor people pictured in stories on all other poverty-related topics, including housing, urban problems, employment programs, old age, unemployment, and legal aid.

Sympathetic Coverage of White Poverty: 1982–83.   The recession of the early 1980s brought America's worst economic performance in decades. Per capita gross domestic product fell over 3 percent between 1981 and 1982, unemployment rose to almost 11 percent, and the poverty rate increased from about 11 percent in 1979 to over 15 percent in 1983 (U.S. Department of Commerce 1993, 414, 445; Patterson 1994, 211). Coincident with this economic downturn came the Reagan administration's domestic spending cutbacks and rhetorical attacks on government antipoverty programs.

The rather dire conditions of America's poor, and the political controversy that erupted in response to President Reagan's efforts to "trim the safety net," led to a substantial increase in the amount of news coverage of poverty. Reflecting the nature of the times, news coverage of poverty during the early 1980s was concentrated on the growing problems of poverty and unemployment, and on debates over the proper response of government to these conditions. This period of widespread public concern with poverty also saw the lowest percentage of blacks in magazine portrayals of the poor of any time since the early 1960s. Overall, only 33 percent of poor people pictured in poverty-related stories during 1982 and 1983 were black.

The two most common themes of poverty stories during this period concerned the growth of poverty and the debates over government cutbacks. Although a few of these stories sought to convince readers that "The Safety Net Remains" (as a *Time* magazine story from February 1982 was titled), most of this coverage was highly critical of the Reagan administration's efforts to trim government programs for the poor. A good example is *Newsweek*'s prominent story titled "The Hard-Luck Christmas of 82," which proclaimed, "With 12 million unemployed and 2 million homeless, private charity cannot make up for federal cutbacks."[14] This story went on to describe the desperate condition of poor families living in camp tents or in automobiles, portraying them as the noble victims "who are paying the price of America's failure of nerve in the war on poverty." Reflecting the general lack of black faces in these sympathetic poverty stories, "The Hard Luck Christmas of 82" included only three African Americans among the 18 poor people pictured.[15] As a whole, blacks made up only 30 percent of the poor people pictured in general stories on poverty and antipoverty programs from 1982 to 1983.

A less common, but important, theme in poverty stories from this period concerned the "newly poor," that is, formerly middle-class Americans who fell into poverty during the recession of the early 1980s. Typical of this coverage is a (white) family of four profiled in a *U.S. News and World Report* story from August 1982. This story describes how the Telehowski family was "plunged into the ranks of the newly poor" when the father lost his job as a machinist with an auto-parts company. No longer able to afford a car or even an apartment, the Telehowskis reluctantly applied for welfare and became squatters in an abandoned house in inner-city Detroit. The Telehowski family, with their two small children and their determined struggle to support themselves, indicate the extraordinary sympathy that the "newly poor" received in news coverage from the early 1980s. *Time* magazine went even farther in proclaiming the virtues of the newly poor, writing, "The only aspect of American life that has been uplifted by the continuing recession: a much better class of poor person, better educated, accustomed to working, with strong family ties."[16]

It is not surprising, of course, that poverty is portrayed in a more sympathetic light during economic hard times. What is noteworthy, however, is that along with shifts in the tone of news reporting on the poor come shifts in the racial mix of the poor people in news stories. As figure 4.2 shows, the true proportion of blacks among America's poor did not change appreciably between the early 1970s and the early 1980s (or indeed, at any time during the past 35 years). But the racial portrayals of the poor in newsmagazines did shift dramatically as media attention turned from highly critical coverage of welfare during 1972–73 to highly sympathetic stories on poverty during the recession of the early 1980s.[17]

This pattern of associating African Americans with the least sympathetic aspects of poverty is consistent with what we found earlier in examining the initial racialization of poverty coverage in the mid-1960s. I next explore the use of poor blacks and poor nonblacks to illustrate stories on different poverty topics from the entire study period of 1950 to 1992.

Racial Portrayals of Subgroups of the Poor

Table 4.1 shows the percentage African American for pictures of poor people in 13 different aggregated subject categories (see Gilens 1999 for details). The story topics shown in table 4.1 relate to members of the poverty population that receive varying levels of public support or censure. For example, surveys show greater sympathy for the poor in general than for welfare recipients, and a stronger desire to help poor children or the elderly than poor working-age adults (Smith 1987b; Cook and Barrett 1992). And despite the negative coverage that the Job Corps received in stories from the mid-1960s, we would expect more sympathetic responses to stories about poor people in employment programs than to stories about nonworking poor adults.

Of the 13 topics shown in table 4.1, 7 fall into a fairly narrow range in which African Americans comprise between 50 percent and 60 percent of all poor people pictured. These include "sympathetic" topics such as poor children (51 percent black) and employment programs (50 percent black), and "unsympathetic" topics such as public welfare (54 percent black). Of those topics that do differ substantially in percentage African American, however, fewer blacks are shown in stories on the more sym-

TABLE 4.1. Newsmagazine Stories by Topic, 1950–92

Topic	Number of Stories	Number of Poor People Shown	Percent Black
Underclass	6	36	100
Urban problems, urban renewal	91	97	84
Poor people, poverty	182	707	59
Unemployment	102	268	59
Legal aid	30	22	56
Welfare, antipoverty programs	399	965	54
Housing/homeless	272	508	52
Children	45	121	51
Employment programs	45	181	50
Education	22	95	43
Medical care	43	36	28
Hunger	52	176	25
Old-age assistance	28	12	0

Note: An additional 79 stories (not shown above) were indexed under miscellaneous other topics; 133 stories (11% of all poverty stories) were indexed under more than one topic. The database includes all stories on poverty and related topics published in *Time, Newsweek,* and *U.S. News and World Report* between January 1, 1950, and December 31, 1992. See Gilens 1999 for details.

pathetic topics of education (40 percent black), medical care (28 percent black), and hunger (25 percent black), while stories about the elderly poor—one of the most sympathetic subgroups of poor people—are illustrated exclusively with pictures of poor whites. In contrast, only African Americans are found in stories on the underclass, perhaps the least sympathetic topic in table 4.1. While the underclass lacks any consistent definition in either popular or academic discourse,[18] it is most often associated with intergenerational poverty, labor force nonparticipation, out-of-wedlock births, crime, drugs, and "welfare dependency as a way of life" (Jencks 1992). In fact, blacks do compose a large proportion of the American underclass, just how large a proportion depending on how the underclass is defined. But even those definitions that result in the highest percentages of African Americans consider the underclass to include at least 40 percent nonblacks, in contrast to the magazine portrait of the underclass as 100 percent black.[19]

With regard to topic of story, then, we find the same tendency that we found in examining changes in media coverage of poverty over time. In both cases, pictures of African Americans are disproportionately used to illustrate the most negative aspects of poverty and the least sympathetic subgroups of the poor.

Television News Coverage of Poverty

The three newsmagazines examined here have a combined circulation of over ten million copies, and 20 percent of American adults claim to be regular readers of "news magazines such as *Time, U.S. News and World Report,* or *Newsweek*" ("Folio 500" 1994, 52).[20] In addition, these magazines influence how other journalists see the world. In one study, for example, magazine and newspaper journalists were asked what news sources they read most regularly (Wilhoit and Weaver 1991). Among these journalists, *Time* and *Newsweek* were the first- and second-most frequently cited news sources and were far more popular than the *New York Times,* the *Wall Street Journal,* or the *Washington Post.*

Despite the broad reach of these weekly magazines, and their role as "background material" for other journalists, there can be little doubt that television is the dominant news source for most Americans. In recent surveys, about 70 percent of the American public identifies television as the source of "most of your news about what's going on in the world today" (Mayer 1993). If the racial content of television news coverage of poverty were to differ substantially from that found in newsmagazines, our confidence in the analysis of newsmagazines would be severely limited.

Unfortunately, tapes of television news broadcasts are unavailable for shows aired before the middle of 1968. Still, we can to some degree determine whether newsmagazine coverage of poverty is unique to that medium by comparing patterns of news coverage on television with those found in newsmagazines for the period in which both sources are available.

Measuring the racial representation of poverty in television news requires the painstaking examination of hours of television news stories. Because it was impossible to code the full twenty-four years of television news, I chose three historical periods: 1968, the earliest year for which television news shows are available and a year in which magazines portrayed the poor as predominantly black; 1982–83, a time when magazine images of poverty contained the lowest proportion of blacks for the entire period studied; and 1988–92, a more recent period that also contained a high proportion of blacks in newsmagazine stories on poverty.

In each of the three periods examined, television news exaggerated the percentage of blacks among the poor to an even greater extent than did the newsmagazines. Equally important, the changing patterns of racial representation found in the newsmagazines was reflected in television news as well. In both media, 1968 contained extremely high proportions of blacks among pictures of the poor: 68 percent for newsmagazines and 93 percent for televsion news. As expected, news stories during 1982–83 contained much lower proportions of blacks at 33 percent and 49 percent in newsmagazines and televsion news respectively. Finally, for both media, the proportion of poor blacks during 1988–92 fell somewhere in between those of the other two periods at 62 percent of all poor people in newsmagazines and 65 percent in television news.

A more complete analysis of poverty coverage in these two media might reveal some important differences. But the data examined suggest that the patterns of coverage found in newsmagazines are not idiosyncratic to that particular medium. Television news also substantially exaggerates the extent to which blacks compose the poor, and as with newsmagazine coverage, the complexion of poverty in television news shifts over time as events draw attention to more sympathetic and less sympathetic subgroups of the poor. In short, it appears that the distorted coverage of poverty found in newsmagazines reflects a broader set of dynamics that also shape images of the poor in the even more important medium of televsion news.

Do the Mass Media Shape Public Perceptions of the Poor?

The racial content of news media images of the poor have changed dramatically over time, and for most of the past three decades have overrepresented the proportion of blacks among the poor. News coverage itself constitutes an important "artifact" of American political culture. But news coverage has a special significance as a cultural product because we know that it not only reflects, but also influences, public concerns and beliefs.

Numerous studies have demonstrated the power of the media to shape public perceptions and political preferences. Media content has been shown to affect the importance viewers attach to different political issues, the standards that they employ in making political evaluations, the causes they attribute to national problems, their positions on political issues, and their perceptions of political candidates (e.g., Iyengar and Kinder 1987; Rogers and Dearing 1988; Krosnick and Kinder 1990; Iyengar 1987, 1991; Bartels 1993). Although most studies of media impact have examined the spoken or textual components of media content rather than the visual components, research has shown that the visual elements of the news—including the race of the people pictured—are highly salient to viewers (e.g., Iyengar and Kinder 1987; Graber 1990; Iyengar 1991; Kenney 1992).

Another indication that the media shape perceptions of the racial composition of the poor concerns the implausibility of the alternative hypotheses. If the media are not the dominant influence on public beliefs about the poor, than these perceptions must be shaped by either personal encounters with poor people or by conversations about poverty with friends and acquaintances. Conversations with others might indeed be an important influence, but this begs the question of how an individual's conversation partners arrived at *their* perceptions. On the other hand, if personal encounters with poor people explain the public's perceptions, then variation in individuals' perceptions should correspond with variations in the racial mix of the poor people they encounter in everyday life.

Although the personal encounter thesis is plausible, survey data show that the racial makeup of the poor in an individual's state appears to have almost no impact on his or her perceptions of the country's poor as a whole. For example, residents of Michigan and Pennsylvania, where African Americans make up 31 percent of the poor, believe that 50 percent of America's poor are black.[21] In Washington and Oregon, blacks constitute only 6 percent of the poor, yet residents of these states believe that the American poor are 47 percent black. Finally, blacks make up only 1 percent of the poor in Idaho, Montana, Wyoming, North Dakota, South Dakota and Utah, yet survey respondents from these states think that blacks account for 47 percent of all poor people in this country. Thus, despite the large state-by-state differences in the percentage of blacks among the poor, personal experience appears to have little impact on public perceptions of the racial composition of poverty.

In sum, then, previous work on related issues shows that the media can have a significant impact on public opinion. And judging by the similarity in public perceptions across states, it appears that differences in personal exposure to poor people of different races has little impact on perceptions of the poor as a whole. People do draw upon other sources of information and imagery about the social world, but it would be hard to deny that the news media are a centrally important source in a society as large and "media-centric" as our own. As Walter Lippmann noted almost 80 years ago, we necessarily rely on the accounts of others to form our beliefs about the world we inhabit. "Our opinions," he wrote, "cover a bigger space, a longer reach of time, a greater number of things, than we can directly observe. They have, therefore, to be pieced together out of what others have reported" (Lippmann 1960, 79). Most of what we know, or think we know, about social and economic issues and conditions we learn from the media. When news reports offer misleading images, it is inevitable that public perceptions and reality will diverge.

Consequences of Public Perceptions of the Race of the Poor

To understand how different racial images of the poor shape attitudes toward welfare, we can compare the views of those Americans who think most welfare recipients are black with those who think most welfare recipients are white. A 1994 CBS News/New York Times survey found that respondents who erroneously believed that most welfare recipients were black held consistently more negative views about welfare recipients' true need and commitment to the work ethic than did respondents who thought most welfare recipients were white. As table 4.2 shows, among respondents who thought most welfare recipients were black, 63 percent said that "lack of effort on their own part" is most often to blame when people are on welfare, while only 26 percent blamed "circumstances beyond their control." But among respondents who thought most welfare recipients were white, 50 percent blamed circumstances and only

40 percent attributed the problem to a lack of effort. Those who saw most welfare recipients as black also expressed substantially more negative views about welfare recipients when asked whether most people on welfare really want to work, and whether most people on welfare really need it (table 2). These differences between respondents with different perceptions of the racial composition of the poor are not caused by differences between theses two groups in other characteristics. When regression analysis is used to control for respondents' age, sex, education, family income, and liberal/conservative orientations, the differences shown in table 4.2 diminish only slightly (Gilens 1999 for details).

Conclusions

It would be naive to expect a "sociologically accurate" depiction of poverty in news stories. Some aspects of poverty and some subgroups of the poor may be more "newsworthy" than others. And news departments, after all, are in the business of selling news. If news photographers seek out the most sensational images of poverty in order to attract readers or viewers, we should hardly be surprised. For most Americans, the

TABLE 4.2. Perceptions of Welfare Recipients

	Think Most Welfare Recipients Are Black	Think Most Welfare Recipients Are White
In your opinion, what is more to blame when people are on welfare . . .		
Lack of effort on their own part	63%	40%
Circumstances beyond their control	26%	50%
Do most people on welfare want to work?		
Yes	31%	55%
No	69%	45%
Do most people on welfare really need it?		
Yes	36%	50%
No	64%	50%

Source: CBS/New York Times Poll, December 1994.

Note: Question wording: "Of all the people who are on welfare in this country, are more of them black or are more of them white?" Respondents volunteering "about equal" are not shown in the table. All differences between respondents who think most welfare recipients are black and those who think most welfare recipients are white are significant at $p < .001$. These differences diminish only slightly and remain highly significant when controls are added for age, sex, education, family income, and liberal/conservative self-identification. "Don't know" and "No answer" responses are excluded from the results shown above.

most powerful images of poverty are undoubtedly the black urban ghettos. These concentrations of poverty represent the worst failures of our economic, educational, and social welfare systems. Yet they also represent a minuscule portion of all the American poor. Only 6 percent of all poor Americans are blacks living in urban ghettos (Jargowsky and Bane 1991, 251).

Furthermore, racial distortions in the portrayal of poverty are not limited to stories on the urban underclass. The overrepresentation of blacks among the poor is found in coverage of most poverty topics and appears during most of the past three decades. Yet just as importantly, black faces are comparatively *unlikely* to be found in media stories on the most sympathetic subgroups of the poor, just as they are comparatively absent from media coverage of poverty during times of heightened sympathy for the least well off.

Journalists are professional observers and chroniclers of our social world. But they are also residents of that world and are exposed to the same stereotypes and misperceptions that characterize society at large.[22] A self-reinforcing cycle exists in which negative images of the black poor feed media coverage of poverty that then strengthens these images in the culture at large. Society's stereotypes are reflected back—and thereby reinforced—by the mass media.

The events of the 1960s played a role in bringing the black poor to the attention of the American public. But the riots of the mid-1960s, the shift in focus of the civil rights movement, and the growing concern over burgeoning welfare rolls did not change the color of poverty in the news in a simple or uniform way. As we saw above, the increased number of black faces in news stories about the poor reflected the growth of *negative* coverage of poverty. Only when stories about the War on Poverty turned negative did large numbers of poor African Americans begin to appear in the news. And as we saw, shifts over time in the tone of poverty coverage have been accompanied by shifts in the racial complexion of poverty images in the news. The overwhelmingly negative coverage of welfare from the early 1970s coincided with extremely high numbers of African Americans in poverty stories, while the decidedly more sympathetic poverty stories from the early 1980s were illustrated primarily with whites.

News coverage of poverty now reflects the close link between blacks and the poor that informs public thinking about poverty and welfare. The poor have indeed "become black" in the national news media. But as the fluctuations in the racial complexion of poverty images over time and the differences across different subgroups of the poor both attest, it is the "undeserving poor" who have become most black.

It may well be that media attention to black poverty was important in mobilizing resources to redress racial inequality. Affirmative action, urban enterprise zones, minority scholarships, and other explicitly or implicitly race-targeted programs have all reflected a concern with black poverty that was absent before the mid-1960s.

Were the media to ignore or downplay black poverty, the public might be led to think that racial inequality was a problem of the past. But the news media's overrepresentation of blacks among the poor and in particular the association of African Americans with the least sympathetic aspects of poverty serve to perpetuate negative racial stereotypes that serve to lessen public support for efforts to fight poverty in general, and black poverty in particular.

NOTES

1. The classic work from this era is Robert Hunter's book *Poverty*, published in 1904 (see Patterson 1994 for a discussion of Hunter and other early authors writing on American poverty). While Hunter spent considerable time discussing the work habits, nutritional needs, and intelligence of the Italians, Irish, Poles, Hungarians, Germans, and Jews, African Americans escaped his attention altogether. Other popular early treatments of poverty similarly fail to mention blacks. These include Hollander 1914; Parmalee 1916; Gillin 1921; and Kelso 1929.

2. For example, I. M. Rubinow's *The Quest for Security* (1934), published in the middle of the depression and often cited in subsequent literature on poverty, made no mention of blacks.

3. Debates still rage over the extent to which later antipoverty programs were a response to ghetto uprisings and growing black political strength, but most observers seem to agree that the Kennedy administration's antipoverty efforts had little to do with either placating blacks or cementing their political allegiance to the Democratic party. See Katz 1989, 81–88; and Patterson 1994, 133–35.

4. One reason that Social Security Survivors' Benefits disproportionately aided whites was that two occupations with large numbers of African Americans—agricultural and domestic workers—were initially excluded from the Social Security program.

5. Since 1995, African Americans have increased as a proportion of welfare recipients. As a consequence of a robust economy and the changes in welfare regulations instituted by the 1996 Personal Responsibility and Work Opportunity Reconciliation Act welfare caseloads fell sharply during the latter half of the 1990s. In 1996, about 5 percent of the U.S. population was receiving welfare; by 1999, that number had fallen to only 2.6 percent (U.S. Department of Health and

Human Services 2000). This decline in welfare use was more pronounced among nonblacks than it was among African Americans. Consequently, the proportion of the welfare rolls accounted for by African Americans climbed from 34.5 percent in 1996 to 37.3 percent in 1998 (House 2000).

6. Of the 1,281 stories on poverty published in these three magazines between 1960 and 1990, a random sample of 234 were examined for any specific mentions of the racial composition of the poor. Only 11 of these 234 stories (or 4.7 percent) gave any concrete information on the proportion of blacks among poor people, AFDC recipients, public housing tenants, or any other subgroup of the poor. Extrapolating from this sample to all of the poverty stories published during this 31-year period, we would expect each magazine to provide this kind of information approximately once every year and a half.

7. On the impact of photographs, see Graber 1987, 1990; and Kenney 1992. On the tendency to be swayed by specific examples rather than statistical information see Brosius and Bathelt 1994; Hamill, Wilson, and Nisbett 1980; and Kazoleas 1993.

8. The reliability of the race coding was assessed by having two coders independently code a random sample of pictures. Using the picture as the unit of analysis, intercoder reliability for percentage black in each picture was .87.

9. A difficult issue in the analysis of news photographs concerns the relative impact that different pictorial content might have on the reader. For example, it is reasonable to assume that other things being equal, a picture of many poor people contains more information, and would have a bigger impact on readers, than a picture of a single poor person. But just how much more of an impact is not clear. Does a picture of 20 poor whites have 20 times the impact on readers' perceptions of the poor as a picture of one poor white?

On the one hand, we might expect each additional poor person in a picture to add somewhat to the overall impact of that picture. On the other hand, it seems likely that beyond some point each additional person would add only slightly to the picture's impact. The simplest approaches would be to count each picture equally in calculating the racial portrayal of the poor, or alternatively to count each person pictured equally. The first approach comes up short because it fails to assign greater weight to pictures with larger numbers of poor people. The second approach is also problematic, however, because it gives the same weight to the fiftieth person in a picture of a large group as it does to the sole individual in a picture of one poor person. In addition, counting each individual equally would allow a few pictures of large groups to dominate the results.

As a compromise, I have adopted the following procedure. In general, each poor person is counted equally, but any pictures that contain more than 12 poor people are adjusted to reflect more accurately the probable impact of the picture on readers, and to prevent pictures of large groups from dominating the results. Specifically, the number of poor people in a single picture is capped at 12. Thus all pictures with 12 or more poor people are coded as containing only 12 poor people. The race of these 12 people are constructed to be proportionate to the race of all the people in the picture. For example, if a picture contained ten poor whites and 30 poor blacks, it would be scored for analysis as containing three poor whites and 9 poor blacks to maintain the percentage of blacks at 75 percent.

Although this system is a fairly crude and imperfect compromise, it derives from the reasonable assumption that in general pictures with more people have a larger impact on readers' perceptions of the poor than do pictures with fewer people. Yet it also recognizes that this tendency has some limit, and that the impact of each individual within a large crowd is less than the impact of lone individuals or of individual people within a small group.

10. The figure for the average percentage of blacks among the poor includes only the years 1960 through 1992, since poverty data broken down by race are not available prior to 1960.

11. In addition to these 54 people for whom race could be identified, this story included 4 others of unidentifiable race.

12. These figures are for *Newsweek* and *Time* combined, for the years 1952 plus 1957 and 1983 plus 1988, respectively. See Lester and Smith 1990, tables 2 and 3.

13. Examining every fifth issue of *Time* and *Newsweek* between January 1963 and December 1965, I found that the proportion of African Americans (excluding advertisements) in newsmagazine photographs increased from 6.4 percent in 1963 to 8.7 percent in 1964 and then decreased to 5.5 percent in 1965. (The total number of individuals coded in the three years was 2,668, 2,744, and 3,115 for 1963, 1964, and 1965 respectively.)

14. *Newsweek*, December 27, 1982, 12.

15. These figures for the "Hard Luck Christmas" story reflect the adjusted counts of poor people using a maximum of 12 poor people per picture (see note 9 above). The raw counts from this story are 73 nonblack and 17 black poor. In this case the adjusted percentage black ($3/18 = 17$ percent) and the raw percentage black ($17/90 = 19$ percent) are quite similar.

16. *Time*, December 27, 1982, 13.

17. African Americans did represent a somewhat larger proportion of welfare recipients in the early 1970s (about 43 percent) than of poor people in the early 1980s (about 28 percent). But this difference is too small to account for the difference in media portrayals, which dropped from 75 percent to 33 percent black.

18. Some argue that the very notion of an underclass is misguided at best and pernicious at worst (e.g., Reed 1991), but this is not the place to debate the utility of this concept. Because the media have adopted the term *underclass,* those interested in understanding public attitudes must acknowledge its importance, irrespective of our feelings about the desirability or undesirability of the concept.

19. One such definition counts as members of the underclass only poor residents of census tracts with unusually high proportions of (1) welfare recipients, (2) female headed households, (3) high school dropouts, and (4) unemployed working-age males (Ricketts and Sawhill 1988). To qualify as an underclass area based on Ricketts and Sawhill's criteria, a census tract must be at least one standard deviation above the national average on all four of these characteristics. By this definition, only five percent of the American poor live in underclass areas and 59 percent of the underclass is African American. However defined, it is clear that the American underclass contains substantial numbers of nonblacks, in contrast to the magazine underclass composed exclusively of African Americans.

20. Readership is gauged by a Times Mirror survey of February 20, 1992, which asked, "I'd like to know how often, if ever, you read certain types of publications. For each that I read tell me if you read them regularly, sometimes, hardly ever or never. . . . News magazines such as *Time, U.S. News and World Report,* or *Newsweek*." Twenty percent of respondents claimed to read such magazines regularly, 38 percent sometimes, 20 percent hardly ever, and 21 percent never.

21. Data on public perceptions come from the 1991 National Race and Politics Study. Figures for the true percentage of blacks among the poor are from the 1990 census (U.S. Department of Commerce 1993).

22. See Gilens 1996b for a discussion of the racial beliefs of news professionals.

CHAPTER 5

Race Matters

The Impact of News Coverage of
Welfare Reform on Public Opinion

JAMES M. AVERY AND MARK PEFFLEY

Since the passage of national welfare reform legislation in 1996, media coverage of welfare has been remarkable in at least two respects. First, given the usual tendency for the media to give short shrift to public policy, news coverage of welfare reform policy has been comparatively intense (e.g., Clawson and Trice 2000). Second, and more important, the tone of coverage has been much more positive.[1] In contrast with the negative focus on welfare "problems" in past decades, many news accounts of welfare reform have already declared it a success, with President Clinton and Republican congressional leaders competing to claim credit for "ending welfare as we know it." Notably, the emphasis in these stories has been on the decline in welfare rolls and the number of women moving from welfare to work, with very little attention to the problems of the newly working poor who continue to struggle to make ends meet.

With more positive news coverage, one might optimistically expect more favorable public attitudes toward welfare and welfare recipients. New evidence of a poverty program that actually puts people to work could revamp traditional public views of welfare as a government "handout" that undercuts the work ethic. Any such optimism would be premature, however, for news coverage of welfare reform is similar to that of an earlier era in one very important respect: news stories about welfare continue to be illustrated with African Americans images and exemplars (Clawson and Trice 2000). And if past research is any guide, such a pattern of media coverage is likely to reinforce public cynicism about welfare rather than reverse it.

In this paper, we examine the various ways that whites' political attitudes are influenced by news coverage of welfare reform. Based on content analyses of news coverage of welfare, several scholars have made the forceful argument that the news media tends to "racialize" welfare policy by disproportionately using images of African Americans to accompany news stories on poverty (e.g., Entman and Rojecki 2000; Gilens 1999; Clawson and Trice 2000). Not only are welfare recipients more likely to be depicted as being African American, but negative coverage of poverty tends to be illustrated with pictures of blacks, while the faces of the poor in more positive stories are predominantly white. As suggested by prior research, the consequences of such coverage are potentially severe: by creating the inaccurate impression that a majority of welfare recipients are black, public support for welfare is likely diminished and negative stereotypes of African Americans as the "undeserving poor" are doubtless reinforced.

But while we know that news coverage of welfare is racially biased, we do not know whether and how such imagery actually affects public opinion. In addition, given the more positive tone of many news stories on welfare reform, it is especially important to investigate the way that racial portrayals interact with the tone (i.e., content) of the story in affecting public opinion. Such questions obviously cannot be answered with the analysis of news content alone. To investigate the impact of biased news portrayals of welfare, we employ an experimental design where we manipulate the content of newspaper stories about welfare reform as well as the photographs that accompany them. The news stories describe welfare reform in either a positive or a negative light, whereas the associated photograph depicts either a white or a black former welfare mother. Our results suggest that identical news stories are interpreted in radically different ways depending on the race of the welfare mother portrayed in the story, with important consequences for public attitudes toward welfare recipients and welfare reform.

We begin with a closer look at research documenting the tendency of the news to overrepresent African Americans in its portrayals of poverty. We then turn to an examination of research on media effects that lends both empirical and theoretical support to the hypothesis that racial portrayals of poverty affect public attitudes toward welfare and welfare recipients. We then test this hypothesis with data from a survey experiment where respondents are randomly assigned to read different versions of a news article on welfare reform that varies both racial imagery and the content or tone of the story. We conclude with a summary of our results and implications for studies of racial bias in the news and its effects on public support for welfare.

Media Portrayals of Poverty

Several studies have documented the tendency for the mainstream news media to disproportionately portray poverty as a "black" problem. In their investigation of television news portrayals of poverty in the 1990s, for example, Entman and Rojecki (2000) found that black people were the dominant visual images appearing in stories about poverty, prompting the authors to conclude that "the imagery of television news suggests poverty is concentrated among blacks, so much so that merely showing a black person on the screen appears to be a code for the involvement of poor people" (105).[2]

Taking a longer historical perspective, Gilens (chap. 4, this volume) examined media portrayals of the poor from 1950 to 1992. He found that African Americans have generally dominated news media depictions of the poor since the late 1960s. About two-thirds of the poor people pictured in major news magazines and network news broadcasts were black—about twice the true proportion of blacks among the nation's poor. Just as importantly, black faces are unlikely to be found in media stories on the most sympathetic subgroups of the poor (e.g., the working poor and the elderly), just as they are comparatively absent from media coverage of poverty during times of heightened sympathy for the poor (e.g., during economic hard times).

Clawson and Trice (2000) extended Gilens's work by examining media portrayals of the poor between 1993 and 1998, during a time when welfare reform was high on the nation's agenda. Like Gilens, they found that pictures of blacks were disproportionately used in news magazine portrayals of the poor, particularly in stories on topics that were not very popular with the public (e.g., welfare reform and pregnancy, public housing, and the welfare cycle of dependency). On the other hand, blacks were less often associated with more sympathetic topics (e.g., welfare reform and children and job training).

Thus, findings from studies covering different media and different time periods converge on a single conclusion: news portrayals of welfare and poverty tend to "racialize" welfare by disproportionately using images of blacks to illustrate the most negative stories about poverty. The consequences of these distortions are held to be severe. Clawson and Trice (2000, 63), for example, conclude that photographic images of poor people in mainstream news magazines "do not capture the reality of poverty; instead, they provide a stereotypical and inaccurate picture of poverty which results in negative beliefs about the poor, antipathy toward blacks, and a lack of support for welfare programs."

Media Effects and Racial Cues in the News

Why are racial portrayals in news coverage of welfare assumed to be so consequential for public opinion? Admittedly, little direct evidence exists at this point. Nevertheless, the circumstantial evidence appears compelling. Most generally, we know that the news media in the United States play a crucial role in shaping the political opinions and behavior of the mass public. Although early studies concluded that the media had only "minimal effects" on public opinion because they did not alter existing attitudes in an obvious way, an avalanche of recent research has shown that news coverage affects public opinion through a variety of more "subtle" pathways. These more subtle effects include agenda setting and framing, both of which can be illustrated with examples of news coverage of welfare policy.

Agenda setting refers to the process whereby the amount of attention the media devotes to an issue or event affects the public's priorities among issues and the problems they want government to solve. Soon after the passage of TANF, for example, a flurry of news stories appeared on welfare reform, making it likely that welfare would be viewed by the public as an important issue. The subtlety of agenda setting is captured best by Bernard Cohen's (1963, 13) famous statement: the press "may not be successful in telling its readers what to *think*, but it is stunningly successful in telling its readers what to think *about*."

Most importantly for our purposes, the media also exerts a subtle effect on public opinion through the way it *frames* news stories (e.g., Iyengar 1991). A news frame is a "central organizing idea or story line that provides meaning to an unfolding strip of events, weaving a connection among them" (Gamson and Modigliani 1987, 143). Citing Entman's (1993) work, Nelson and Kinder (1996) write that "frames spell out the essence of the problem, suggest how it should be thought about, and may go so far as to recommend what (if anything) should be done about it" (1057). Thus, the way reporters frame stories on welfare reform is likely to affect the way the public thinks about the problem. Welfare could be framed as a temporary means to allow the disadvantaged to help themselves, or as an unearned handout to people who don't want to work (Gamson and Lasch 1983). Obviously, the former frame is more likely to encourage support for welfare than the latter.

Against this backdrop of strong media effects, it is easy to appreciate how racial images in news coverage of welfare can be so consequential for public opinion. A considerable body of media research points to the power of visual images to trump auditory and text messages. Moreover, media imagery helps to *frame* media content. Visual images in the news, for example, tend to be more vivid, salient, and memorable than auditory or textual information (e.g., Graber 1990; Neuman, Just, and Crigler 1992). Gamson and his colleagues (Gamson 1992; see also Gamson and Lasch 1983) argue that visual images play an important role in defining and illustrating particular *issue frames*. In other words, images or pictures help to frame the content of the news. In their study of issue framing of affirmative action policy, for example, Nelson and Kinder (1996) found that photographs of blacks versus whites represented different issue frames that affected attitudes toward affirmative action. According to Clawson and Trice (2000, 55), "[News] photographs are symbolic of the "whole mosaic" [of the story], . . . providing texture, drama and detail, they illustrate the implicit, the latent, the "taken for granted" and the "goes without saying."

Especially relevant here is the growing body of experimental research that shows the race of an individual pictured in the news is a salient and powerful cue in affecting public opinion. Shanto Iyengar and Donald Kinder (1987), for example, found that when people are presented with a television news story about unemployment that featured a black individual, they were significantly less likely to think that unemployment is a pressing national issue than when the story features a white person. In another experimental study Iyengar (1991) found that racial imagery in a news story about poverty affected the kinds of solutions people proposed to deal with unemployment. After watching a story about a poor black person, people suggested poor people need to work harder, while societal solutions were recommended after watching a similar story about a poor white person.

In the related domain of crime policy, experimental research demonstrates that negative images of blacks have the power to influence public opinion toward criminal suspects and crime policy (e.g., Peffley, Shields, and Williams 1996; Gilliam and Iyengar 2000). Crime, like welfare, is an ostensibly race-neutral issue that has become racialized, in part, by news coverage that portrays the average criminal as African American (Entman 1992). Experimental evidence suggests that even a brief visual image of a black male in a typical nightly news story on crime is powerful and familiar enough to activate viewers' negative stereotypes of blacks, producing racially biased evaluations of black criminal suspects (Peffley, Shields, and Williams 1996). In their experimental studies manipulating the skin color of a male perpetrator in a local news broadcast, Gilliam and associates (Gilliam et al. 1996; Gilliam and Iyengar 2000) found that when the perpetrator was African American, more subjects endorsed punitive crime policies and negative racial attitudes after watching the news broadcast.

Contemporary News Coverage of Welfare Reform

Clearly then, prior research provides strong support for the hypothesized effects of racially biased news portrayals of welfare. As suggested by extant research, illustrating negative news stories about welfare with African Americans is likely to diminish whites' support for welfare programs as well as reinforce pejorative beliefs about blacks and the poor. But this hypothesis needs to be reconsidered in light of contemporary news coverage of welfare reform. Because while blacks continue to be overrepresented in news stories about poverty, news coverage of welfare reform (since the passage of the welfare reform act) has been more positive, emphasizing the success with which people have moved from welfare to work. Like most political news, stories about welfare reform tend to rely heavily on "official sources," and in this case a bipartisan consensus quickly emerged hailing welfare reform as a success. President Clinton, who signed the Personal Responsibility and Work Opportunity Reconciliation Act (PRWORA) in 1996 with some misgivings, later was adamant in proclaiming welfare reform a success and, of course, taking credit for it. In a speech in August 1997, for example, he concluded, "A lot of people said that welfare reform would never work. . . . But a year later, I think it's fair to say *the debate is over. We now know that welfare reform works*" (*Washington Post*, August 13, 1997; emphasis added).

The standard for success in this case is the much-heralded drop in the welfare rolls and the increase in the number of people moving from welfare to work. More equivocal evidence bearing on the success of welfare reform legislation has received scant attention in the news. The fact that many women moving from welfare to work continue to live in poverty or struggle to make ends meet has been virtually ignored. Moreover, the role of the surging economy in shrinking welfare rolls, independent of any effect of welfare reform legislation, is rarely considered in such news coverage. It may be understandable for journalists to emphasize what's "new" about welfare, but, as many scholars point out, the real test of any poverty program occurs during an economic downturn when more people are in need of assistance, not during one of the longest economic expansions in U.S. history.

The important point for our purposes is that, in the contemporary context, the tone as well as the racial imagery of the story is likely to affect public opinion. Indeed, one can imagine a number of different paths through which racial imagery and story content could affect public opinion. Race and tone, may, of course, have independent, additive effects. A more interesting possibility is suggested by research on framing. If visual cues tend to frame stories on welfare reform, identical stories are likely to be interpreted very differently depending on whether the story is illustrated with a black welfare mother or a white welfare mother. A white mother in a story about the problems of welfare reform may suggest the hardships of a struggling family, while the same story illustrated with an African American may generate an unsympathetic response to a "less deserving" individual.

Methods, Data, and Estimation

In the study that follows, we provide a more direct test of how the race of the individual depicted in a news story about welfare reform—as well as the tone of the story—affects whites' evaluations of welfare and its recipients. We embedded a news story experiment into a nonprobability survey of 603 nonstudent white adults interviewed by trained college students in the spring of 2000.[3] Respondents were randomly assigned to read one of four different versions of a newspaper article evaluating welfare reform (see the appendix). They were then asked several questions about the woman in the article as well as various background questions.

Experimental Manipulations

For the experimental treatment we use a two-by-two design, independently varying both the race (either *black* or *white*) of the woman (and her child) depicted in the article and tone of the article (either *success* or *problems*). Thus, a random half of the respondents read an article with an accompanying photograph of a *white* woman (Mary Ellsworth) and her child and the other half read an article with a photo of a *black* woman (Lashanda Washington) and her child. In addition, a random half of the respondents read an article that described welfare reform as a *success* ("Welfare Reform's Triumph Is Affirmed") while the other half read about the *problems* of welfare reform ("Welfare Reform's Problems Are Confirmed").[4] In both the *success* and the *problems* versions of the article, the woman featured has moved from welfare to work and is described as "the perfect example" of welfare reform. In the *success* version, however, the mother reports that she is now able to provide for her family on her own, while in the *problems* version she reports that since leaving the welfare rolls she is having problems providing for her family. The body of the article cites a comprehensive study by the "Urban Institute" that either "highlights the economic problems experienced by former welfare recipients" (in the *problems* condition) or "affirms the early optimism" of the program's authors (in the *success* condition).

This difference in tone is characteristic of the debate surrounding the effects of welfare reform. Critics do not deny that the welfare rolls are decreasing; rather, the debate revolves around the question of whether the conditions of those leaving the welfare rolls are actually improving after joining the ranks of the "working poor." The articles also reflect the way the media tend to cover welfare reform. Most articles tend to combine elements of episodic and thematic frames in discussing welfare reform (Iyengar 1991) by leading with a featured exemplar that introduces a more thematic discussion of welfare reform.

It is also worth noting that while the tilt of the article favors either a positive or a negative evaluation of welfare reform, there is some attempt to give the appearance of "balance" at the end of the article by briefly touching on the "problems" of welfare reform in the *success* version and the successes of the reforms in the *problems* version.

Dependent Variables

After reading one of the four news articles, respondents were asked to make evaluations of the woman in the story, of welfare reform, and of welfare in general. Two questions were used to tap evaluations of the woman's work ethic in the article. The first item, Blame Mother, asks respondents, "If you learned that the woman in the article lost her job, would you guess that it was due more to the failure of the woman" (at point 1), or "to the failure of welfare reform" (7) on a seven-point scale. The second item, Back on Welfare, asks respondents to rate on a seven-point scale the degree to which, "If the woman in the article lost her job," she would be more likely to "try hard to look for a new job" (1) or "try to go back on welfare" (7).

In assessing evaluations of welfare reform, the Limit Welfare item asks respondents to rate on a seven-point scale whether the five-year lifetime limit for receiving welfare benefits, "[u]nder the current law," is "much too short" (1) or "much too long" (7). Lifetime limits on the maximum number of years recipients are eligible to receive assistance marks one of the key differences between the former welfare system under AFDC and the current system under TANF.

Finally, we use two questions to assess evaluations of welfare in general. The first item, Without Welfare, asks respondents the extent to which they agree or disagree on a seven-point scale with the following statement: "Most people on welfare could get by without it if they really tried." The second item, Welfare Spending, asks respondents whether they would rather see spending on welfare decrease (1), increase (7), or kept the same (4).

Independent Variables

The race of the mother depicted in the photograph is indicated by a dummy variable, Race, coded 1 if the mother is black and 0 if the mother is white. The Tone of the article is coded 0 if respondents were assigned to the success condition and 1 if they were assigned to the problems condition. Because the way respondents react to the tone of the article is likely to be affected by the race of the mother in the article, we created an interaction term, Race × Tone, by simply multiplying Race times Tone.

Estimation

Two models are estimated for each dependent variable, with the first examining the additive effects of Race and Tone and the second model including the interaction term. In addition, party ID, Ideology, and several demographic variables (education, gender, income, and age) were included in the model.

Results

Evaluations of the (Former) Welfare Mother

Table 5.1 displays the OLS results obtained from regressing evaluations of the former welfare mother on the Race and Tone of the story, along with the other predictors. Looking first at results for the Blame Mother question, the first column of coefficients reveals that neither Race nor Tone has a significant additive effect on evaluations of whether the mother or welfare reform is more to blame if the woman loses her job. As revealed by the second column of coefficients, however, the interaction between Race and Tone is highly significant.

How should this interaction be interpreted? The upper panel of figure 5.1 displays the prediced values of blame for each of the four versions of the article.[5] Clearly, when welfare reform is described as a success, the race of the welfare mother has no effect. When welfare reform is described as having problems, however, substantial differences emerge in the evaluation of the welfare mother, depending on her race depicted in the photograph. In this context, the black woman is more likely to be blamed if she lost her job, while blame is more likely to be directed at the problems of welfare reform when the woman is portrayed as being white.

TABLE 5.1. Effects of Race and Story Content on Evaluation of Former Welfare Mother

	Evaluation of Former Welfare Mother			
Predictors	Blame Mother		Back on Welfare	
Race (1 = Black Mother)	−0.20	0.15	0.51***	0.66***
	(0.13)	(0.18)	(0.14)	(0.20)
Story Tone (1 = Still Problems)	0.05	0.39**	1.78***	1.93***
	(0.13)	(0.18)	(0.14)	(0.20)
Race × Tone		−0.71***		−0.32
		(0.26)		(0.28)
Constant	3.21***	3.06***	3.24***	3.16***
	(0.51)	(0.51)	(0.12)	(0.13)
Adj. R^2	0.017	0.025	0.289	0.289
N	512	512	513	513

Note: Table entries are unstandardized regression coefficients with standard errors in parentheses. Each regression equation included Party ID, Ideology, Education, Gender, Income, and Age.

**$p < 0.05$ \qquad ***$p < 0.01$

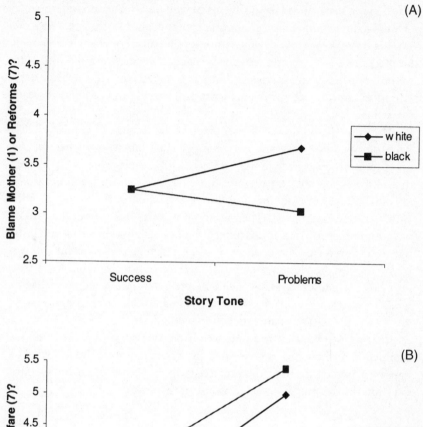

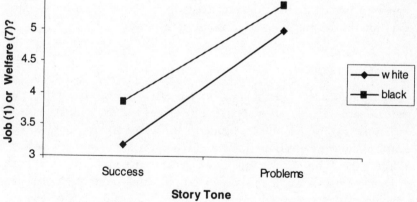

Fig. 5.1. Effects of race and story tone on evaluation of former welfare mother. *(A)* If lost job, due to failure of woman or reform? *(B)* if loses job, likely to look for new job or back on welfare?

Thus, in the story about the problems of welfare reform, altering the race of the welfare mother in the photograph appears to affect the way the story is framed by many of our white respondents. For the white welfare mother, there is more of a tendency to deflect blame for a job loss onto welfare reform, whereas responsibility is targeted more to the black welfare mother even after problems with welfare reform are highlighted in the article.

The right-hand side of table 5.1 displays the results of a similar model, Back on Welfare, this time explaining evaluations of whether, in the event the former welfare mother loses her job, she is more likely to "try to find a new job" or "try to go back on welfare." In this case, both race and story tone have significant additive effects on evaluations. In other words, as one might expect, people are more optimistic about the former welfare mother looking for another job after reading the article describing welfare reform as a success; a more pessimistic assessment follows from reading about the problems of welfare reform. The mother's race also has a significant, albeit smaller, effect on such evaluations, with white respondents expecting the black woman to be more likely to try to go back on welfare than the white woman. In the next column of coefficients, we see that the interaction between Race and Tone is not significant, a result that is confirmed by inspection of the lower panel of figure 5.1, which displays the predicted values for the Back on Welfare question for the four different versions of the article.

Evaluations of Welfare

Although one may expect a news story to affect evaluations of the individual featured in the story, research by Gilens and others suggests that visual portrayals also influence support for welfare *policy*. In table 5.2, we examine the effects of Race and Tone on evaluations of welfare reform (the Limit Welfare question), general attitudes toward welfare recipients (the Without Welfare question), and support for welfare spending (Welfare Spending). Focusing first on evaluations of welfare reform, perhaps the single most important difference between AFDC and the current system under TANF is the new limit on the maximum number of years families are eligible to receive assistance. As can be seen by the first column of coefficients for the Limit Welfare equation, the race of the woman depicted in the article significantly affects evaluations of whether a five-year lifetime limit on welfare benefits is judged to be too short or too long. Overall, white respondents are more likely to view the five-year limit as being *too long* when the *black* (former) welfare mother is portrayed in the story.

Interestingly, the interaction between race and tone is also significant (the second column of coefficients for the Limit Welfare question). To interpret this interaction, we turn again to the predicted values for the different versions of the article displayed in the upper panel of figure 5.2. Here we see that the race of the mother makes no difference when welfare reforms are described as a success. But when the reforms are described as having *problems,* people are more likely to think the lifetime limits on receiving welfare are *too long* when the mother is *black*. When a *white* former welfare mother is portrayed as facing hardships, however, respondents are more likely to view a five-year limit as being *too short.* These results are similar to those of the Blame Mother question in table 5.1, where the complexion of the former welfare mother also appeared to shift the frame of the story. Not only was the black woman held more responsible for losing her job (table 5.1), but she prompts a different policy remedy for the general problems of welfare reform that she portrays: eligibility for assistance needs to be tightened when the exemplar is black, but expanded when the exemplar is white.

Racial portrayals of poverty are also hypothesized to affect more gen-

TABLE 5.2. Effects of Race and Story Content on Evaluation of Former Welfare Mother

Predictors	Evaluation of Welfare Reform		Evaluation of Welfare in General			
	Limit Welfare		Without Welfare		Welfare Spending	
Race (1 = Black Mother)	0.31***	0.02	0.23*	0.34*	0.10	0.14
	(0.12)	(0.17)	(0.14)	(0.20)	(0.11)	(0.15)
Tone (1 = Still Problems)	0.11	−0.17	−0.003	0.11	0.06	−0.09
	(0.12)	(0.16)	(0.14)	(0.20)	(0.11)	(0.15)
Race × Tone		0.58***		−0.23		−0.09
		(0.23)		(0.28)		(0.22)
Constant	4.36***	4.47***	4.51***	4.43***	3.90***	3.88***
	(0.10)	(0.11)	(0.12)	(0.13)	(0.41)	(0.41)
Adj. R^2	0.053	0.062	0.102	0.102	0.163	0.147
N	512	512	513	513	508	508

Note: Table entries are unstandardized regression coefficients with standard errors in parentheses. Each regression equation included Party ID, Ideology, Education, Gender, Income, and Age.
$*p < 0.10$ $**p < 0.05$ $***p < 0.01$.

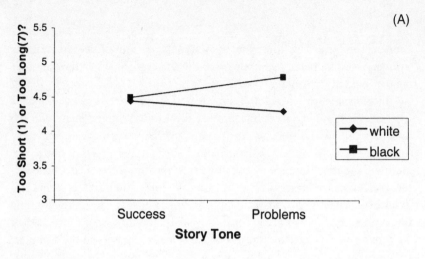

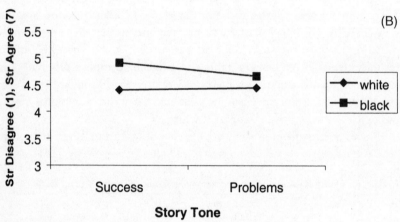

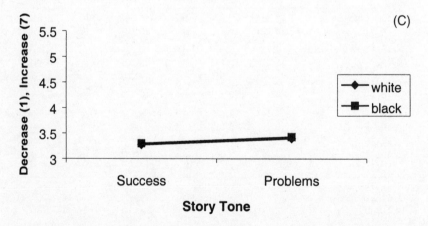

Fig. 5.2. Effects of race and story tone on evaluation of welfare policy. *(A)* Five-year limit too short or too long? *(B)* most people could get by without welfare? *(C)* spending on welfare?

eral attitudes about welfare recipients and support for welfare. In the third column of coefficients in table 5.2 (the Without Welfare question), we use the same predictors to explain agreement with the general belief that "Most people on welfare could get along without it if they tried." Race is a significant predictor of such attitudes in the additive model, but only at the .10 level. Although the interaction between Race and Tone is not statistically significant either (the fourth column of coefficients), the middle panel of figure 5.2 suggests a slight tendency for racial imagery once again to alter the interpretation of the article. This time, however, the race of the woman has a greater impact for the story describing welfare as a success. When the black woman is portrayed in a story about welfare reform being a success, respondents are more likely to agree that "most people could get by without welfare." In other words, describing welfare reform as a success more strongly encourages conservative attitudes on welfare when the woman is black than when she is white.

As a final test of the power of racial portrayals to affect support for welfare, we present estimates for a third dependent variable in table 5.2, the Welfare Spending question. In this case, neither Race nor Tone significantly affects the general desire to increase or decrease spending on welfare. None of the coefficients in table 5.2 are significant, a "nonfinding" that is confirmed by the third panel in figure 5.2. It may be that the impact of the manipulated elements of the story diminish as the focus shifts to more general evaluations of welfare (Without Welfare and Welfare Spending) with less direct relevance to the article respondents read. Treatment effects decline as the focus of evaluation shifts from evaluations of the mother (i.e., the Blame Mother and Back on Welfare assessments in table 5.1) to welfare reform (Limit Welfare) to welfare in general (Without Welfare and Welfare Spending).[6] Overall, despite these "nonfindings," the effects of reading a single story on evaluations of welfare and welfare recipients seem impressive by almost any standard.

Conclusions

Summary and Implications

One conclusion of our study stands out from our findings: racial portrayals of poverty in the media clearly do matter. Studies of media portrayals of poverty have consistently documented a tendency for the media to "racialize" welfare policy by disproportionately using images of African Americans to accompany news stories on poverty. Our experimental study shows that this racially biased imagery is not without consequence. By randomly varying the race of the woman depicted in identical stories about welfare reform, we were able to show conclusively that racial imagery has a powerful effect on the way whites respond to the news articles. Generally speaking, respondents who read a story with an accompanying photograph of a black (versus a white) woman and her child were decidedly more harsh in their evaluations of welfare recipients and welfare in general. This finding is very much in keeping with the hypothesized effects of racial portrayals in content analysis studies.

Our findings also demonstrate that the content of the story affects readers' reactions, as well. Content analysis studies have documented a clear pattern for journalists to use photographs of African Americans to portray negative stories about poverty that are likely to generate unsympathetic responses from the public. To estimate the effects of the tone of the story in addition to racial imagery, we also randomly assigned respondents to read either a story describing welfare reform as a *success* in moving women from welfare to work or as creating *problems* for the newly working poor who continue to struggle to make ends meet. We found the tone of the story to exert a simple additive effect on assessments of the work ethic of the former welfare mother portrayed in the article. Thus, in the Back on Welfare model, reading about the success of welfare reform prompted more optimistic assessments of the former welfare mother's ability to hold down a job without going back to welfare. And in the Blame Mother model, reading the story about the successes of welfare reform led respondents to place more of the blame on the mother if she lost her job. Based on these results, we might speculate that the tendency of the media to portray welfare reform as an unmitigated success may convince the public that governmental assistance is not needed in light of the opportunities for employment greeting women who leave welfare.

On the other hand, in most cases the story content failed to exert a simple additive effect on respondents' evaluations of welfare and welfare recipients. Rather, the tone of the story was found to interact with racial imagery in shaping responses to welfare and welfare recipients. Depicting the woman as black or white appeared to alter drastically the frame of the story. Thus, stories identical in content or tone had very different effects on political evaluations depending on the race of the mother and her child depicted in the story. Consistent with the arguments of content analysis studies, associating a black woman with a story about the problems of welfare tended to produce the most cynical public evaluations of welfare recipients and welfare policy. When a black woman is placed in the stigmatizing context of a story about the problems of welfare reform, she is held more responsible for losing her job (Blame Mother model), and respondents are more likely to favor more stringent eligibility limits for welfare assistance (Limit Welfare). Because research finds that African Americans are more likely to be used by journalists to portray the problems of welfare (Gilens, chap. 4, this volume; Clawson and Trice 2000), our findings confirm that such portrayals tend to produce the most cynical responses to the poor and to welfare programs. Though journalists may intend to create a more sympathetic public response with their stories, our findings suggest that such news stories are likely to have just the opposite effect on their audience.

Caveats

Several caveats about our findings are in order. In the first place, while our experimental design offers a useful balance between internal and external validity, it is by no means perfect. Although our sample is large and diverse in comparison with most laboratory studies, it was not selected randomly, and so we lack the benefit of being able to generalize our findings to a known population. In addition, while respondents were asked to read the news story as they would any newspaper article, respondents may have paid more attention to the content of the story than they would in a more natural setting. It may be that in a low-attention setting, visual images are weighed more than story content in determining responses to the news. Alternatively, neither image nor story content may affect responses as much as the did in our study, where respondents were asked to read a news story. In addition, our respondents read a single news story, while the effects of racially biased news portrayals of poverty may emerge after being exposed to a pattern of bias in dozens of news articles over a period of years. The fact that we did not find powerful effects of race in every single instance, therefore, should not be viewed as a refutation of the power of news to affect public opinion. Rather, the fact that a single news story had such important consequences should give one pause. Repeated exposure to a similar pattern of news stories can only reinforce the racialization of welfare over the longer haul.

Recent trends in the makeup of the welfare population are likely to magnify racial biases in news coverage of welfare. Welfare rolls are becoming increasingly skewed toward people of color (Zedlewski and

Alderson 2001). In 1998, white families made up only 33 percent of the nation's welfare caseload, down from 42 percent in 1997. Black families, however, made up 46 percent of the nation's caseload in 1998, up from 34 percent in 1994. As the caseload under TANF becomes less white, African Americans are increasingly likely to be used by the media to portray the problems associated with welfare. The results of our paper strongly suggest that if this trend continues, public evaluation of welfare recipients and welfare policy are likely to become even more racialized and more negative.

APPENDIX

News Treatments

Success

Welfare Reform's Triumph Is Affirmed
By Staff Reporters

Wednesday, February 2, 2000; Page A1

[*Photo of white (black) woman and child goes here*]

Mary Ellsworth (Lashanda Washington), a former welfare mother of Milwaukee, Wisconsin, describes herself as a living example of the success of welfare reform. The welfare reform law, passed by Congress and signed by the President in 1996, ends assistance after a maximum of five years. "Today, I'm working as a machine operator, providing for my family," Ms. Ellsworth (Washington) said. Pointing to her three children, she said, "Now I tell my kids that this is what you get when you do your homework."

Almost four years after a radical overhaul of the nation's welfare system, the most comprehensive independent study to date confirms that Ms. Ellsworth (Washington) is not alone: nationally, the welfare rolls have fallen more dramatically than anyone expected. Conducted by the Urban Institute, this first thorough national assessment of welfare reform in many respects affirms the early optimism of the program's authors. According to the Urban Institute, there are now some 7.3 million people on welfare nationally—down from 12.2 million when President Clinton signed the Republican-drafted welfare overhaul in August 1996. That experiment is proving largely successful in its early stages, according to the Urban Institute review.

The Urban Institute study, however, also includes some warnings about the precarious position of the poor at a time of general national prosperity, and suggests that many people who leave public assistance remain trapped on the lower rungs of the economy. Nevertheless, Mary Ellsworth (Lashanda Washington), and many other former welfare mothers like her, are examples of the many women who have made the successful transition from welfare to work.

Problems

Welfare Reform's Problems Are Confirmed
By Staff Reporters

Wednesday, February 2, 2000; Page A1

[*Photo of white (black) woman and child goes here*]

Mary Ellsworth (Lashanda Washington), a former welfare mother of Milwaukee, Wisconsin, describes herself as a living example of the problems with welfare reform. The welfare reform law, passed by Congress and signed by the President in 1996, ends assistance after a maximum of five years. "Today, I'm off welfare and working full time, but I have more trouble finding money for rent, food, and medical things for my kids," said Ms. Ellsworth (Washington), pointing to her three children.

Almost four years after a radical overhaul of the nation's welfare system, the most comprehensive independent study to date confirms that Ms. Ellsworth (Washington) is not alone: while the welfare rolls have fallen, many of those leaving welfare for the work force struggle to afford basic life essentials. Conducted by the Urban Institute, this first thorough national assessment of welfare reform highlights the economic troubles experienced by former welfare recipients. After interviewing thousands of women who reported leaving the welfare rolls after the reforms were passed, the Urban Institute concluded that "most people who leave public assistance remain trapped on the lower rungs of the economy." In particular, most women who leave welfare are working in low-wage service jobs, and a significant minority say they have trouble providing food and medical care for their families or paying rent, the study concludes. According to the Urban Institute, there are now some 7.3 million people on welfare nationally—down from 12.2 million when President Clinton signed the Republican-drafted welfare overhaul in August 1996. While that experiment was initially hailed as a success in its early stages, cases like Mary Ellsworth (Washington) are sobering examples of the many problems with welfare reform.

NOTES

The authors would like to thank Jason Glass, Richard Fording, and Steven Voss for a variety of helpful comments. We also wish to thank Mary Beth Beller for her help in collecting the survey data.

1. Although our content analysis of welfare reform stories is in its early stages, on balance, more stories appear to be characterized by a positive tone (noting the successes of reform) than a negative one (focusing on the problems of reform).

2. See also Entman 1992, 1995.

3. While an examination of the effect of racialized media coverage of welfare reform on attitudes among African Americans would be a worthy undertaking, the limited number of African American participants in our study does not allow us to do so here. Thus, this chapter is specifically interested in the attitudes of whites.

4. Portions of the fictitious articles describing the problems and success of welfare reform were taken from Rosin and Harris 1999.

5. Predicted values were computed based on the interactive model in table 5.1, varying race and tone and holding the control variables at their means.

6. It may also be that describing welfare reform as a success (versus having problems) is less relevant for the specific question of whether spending on welfare, in general, ought to be cut. For some respondents, a successful program to reform welfare may suggest welfare (and welfare spending) is a good program that helps put people back to work and therefore deserves an increase in spending; for others, a successful welfare reform effort may imply that welfare (i.e., assistance) could be cut without serious consequences for people who really want to work.

CHAPTER 6

Racial Context, Public Attitudes, and Welfare Effort in the American States

MARTIN JOHNSON

For decades, social scientists have recognized a connection between the politics of race and welfare policy. Researchers consistently find a strong relationship between the size of a state's minority population and its generosity to social welfare recipients (Howard 1999). States with larger proportions of minorities tend to be less generous in extending benefits to welfare recipients (Wright 1976). In a somewhat different research setting, students of public opinion and political psychology have demonstrated that at the individual level, feelings white Americans express about the minorities they perceive to be the main recipients of welfare benefits influence their support for these programs (Gilens 1998; Peffley, Hurwitz, and Sniderman 1997). While scholars have suggested that these lines of research, with their conceptual similarities, must be connected (as Fording discusses in chapter 3 of this volume), it has not been until recently that we have been able to assess how they might fit together.

This chapter extends previous work investigating the influence a state's racial composition has on white attitudes about minorities and welfare spending, and how these attitudes subsequently affect state welfare programs (Johnson 2001). Aggregate white attitudes about minorities represent a facet of public opinion distinct from their judgments of the appropriate scope of welfare spending and mass political ideology.

State policymakers are sensitive to these aspects of public opinion, with attitudes about welfare influencing the reduction of welfare rolls in the states and racial attitudes affecting the amount of support program beneficiaries receive.

Linkages between Public Opinion and Policy in the States

From the early work of Miller and Stokes (1963) to more recent scholarship on representation, much evidence connects public opinion and government output in the United States. In particular, Erikson, Wright, and McIver (1993) demonstrate that the general ideological orientation of mass publics in the states influences the types of policies their governments adopt. Beyond identifying this general connection between public opinion and policy outputs, however, research has not extensively explored the effect specific facets of public opinion have on public policy in the American states. Part of the problem has been a lack of suitable public opinion data collected at the state level. For more than a decade, researchers have had access to a well-constructed, demonstrably stable and reliable measure of mass ideology, but little data on other elements of public opinion in the states. Recent work building on the strategy Erikson, Wright, and McIver (1993) used to gauge state ideology and partisanship has provided researchers access to measures of specific public preferences and attitudes in the American states (Brace et al. 2002). Similarly, Norrander (2001) has constructed measures of aggregate state-level attitudes about the death penalty, abortion, and several other policy areas using public opinion data from the National Senate Election Study.

Given what we have learned about the general relationship between public opinion and policy, I expect policymakers to be sensitive to other mass attitudes expressed by the majority of their constituents. Using data from the General Social Survey (GSS), I am able to explore how public opinion among the racial majority of American states has influenced welfare programs and reform in the states. If the psychological relationship between race and welfare manifests itself in aggregate public opinion, and this public opinion is represented in the policy-making process as we might expect, interstate variation in these attitudes could help explain variation in state welfare policies. This is particularly important given the role states have played in administering programs such as Aid to Families with Dependent Children (AFDC) and their increased responsibilities during the recent transition to its successor, Temporary Assistance for Needy Families (TANF).

Context, Contact, and Attitudes about Race and Welfare

Since the time of V. O. Key's (1949) influential study of the American South, a great deal of evidence indicates the racial composition of a polity influences the racial attitudes of its residents, particularly the racial attitudes of majority group members about minorities. This "group threat" hypothesis suggests that when a minority group constitutes a small fraction of a population, it poses only a small threat to the interests of the majority racial group. Increased numbers imply increased threat—a minority more competitive in the economy and in politics. This increased threat leads to increased animosity toward minorities among those in the majority. In the contemporary South (Glaser 1994; Giles and Buckner 1993), across the United States (Huckfeldt and Kohfeld 1989), and in Europe (Quillian 1995), larger minority populations appear to be associated with antiminority hostility and less desirable policies for those minorities, such as stricter voter registration laws. Further, these feelings of threat appear to be exacerbated by economics: as economic conditions in a community worsen, members of the racial or ethnic majority grow less supportive or tolerant of the minority due to their financial insecurity (Oliver and Mendelberg 2000).

Contrary to the expectations of "group threat" theorists, students of intergroup contact argue that isolation from members of other races rather than exposure to them aggravates prejudice among members of the majority. They find that increased interaction among members of different races combats stereotyping and reduces prejudice (Allport 1954; Kinder and Mendelberg 1995). Forbes summarizes this literature well: "liking and association go together" (1997, 111). For example, Carsey (1995) finds that white voters living in diverse precincts were more likely to support an African American mayoral candidate than whites living in homogeneous districts. Similarly, Voss (1996) demonstrates that the white residents of racially diverse areas of Louisiana were not particularly responsive to David Duke during his early-1990s political campaigns, with more support for the former Ku Klux Klan leader coming from predominantly white suburban areas of the state.

While appearing contradictory, the context literature and studies of interracial contact may not be irreconcilable. For example, Hero (1998) identifies a consistent relationship between the racial diversity of states and a number of state policies and social outcomes: States with homogeneous white populations and those with the largest minority populations appear to produce policies most hostile to minorities. Heterogeneous states offer outcomes less hostile to minorities. His findings, along with others (Branton and Jones 1999; Fording 1997; Taylor 1998), suggest the relationship between the size of minority populations and social outcomes disadvantageous to them is curvilinear. This curve-shaped relationship between diversity and social outcomes for minorities that Hero and others have found may be able to help us to integrate these seemingly divergent expectations about contextual threat and social interaction.

If we assume that in homogeneous social environments in the United States, the white majority's lack of interaction with minorities and their subsequent ignorance about people of other races breed fear and intolerance, the presence of minorities should provide increased opportunities for interaction and ultimately ease racial conflict. However, past some population level of minorities, whites may feel that their interests are threatened. These cross pressures could intersect to create the observed curvilinear relationship. In this vein, Stein, Post, and Rinden (2000) find a strong positive relationship between the proportion of minorities in a county and the frequency with which whites report social interaction with nonwhites. Underlying their analysis is the expectation that meaningful interracial interaction is not possible without a sufficiently diverse population. Focusing on Anglo-Latino relations, they use these insights to model white attitudes about immigration as a function both of patterns of social interaction and the proportion of an area made up of members of the ethnic minority.

Consistent with these literatures, I expect white attitudes about African Americans in the states to be influenced both by patterns of interracial interaction and the potential threat posed by populations of minority residents. While proximity to minorities should provoke feelings of threat among members of a polity's white majority, it should also provide avenues for interracial exchange and a smoothing of racial hostilities. Whites in states with larger populations of African Americans and other minorities are expected be less supportive of the social inclusion of these groups among members of the white majority. But meaningful social interaction among members of different races may only be possible when a state is sufficiently diverse. Where it is possible, interracial interaction should improve race relations and generate more support for the social inclusion of minorities. Taken together, these threat and contact effects may help explain the curvilinear shape of the relationship between racial composition and white attitudes, public policy and social outcomes found in the racial context literature.

Contact, Racial Attitudes, and Beliefs about Welfare Spending across the United States

This research on interracial interaction and group threat suggests two specific hypotheses about aggregate public opinion among whites about African Americans. First, other things equal, whites in states with larger populations of African Americans should have less positive attitudes about minorities. Second, whites should be friendlier to blacks in states where there is greater interaction among members of different races. To test these hypotheses, I measure white attitudes about African Americans and patterns of interracial interaction in the states generated using data from the GSS cumulative file, 1974–98 (Brace et al. 2002).[1] These measures are constructed by creating individual-level indicators and aggregating the scores on each of these indicators by state, discussed in the appendix. *Racial Tolerance* is an index of white attitudes[2] toward desegregated schools and neighborhoods, interracial marriage, hosting African American guests, and perceptions of blacks pushing "where they are not wanted." Ranging between 0 and 1, larger scores on the measure indicate friendlier white attitudes toward minorities. *Interracial Interaction* is a measure of self-reported social contact between whites and blacks: attending an interracial church, dining together, and living in a multiracial neighborhood.

Measuring state racial composition as the percentage of a state's population made up of African Americans (U.S. Department of Commerce 1990), the analysis presented in table 6.1 indicates that controlling for education, income, and mass ideology, the white residents of states with higher proportions of black residents tend to be less supportive of their social inclusion.[3] However, in states where whites report having greater interaction with African Americans, we observe less hostile aggregate attitudes toward minorities.[4] These variables account for more than half of the variation in state racial attitudes (adj. $R^2 = 0.56$). While this particular analysis makes use of aggregate data, an individual-level model reveals the same pattern: individuals in diverse states are less supportive of racial integration, while whites who report having some form of contact with African Americans have more tolerant racial views.[5]

But how are these racial concerns related to public judgments expressed about welfare spending? The literature on attitudes about welfare among whites finds that opposition to social spending is influenced by the acceptance of racial stereotypes (Peffley, Hurwitz, and Sniderman 1997). At the individual level, Gilens finds racial attitudes are "the most important source of opposition to welfare among whites" (1995, 994). In the aggregate, I expect to find similar relationships between racial tolerance and white attitudes about welfare. To measure attitudes about welfare spending, I aggregate at the state level the answers white respondents give to a GSS question about social spending. Larger numbers indicate that on average white respondents in a state feel more government funds should be spent on welfare programs.

The measures used here are quite different from those used by others to explore linkages among white attitudes about race and welfare, which have focused on the acceptance of racial stereotypes rather than the social inclusion of minorities. As mentioned above, the number of public opinion measures that can be developed is constrained by the questions GSS has asked regularly over time. Thus, while many of these stereotyping questions have appeared on the GSS, they have not been presented to respondents with the frequency of the social integration question. In addition, the relationship between individual racial attitudes and attitudes about welfare spending may be blunted by the process of aggregating them to the state level (Langbein and Lichtman 1978, 10).

TABLE 6.1.   State Racial Attitudes and Beliefs about Welfare

	Racial Tolerance		
	Slope	SE	Standardized Slope
Percent Black	−0.005***	(0.002)	−0.374***
Interracial Interaction	0.243*	(0.168)	0.208*
Mass Ideology	0.003	(0.002)	0.234
Per Capita Income	0.0000002	(0.000)	0.007
Education	0.015**	(0.007)	0.331**
Constant	0.503**	(0.144)	
Adj. $R^2 = 0.558$			

Note: N = 43. Table reports OLS coefficients for models weighted by the number of respondents included in the GSS cumulative file, 1974–98.

*p < 0.10   **p < 0.05   ***p < 0.001 (one-tailed tests)

In spite of these concerns about the data and measures used here, there is a modest correlation between white attitudes about blacks and support for additional welfare spending (Spearman's ρ = .26, p < .05, one-tailed test). White welfare attitudes are modestly related to the proportion of welfare rolls made up of African Americans, with higher proportions of minority clients associated with less support for welfare spending (Spearman's ρ = .36, p < .01, one-tailed test). Support for welfare is also associated with state mass ideology, as measured by Erikson, Wright, and McIver (1993), with whites in more liberal states tending to be more supportive of additional welfare spending (Spearman's ρ = .21, p < .10, one-tailed test).

Benefit Payments and the Leaning of Welfare Rolls in the American States

Given the expectation that democratically elected policymakers in the states will be responsive to majority public opinion, understanding the forces that shape attitudes about race and welfare policies should also help us understand certain policies and social outcomes. Elsewhere, I have shown that state welfare generosity—the size of monthly AFDC payments per recipient—is influenced by racial composition and white racial attitudes in the states (Johnson 2001). The analysis below extends that work in two ways. It expands the basic model to include the indicator of support for welfare spending itself. This allows me to ask whether policymakers respond to public opinion when setting welfare policy and, if they do, which aspects of public opinion are relevant. Are policymakers sensitive to judgments about the welfare spending, or to the racial views of their constituents when setting welfare policy? I also examine two different facets of state welfare policy. A great deal of scholarship on AFDC has focused on state spending (Howard 1999). However, Hero strongly advocates the use of measures that indicate how public policies affect people (1998), and Hanson (1983) urges scholars to focus on the content of social policies in order to bring issues such as eligibility for benefits, or "who gets what," to the fore. In addition to examining the average monthly benefit payment in 1990, I examine the overall change in state welfare rolls between 1993 and 1999 (U.S. Department of Health and Human Services 2000c). The average state's welfare population decreased by almost 57 percent during this time period. These changes serve as a proxy both for the effect of welfare reform on program beneficiaries and the effort policymakers have invested in reducing the number of people in their state receiving benefits.

These two indicators represent quite different aspects of welfare policy-making. The change in the number of clients served by a state reflects government judgments about how many people it is willing to subsidize and for how long. The spending variable, on the other hand, indicates the treatment this pool of beneficiaries will receive, once it is defined. However, given that these indicators are rooted in government policy decisions, similar forces such as public opinion and symbolic politics could influence each. My expectation is that welfare policymakers will be responsive to public opinion, measured by *Racial Tolerance* and *Welfare Attitudes,* as well as the racial composition of state welfare recipients measured by the percentage of AFDC families in 1990 headed by an African American (U.S. Department of Health and Human Services 1994).[6] Racial composition measures are often included in an analysis of this kind as a proxy for attitudes about African American welfare recipients (Fording, this vol., chap. 3). However, here it allows us to examine the response of policymakers to the composition of welfare populations independent of these attitudes, as well as the cumulative effects of racial composition on public policy discussed by Hero (1998).

This analysis also incorporates factors found elsewhere to affect welfare policy in the states (Howard 1999). Some students of state public policy have found socioeconomic factors to dominate welfare policy-making (Dye 1984), while others have combined socioeconomic and political variables in more complex models explaining welfare policies (Plotnick and Winters 1985). I include socioeconomic variables similar to controls used by Hero (1998): *Per capita Personal Income, Urbanization,* and *Education* (U.S. Department of Commerce 1999). The models also contain political characteristics thought to influence social policy, namely *Party Competition* (Cnudde and McCrone 1969; Holbrook and Van Dunk 1993) and voter turnout among less affluent citizens—*Low SES Turnout* (Hill, Leighley, and Hinton-Andersson 1995).

Students of welfare policy have also found a relationship between social spending and political ideology. Left-leaning states are more supportive of expansive welfare policies than more conservative states (Hill, Leighley, and Hinton-Andersson 1995). Consequently, the models reported below include measures of *Elite Ideology* and *Mass Ideology* provided by Erikson, Wright, and McIver (1993). Finally, Howard's (1999) review of scholarship on welfare in the American states emphasizes the importance of need and state capacity as influences on state welfare policy. A state with a high *Poverty Rate* may have a greater objective need for welfare relief, but its policymakers may fear attracting more impoverished people and be less progressive in their provision of welfare benefits (Peterson 1995). Governments with greater administrative capacity are more capable of managing social programs and thus more likely to develop them (Skocpol 1992). I use *Bureaucratic Professionalism* as a tracer for state capacity, measured as a state government's total payroll by its number of full-time equivalent employees (U.S. Department of Commerce 1992).

Table 6.2 reports regression models testing each of these explanations for both welfare recipient benefit payments and the percentage change in the number of people on welfare in each state. Even controlling for com-

TABLE 6.2. Racial Composition, White Public Attitudes, and Other Explanations for Welfare Effort

	Average Monthly Benefit		Change in Welfare Rolls	
	Slope	SE	Slope	SE
Percent AFDC Black	−1.159**	(0.672)	−0.202*	(0.126)
Racial Tolerance	248.664*	(159.347)	−9.453	(30.027)
Welfare Spending	−390.168	(403.144)	159.751**	(75.967)
Socioeconomic				
Per Capita Income	0.0003	(0.009)	0.003**	(0.002)
Urbanization	−0.015	(0.980)	−0.089	(0.185)
Education	−3.533	(7.472)	−1.770	(1.408)
Ideology				
Mass Ideology	5.584*	(3.429)	−0.682	(0.646)
Elite Ideology	7.434	(16.086)	0.144	(3.031)
Political				
Party Competition	0.569	(1.500)	−0.087	(0.283)
Turnout (Low SES)	5.062***	(1.362)	0.219	(0.256)
Need				
Poverty	−1.018	(4.837)	0.074	(0.912)
Capacity				
Bureaucratic Professionalism	0.069	(0.054)	0.010	(0.010)
Constant	49.059	(200.729)	−136.788***	(37.824)
	Adj. R^2 = 0.832		Adj. R^2 = 0.200	

Note: N = 42. Table reports OLS coefficients for models weighted by the number of respondents included in the GSS cumulative file, 1974–98.

*$p < 0.10$ **$p < 0.05$ ***$p < 0.001$ (one-tailed tests)

plementary and alternative explanations of welfare policy-making, race, racial attitudes, and public beliefs about welfare spending are influential to the decisions of state policymakers. Support for the social inclusion of African Americans and the racial composition of welfare recipients influence benefit payments, while welfare spending attitudes have a large impact on the overall pace of welfare reform in a state.

State Welfare Spending

The first two columns of table 6.2 report regression results for *Welfare Spending*. The model explains more than four-fifths of the variation in state welfare benefit levels (adj. R^2 = 0.83). State welfare spending per recipient has little to do with public judgments about how much the government should spend on welfare. Instead, policymakers appear responsive to the racial attitudes of their constituents and the proportion of minorities among program beneficiaries. Beyond these racially oriented influences on policymakers, state mass ideology, voting behavior, and administrative capacity appear to have strong influences on state benefit levels. These variables are included in the reduced model of monthly benefit payments in table 6.3. In states where white residents have progressive attitudes about the social integration of African Americans, welfare payments are higher than they are in states with white residents less friendly to social inclusion. States with residents who tend to have a left-leaning political ideology, with high rates of voting among people with lower socioeconomic status, or with greater bureaucratic capacity are

TABLE 6.3. Reduced Average Monthly Benefit Model

	Average Monthly Benefit		
	Slope	SE	Standardized Slope
Percent AFDC Black	−1.275**	(0.502)	−.189
Racial Tolerance	207.807**	(117.624)	.155
Mass Ideology	7.353***	(1.989)	.370
Low SES Turnout	4.509***	(1.174)	.252
Bureaucratic Professionalism	0.087**	(0.035)	.274
Constant	−18.699	(124.191)	
Adj. R^2 = 0.845			

Note: N = 43. Table reports OLS coefficients for models weighted by the number of respondents included in the GSS cumulative file, 1974–98.

$*p < 0.10$ $**p < 0.05$ $***p < 0.001$ (one-tailed tests)

associated with higher welfare benefit levels. States with larger percentages of African Americans on their welfare rolls offer systematically lower welfare benefit payments.

In order to better characterize the influence of the racial composition of states on monthly benefits, figure 6.1 graphs a causal diagram (Asher 1976) incorporating the relevant regression results presented in this chapter. The model includes the standardized regression coefficients from the reduced model shown in table 6.3, and the regression predicting interracial contacting reported in note 4. State policymakers' direct response to the presence of minorities on its welfare rolls is captured by the standardized regression coefficient between that variable and the welfare benefit payment. The indirect effects of racial composition are estimated as the product of each standardized coefficients on the path through which the variable of interest moves. The total effect of the racial composition of states on welfare benefit payments is the sum of these direct and indirect effects.

The sum of the path products between percentage of a state's residents who are African American and welfare benefit payments, mediated by interracial contact, black AFDC participation, and racial attitudes, is –0.22. A one-standard-deviation increase in a state's African American population is associated with a decrease in welfare spending by about one-fifth of a standard deviation. Translated into meaningful units, this suggests that a 9.34 percent increase in the number of African Americans in a state would be associated with a $10.25 decrease in the state's monthly welfare payment. This is more than an 8 percent cut in the average monthly benefit a welfare recipient received in 1990, $121.25.

Changing Welfare Rolls

Table 6.2 also shows that the cumulative results of state policymakers' efforts to reform welfare and reduce the number of beneficiaries in a state are responsive to white attitudes about welfare spending.[7] Where aggregate public opinion supports increased spending on social programs, state policymakers have been less vigorous in their efforts to lean welfare rolls. With all variables set to their average values, the regression equation predicts the average state would see a 55.1 percent reduction in the number of clients served by welfare programs. Other things equal, when support for welfare spending is set to its lowest observed level, the model predicts a 79.6 percent reduction in the number of beneficiaries. However, where state residents think government should spend more on wel-

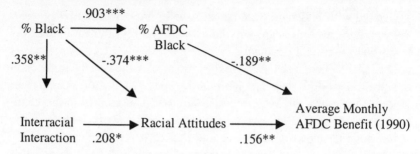

Fig. 6.1. Average monthly welfare benefit causal model. Diagram includes path coefficients from tables 6.1 and 6.3 and note 4. The racial composition of a state's AFDC recipient population is based on the race of the head of household or in child-only cases, the race of the youngest child of the unit. (*Source:* Lower-Basch 2000.) *$p < .10$, **$p < .05$, ***$p < .001$ (one-tailed tests).

fare, this model predicts a less aggressive reform effort, the removal of 41.0 percent of recipients from the state's welfare program.

Conclusion

This chapter has examined two distinct aspects of welfare policy-making: the cumulative result of efforts to reduce welfare rolls and the average size of cash assistance benefits themselves. The overall picture presented here suggests that politics of welfare are not entirely dominated by racial concerns, but that race clearly matters to state policymakers. Outcomes associated with welfare reform and many policy choices are influenced by what appear to be ideological public judgments and are not as strongly determined by the racial attitudes of the white public. Public judgments about social spending establish an appropriate size for a state's welfare system and, given their increased authority under TANF, how aggressive each should be in removing people from the system.

However, the politics of race strongly affect how the population of beneficiaries, once defined, is treated. For example, the actual size of the benefit payment each receives is related to race. Consistent with Hero's (1998) proposition that racial politics has a pervasive, cumulative effect on state policy outputs and social outcomes and my expectation that policymakers react to the presence of minorities in the population of welfare recipients in addition to white attitudes about race, the racial composition of the pool of welfare clients has a large independent effect on facets of welfare and welfare reform in the states. And as Gilens's research underscores, welfare remains a "racialized" policy, perceived as benefiting mostly African Americans and other nonwhites. This affects the treatment of program clients.

The white majority in the United States appears to be quite sensitive to the presence of racial minorities. This sensitivity manifests itself both in increased hostility toward minorities as they increase in number. However, whites are also more likely to support the social inclusion of minorities when they have an opportunity to meet and interact with them, as the literature on racial contacting suggests. Holding everything else constant, the total effect of increased diversity on racial attitudes is a reduction of support among whites for racial integration, consistent with the group threat hypothesis.

The results reported in this chapter have important implications for the study of the responsiveness of state governments to public opinion. State governments are quite representative of public preferences. This responsiveness is as multifaceted as public opinion itself. However, a troubling impression that emerges from the evidence presented here is that policymakers are primarily responsive to the expressed will of the white majority. Given the limitations of this source of opinion data,[8] we are still unable to determine the extent to which state policymakers are responsive to the preferences and needs of their minority constituents. That said, it appears that policymakers have a different relationship with the racial majority in their states than the racial minority: They *respond* to whites and *react* to the presence of African Americans.

APPENDIX: INDICES AND ITEMS

Racial Tolerance. This measure uses five GSS items about the appropriateness of various forms of racial integration (Cronbach's $\alpha = .710$):

"Do you think white and black students should go to the same school?" $0 =$ No, $0.5 =$ DK, $1 =$ Yes

"Blacks should not push where they are not wanted." $0 =$ Agree, $0.5 =$ NA, $1 =$ Disagree

"Do you think there should be a law against marriages between members of different races?" $1 =$ No, $0.5 =$ Don't Know, $0 =$ Yes

"White people have a right to keep blacks out of their neighborhoods if they want to." $0 =$ Agree, $0.5 =$ NA, $1 =$ Disagree

"How strongly would you object if a member of your family wanted to bring a black person to dinner?" $0 =$ Strongly/Mild, $0.5 =$ DK, $1 =$ Not Strongly

The individual-level index is the respondent's average answer across the five items and ranges between 0 and 1, with 1 representing strong support for integration. These individual scores were then averaged for all respondents in each state. Thus, a straightforward interpretation of the absolute values of this scale is not possible. We can only speak in relative terms about states and their scores on the index and recognize that a state scoring a 0.83 (Oregon) has more aggregate support for racial integration than a state with a score of 0.38 (Alabama).

Welfare Spending. Aggregate support for welfare is computed using the mean state response to the question:

> "We are faced with many problems in this country, none of which can be solved easily or inexpensively. I'm going to name some of these problems, and for each one I'd like you to tell me whether you think we're spending too much money on it, too little money, or about the right amount. Are we spending too much money, too little money, or about the right amount on welfare?" 1 = too little; 0.5 = right amount, don't know; 0 = too much money.

Intergroup Interaction. For almost two decades, the NORC has asked white respondents about their social contact and experience with blacks. More recently, they have directed these questions to members of all races. For this study, however, I considered only the white respondents in the cumulative file. I calculated an index averaging white responses to these contacting questions (Cronbach's α = .379):

> "Do (Blacks/Negroes/African Americans)/Whites attend the church that you, yourself, attend most often, or not?" Yes, attend; No, do not attend; No church; Don't know; No answer.
> "During the last few years, has anyone in your family brought a friend who was a (Negro/Black/African American) home for dinner?" Yes; No; Don't Know; No answer.
> "Are there any (Negroes/Blacks/African Americans) living in this neighborhood now?" Yes; No; Don't Know; No answer.

Affirmative responses to these questions were coded 1, indicating that either church, dining, or neighborhood of residence provided a venue for interracial association. All other responses were coded 0.

Auditing the Measures

In order to calculate the appropriate split-half reliability and stability tests for each of these measures (Carmines and Zeller 1979; Erikson, Wright, and McIver 1993), the GSS file was divided into early (1974–85) and late (1986–98) samples, as well as divided into even and odd years. Pearson's *r* correlations between the even- and odd-year sample halves were used to calculate the reliability of measures, while early and late period scores were used to establish their stability. These were converted into stability and reliability statistics via the Spearman-Brown prophesy formula:

$$\text{Spearman} - \text{Brown} = \frac{2r_{12}}{1 + r_{12}}.$$

The Spearman-Brown statistics indicate that racial attitudes are measured reliably (0.95), as are instances of interracial contact (.78), with the welfare attitudes measure appearing less reliable (.68). Self-reported interracial interaction is less stable (.68) than racial attitudes (.88). There is no significant correlation between early and late welfare scores in the states.

However, in addition to these measures of reliability, Jones and Norrander (1996) recommend a generalizability diagnostic test for aggregate-level data created from individual-level observations. One-way ANOVA was used to determine the mean sums of squares between aggregate units, as well as the mean sums of squares within aggregate units, and

$$E\rho^2 = \frac{MS(a) - MS\,(r:a)}{MS(a)}.$$

where $MS(a)$ is the mean between sums of squares and $MS(r:a)$ is the mean within sums of squares. The test suggests the extent to which each measure is generalizable: *Racial Tolerance*, $E^2 = .98$, and *Interracial Interaction*, $E^2 = .97$, appear quite generalizable. *Welfare Attitudes* has a more modest score on this generalizability measure, $E^2 = .58$. Together these tests suggest that we should be particularly cautious drawing inferences based on the aggregate measure of white attitudes toward welfare presented here. However, given the present paucity of alternative public opinion measures and its performance in the models reported, *Welfare Attitudes* will suffice for now, pending future innovations in the estimation of state public attitudes about social programs.

NOTES

1. Following Jones and Norrander (1996) and Erikson, Wright, and McIver (1993), Brace and his coauthors (2002) create a variety of indicators of public opinion in the states. While this provides researchers access to new public opinion measures, they are limited to subset of GSS questions that have been asked regularly over the years and on those issues for which public opinion can be demonstrated reliable and generalizable. Also, most of the analyses in this study are limited to data from 42 states because the GSS cumulative file (1974–98) contains insufficient responses from Alaska, Hawaii, Idaho, Maine, Nebraska, Nevada, New Mexico, and Wyoming to compute each of the public opinion and self-reported behavior variables used.

2. While this index is not a direct measure of prejudice or acceptance of

racial stereotypes, the works cited suggest it can be a valid surrogate for racial views, specifically whether white respondents are more or less supportive of racial integration. The choice of this measure was also driven by the frequent recurrence of these five questions in the GSS since the early 1970s. It would be beneficial to have more items about racial stereotypes and white attitudes toward other racial groups, but I am constrained by the availability of data in the GSS.

3. Because these public opinion indicators are averages of individual responses at the state level, regressions reported in this chapter using the aggregate opinion scores are inversely weighted by the number respondents the GSS has drawn from in each state over time. As Brace et al. (2002) discuss, the size of the state samples or the number of primary sampling units the GSS has used in each state is a potential source of nonconstant error variance in models utilizing this aggregate opinion data. Weighting the models with the state sample sizes is intended to address this concern (Gujarati 1992). However, the results of these weighted regressions are substantively quite similar to unweighted models (Johnson 2001).

4. Interracial interaction is itself influenced by the racial composition of states. Controlling for socioeconomic characteristics of states (Hero 1998, 37), contact between white and black state residents increases in states with larger African American populations.

	Interracial Interaction		
	Slope	SE	Standardized Slope
Percent Black	0.004**	(0.001)	0.357
Urbanization	0.001	(0.001)	0.154
Education	0.016**	(0.006)	0.401
Per Capita Income (in thousands)	0.007	(0.007)	0.219
Constant	–0.055	(0.081)	
Adj. R^2 = 0.418			

Note: N = 44
**$p < 0.05$ (one-tailed tests)

5. Johnson (2001) also reports a 2SLS analysis that supports his contention that interracial interaction has a greater effect on racial attitudes than these have on an individual's propensity to engage members of other races. After purging each measure of the effects of the other, racial attitudes are not a significant predictor of contacting behavior, while the hypothesized influence of contacting on racial attitudes remains.

6. The percentage of state populations made up of African Americans is strongly related to the percentage of AFDC recipients who are black (Pearson's r = 0.903, $p < .001$).

7. While it would be preferable to present a fully dynamic model of change in welfare rolls over time, there is precedent in public policy literature for the cau-

tious use of cross-sectional data in making inferences about dynamic processes (Feiock 1991).

8. While the GSS has frequently oversampled black populations, there are insufficient observations available to use in order to generate measures of aggregate black attitudes about whites at the state level, although the GSS appears useful in estimating the attitudes of black respondents in selected metropolitan areas (Gibson 1995).

Discourse

CHAPTER 7

Queens, Teens, and Model Mothers

Race, Gender, and the Discourse of Welfare Reform

HOLLOWAY SPARKS

Are you trying to get people off welfare by solving problems or are you punishing them for the choices that you disagree with? If you are trying to solve the problem, go back to the drawing board, and listen to people like me.
—*Tandi Graff, former welfare recipient,*
to members of Congress, 1995

For democratic theorists and other scholars interested in theorizing the promise and pitfalls of citizen participation in the contemporary public sphere, the welfare reform debate surrounding the Personal Responsibility and Work Opportunity Reconciliation Act of 1996 (PRWORA) provides an emblematic case study. In the period preceding the passage of the PRWORA, a lively public discussion on the shortcomings of the welfare system and Congress's proposed solutions filled the airwaves and other venues of public communication. Strikingly absent from this debate, however, were the voices of welfare recipients themselves. Congress and the media showcased the arguments of welfare administrators, politicians, business lobbyists, academics, and pundits, but welfare activists and other critics of "the end of welfare as we know it" often had a difficult time getting their views heard. Marginalized at congressional hearings and mostly ignored or discounted by the press, welfare recipients ended up primarily on the sidelines of this critical dialogue.

In their absence, commentators regularly invoked racist and gender-biased images of "welfare queens" out to cheat taxpayers and of irresponsible teenage girls bearing children out of wedlock as the quintessential justifications for punitive welfare reform. The only seemingly positive public role for recipients during this debate was as a "welfare to work" success story. Politicians and journalists delighted in telling rags-to-riches morality tales about "model mothers" whose compliance with the new welfare regime meant they could leave the welfare rolls, provide better lives for their children, and become "respectable" citizens. Welfare recipients who opposed any part of the reforms, in contrast, were portrayed as troublemakers, not as citizens who might have important insights into public policy.

The exclusion and stereotyping of welfare recipients during the PRWORA debate reveals a serious distortion in the contemporary American public sphere. In spite of widespread assertions that the United States enjoys one of the most open democratic societies in the world, it nonetheless remains extraordinarily difficult for poor people to participate in democratic decision making. The fact that the absence of the poor was not widely questioned during the PRWORA debate only confirms the pervasiveness of the problem. The result of this distortion is that some citizens' voices are consistently amplified in the context of democratic discussions, while others are muffled or silenced altogether.

This distortion, moreover, has racist and sexist contours. Although the discourses of personal responsibility and citizenship used to frame the reform debate appeared neutral on the surface, these discourses in fact masked the racially specific content of the stereotypes about welfare recipients that so influenced this debate. The stereotypes, furthermore, were not simply negative images of people of color, but were primarily negative images of *women* of color. The portrayal of poor women of color—and particularly African American women—as abusers of the system, immoral, and badly in need of discipline essentially destroyed their ability to appear as legitimate and authoritative participants in democratic deliberations about welfare. Since nearly one-third of all African American women are poor, and women of color and their children account for half of all welfare recipients (Albeda and Tilly 1997, 24–28), such stereotyping meant that the citizens with the most at stake in this policy discussion were the least likely to have input. For democratic theorists and others concerned about the legitimacy of our political institutions, such exclusions should raise fundamental questions about the quality of democratic life in the United States.

This essay analyzes the welfare reform debate of 1995–96 as a case study of public deliberation, and pays particular attention to how the construction of racist and sexist stereotypes affected the political participation of the poor. My argument has five steps. To ground my analysis, I begin with some contemporary theories of citizen participation and democratic discourse prominent in the field of political theory. Second, I explore the racist images and stereotypes of the poor invoked during congressional discussions of welfare reform in 1995–96 that undermined the meaningful participation of poor citizens. In the third section, I examine the unsuccessful efforts of current and former welfare recipients to introduce an alternative understanding of welfare into the PRWORA deliberations through congressional hearings. Fourth, I analyze the contractual theory of citizenship that helped justify the withdrawal of rights from poor women of color. And finally, I reflect on the lessons that scholars and activists might draw from this analysis in the service of reframing the public discourse on race, welfare, and citizenship in the future.

Democratic Theory, Citizen Participation, and the Contemporary Public Sphere

In recent years, democratic theorists have explored how we might encourage and expand citizen participation in settings where individual rights, regular elections, and representative democracy have already been institutionalized. One of the most influential versions of this project comes from theorists attentive to what Jürgen Habermas and others call the "public sphere."[1] In Nancy Fraser's words, the public sphere

> designates a theater in modern societies in which political participation is enacted through the medium of talk. It is the space in which citizens deliberate about their common affairs, and hence an institutionalized arena of discursive interaction. This arena is conceptually distinct from the state; it is a site for the production and circulation of discourses that can in principle be critical of the state. The public sphere in Habermas's sense is also conceptually distinct from the official economy; it is not an arena of market relations but rather one of discursive relations, a theater for debating and deliberating rather than for buying and selling. (Fraser 1997, 70)

Theorists drawing on this idea have defended a conception of democracy variously termed *deliberative democracy, discursive democracy,* or *communicative democracy* (Benhabib 1996; Cohen 1989; Dryzek 1990; Fishkin 1991; Habermas 1996; Mansbridge 1992, 1993; Young 1996, 2000). Deliberative theorists generally accept the continued necessity of representative institutions given the large size of most modern democracies, but as a complement to these institutions, they insist that democracies should promote significant citizen participation in public sphere deliberation about matters of common concern.

In spite of the participatory principles embodied in these theories, some deliberative democrats have given inadequate attention to the barriers to public sphere participation confronted by marginalized citizens. Activists, dissidents,[2] racial and ethnic minorities, and particularly poor citizens are regularly excluded from both decision-making and deliberative venues, but this problem is often sidestepped in the mainstream theoretical literature by theorists who downplay the effects of social and economic inequality on public participation (see, e.g., Barber 1984; Cohen 1989; Dryzek 1990). The claim that we can effectively bracket inequality in the public sphere, however, has been strongly criticized recently by a group of theorists explicitly concerned with problems of democratic inclusion. These scholars, including James Bohman (1996), Nancy Fraser (1997), Jane Mansbridge (1991, 1999), and Iris Young (1993, 1996, 2000), have emphasized the fact that formal political equality does not guarantee equal authority in or even access to the public realm.

Iris Young, for example, has identified two forms of exclusion that prevent citizens from fully participating in democracies. What she calls *external* exclusion "names the many ways that individuals and groups that ought to be included are purposely or inadvertently left out of fora for discussion and decision-making" (2000, 53–54). External exclusion can be as blatant as deliberately failing to invite certain groups to important meetings, or can take more subtle forms such as the way economic inequalities affect access to political institutions. As Nancy Fraser has noted, in societies like the United States in which the publication and circulation of political views depends on media organizations that are privately owned and operated for profit, those citizens who lack wealth will also generally "lack access to the material means of equal participation" (1997, 79). This criticism has obvious salience for families living on welfare budgets. On a more basic level, money and time are also necessary for participation in putatively "free" political institutions. Poor parents with young children, for example, might not have the resources to purchase child-care in order to attend a town council meeting at which important political decisions are made.[3]

Internal exclusions, in contrast, "concern ways that people lack effective opportunity to influence the thinking of others *even when they have access* to fora and procedures of decision-making" (Young 2000, 55; emphasis added). Citizens may find that "others ignore or dismiss or patronize their statements and expressions. Though formally included in a forum or process, people may find that their claims are not taken seriously and may believe that they are not treated with equal respect" (55). Internal exclusion can take the form of public ridicule or face-to-face inattention (Bickford 1996), but it can also stem from less obvious sources, such as the norms of articulateness, dispassionateness, and orderliness that are often privileged in political discussions (Young 2000, 56). As Young observes,

> In many formal situations the better-educated white middle-class people
> . . . often act as though they have a right to speak and that their words
> carry authority, whereas those of other groups often feel intimidated by
> the argument requirements and the formality and rules of parliamentary
> procedure, so they do not speak, or speak only in a way that those in
> charge find "disruptive." . . . The dominant groups, moreover, often fail
> entirely to notice this devaluation and silencing, while the less privileged
> often feel put down or frustrated, either losing confidence in themselves
> or becoming angry. (1996, 124)

Since "unruly" forms of speech tend to be used primarily by women, racial minorities, and working-class people, large groups of citizens face the devaluation of their political participation.

Young's solution is what she calls "communicative democracy," a form of deliberative democracy that expands the range of legitimate speaking and argument styles to include not only traditional arguments, but also practices such as the use of rhetoric and storytelling (1996, 129–32; see also Young 2000, 57–77).[4] Young's hope is that making room at the democratic table for narratives that exhibit "experience and values from the point of view of the subjects that have and hold them" (1996, 132) will mitigate the problem of internal exclusion. During public deliberation about welfare programs, for example, this might mean that legislators and other citizens would welcome and value (as opposed to dismissing or merely tolerating) poor people's narratives about the sources of poverty, the dilemmas created by the welfare system, and their views on acceptable solutions.

Other political theorists, however, take a somewhat more skeptical view of the power of disadvantaged citizens to command meaningful public attention with narratives. These theorists, including a wide range of feminist, postcolonial, queer, and other theorists influenced by post-structuralist and postmodern theory, view the consciously used narratives and rhetorical strategies that Young discusses as part of a broader and more complex category of communicative practices visible when we turn our attention to political discourse (see, e.g., Fraser 1989, 1997; Laclau and Mouffe 1985; Naples 1997; Phelan 1994). These theorists suggest that discourse, or the language, concepts, idioms, vocabularies, narratives, and social practices used to "construct what is taken to be real, natural, and true" (Schram 1995, xxiv), helps create and reinforce the power inequalities that affect participation (and thus inclusion).

While some discourses are hegemonic, officially sanctioned, and uncontroversial, others are nonhegemonic, officially discounted, and hotly contested (Fraser 1989, 165). In the context of welfare policy, for example, a discourse that constructs children as the innocent victims of poverty has remained solidly hegemonic for most of the twentieth century. In contrast, the discourse that constructs poor mothers who raise their children alone as noble heroines has almost disappeared under the recent onslaught of hostility directed at welfare recipients. Because such discourses both reflect and constitute power relations among the people who use them, and especially because they position "the people to whom they are addressed as specific sorts of subjects endowed with specific sorts of capacities for action" (Fraser 1989, 165), discourses deeply influence the forms citizen participation in the public sphere can take.

One particularly powerful way that discourses enter public sphere discussions is through stereotypes, or what Patricia Hill Collins has theorized as "controlling images" (2000, chap. 4; see also Lubiano 1992). Controlling images, Collins suggests, are socially constructed images "designed to make racism, sexism, poverty, and other forms of social injustice appear to be natural, normal, and inevitable parts of everyday life" (2000, 69). The examples Collins discusses—mammies, matriarchs, welfare queens, and hoochies—objectify and subordinate black women.[5] These images serve as a kind of shorthand for interpreting, shaping, stigmatizing—and thereby controlling—the actions of marginalized groups. For example, Collins notes that single black women who work outside the home to support their families are called "matriarchs," and instead of being praised as good providers are blamed for driving their men away and for not being home to supervise their children adequately. Single black women who do stay home to supervise their children are stigmatized as "welfare queens" and are viewed as lazy rather than as good parents. In both cases, the controlling image constructs the woman as the problem, which draws attention away from structural reasons for poverty, and from the gender, race, and class discrimination that hinders the ability of black women to support and care for themselves and their families in the first place (2000, 72–84).[6]

Controlling images and stereotypes are used in turn to reinforce larger, overarching narratives about social and political issues. For example, as I discuss in the next section, controlling images of welfare recipients as loafers and drug addicts have supported a narrative that portrays poverty as the result of individuals' bad decision making and learned "dependency." This narrative in turn supports policy programs that sanction participants for failures of "personal responsibility." If a controlling image is widely taken as true, then opponents will have more difficulty challenging either the discourse or the policy prescription that has been constructed to solve the "problem" posed by the stereotyped group (Naples 1997).

For democratic theorists concerned about citizen participation, attending to the discourses and controlling images used in the context of public sphere discussions clearly augments approaches that attend to more obvious practices of exclusion. The power to construct potent controlling images and discourses about other citizens, if unchallenged, not only shapes the way those citizens' speech is heard, but also affects whether they even try to speak in the first place. Such power can thus significantly affect who participates and how in public sphere discussions. While some advantaged citizens have an easy time both with gaining access to political discussions and being heard as authoritative once there, others face nearly insurmountable challenges on both fronts. The result is a public sphere in which some citizens have a far more powerful voice than they should.

As I show next, such inequities played an important role in the welfare reform debate of 1995–96. I begin with the controlling images that dominated congressional and media discussions of the poor and undermined the participation of poor citizens during the PRWORA debate.

Wicked Queens, Unwed Teens, and Deadbeat Dads: The Discourse of Welfare Reform in the 104th Congress

As one of the most popular features of the Republicans' "Contract with America," welfare reform was one of the first items on the agenda of the

104th Congress. Capitalizing on President Clinton's 1992 promise to "end welfare as we know it," Republicans pledged to "revolutionize the system from top to bottom" and "make the tough decisions that must be made" (House 1995b, 7). The dominant narrative about welfare reform they subsequently presented framed the "problem of welfare" as first and foremost a problem with "welfare dependency." According to this discourse, welfare recipients were poor primarily because they were individually lazy and irresponsible, not because of a lack of child-care options, job shortages, racism, or other forms of discrimination.[7] The solutions to poverty offered as a result focused on reforming the behavior of the poor.[8] Republicans and Democrats alike agreed that welfare recipients— and especially welfare mothers—needed discipline, or what some legislators preferred to characterize as "tough love" (House 1995b, 675). Left to their own devices, these legislators argued, welfare mothers would refuse to work, continue to bear children without regard to their ability to support them, and continue letting the fathers of their children off the financial hook.

This discourse vilified all welfare recipients, but specifically relied on and reinforced racist views of people of color in general, and African Americans in particular, as unmotivated shirkers, drug addicts, and irresponsible parents. The scapegoating of poor women of color took several forms in this discourse, but one of the most influential controlling images presented was that of the "welfare queen."[9] Countless legislators and witnesses portrayed welfare recipients as black (or occasionally Hispanic) women who avoided paid employment, spent their welfare checks on drugs and liquor, and neglected their many children.[10] Legislators repeatedly referenced "people who refuse to work" and people "who think they are owed the money for doing nothing" when advocating strict new rules for welfare recipients (see, e.g., *Cong. Rec.* 1995, H3581).[11] Senator Phil Gramm told a cheering Texas crowd he wanted "able-bodied men and women riding in the welfare wagon to get out and help the rest of us pull" (Yepsen 1995).[12]

Legislators also portrayed welfare queens as cheaters. Representative Nick Smith (R-Mich.) encouraged House members to end the "widespread abuse" of the Supplemental Security Insurance program by welfare mothers who coached their children to mimic the problems of "slow learners" so they could collect disability payments along with their regular welfare check (House 1995b, 671–73). Others argued vehemently against expanding the food stamp program because of rampant "waste, fraud, and abuse" (see, e.g., *Cong. Rec.* 1995, H3742).

Legislators and welfare experts also repeatedly linked welfare use by poor women with drug abuse. As former drug czar William Bennett told a House committee:

> I think any police sergeant in the country will tell you that the day the welfare checks go out is a big day for drug buys. . . . When I was Drug Czar, . . . I would ask to be taken to the worst place. The place I almost always ended up was public housing . . . There were no men there [on a regular basis except] . . . the drug predators who were waiting to make their easy hits. (House 1995b, 163)

In talking about welfare recipients this way, Bennett indiscriminately portrayed welfare recipients as drug addicts and further reinforced the popular perception that most welfare recipients are African Americans living in "drug-infested" public housing (see Gilens 1996 and chap. 4, this volume).

Drug use by welfare mothers was also linked to child neglect. Representative Nancy Johnson (R-Conn.) blamed "parents' drug addiction, subsidized with taxpayer [welfare] dollars" for the high turnover rates in urban schools that compromised poor children's education (*Cong. Rec.* 1995, H3581). The view of welfare recipients as unfit mothers was also supported by high-profile media stories about child abuse. In 1994, for example, CNN, ABC, and most of the major national papers extensively covered a story about five African American welfare mothers and one African American man accused of neglecting and abusing nineteen children found in a Chicago apartment during a drug raid (Williams 1995, 1164–66). The influence of stories like these was immense, since many news outlets repeatedly used the "Chicago 19" as backdrops to stories about Republican and Democratic welfare reform proposals throughout the PRWORA debate (Williams 1995, 1166).[13]

Another way that welfare mothers were portrayed as harming their children was by "refusing" to get married. Commentators criticized not only the number of children welfare recipients (supposedly) had, but the fact that they had children by multiple men and were rarely married to them.[14] Poor unmarried mothers were also censured for the fact that children who grew up in households without fathers seemed more likely to be suspended from school, have emotional problems, and display antisocial behavior (see, e.g., the testimony of James Q. Wilson, House 1995b, 151–52). In addition, women who had children out of wedlock were portrayed by many as the primary *cause* of poverty. The House Ways and

Means Committee, for example, held an entire day of hearings called simply "Causes of Poverty, With a Focus on Out-of-Wedlock Births" (House 1996a). Although some legislators challenged the argument that illegitimacy caused poverty and not the reverse, influential congressional witnesses like Robert Rector of the Heritage Foundation argued that the only real solution to the poverty problem was "marriage and reducing out-of-wedlock births," not "training and putting a lot of people in the labor force" (U.S. Senate 1995a, 30).[15]

The overwhelming concern with what many called "the crisis of illegitimacy" (U.S. Senate 1995a, 46–47) greatly influenced the construction of a second but closely related set of scapegoats in the dominant discourse about welfare during the PRWORA debate: teen mothers. As Senator Byron Dorgan (D-N.D.) told the Senate, "There is an avalanche of teen pregnancies in this country, and too many of them end up on welfare and are unprepared to take care of children" (*Cong. Rec.* 1996, S8076). The number of unmarried teen mothers actually receiving AFDC in 1994–95 was extraordinarily low (less than 0.5 percent of the total caseload, and just 2 percent of all parents on AFDC [U.S. Department of Health and Human Services 1995]), but legislators repeatedly cited studies showing that unmarried teens who had children were far more likely to get on welfare and to stay on welfare for longer than average periods of time.[16] As a result, "children having children" loomed large in the discourse surrounding welfare reform.

Republicans and Democrats alike chastised unmarried teens for having sex at all, for failing to use birth control properly, and most of all, for intentionally becoming pregnant. Delaware Governor Thomas Carper, in his testimony before the House Ways and Means Committee about ways to "turn off the spigot" of teen pregnancy, argued that "we have a situation where a lot of young girls need and want somebody to love them and the idea of having a baby who will love and want and need them is desirable" (House 1995b, 15). David Burgess, a father's rights advocate, criticized teenagers who deliberately got pregnant because it was "in," and who used pregnancy as a way to get attention and love (House 1995b, 1245–63).

Like the welfare queen stereotype, this controlling image was also racialized, both because the average citizen wrongly assumed most teen welfare mothers were African Americans, and because legislators often closely juxtaposed statistics about teen pregnancy with statistics on illegitimacy in the African American community (see, e.g., House 1995b, 133–34). The proximity of such figures elided the fact that the majority of all nonmarital births (69 percent) occur to older women, not teens, and that white teens are responsible for 70 percent of all teen births (Albeda and Tilly 1997, 193). But with legislators portraying unmarried, apparently African American teen mothers as the driving force behind "a tangle of social pathologies, including school dropout, welfare use, unemployment, drug addiction and crime" (House 1995b, 134), lamentations about teen mothers easily fed racist stereotypes about welfare, crime, and sexual promiscuity.

Some legislators were equally critical of male teens who fathered children out of wedlock. In fact, "deadbeat dads" emerged as a third category of welfare miscreants during the PRWORA debate. As Senator Dorgan told the Senate, "There is an army of deadbeat dads in America, men who have babies and leave. . . . Guess who pays for that child? The American taxpayer" (*Cong. Rec.* 1996, S8076). Young deadbeat dads were particularly criticized for engaging in reckless virility rivalries with other teens. William Bennett advocated stigmatizing the young men "who think it is a show of macho maleness to impregnate five women" they cannot support (House 1995b, 170). Senator Joe Lieberman and others advocated particularly harsh penalties for the men over twenty who preyed on teen girls, then failed to financially support them or their babies (*Cong. Rec.* 1996, S8409).

A fourth category of welfare recipients portrayed as cheating the welfare system were "noncitizens." Robert Rector, one of the original advocates of the exclusion of legal immigrants from welfare, testified in the Senate about how elderly noncitizens, particularly from southern China, Hong Kong, and Taiwan, were coming to the United States and living on welfare. "The United States taxpayer," he argued, "simply cannot allow the U.S. welfare system to become a deluxe retirement home for elderly people from the Third World" (Senate 1995a, 22). Senator Phil Gramm (R-Tex.) made this point more succinctly: "I want people, when they come to America, to come with their sleeves rolled up and not their hands held out" (Yepsen 1995).[17]

Perhaps the biggest villain constructed by the dominant discourse on reform, however, was the welfare system itself. No one was satisfied with the welfare system as it was, but Republicans in particular portrayed the AFDC program and the federal welfare entitlement (with their Democratic heritage) as fundamentally responsible for the dependency of millions of welfare recipients. Notably, this framing of the welfare problem was the only context in which adult welfare recipients ever appeared as victims. In Senator Kay Bailey Hutchison's (R-Tex.) words, "What we have created . . . is a self-perpetuating monster that sustains the most distressing ills of our society—illegitimacy, the disintegration of the family, weakening of the work ethic, and crippling dependency. Indirectly, it feeds ever-rising levels of functional illiteracy, violence, and juvenile crime" (*Cong. Rec.* 1995, S11754). This monster "savaged" the poor (House 1995b, 80), and repeatedly "lure[d] young mothers and fathers into creating a family they cannot support" (House 1995b, 134).

The solution to this nightmare was to cut "ensnared" adults free from the "welfare trap," and to reinstate their natural independence (*Cong. Rec.* 1996, S8076). Representative John Mica (R-Fla.), argued this point by way of a controversial analogy:

> I represent Florida where we have many lakes and natural reserves. If you visit these areas, you may see a sign like this that reads, "do not feed the alligators." We post these signs . . . because unnatural feeding and artificial care creates dependency. . . . Now, I know people are not alligators, but I submit to you that with our current handout, nonwork welfare system, we have upset the natural order. . . . We have created a system of dependency. (*Cong. Rec.* 1995, H3742)

These portrayals of poor adults as helplessly stuck in the "vicious cycle of poverty" helped justify the "tough love" of the PRWORA, and removed them from the category of people who needed to be consulted as competent, full citizens with a legitimate stake in public policy.

Although the most visible victims constructed during the welfare reform debate were the children who suffered from their parents' mistakes and the savagery of the system (see, e.g., *Cong. Rec.* 1996, S8073–74), another group of victims created by the dominant discourse on welfare were taxpayers, working people, and "decent middle class Americans." These citizens were cast as the unsung heroes of America paying for a system that cheated them out of their hard-earned money. As Representative Robert Walker (R-Pa.) argued during a House debate:

> Do you agree with the present system that robs working people of the treasure of their work in order to support people who refuse to work? . . . It is immoral to take money from decent, middle-class Americans who work for everything they have and give it to people who think they are owed the money for doing nothing. (*Cong. Rec.* 1995, H3581)

These taxpayers were portrayed as wanting to give the poor "a helping hand," but as impatient after "30 years and $5 trillion" spent on a system that rewarded immorality and indolence (*Cong. Rec.* 1995, H3398).

Given the controlling images of welfare recipients that dominated congressional and media discussions of welfare, it is little wonder that few poor people were able to or perhaps even interested in joining this public sphere debate. The prevailing stereotypes of welfare recipients in effect created a hostile environment; recipients who wished to participate in the public discussion about welfare risked being heard only as the loafers, lawbreakers, and immoral mothers portrayed by the dominant discourse. It is likely no accident, then, that most of those who did participate were *former* recipients, women who could claim the same hard-working self-reliance as middle-class taxpayers. These women could legitimately speak about welfare in the public sphere only because they had rejected and then conquered the system.[18]

Legislators enjoyed citing these success stories as support for their reform plans, and typically celebrated two kinds of model mothers. First were the plucky heroines who had bucked the old system and outsmarted the welfare trap. These recipients were often women with middle-class backgrounds, good educations, and marketable skills who rebelled against attempts to steer them away from paid employment or further education. In an irony not lost on critics of the PRWORA, many of these women had benefited from programs that the PRWORA would disallow, including programs that allowed women to draw welfare while attending college rather than immediately forcing them to search for paid work (see, e.g., House 1995b, 178–95). Nonetheless, these women were effusively praised by legislators for "their tremendous show of courage" in resisting the welfare system's best efforts to trap them into poverty (House 1995b, 180; Senate 1995b, 4).

The second group of success stories were the new model mothers, the women who overcame bad habits, complied with new state-based "welfare-to-work" programs, and became self-sufficient for often the first time in their lives. Three of these women, including a nurse, a welder, and receptionist, appeared in a hearing called simply "Welfare Reform Success Stories" (House 1995c; see also Senate 1995c). Legislators also sometimes read media accounts of success stories into the record during debates (see *Cong. Rec.* 1996, S8073). Other welfare-to-work model mothers appeared at press conferences held by welfare administrators (Tumulty 1994) or on morning news shows ("People on Welfare" 1995;

"Chicago Program"1995; "Welfare Mom Works Hard" 1996; "From Welfare to Work" 1996).

These women sounded sincerely grateful for the opportunity to work for wages, and seemed generally satisfied with the welfare-to-work programs in which they participated, even if they criticized remaining glitches. Several of the former recipients who testified before Congress, in contrast, expressed far more serious reservations about the changes in welfare law proposed under the PRWORA. I turn next, then, to the counterdiscourse of reform put forward by welfare mothers themselves.

"Everyone Needs Help Sometimes": Welfare Mothers Go to Washington

Hearings on welfare reform were held by more than a dozen committees and subcommittees across the House and Senate and gave hundreds of people an opportunity to talk to legislators about welfare reform. Committee members heard from Health and Human Services Secretary Donna Shalala, more than 160 members of Congress, a dozen governors, a half dozen mayors, two dozen welfare administrators, at least 60 academic experts, more than 75 representatives from nonprofits, 100 business representatives, and a host of other interested groups. Of the nearly 600 witnesses, however, only 17 were welfare recipients.[19] Even this figure overstates the participation of welfare recipients because just four of these witnesses were actually still receiving AFDC at the time of their testimony. Four more were receiving transitional benefits such as child-care assistance, and the remaining nine were former recipients. This latter group included one member of Congress, Representative Lynn C. Woolsey from California.

The fact that so few welfare recipients participated in congressional hearings would not have mattered as much if the testimony these women provided had been attended to more seriously. The counterdiscourse that they offered was unique. It expanded the list of reasons women needed welfare, argued for the continued necessity of a "safety net" for poor women and their children in distress, and challenged the stereotypes about welfare recipients so common in mainstream discussions about welfare reform. Their analysis of the welfare system, however, was mostly dismissed or simply ignored by defenders of the dominant discourse, perpetuating the patterns of external and internal exclusion apparent in the broader public sphere debate.

Like many Republicans and Democrats, the welfare mothers who did testify were highly critical of the administrative catch-22s that made it hard for women to escape the "welfare trap." But most of these women also condemned legislators for misunderstanding the reasons women needed welfare in the first place. Some recipients, for example, criticized the PRWORA for failing to include stiff child support enforcement mechanisms. As former recipient Pamela Cave put it, "Every AFDC case is a child support case" (House 1995b, 1213). Cave blamed her welfare stint on an irresponsible husband who left without warning, and the legal system that made it nearly impossible to collect the child support he owed across state lines. A few recipients supported garnishing fathers' wages, mandatory work programs, or even prison time for "deadbeat dads" (House 1995b, 181), but most of the mothers simply advocated better enforcement of already existing laws.[20]

A second strand of the counterdiscourse emphasized that many women needed welfare because of domestic violence or abuse, a fact that only rarely made it into the welfare reform discussion by way of legislators or expert witnesses. In fact, in one of the few flashes of protest evident in weeks of welfare hearings, two young welfare mothers were "escorted" from a hearing room after interrupting testimony from high-profile welfare experts who failed to acknowledge the high percentage of welfare recipients trying to exit abusive relationships (see House 1995b, 173–77). In a later hearing, former recipient Tamara Elser described leaving Florida to escape her abusive ex-husband, and discussed how welfare programs in Vermont "provided a bridge from destitution and abuse to independence and safety for my children and myself" (Senate 1995c).

Welfare mothers also strongly contested the view that simply getting a job—any job—would end women's need for welfare. Mother after mother told legislators that they wanted to work, but that too many jobs failed to pay a living wage, and the high cost of child-care meant that going to work often harmed the family rather than helping it. As Karolin Loendorf, a former welfare recipient from Montana, put it, "If you choose to try and regain your self-worth, self-esteem, dignity and self-respect and go out and become a tax paying citizen, you then also choose to take food out of your children's mouths, provide less clothing, [and] create more stresses in the home" (House 1995b, 1217). Cheri Honkala, a recipient and welfare activist from Philadelphia,[21] pointed out that job hunting required money that welfare mothers often didn't have, but the real trick for poor women was keeping a job once they had it:

The low-paying jobs I've gotten don't have health care benefits or sick days and don't pay enough to cover the costs of decent child care and transportation to work.

. . . If your kids get sick, you have to miss work. If your child care provider gets sick, you have to miss work. I know many women who were fired when they missed work because of an ill child or a sick elderly parent. (House 1995b, 1113)

In trying to take care of their responsibilities as both caretakers and wage earners, these women maintained, they were repeatedly caught in no-win situations.

Given these sorts of obstacles, welfare recipients argued, the safety net that the old welfare system provided had to be preserved. Representative Lynn Woolsey made this argument on the floor of the House:

Twenty-eight years ago, I went from being a married woman with complete health care coverage for my children to being a single mother with three small children receiving no child support. . . . Thankfully, I was able to turn to Medicaid and other forms of public assistance to add to my salary so I could provide my children with the health care, child care, and food they needed. Mr. Chairman, that safety net is what helped my family get back on their feet. But I will never, not for 1 minute, think that just because my family made it, so can the millions of families who are in similar or worse situations than we were today. (*Cong. Rec.* 1995, H10781)

The real point of welfare reform, Woolsey insisted, had to be reducing "the need for assistance, not the availability of assistance" (House 1995b, 698). In the words of Pam Harris White, "If it had not been . . . for the system being there, even in the condition that it is in, how would I have fed my kids? How would I have been able to support them? What would have happened to their medical needs? It is a need, it is definitely a need" (House 1995b, 189).

For White, Cave, and a few others, the safety net was necessary to temporarily protect traditional women (those who had gotten married and been stay-at-home mothers) until child support payments began. Other welfare mothers argued that the safety net had to give women with children the time and help they needed to achieve *permanent* self-sufficiency. As a result, these women argued strongly against what they viewed as the "one size fits all" model contained in the PRWORA. They were particularly troubled by the two-year time limit on education and training mandated by the bill. Karolin Loendorf, Tamara Elser, Amy Hendricks, and Tandi Graff all testified that two years would not have been enough time to gain the skills or degrees necessary for the living wage jobs they now held (see, e.g, House 1995b, 191, 695, 1227). Lynn Woolsey made the same argument on the floor of the House: "We must be flexible about transition from welfare to work. It took me 3 years to get off welfare and I was educated, healthy, and working" (*Cong. Rec.* 1995, H3742).

The welfare mothers who testified in the House and Senate saved some of their strongest criticisms for those who stereotyped welfare recipients. As welfare mother Lea Higashi wrote to the House Ways and Means Committee:

> For 18 years I was a decent, responsible middle class American. I stood tall in the knowledge that my tax dollars helped provide a safety net to families. . . . Now that I need a hand up, I am labeled a deadbeat, lazy, unmotivated, un-willing to work, looking for a free ride, irresponsible, this is not true! What I need is a time frame that fits the *NEEDS* of my family. Not a[n] arbitrary 2-year time limit created by someone who has little *understanding* of the realities I face. (House 1995b, 1511)

Tandi Graff criticized members of Congress who claimed welfare recipients were living the high life: "I challenge you to hand in your paychecks for 1 month and live on welfare. You will discover that it is not a luxurious lifestyle" (House 1995b, 695). And Cheri Honkala took on people who characterized welfare recipients as bad mothers:

> You may look at me that think that because I'm on welfare there must be something wrong with me, that somehow it's my fault that I'm poor. I am here to tell you that there is nothing wrong with me. I am a hard working person and a good mother. Everyone needs help sometimes. (House 1995b, 1108–14)

For these welfare recipients, the true model mothers weren't only the women who had outsmarted the welfare monster or complied with new welfare-to-work programs. They were also women who believed, like Tamara Elser, that their top priorities were "proper parenting," self-respect, and self-sufficiency (Senate 1995c). But even though these individual women were sometimes commended and applauded by the legislators who heard them speak, their counterdiscourse was nonetheless overwhelmed by the discourse of dependency and the stereotypes of recipients they tried so earnestly to dislodge.

Gender, Race, and Contractual Citizenship

Why was the dominant discourse on welfare so hard to displace? Deeply entrenched views about welfare recipients as part of the "undeserving" poor certainly played a role (Fraser and Gordon 1993), but an additional factor was the discourse of citizenship invoked by supporters of the PRWORA. One of the main sources of this discourse was political scientist Lawrence Mead's influential books *Beyond Entitlement: The Social Obligations of Citizenship* (1986) and *The New Politics of Poverty* (1992). Mead's basic argument was that the "most vulnerable Americans need obligations, as much as rights, if they are to move as equals on the stage of American life" (1986, 17). In Mead's view, "federal programs that support the disadvantaged and unemployed have been permissive in character, not authoritative. That is, they have given benefits to their recipients but have set few requirements for how they ought to function in return" (1986, 1). Mead suggested that requiring employable recipients to work in return for support would help those recipients "function better," and would also allow them to meet their social obligations to other citizens (1986, 1; see also chap. 11).

Here we find the basic outline for the contractual relationship constructed by the PRWORA. In Mead's words, "The idea is that parents are responsible in some sense for themselves and the families they have brought into being" (1986, 244). Those who make "an honest effort to support their families" and abstain from "moral offenses" such as "nonpayment of child support, and fraud or abuse of programs by recipients" (244) are judged to have met their social obligations to other citizens. Those who fail to comply with these obligations should face strong sanctions.

Mead explicitly acknowledges the paternalism that would be required to run programs that force the poor and unemployed to work and be "moral" in exchange for support (246). In the context of experimental welfare-to-work programs in the states prior to the PRWORA debate, however, Mead's ideas were translated almost exclusively into the language of contract. Governor John Engler of Michigan and Governor Thomas Carper of Delaware, the first two witnesses on welfare reform before the House Ways and Means Committee in the 104th Congress, proudly told their audience about the "social contract" that Michigan and Delaware now required AFDC recipients to sign. Carper described this "social contract of mutual responsibility" in detail:

> I am the welfare recipient, you are the State. For example, you, the State, offer to do certain things to help me, the welfare recipient. For example, you will help me with my education, to get my high school degree, help with job training, with job placement, maybe help me with some transportation to the job, some child care for my kids and make sure that we still have health care.
>
> . . . My responsibilities would be to take advantage of the education, take advantage of the job training, take the job that is presented to me, even a minimum wage job, make sure my kids are in school and once I have a job, to work, not to quit the job. If I do, I will face sanctions. In some cases, I will face the complete total lifetime cut-off of AFDC eligibility. (House 1995b, 16–17)

Other aspects of Delaware's new welfare regime required that both parents support their children, and encouraged the "maintenance and sustenance of two-parent families" (17).

The debt to Mead's argument is clear, but the portrayal of this relationship as one of contract (a portrayal resonating, of course, with the language of "The Contract with America") is problematic. In most contexts, a contract implies that there is a free exchange between equals, and that both parties can either negotiate the agreement to their satisfaction, or can walk away if they don't like the terms. The social contracts of Michigan and Delaware, however, were hardly transacted between equal partners. On one side was the state, with the power to determine the contours of the "agreement," to judge compliance, and to unilaterally withhold resources. On the other side was the welfare recipient, usually lacking even the most basic means of subsistence, and positioned only to say yes or no to the "agreement" (Fraser and Gordon 1993, 63–64). The result was at best a lopsided contract, and perhaps more accurately, an illegitimate contract.

These social contracts, however, clearly served as models for the legislators who crafted the PRWORA. The resulting contract constructed by the PRWORA could be abridged as follows:

If work
And morals
Then rights.

In other words, if a poor person works for pay (or in the case of a woman, is supported by a man who works for pay) and behaves morally (is heterosexual, monogamous, law abiding, and preferably married or formerly married), then that person will be granted respect and the full rights of citizenship (including procreative rights, privacy rights, vocational liberty, and political participation rights). If a poor person does *not* work, or does *not* conform to the moral standard, then he or she will not deserve or be granted the respect or rights that other citizens enjoy. Senator John Ashcroft made this contractual view of citizenship clear during one of the final debates on welfare reform in the 104th Congress:

> I think it is time for us to limit the amount of time that people can be on welfare. It is time for us to provide disincentives to bear children out of wedlock. It is time for us to provide powerful incentives for people to go to work. It is time for us to say that, if you are on welfare, you should be off drugs. It is time for us to say that, if you are on welfare, your children should be in school. . . . You have to be responsible for what you are doing. We are not going to continue to support you in a way in which you abdicate, you simply run from, you hide from, *your responsibility as a citizen*. (*Cong. Rec.* 1996, S8081; emphasis added)

A central problem with this contractual account of citizenship and rights, however, is that it's a selectively applied contract. In spite of being framed in the universalist language of citizenship, this contractual discourse is in fact gendered, raced, classed, and heterosexist. There are, for example, significant gender differences in how the "work test" part of this contract plays out. As Gwendolyn Mink has argued, the caregiving work women do for their own families is generally not accorded economic value, but in the case of poor single mothers, that work "*is not considered work* at all" (Mink 1998, 134). This is evident in the line used incessantly by legislators from both sides during the PRWORA debate: "Our plan puts welfare mothers to work" (see, e.g., *Cong. Rec.* 1995, S19154). To count as real, valuable, productive work, in other words, "work" has to be paid work. Since women consistently perform far more unpaid work than men do, a contractual account of citizenship that privileges paid work seriously disadvantages women citizens.

The exceptions to the requirement that valuable work must be paid work reveal the racial and heterosexist dimensions of this contract. There are women whose unpaid work in the home *is* publicly supported: widows. Mothers with children in the Survivor's Insurance (SI) program receive both unstigmatized *and* far more generous benefits than mothers with children in AFDC (now TANF) programs. As Mink observes, "Where the welfare law tells unmarried mothers to get to work outside the home, SI underwrites the widowed mother's decision to devote herself to the care of her children" inside the home (1998, 124). SI's liberal earnings exemption also means widows can choose a combination of paid work and caregiving work as they see fit. It is no coincidence, Mink suggests, that SI recipients have been disproportionately white and AFDC/TANF participants have been disproportionately black (28).[22]

Another example of how the value "assigned to mothers' work inside the home has depended on the class and color of the mother" (Mink 1998, 28) is shown in Congress's decision to grant wives who work at home the right to establish their own Independent Retirement Accounts (IRAs). In an ironic twist, this new law, which allows stay-at-home wives to set aside a portion of their "earned income" for retirement, was passed the same week as the PRWORA (Mink 1998, 28–29). Again, the women this publicly financed tax break benefits are far more likely to be white, well-off, and married. The bottom line is that primarily white widows and middle and upper-class wives are allowed to stay home with their children without stigma and are not required to relinquish their procreative autonomy or their privacy rights even though they don't "work." Poor women are not given these options.

The morals test in the PRWORA contract is also selectively applied. Poor women (and more recently, poor men) who have children out of wedlock are judged to fail the morals test and are sanctioned with the loss of income, privacy, and autonomy. Wealthy heterosexual men, in contrast, do not face the same penalties. As an example, Jesse Jackson might well lose moral clout for fathering a child outside of wedlock, but he is unlikely to lose rights in the way that poor welfare recipients do under the PRWORA. Most wealthy heterosexual women enjoy the same ability to retain rights when they fail to pass the morals test.

Both the "work" test and the "morals" test of the PRWORA's contract thus help justify a racist, sexist, heterosexist, and classist withdrawal of rights from welfare recipients. As Uma Narayan has argued, such contractual models of rights and citizenship ultimately stem from the view that rights should depend on one's contributions to public life (1997). Whether this contribution comes via waged work (Shklar 1991) or unwaged care-work (Mink 1998), Narayan suggests that we should instead "insist that dignity, worth and social standing matter to all who are *participants* in national life, that is, *who are part of the national com-*

munity, independently of how they *contribute* to it" (Narayan 1997, 52). Such a view of rights and citizenship as based on participation rather than contributions might well help displace the paternalistically constructed obligations that some powerful citizens have been able to impose on others through the Personal Responsibility Act.

Conclusion

How do the insights of discourse analysis and democratic theory help us better understand the politics of race and welfare in the United States? In an age when direct appeals to racism have lost their acceptability in most public venues, analysis of the seemingly neutral discourses used in public sphere debates remains a critical tactic for unmasking the indirect appeals to racism that still influence public policy. Although the discourses of citizenship and responsibility clearly resonated with many Americans during the welfare reform debate, they were buttressed by racist and sexist stereotypes. By portraying welfare recipients as drug-addicted, immoral, inner-city welfare queens and unwed teenage mothers, the dominant discourse reduced the complexity of American poverty to a simplistic, racist caricature. Practitioners of discourse analysis can reveal the continued salience of racism and sexism in the public discourse about welfare, and can aid in the effort to usefully complicate public understanding of the welfare system and its participants.

Democratic theorists, in turn, sensitize us to the patterns of political exclusion that such caricatures reinforce, and encourage us to keep a watchful eye on who actually participates in decision making in established democracies. Welfare recipients ultimately had little effect on the dialogue about reform in spite of their firsthand experience with AFDC and their immediate interest in the outcome of the reform process. The hostility toward welfare mothers generated by the dominant discourse and its attendant stereotypes certainly might have encouraged some recipients to remain silent, but even when recipients like Tandi Graff challenged legislators to "listen to people like me," those demands were easily (if arbitrarily) dismissed. Democratic theorists remind us that the passage of a policy like the PRWORA without the meaningful participation or consent of the poor represents a failure of democracy.

The barriers to poor people's authoritative participation analyzed here should raise distressing questions for a society that claims to be democratic, and suggest at least one potential goal welfare recipients and their allies might pursue in future efforts to revamp the U.S. welfare system. Although the provision of an adequate income and the protection of individual civil rights are critical measures of the success of any welfare program,[23] democratic theory suggests a third criterion: the meaningful political participation of the poor in democratic deliberation and decision making, particularly regarding the welfare system. We should not submit to the argument that poor people lack the moral standing or competence to participate in political life, nor should the joys and burdens of participation in democratic life become the exclusive privilege of the wealthy.

NOTES

I am grateful to the editors, Maxine Eichner, and Marnina Gonick for their helpful comments on an earlier version of this essay, and to George Davis and Challen Nicklen for outstanding research assistance.

1. Two other groups of scholars who have advocated increased citizen participation are theorists of "participatory democracy," including Carole Pateman (1970) and Jane Mansbridge (1980), and civic republicans such as Hannah Arendt (1958) and Benjamin Barber (1984). Participatory theorists have generally argued for the expansion of democracy to areas of life *beyond* formal political institutions, while civic republicans have concentrated on making those formal political institutions themselves more participatory.

2. I have examined the political participation of activists and dissidents in more detail in Sparks 1997.

3. Some of these issues could obviously be addressed with better institutional arrangements (e.g., free on-site child or elder care), but few public institutions have made such accommodations.

4. For additional perspectives on the political importance of storytelling, see Disch 1994; and Lara 1998.

5. Although Collins does not make this point explicitly, other subordinated groups clearly confront controlling images as well. African American men, for example, have encountered the controlling image of the violent, oversexed would-be rapist.

6. Anne Schneider and Helen Ingram have made a parallel but more general argument about the "social construction of target populations" (1993).

7. This discourse drew heavily from older "culture of poverty" arguments first developed in the 1960s (e.g., Moynihan 1965; see also Mead 1986, 1992). For more detailed critiques of the discourses of poverty used in the transition to TANF, see Mink 1998; Naples 1997 (discussing the 1987–88 reforms but also applicable to TANF); and White 1997.

8. See Naples 1997 and Stoesz 2000 for analyses of the individualist and behaviorist assumptions built into mainstream views of welfare reform.

9. My discussion relies on the work of feminist scholars who have carefully

analyzed both the gendered character of U.S. welfare programs and the inseparability of race and gender in the context of welfare politics. See especially Abramovitz 1988; Albeda and Tilly 1997; Gordon 1990, 1994; Mink 1998, 1999; and Quadagno 1994.

10. Ronald Reagan is often credited as the original author of the "welfare queen" stereotype. In numerous speeches in the late 1970s and early 1980s, he told the story of a "Chicago welfare queen" (apparently an African American woman named Linda Taylor) who supposedly drove a Cadillac, bought thick steaks with food stamps, and vacationed in resorts on taxpayer funds. Reporters found many discrepancies between the facts of the case and Reagan's story (see, e.g., *New York Times,* January 9, 1977, 39), but the image proved extraordinarily resilient.

11. The term *welfare queen* itself was not invoked all that often during the 104th Congress; there are less than a dozen references during the floor debates. Those who did use the term had two quite different purposes. One group invoked the label in order to argue that they weren't stereotyping recipients but were dealing with "real problems." Their listing of recipients' failings, however, would then closely track the welfare queen stereotype. See, for example, the speech by Senator Dorgan (*Cong. Rec.* 1996, S8094). A second group of legislators explicitly criticized the welfare queen stereotype as a myth. See, e.g., the speech by Representative Coyne (*Cong. Rec.* 1995, H15530).

12. Although some legislators spoke as though the welfare rolls were full of able-bodied men, adult men accounted for just 4 percent of the AFDC population in FY 1995. The vast majority of welfare recipients then as now are in fact children; they accounted for 69 percent of all welfare recipients in 1994–95 (U.S. Department of Health and Human Services 1995).

13. Lucy Williams has analyzed the one-sided character of much of the news coverage of the Chicago 19 case and similar situations to criticize both how the media creates an image "which is not false or exclusive, but is dissembling in its uniqueness—and the public's selective gravitation to that image in order to validate its own race and gender perceptions" (1995, 1161).

14. The average welfare mother had only two children (Department of Health and Human Services 1995).

15. Even legislators who noted that out-of-wedlock births were on the rise in most Western democracies and that the phenomenon certainly wasn't limited to poor people often agreed that the "disastrous" results of illegitimacy justified sanctions against poor women who had children outside of marriage (see, e.g., Senate 1995b). This is a rather remarkable reassertion of the norm of the heterosexual nuclear family in a context in which fewer than half of American families now adhere to this idealization.

16. The average welfare stay for all AFDC recipients in the years prior to the passage of the PRWORA was just over two years, but women who had their first child while a teenager were three times as likely to be on welfare for ten or more years (Senate 1995b, 4).

17. Although many legislators objected to the fact that the PRWORA eliminated benefits for virtually all legal aliens (including refugees from Cuba and other politically sensitive groups), the final version of the PRWORA included stricter sponsorship requirements and higher barriers to welfare support for legal

immigrants. For a more detailed analysis of the racial politics of welfare reform and immigrant communities, see Fujiwara 1999.

18. Compare also Mead's argument that most Americans believe only *workers* have the right to press claims for equality against the government or their employers (1992, 60).

19. Two of the recipients appeared twice, for a total of nineteen appearances. This figure is based on a search of the published hearings of the 104th Congress. Since former welfare recipients were often listed with their new job title, it is possible that a few have been missed. Three additional recipients submitted statements to committees for inclusion in the record. All of the recipients were adult women.

20. Pamela Cave was one of the most conservative welfare recipients to testify during the PRWORA debate. She described herself as an "avid" Rush Limbaugh listener, even though she criticized his regular practice of saying "good morning" to "those welfare recipients who are just getting up" several hours into his broadcast (House 1995b, 1210).

21. Cheri Honkala appears to be the only welfare activist who actually testified during 1995–96; two other participants in a welfare rights organization submitted letters to the House Ways and Means Committee (see House 1995b, at 1511 and 1709).

22. See also Soss 2000 for a fascinating study of how the different designs of AFDC and SSDI (Social Security Disability Insurance) affect the political marginality of different welfare populations.

23. See also Schram and Soss 2001 for an analysis of the political construction of "success" in the context of welfare policy.

CHAPTER 8

Putting a Black Face on Welfare

The Good and the Bad

SANFORD F. SCHRAM

"Everyone who knows anything about welfare knows that most recipients are white." This is a common statement often made in conversation among people concerned about racist representations of welfare in the mass media. It often goes unchallenged. In fact, in recent years it seems to have taken on the status of an unquestioned truth among those who claim to know better than to buy into the myths in popular culture. This statement has been used repeatedly to undermine the prevalent notion that welfare is largely a "black program" needed because African Americans are trapped in a "black underclass," mired in a "culture of poverty," bereft of "personal responsibility," and unable to break out of an intergenerational cycle of "welfare dependency."

Yet this statement increasingly is factually questionable; and under welfare reform, it is politically problematic. In what follows, I argue that in debates about welfare reform, failure to acknowledge the racial composition of the welfare population compounds the problems social policies pose for people of color, African Americans in particular. I argue that such reticence will only "whitewash" the racial disparities in the U.S. economy that in recent years have increased the extent to which low-income persons of color rely on public assistance. Frank discussion is needed because welfare discourse in recent years has come to be increasingly encoded with racial connotations (Schram 2000). It is important to recognize that, contrary to the conventional understanding, there are both good and bad ways to highlight the color issue in welfare.

In other words, analysis suggests that putting a "black face" on welfare is not as clear-cut an issue as it is often depicted.[1] There are pitfalls either way. Emphasizing the disproportionate numbers of persons of color on public assistance can reinforce attempts to denigrate welfare as a "black program" for those "other" people who are too irresponsible to conform to the standards of white, middle-class society. Yet going along with depictions of welfare that do not account for race leaves unchallenged the racial disparities reinforced by welfare policy. White or black, the face of welfare that we project poses political risks.

I will note recent scholarship that shows how racial representations of welfare undermine support for public assistance, but I also suggest that such scholarship can overlook the political complexities of race and welfare. In particular, it does not sufficiently examine the artificiality of racial categories, the political uses of different constructions of race, and the ways in which "race talk" about welfare—or the lack thereof—can be self-defeating. These problems spill over into questions of advocacy. I conclude that racial representations of welfare involve layers of political consideration and pose strategic problems for political activism. More stress should be given, not to the frequency of racialized depictions of welfare in the mass media, but to how prevailing modes of perception prime people to rely on tendentious racial categorizations to interpret issues of race and welfare (see Mendelberg 1997). My recommendation is not to avoid racial categories in discussions of welfare but to deploy such constructions in politically sensitive ways. Putting a black face on welfare risks reinforcing racial stereotypes, but only by acknowledging the disproportionate numbers of persons of color relying on welfare can we challenge racial inequality in the economy.

I undertake this line of inquiry to suggest that understanding the racial dimensions of welfare can promote racial justice. To get more racial justice, we need to ask hard questions and break with conventional wisdom. Because racial connotations are encoded in welfare discourse, we need to call them out. Because welfare reform has disproportionately affected persons of color, the need to highlight the racial dimensions of welfare has intensified. Taking race into account is more necessary now than before.

The Moynihan Problem

Breaking with the conventional wisdom on racialized depictions of welfare has its own pitfalls. The risk here is the "Moynihan problem"; that is, looking into welfare along racial lines may be associated with Daniel P. Moynihan's controversial work on the subject, *The Negro Family* (1965). This short (78-page) internal U.S. Department of Labor report, emphasizing the then well-accepted theme of pathology among economically marginalized African Americans, was leaked to the press by Moynihan himself (Lemann 1991, 171–72).

The report's distinctive claim was that welfare dependency among single-parent African American families was starting to spiral out of control due to a breakdown in values in black communities. While the number of families on welfare historically had tracked the black male unemployment rate, in the early 1960s, Moynihan suggested, the welfare participation rate for African Americans was becoming "unglued." The link between the black male unemployment rate and welfare caseloads was becoming weaker. Black poverty was turning into an autonomous problem disconnected from the status of the economy, indicating that the black family was becoming wrapped in a "tangle of pathology" (Katz 1989). To underscore its importance as a finding of social science, Moynihan would in time proudly call this phenomenon the "Moynihan Scissors" (Moynihan 1985). His analysis has been criticized on methodological grounds for tying the unemployment of black males with the welfare caseload for all races, and subsequent research has shown the correlation to be unsubstantiated (O'Connor 2001, 205–6). The report reached bad conclusions on the basis of bad research.

Moynihan may have intended to highlight racial unfairness in the broader society (O'Connor 2001, 203–10), but that is not how his effort was received. Instead, the report was criticized for essentializing racial differences, reinforcing racist attitudes, and promoting the idea of a self-created "culture of poverty" in which low-income African American families were mired—making them personally responsible for their own plight. In particular, the report was condemned for stressing racial background as the key factor in producing poverty among African American families and neglecting its political and economic roots. Although Moynihan was rarely labeled a racist, his work was seen as "blaming the victim" (Ryan 1971).

The report deserved such interpretations, in its effects if not intention. Conservatives appropriated it to justify cutbacks in public assistance on the grounds that it promoted "welfare dependency" and undermined "personal responsibility" among African American families (O'Connor 2001). The Right campaigned on this theme for three decades, finally ending welfare as an entitlement in 1996. In spite of Moynihan's own pained resistance to that disentitlement, the seeds for the Personal Responsibility and Work Opportunity Reconciliation Act of 1996 were sown in the Moynihan report (Katz 2001).

William Julius Wilson (1987) has trumpeted Moynihan as a prophet who was unfairly castigated for pointing out the growing problems of social breakdown among the "black underclass." Wilson believes that criticism of the Moynihan report may have induced self-censorship among social scientists who feared being labeled racist for discussing family formation among African Americans. Adolph Reed and others have questioned whether this self-censorship really happened (Reed 1999, 93; Schram 1995, 31). A better explanation may be that in the wake of the controversy over the Moynihan report, researchers avoided the canard that low-income African American families were the source of their own poverty. Researchers instead sought to understand how poverty could create conditions that made it difficult to adhere to conventional moral standards of personal responsibility. Rather than speculate that an underclass had come to indulge in a culture of poverty, researchers found ways to understand the causes of what was previously called "pathology." The Moynihan controversy therefore was not, as Wilson suggested, a cautionary tale about the premature dismissal of good research that predicted the demise of the traditional nuclear family among low-income African Americans. Instead, it showed that emphasizing race as a factor in welfare may be correctly interpreted as blaming the victim.

The Negro Family provides a reminder of the dilemmas associated with raising issues of race and welfare: there are good reasons to be sensitive about introducing race into one's analysis. Yet there are problems in the other direction as well. Analysis of the disproportionate use of public assistance by African Americans cannot be left in the dust, for there are pitfalls to *not* putting a black face on welfare, as I demonstrate in the following.

Myths about Myths

In 1996 the PRWORA ended welfare as an entitlement. As part of the battle to prevent this outcome, efforts were made to inform the public about the real facts on welfare. Most of this work was quite good in correcting popular misunderstandings. Yet analyses that were sound in other respects often mischaracterized the racial composition of the welfare population. These studies added fuel to the tendency in informal conversation to claim that "most recipients are White." An instance is *Welfare Myths: Fact or Fiction? Exploring the Truth about Welfare,* published in 1996 by the Welfare Law Center. Even this scrupulously researched and clearly presented publication parsed its statistics on race and welfare in a problematic way.

> *MYTH:* Almost all of the families receiving AFDC are Black or Hispanic.
> *FACT:* Many more White families than Black families or Hispanic families are helped by the AFDC program.

In the Internet version, to the left of "MYTH" is a button to push for "More Info." That additional information turns out to be statistics that cover the "facts," such as the percentage of Black families and of Hispanic families that receive cash assistance is larger than the proportion of White families who do, as is the proportion of Black and Hispanic families that are in poverty. Yet, the main point emphasized is that even though poverty forces African Americans and Latinos to rely on welfare more frequently than whites, whites make up a majority of welfare recipients. The factual basis for this claim is reported as follows:

> A study of families receiving AFDC between January 1990 and June 1992 found that less than 3 in 10 women receiving AFDC for the first time were Black and 1.6 in 10 were Hispanic. Looking at all families receiving aid during a given period of time, White families still outnumber Black families, although the percentage of Black families in the total caseload is higher than the percentage among first-time recipients. White families make up 38.3% of the caseload, Black families 36.6%. Hispanic families account for 17.8% of all families receiving aid while Asians and Native Americans amount to a total of 4.2%.

There are numerous problems with this "myth vs. fact" presentation. First, the study from which supporting calculations are drawn is cited nowhere in the publication. Second, the primary statistic used by the report is about the percentage of first-time users of welfare; this measure neglects to count people who are reapplying after having been off. These recyclers are left out of this statistic and are not counted at all. This measure also does not count people who are still receiving assistance they initiated before the start of the time period studied. In short, this statistical claim that most recipients are white is highly selective.

There are many ways to measure the racial composition of the welfare population. While none is perfect, several are an improvement over looking at first-time users. One common approach is to examine the racial composition of the rolls in a representative month (say January or June, or better, the average monthly breakdown for 12 months in that year). This approach is reported in figure 8.1.

The data in figure 8.1 are the more commonly reported data from the federal government and indicate that for the decade before welfare reform, roughly equal proportions of recipients at any one time were white or African American, with Latinos at a lower but increasing rate during the 1985–99 period. These data are by no means consistent with the popular claim often made in political discussions that most welfare recipients are white, indicating as they do that whites and blacks received welfare in approximately equal numbers for most of the years since 1985 and the number of Hispanic recipients was somewhat lower. Data on the number of recipients indicate that since the mid-1990s, the number of recipients for all three groups has declined, fastest for whites and slowest for Hispanics, so that blacks were the largest group by the end of the 1990s. It deserves emphasis that a major part of the explanation for the disparity between these data and those reported in *Welfare Myths* is that the federal government data include the people on the rolls at any one point in time, regardless of whether they are using assistance for the first time.

The federal government, however, is excluding people who have gone off the rolls but had received welfare during that year. Therefore, we may want to try still another method, which estimates the racial composition all family heads that received any assistance during a calendar year, regardless of whether it was their first time or not. Table 8.1 presents data from the Panel Study of Income Dynamics (PSID) on the racial breakdown of welfare recipients. The PSID is a national longitudinal study with a sample population in any one year exceeding 2,000 families.[2] The data are weighted to ensure representativeness by race.[3]

The figures in table 8.1 are from the annual PSID waves for selected years 1970–93.[4] The figures presented are the percentage of all the PSID married women or independent female heads of households with children who indicated receiving any amounts of public assistance at any time during the preceding calendar year. In these figures, blacks outnumbered whites in 1970. Whites slightly outnumbered blacks in 1975 and

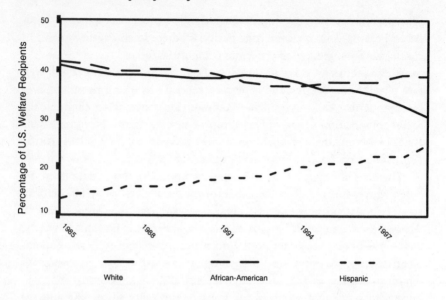

Fig. 8.1.   Distribution of U.S. welfare recipients by race, 1985–99. (Data from U.S. Department of Health and Human Services, <http://aspe.os.dhhs.gov/hsp/leavers99.race.htm#tab2>).

TABLE 8.1.   Welfare Receipt by Race, 1970–93

	1970	1975	1980	1985	1990	1991	1992	1993
Black	46	44	46	50	54	57	53	50
White	45	50	50	49	45	42	43	46
Other	9	6	4	1	1	1	4	4
Total	100	100	100	100	100	100	100	100
N	281	361	350	304	301	302	314	292

Source: University of Michigan, Panel Study of Income Dynamics (PSID), annual waves. Calculations provided by Thomas P. Vartanian.

Note: Married Mothers and Independent Female Heads of Households Who Received Welfare During the Calendar Year (in percentages).

1980. Blacks outnumbered whites in each year after 1980. For 1991, 57 percent of all the mothers who indicated receiving any public assistance were black, 42 percent were white, and 1 percent were other races. In 1992, 53 percent were black, 43 percent were white, and 4 percent were other races. In 1993, 50 percent of recipient families were black, while 46 percent were white and 4 percent were other. These calculations sort by race identification alone, so Latinos, for instance, are sorted into either black or white categories, and the "other" category refers to Native Americans, Asians, and other racial groups designated neither white nor black. The calculations are based on all the married women and independent heads of households who had children and had received any welfare benefits in the preceding calendar year. Therefore, this is an inclusive sample that maximizes the chances of counting even a middle-class, suburban woman who received only a partial welfare benefit for one month while, say, making the transition from being in a marriage to being divorced. This calculation therefore does not systematically exclude whites. Still, the percentages indicate that *in each year examined from 1985 on, more black than white women received assistance.*

These larger PSID numbers for blacks were for essentially the same time period covered by *Welfare Myths* data. During that time period, the average number of whites and blacks receiving welfare at any one point in time (e.g., in any one month) was essentially the same according to government statistics (U.S. Department of Health and Human Services 2000c). Yet, according to the PSID data, the total number of blacks who had received assistance during the calendar year exceeded the number of whites.

These data are therefore different from both the *Welfare Myths* data and those reported by the federal government. Part of the explanation is that the government and the *Welfare Myths* data report Latinos separate from race. Another difference that is important for the contrast with both the *Welfare Myths* and federal government data is that the PSID data account for recycling back onto welfare, while still only counting each family only once. Looking only at first-time users ignores the fact that compared to whites, African Americans who have left public assistance are more likely to return later as second- or third-time users (largely due to lower marriage rates) (Edin and Harris 1999). Therefore, presenting a racial breakdown of the first-time users, as is done by *Welfare Myths*, cuts out more African American than white families. In the case of the federal data, not counted are all the people who are not currently receiving assistance, including recyclers who are disproportionately nonwhite.

Another difference with the *Welfare Myths* data is that by only concentrating on people who initiate the receipt of welfare, those data miss people who began using welfare before the time period covered. This leaves out longer-term users who are already welfare recipients. According to available research, these people are more likely to be nonwhite (Blank 1997, 154; and Duncan, Harris, and Boisjoly 2000). This is critical especially since long-term use has for years been the main source of concern about welfare in the mass public. Therefore, looking only at first-time receipt or only at who is on welfare at any one point in time takes the focus off the more controversial, long-term welfare population, which happens to be even more disproportionately nonwhite.

The PSID data, however, do not fully solve these problems. These data produce a small sample, making their generalizability suspect. In addition, the inclusion of anyone who receives welfare for even the shortest period of time and the smallest amounts fails to address the claim that longer-term users are the more significant population. An even better estimate would weight the population by how long each family received welfare and how much they received. When this is done, the racial composition of the welfare population would in all likelihood be even more heavily skewed toward persons of color because, as mentioned, various studies have indicated that nonwhites are likely to have longer spells of welfare receipt (Blank 1997, 154).

Therefore, I would suggest that the data on the racial breakdown of those receiving welfare is subject to much debate. One thing is clear: in the run up to welfare reform it was questionable to claim, as many did, that most welfare recipients were white. This claim operated as its own unquestioned myth among those seeking to repudiate the equally suspect notion that welfare was a "black program" for those "other" people who were not conforming to white, middle-class work and family values.

There was, however, a good rationale for the myth-busting about race even if it was factually suspect. Martin Gilens (1999) has effectively demonstrated that beginning in the 1960s, the mass media—both print and electronic—began to overrepresent African Americans in negative stories about poverty and, to a lesser extent, about welfare. Gilens also notes that beginning at that time, the mass public began to regard welfare as a "black program" that coddled low-income black families and rewarded them for not adhering to middle-class work and family values. Gilens goes on to demonstrate persuasively that both the mass public and journalists were likely to grossly overestimate the proportion of welfare recipients who were black. There came a need to challenge the highly racialized image of welfare recipients that was and continues to be ascendant in the culture and among the people in positions to influence opinion.[5]

Gilens's work is important in highlighting the role of the mass media in providing a racially distorted image of the welfare population. He effectively suggests that media representations encouraged the denigration of welfare as a program for "other" people who did not adhere to white middle-class work and family values. Yet there is a need to go beyond discussing whether mass media depictions are affecting attitudes toward welfare (Neubeck and Cazenave 2001). We need to recognize that the problem transcends such racialized depictions. What do we do when these depictions become accurate because the welfare population has in fact become disproportionately nonwhite? We need to ask: Why is the mass public reluctant to see black welfare recipients as deserving? In other words, we need to examine why some segments of the white population are predisposed to looking negatively upon blacks receiving welfare and are therefore already primed to respond negatively to media depictions of them (see Mendelberg 1997).

As the "most recipients are white" mantra of popular discourse cited at the outset becomes a more and more popular myth-busting claim among antipoverty advocates, less attention is given to how welfare recipients are "different" in racial composition and other ways, especially in how society treats them. As a result, less attention is given to how this relatively distinctive group came to require assistance. The lure of "Most recipients are white" is the prospect of unracializing welfare, of "whitening" it. If that can be accomplished, an opportunity is created for more equity in the treatment of welfare recipients. Further, if advocates can make the case that the racial composition of the welfare population is no different from that of the society overall, there is a stronger empirical base for insisting on more equitable treatment of recipients because they do not need to be treated as an alien group to be singled out for distinctive treatment under a punitive welfare system. The goal of equitable treatment is laudable and well established among advocates for a more progressive welfare state. But trampling over basic demographics and creating a distorted image of the racial composition of the welfare population is a doomed strategy. It will founder on the shoals of factual disputation, which will not help realize the larger goal of equity.

In addition, while we may want to downplay race as socially constructed, it has real consequences as a way of organizing social life (Loury 2002). Ignoring the racial composition of the welfare population on the grounds that race should not count unfortunately overlooks that it does. Therefore, we need to recognize how it counts, and deal with the consequences. As much as we want to sweep the fictions of race into the dustbin, they continue to haunt social life. A disproportionately black welfare population is a subject that needs to be addressed for no other reason than to resist racist interpretations of welfare. When the welfare population becomes so disproportionately nonwhite that the myth-busters' myth can no longer be sustained, where are we then?

One answer is: the present. That is exactly where we are right now. Today, we confront the prospect of arguing for equity on grounds other than the distorted image popular in advocacy discourse that the demographic profile of welfare recipients mirrors the general population. It has not for a long time, and it increasingly does not. While during much of the 1980s whites and blacks were about equal in the government's monthly tabulations of welfare recipients, they no longer are. As Michael Brown in this volume and others have emphasized, with welfare reform in 1996, the welfare rolls declined dramatically through 2000, with whites leaving welfare faster than other groups, making the welfare population even more disproportionately nonwhite and creating an even greater prospect that welfare will be marginalized as a "black" program for "other" people (also see Neubeck and Cazenave 2001).

The main source for tracking this change has unfortunately been the aforementioned federal government's statistics on the characteristics of the welfare population (U.S. Department of Health and Human Services 2000c). These data combine race and ethnicity to report not only on "whites" and "blacks," but also on "Hispanics," which is not a racial designation. Nonetheless, these data supply the evidence that, since welfare reform was enacted in the mid-1990s, the proportion welfare recipients who are nonwhite has increased rapidly, even if one makes the conservative assumption that about half of Hispanics on welfare are nonwhite (Grieco and Cassidy 2001). In 1985, for the average month, 40.8 percent of adult recipients were white, 41.6 percent black, and 13.6 percent Hispanic. In 1999, the percentage of whites had fallen sharply to 30.5, while the percentage of blacks had only dropped to 38.3 and the percentage of Hispanics had risen to 24.5 (Lower-Basch 2000). (See table 8.2.) The U.S. Department of Health and Human Services noted in its report on these figures:

> The racial composition of welfare families has changed substantially over the past ten years. In 1990, it was 38 percent whites, 40 percent blacks and 17 percent Hispanics. In 1999, however, it was 31 percent whites, 38 percent blacks and 25 percent Hispanics. In addition, the small percentage of the welfare population which is Asian has grown slowly but steadily over the period from just under 3 percent to about 3 and one-half percent. Viewed over the decade there has been a shift from white to Hispanic families which is consistent with broader population trends. This shift has been accelerated since 1996 and is particularly pronounced in California, New York and Texas. Thus, in 1999, 70 percent of all His-

panic welfare families were in three large States (California, New York and Texas), as compared to 65 percent in 1996. In California, the proportion of Hispanic welfare families increased to 46 percent in 1999 from 38 percent in 1996. In addition, black families which had been a declining proportion of the caseload have trended up slightly since 1996. The upshot of these changes is that the proportion of welfare families that were minorities has increased from three-fifths to just over two-thirds over the decade, primarily driven by the growth in Hispanic families. (U.S. Department of Health and Human Services 2000c)

Given the racial diversity of the Latino population, we can conclude that part of its growth as percentage of recipients adds to the increase in the nonwhite proportion of the welfare population. With welfare reform, blacks have increasingly been established as the largest group, and nonwhites as the overwhelming majority, of recipient families at any one point in time. (See table 8.2.)

These figures, however, point to an even less discussed dimension of the issue. Comparing these figures to raw population numbers, we can suggest that the probability that African Americans rely on welfare is much greater than it is for whites. We can estimate that on average, in any single month in 1999, 1 out of 100 whites and 8 out of 100 blacks were receiving welfare, an eight times higher probability of using welfare.

What are we to do now, under these circumstances, with a welfare population as racialized as this one? The welfare population remains diverse but increasingly composed of nonwhites. Arguments by advocates for equity based on a distorted image of the welfare population as largely white or like the population overall were always questionable; now they are irrelevant.[6] How are we now to build the case for equitable treatment of welfare recipients? For a long time, equity arguments should have been made on other than the misleading grounds that most welfare recipients are white; for a long time, they needed to be made not by

TABLE 8.2. Percentage Distribution of TANF Families by Race, October 1998– September 1999

Total Families	White	Black	Hispanic	Native American	Asian	Other	Unknown
2,648,462	30.5	38.3	24.5	1.5	3.6	0.6	1.0

Source: U.S. Department of Health and Human Services 2000 (last updated on 08/27/2000). Figures are for the average month.

neglecting race but by explaining why African Americans in particular, but other racial minorities as well, were more likely to be living in poverty and in need of public assistance at higher rates. Equity arguments need to be urgently made now that take race into account, indicating that there are good reasons why African Americans and Latinos need to rely on public assistance more frequently and that they *should* be seen, if only in this regard, as "different." They confront different circumstances, often facing greater need, and more often requiring the assistance of welfare. The situation is critical since research indicates that blacks constitute a large majority of the recipient families that will be affected by the new time limits under welfare reform. Greg Duncan, Kathleen Harris, and Johanne Boisjoly (2000) estimate that blacks constitute over two-thirds of the families who will reach the newly imposed 60-month federal limit for the receipt of welfare. Taking race into account is now an unavoidable necessity.

As long as advocates cling to the myth of a white welfare population, we will neglect the problems of racism, the issue of racial barriers, the extent to which race-related differences need to be addressed (Loury 2002). Such neglect is dangerous; it can ignore the systemic sources of poverty for low-income families of color. Yet this failure is not just a conservative deficiency but part of a pattern of political inadequacy among liberals unwilling to discuss what they see as troubling facts about welfare recipients.

While this gentility is understandable, it is also harmful. The unwillingness to address more forthrightly the racial composition of the welfare population springs in part from a fear that conservatives will use such information to reinforce their arguments that welfare recipients are "different." This reticence extends to discussing the "differences" associated with all single mothers on welfare, black or white, thereby often leaving the field open to conservatives to decide how differences are interpreted.

There are many parallels for this sort of reticence. For years liberals were reluctant to examine seriously what was alleged to be "welfare fraud" when recipients were not reporting all of their other small sources of income. For years, the topic was dominated by conservative viewpoints that led to the development of obsessive practices by states to hunt down and punish violators who failed to report all of their income even if it was minimal. "Welfare fraud" became another way to harass economically distressed welfare recipients and depict them as undeserving. Finally, after decades of a crackdown on these alleged abuses of welfare, studies such as the one by Kathryn Edin and Laura Lein (1997) offered an alternative perspective, showing that low benefits left recipients no choice but to supplement their welfare checks with unreported income. Unfortunately, by the time that Edin and Lein published their findings in 1997, the campaign to combat fraud and withhold aid from "cheaters" had held down welfare benefits for over two decades so that they had on average declined in real value by over 40 percent since the early 1970s (Moffitt 1992). The prior failure to join the discussion about the issue of "welfare fraud" was therefore at best unhelpful. At worst, this lapse in political courage provided an opening for conservatives to frame the issue of unreported income in the worst possible light as "welfare fraud." This in turn enabled states to tighten access and reduce benefits, in effect punishing people in most cases for trying to survive by combining inadequate welfare benefits with small amounts of unreported income.

Reluctance to discuss particular issues about welfare and poverty can have its negative effects. But the whole point of getting involved and discussing potentially difficult issues about welfare and poverty is to prevent those issues from being framed in tendentious ways. Talking about the disproportionate numbers of nonwhites receiving welfare does not have to involve Moynihan's "tangle of pathology" perspective. Yet, if only the Moynihans of the world get involved in highlighting the racial composition of the welfare population, that is just what may happen. Others need to engage these issues, not just to check the facts about the racial composition of the welfare population, but more importantly to address how the facts are being framed and how assumptions of otherness inform the interpretation of those facts.

Visualizing Race

The issue of racialized depictions of welfare recipients is not just a problem of numbers. It is perhaps an even greater problem when we turn to visual culture. For a long time, there has been a great concern that showing pictures of African Americans on welfare reinforces the stereotype that welfare is strictly a "black" program. Such pictures inevitably risk reinscribing the notion that only blacks use welfare because there is something in their personal characteristics, behavior, and culture that leads them to rely on welfare. These images reinforce the worst racist stereotypes about why African Americans use welfare.

A cultural dynamic underlies racialized images. The denigration of "black" supports the privileging of "white." The socially constructed designation of "black" is continually manufactured and given life largely to sustain the privileges associated with the category of "white." Therefore, if "black" had not existed, then in the quest to validate "white" identity and culture, something else would have been created. Hortense Spillers has stated: "Let's face it. I am a marked woman, but not everybody knows my name. . . . 'Sapphire' . . . or 'Black Woman at the Podium': I describe a locus of confounded identities, a meeting ground of investments and privations in the national treasury of rhetorical wealth. My country needs me, and if I were not here, I would have been invented" (quoted in Lubiano 1992, 323). In a more abstract register, Slavoj Žižek has pointed toward how the "black welfare queen" has been constructed out of need for an "other" to legitimate the middle-class white man of virtue who practices personal responsibility and has no need for assistance from the government. Žižek adds:

> [E]ach universal ideological notion is always hegemonized by some particular content which colours its very universality and accounts for its efficiency. In the rejection of the social welfare system by the New Right in the US, for example, the universal notion of the welfare system as inefficient is sustained by the pseudo-concrete representation of the notorious African American single mother, as if, in the last resort, social welfare is a programme for black single mothers—the particular case of the "single black mother" is silently conceived as "typical" of social welfare and of what is wrong with it. . . . Another name for this short-circuit between the Universal and the Particular is, of course, "suture": the operation of hegemony "sutures" the empty Universal to a particular content. (Žižek 1997, 28–29)

Žižek emphasizes that the abstract categories need to be filled with content from the experienced world of social relations. The idea of a welfare queen is one of black single mothers who rely on public assistance, making the abstract idea seem more credible and consistent with real life. Yet most women on welfare are not as the stereotype depicts—that is, they are not lazy, unmotivated, irresponsible, promiscuous, and so on. They are often actually "heroes of their own lives," exercising initiative and independence by putting themselves on welfare in order to make the best of a bad situation and provide for their children (Gordon 1988). Furthermore, most white middle-class "men of virtue" rely on the government for various tax advantages, subsidies, and other forms of assistance. Nonetheless, the contrast between "black welfare queen" and "white middle-class man of virtue" resonates very strongly in popular culture, scholarly critiques notwithstanding.

Images of women on welfare reinforce this biased distinction and reinscribe black inferiority and white supremacy. The history of depictions of African Americans in the United States has created a reservoir of racist iconography, and the exploitation of black images to access white privilege is a recurrent pattern in our culture. We need reach no farther than the now repudiated practice of white entertainers performing in blackface, beginning in the 1840s in minstrel shows and becoming popular first among Irish, and eventually among Jewish, entertainers.

> Blackface is a form of cross-dressing, in which one puts on the insignias of sex, class or race that stands in binary opposition to one's own. . . . Assimilation is achieved via the mask of the most segregated; the blackface that offers Jews mobility keeps blacks fixed in place. Rabinowitz turns into Robin, but the fundamental binary opposition nevertheless remains. That segregation, imposed on blacks, silences their voices and sings their names. (Rogin 1996, 30, 112)

Blackface facilitated assimilation for white immigrants, demonstrating their whiteness—after all, they needed to paint their faces to look black. The Jew was white because he was not black until painted. In this way, the cultural dynamic of invoking black in order to privilege white is enacted once again.

The creation of whiteness via the denigration of blackness is an immense topic that has only begun to receive serious study by white scholars in recent years (Roediger 1991; Frankenberg 1993; Ignatiev 1995). Yet African American intellectuals have been commenting on it for decades, highlighting that becoming white was the goal of many immigrants. This made the American Dream something that was inaccessible to African Americans. James Baldwin once emphasized:

> No one was white before he/she came to America. . . . It took generations and a vast amount of coercion before this became a white country . . . There is an Irish community. . . . There is a German community. . . . There is a Jewish community. . . . There are English communities. There are French communities. . . . Jews came here from countries where they were not white, and they came here in part because they were not white. . . . Everyone who got here, and paid the price of the ticket, the price was to become "white." (1984, 90–92)

The use of "black" to legitimate "white" has in recent years remained prevalent. In a controversial photograph, Christie Todd Whitman, former governor of New Jersey, was caught on film frisking an innocent black man, for what purpose remains unknown. One possible explanation is the imbrication of race and gender: a female Republican governor felt the need to prove she was as tough as some of her white, male conservative party members when it came to cracking down on crime. In the photo Whitman is dressed in white, frisking a black male, underscoring her claiming access to white male privilege. As a woman, she was adopting the traditional role of the white male overlord. She was exploiting a black man to prove she was tough enough to be like a white man herself. She erased her gender on the back of a black man.

With this visual display, her wish to be not just Governor Whitman but also Governor *White*man was fulfilled.[7] In the process, she unwittingly ratified the practice of racial profiling by the New Jersey state troopers. The systematic stopping and harassing of African American motorists on the New Jersey Turnpike was to continue even after the state settled out of court in a controversial case on the matter. In that case, the state all but admitted responsibility for the shooting of two black and one Latino young males. Sufficient evidence had been produced, including the picture, about the state's willingness to allow racial profiling to continue (Peterson and Halbfinger 2001). The racist practices of the state police were not to be repudiated until Whitman left to assume the head of the federal agency that was dedicated to making our environment clean. The racial connotations, from white clothes to clean environment, make the Whitman photo all the more troubling.

Therefore, racialized images have a long history of reinforcing white privilege in the broader society and not just in welfare. This history makes thoughtful people understandably reluctant to put a black face on welfare. The photograph in figure 8.2 is on the cover of Martin Gilens's book on the racialization of welfare promoted by the media from the 1960s. His editors probably did not put an African American woman on the cover in part because his main thesis is that beginning in the 1960s, the overrepresentation of African Americans in stories and accompanying pictures about welfare led to increased opposition to the welfare program.

Yet Gilens's cover suggests that something else is at work as well. The hand shown is ambiguously multishaded, forcing viewers to make their own judgment about who is taking welfare and why. In this sense, the photograph is what W. J. T. Mitchell (1994) calls a "metapicture"—a representation that refers not so much to a visualized object but more

Fig. 8.2.   The cover of *Why Americans Hate Welfare* by Martin Gilens (1999).

importantly to the process of visualization. This metapicture suggests that all representations require the work of viewing subjects to make the viewed object coherent and that these judgments are to varying degrees grounded in the prevailing culture.[8] White viewers were often thinking negatively about persons of color on welfare even before reading slanted news stories. As it turns out, the racially ambiguous hand proved to be too troublesome an image and was removed from the cover with the publication of the paperback version of the book (Tryneski 2001).

Racialized images of women on welfare are often interpreted in ways that reinforce prevailing biases against persons of color, women, and public assistance (Schram 2000). Such images are critical to reinforcing white privilege in society. Yet my major point is that these pictures do not do this all by themselves. They require an act of supplementation. Paul de Man (1986) once defined reading as supplying what is missing to a text. Texts are inert until they are read; reading breathes lives into them, making them interpretable. The net result is that each reading supplies its own text, making the idea of one objective reading of any text unattainable and the definitive meaning of any text something that is infinitely deferred and ultimately undecidable. And we are in turn are shaped by texts in less than predictable ways. The same is true with pictures. Pictures are nothing until they are seen. What we see is an act of visualization, as multivalent and polyoptic as texts are undecidable. Every picture produces as many visualizations as the number of people who see it. Maybe more. This is Mitchell's point about what the metapicture tells us. It teaches us about visualization in the abstract, overall, in general; and part of that act of visualization is its unavoidably subjective character inevitably destined to produce multiple readings that loop back to influence their viewers in multiple ways.

A larger point here is that visualization is a dynamic process; it is not one in which pictures impose their imagery on passive viewers. Viewers must be enlisted into the viewing process in order for visualization to occur. Pictures of black women on welfare do not in and of themselves mean anything in particular. They need to be visualized; they need viewers to interpret them before they can become meaningful representations. And when viewers draw on the rich cultural traditions of reconstructing white privilege on the backs of black people, then pictures of African American women on welfare take on an added significance, signifying black inferiority in the name of consolidating white supremacy (see Mendelberg 1997).

Therefore, we need to go beyond Gilens's analysis. It is not enough to emphasize that the mass media exaggerate the extent to which the welfare population includes African Americans. We need also to explain how our culture primes people to read news reports and images in a certain way. Of one such image that appeared in the press in the wake of welfare reform, I have written (Schram 2000):

> The woman depicted . . . had in 1997 been sanctioned to the point where she was being removed from the welfare rolls. Reduced to cooking family meals on an outdoor grill, she sits outside and stares blankly away from the camera while her teenage son looks on. She seems to be an

enigma, refusing to work and claiming undetectable maladies, though not even trying to defend herself against a welfare bureaucracy that rejects her story. Her inscrutability creates doubts in our minds, allowing us to decide that she is incorrigible in her insistence on taking welfare. Her passivity becomes a form of active defiance. Her blank face is a blank slate on which welfare discourse can write its stigmatizing story of the welfare queen. Her body language is therefore not of her own making but a discourse that reads her a certain way. Simply being there, in poverty, on the welfare rolls, in the backyard, cooking on the grill, she is open to being read by welfare policy discourse. Without knowing anything about her life, her personal experiences, or her hopes and fears, welfare policy discourse appropriates her body and judges her passivity as a willfully chosen dependency. (54–55)

Therefore, it is important to emphasize how the prejudices operating in society prime people to read racialized images of welfare recipients in particular ways. I also want to highlight how the prejudices of the culture not only reinforce negative views of welfare-taking by persons of color but also necessitate the greater frequency with which persons of color are forced to rely on public assistance. I feel it is necessary to put a black face on welfare *and* to make more visible how those biases are operating and to what effect.

Such pictures appropriately framed and placed may have several redeeming features. They can highlight in politically constructive ways how race and welfare are often connected. They can also if done in a sufficiently self-reflective fashion remind us that the act of viewing demonizes welfare recipients at least as much as the picture itself. If such photos even when they show women of color in uncritical ways are frequently read as telling the same old tendentious tale of black insufficiency, then we need to ask how and why these photos are read in such a demonized way. The answer, one suspects, will be found more in our hearts and in our heads than on the page or in the photo. And until we are willing to interrogate the rich cultural reservoir that funds such prejudice, the manufacturing and demonizing of black welfare queens will surely continue.

Putting a Face on Advocacy

The issues of representation spill over into questions of advocacy. A common dilemma among advocacy and welfare rights groups is who should represent welfare recipients in public forums. One response is to choose white, single mothers who have been divorced, who have only one or two children, who are in transition from welfare to work (Brenner 2000). The goal is often to suggest that welfare recipients are not different from the average middle-class family and that all families should be supportive of welfare because it is really a program for all of us, and all our families may need to rely on it at some time in our lives. This of course is not true. Most families will never need welfare, even during divorce. Many women do go on welfare for short periods of time during divorce; however, they do not comprise a majority of divorcing families, let alone all families, nor do divorced families make up a sizable proportion of welfare recipients (Duncan and Hoffman 1995; Hoffman and Duncan 1991).

Yet, there are more serious problems than the factual misrepresentations. Putting a white face on welfare and then pretending that recipients are just like middle-class families risks encouraging policymakers to reform welfare on the basis of that assumption. Then, we face the prospect that welfare policies will be even less attuned to the real circumstances and struggles that the families who need welfare actually confront. If we represent welfare mothers as people who are "job ready," who are only going to need to rely on welfare for a short period of time while they transition to paid employment, then we are more likely to get public policies that are insensitive to the fact that some mothers will need to rely on welfare for extended periods of time. Our policies may then neglect that many are not able or ready to secure employment that can pay them enough while they maintain full responsibility for their children on their own. This is exactly the kind of welfare reform we have been getting—reform that seems to be oblivious to the realities that most welfare mothers, of any color, confront. Presenting the welfare population as being just like the middle class leads to public policies that assume that welfare mothers can begin acting middle class tomorrow, when in fact many mothers on welfare confront dire circumstances that make that assumption ludicrous.

The more effective responses lie in recognizing the diversity of welfare recipients. Neither white nor black, divorced or unmarried, "job ready" or not, will do. Only when we begin representing welfare families in all their diversity, in all their colors, highlighting how many of them are confronting numerous social and economic obstacles, will we begin to understand the barriers they confront and can we begin to convince others to join us in trying to remove those barriers. In particular, we need to highlight that large numbers of welfare mothers are in very difficult circumstances that are often the result of having been marginalized by class, race, and gender discrimination. They are not ready to act middle class because the structure of society has ensured that their inequitable access to education, their lack of opportunities to form traditional families, their lack of economic opportunities, and their overall poverty were not of their own making but a result of being left out of the mainstream of society. Only when welfare recipients in all their diversity get to articulate in their own voices that they have been marginalized will we begin to see how putting a full face on welfare is a better alternative than whitewashing the welfare population with strategic misrepresentations.

Conclusion

The United States has a bifurcated welfare state (Nelson 1990). In this bifurcated state, citizens qualify for the more generous social insurance programs on the basis of their participation in the labor market, requiring others to settle for the inadequate benefits of public assistance programs. The privileged under this system can qualify for retirement benefits, survivor benefits, disability insurance, and unemployment compensation; those who have not worked enough in the right jobs or were not married to someone who worked enough in the right jobs must rely on welfare.

This bifurcated welfare state is based on invidious distinctions, socially constructed to achieve the political effect of privileging some families as more deserving than others. The deservingness of top-tier families is not the result of politically neutral, fair economic processes. Instead, the distinctions between deserving and undeserving are politically suspect, reinforcing long-standing class, race, and gender biases about which types of people and families are more appropriate for our social order. The traditional two-parent family with a "breadwinner" and a "homemaker" is privileged, especially families where the breadwinner worked in an appropriate job long enough to qualify for benefits. This privileged status was more often accessible to white middle- and upper-class families. It is no surprise, then, that the bottom rungs of the welfare state are disproportionately populated with low-income, non-white single-parent families where a mother is left to do the double duty of being a breadwinner and a homemaker for her children, in ways that make her less likely to qualify for top-tier benefits.

Writing about the conservative push for welfare reform in the early 1980s, Frances Fox Piven and Richard A. Cloward wrote:

217

[W]hen the several major policy initiatives of the Reagan administration are laid side by side, something of a coherent theory can be detected. . . . [T]he coherent theory is about human nature, and it serves the class interests of the Reagan administration and its business allies. It is the archaic idea the people in different social classes have different human natures and thus different basic motivations. The affluent are one sort of creature and working people are another. It follows that these different sorts of creatures require different systems of incentives and disincentives. The affluent exert themselves in response to rewards—to the incentive of increased profitability yielded by lower taxes. Working people respond only to punishment—to the economic insecurity that will result from reductions in the income support programs. (1982, 38–39)

There are therefore institutional roots behind the concern of reinforcing the idea that welfare recipients are these "other" people (Rank 1994). Highlighting that welfare recipients are different in any relevant way, including their racial composition, is at risk of being appropriated in service of the right-wing agenda to construct welfare recipients as these "other people." This easily slides into more ambitious attempts to "other" welfare recipients as deviants who fail to conform to white middle-class work and family values. Focusing on difference between welfare recipients and others can reinforce attempts to blame welfare mothers for their own poverty, allegedly attributable to their failure to try to be like the rest of us.

Yet, there is also the risk that if we fail to indicate how welfare recipients are different and why, those differences will not be taken into account when fashioning welfare reforms. Social policy becomes even more obtuse than it normally is, imposing an intensive set of assumptions on recipients and expecting them to live up to them immediately. Welfare reform becomes focused on enforcing work and family values on welfare recipients when they are not always ready immediately to take a job and work their way off welfare and out of poverty. Obtuse welfare reform that fails to account for difference can end up insisting that welfare recipients be "job ready," make "rapid attachment" to the labor market, take paid employment, and so on, without noting that recipients may, for instance, face race and gender biases and barriers in the workforce and on the job. In fact, that is what we have today: obtuse welfare reform that in its ostensible neutrality masks the extent to which it reinforces racial inequities. Such a racially encoded welfare policy fails to account for difference, fails to understand why the welfare population is disproportionately of color, and fails to try to do anything worthwhile to address the racial dimensions of our social and economic life that make race the salient reality of welfare today.

We need to learn to be able to walk and chew gum at the same time. One would think we could do that. We need to learn to see the difference among welfare recipients, including the racial difference, but not be so blinded to immediately assume that traits specific to these different individuals account for their being on welfare. We need to challenge how we see and how we think. Otherwise we will remain blind and ignorant.

In other words, it takes more than numbers and images to create racism. It takes more than statistics and pictures of black women on welfare to reinforce that they are undeserving. The racist premises that inform such interpretations must already be available before these pictures can do their work. Yet, given that those prejudices are there, racial representations of welfare need to be sensitive that they will possibly tap those reserves and reactivate such tendentious interpretations of why some people need to use public assistance more than others.

There is a need to acknowledge that race does figure into the use of welfare. The difficulty is in introducing such topics in a culture that is predisposed to talk about such issues in the worst possible ways, serving to further reinscribe the prejudices and racial barriers that create the racial injustice in the first place. Yet, until we find ways to talk about race and welfare, the predicament will continue. Persons of color, African Americans and Latinos in particular, will continue to be overrepresented in the welfare population; however, our willingness to openly discuss the racism and racial barriers that put them there will remain off the public agenda. The dilemma is that if we take race into account, we risk reinscribing racial prejudice; however, if we do not, we risk not calling such prejudice into account for the crimes of poverty that it has inflicted on some groups more than others.

Under welfare reform, as the welfare population becomes increasingly nonwhite, the dilemma intensifies. To get equity for welfare recipients, we need to begin highlighting their differences and their often inequitable situations. We cannot afford not to talk about race. In particular, we cannot afford not to talk about the assumptions about race that infiltrate discussions of welfare. Just as it takes more than numbers and images to create racism, it takes more than numbers and images to undo it. Examining these assumptions, more than waging wars of images and numbers, becomes critical to advocacy for racial justice in welfare in particular and in social relations more generally. As Paul Gilroy (2000) has suggested, to be "against race," we need to account for and take responsibility for it in explicit terms.

NOTES

1. Linda Williams (2001) uses Leslie Fiedler's distinction to suggest that in the United States historically race relations have unavoidably been dramatized in melodramatic terms of either "Tom" or "Anti-Tom" (as in "Uncle Tom"). Williams suggests that the entirety of race relations is always at risk of being discussed melodramatically in ways that do real injustice to its subject matter. She suggests that Americans to a great degree cannot talk about race but in melodramatic terms. Americans are continually talking about race melodramatically if for no other reason than that race itself is a melodramatic construction of questionable politics. This makes the choice to take race into account or not to fraught with political pitfalls that must be negotiated.

2. "The PSID is a longitudinal survey of a representative sample of US individuals and the families in which they reside. It has been ongoing since 1968. The data were collected annually through 1997, and biennially starting in 1999. The data files contain the full span of information collected over the course of the study. PSID data can be used for cross-sectional, longitudinal, and intergenerational analysis and for studying both individuals and families. The PSID sample, originating in 1968, consisted of two independent samples: a cross-sectional national sample and a national sample of low-income families. The cross-sectional sample was drawn by the Survey Research Center (SRC). Commonly called the SRC sample, this was an equal probability sample of households from the 48 contiguous states and was designated to yield about 3,000 completed interviews. The second sample came from the Survey of Economic Opportunity (SEO), conducted by the Bureau of the Census for the Office of Economic Opportunity. In the mid-1960s, the PSID selected about 2,000 low-income families with heads under the age of 60 from SEO respondents. The sample, known as the SEO sample, was confined to Standard Metropolitan Statistical Areas (SMSA's) in the North and non-SMSA's in the Southern region. The PSID core sample combines the SRC and SEO samples. From 1968 to 1996, the PSID interviewed and reinterviewed individuals from families in the core sample every year, whether or not they were living in the same dwelling or with the same people. Adults have been followed as they have grown older, and children have been observed as they advance through childhood and into adulthood, forming family units of their own." See http://www.isr.umich.edu/src/psid/ (accessed June 9, 2001).

3. The PSID's representativeness is subject to some debate since some families over time leave the study and the PSID did not include new immigrants arriving after its start in 1968. Yet, John Fitzgerald, Peter Gottschalk, and Robert Moffitt (1998) found "no strong evidence that attrition has seriously distorted the representativeness of the PSID . . . and considerable evidence that its cross-sectional representativeness has remained roughly intact."

4. The calculations in table 8.1 were graciously provided by Thomas Vartanian.

5. Boisjoly, Harris, and Duncan (1998) find, using the PSID, that the percentage black of all children receiving welfare in any one calendar year gradually moved upward from 1973 to 1990 from the low 40 percent range to 52 percent, suggesting that the black proportion of the welfare population was lower back when the press began to overrepresent welfare as a "black program" in the 1960s and 1970s.

6. For an alternative perspective, see Clawson and Trice 2000. They provide evidence that the mass media continued to overrepresent blacks in news stories about poverty and welfare in the 1993–98 period when welfare reform was being debated and assessed. While this is certainly correct for poverty, it is less so for welfare, if we compare their calculations to the various data presented in this chapter.

7. Steven Levine provided the point in conversation that Christie Whitman suffered from *e* envy. Lacking an *e* in her last name prevented her from being a *Whiteman*.

8. Michel Foucault (1973) has emphasized that pictures only become coherent by virtue of a "cycle of representation" whereby a circuitry connects a picture to interpretations by the viewing subject that are needed to visualize the viewed object. Foucault goes on to stress that the cycle of representation necessarily combines the *image* of a picture with the *text* of interpretations to make the viewed object that is therefore better conceived as a text/image, or what Foucault calls a "calligram."

Policy Choice &
Implementation

CHAPTER 9

The Hard Line
and the Color Line

Race, Welfare, and the Roots
of Get-Tough Reform

JOE SOSS, SANFORD F. SCHRAM,
THOMAS P. VARTANIAN, AND ERIN O'BRIEN

The Social Security Act of 1935 laid the groundwork for something poor families had never had in the United States: a federal entitlement to public aid.[1] Thirty-five years later, in the wake of legal victories in the 1960s, this entitlement began to bear fruit in the form of greater access and equity in the Aid to Families with Dependent Children (AFDC) program. By the 1990s, however, the political tides had turned. The Personal Responsibility and Work Opportunity Reconciliation Act of 1996 (PRWORA) abolished the federal entitlement to aid. In its place, federal lawmakers created Temporary Assistance for Needy Families (TANF), a system of block grants that gave states more freedom to select among policy tools but also imposed a forceful mandate to promote work, reduce welfare usage, and change poor people's behaviors. Public officials in many states moved quickly, and with considerable public support, to implement tough new policies consistent with these federal TANF goals.

In this chapter, we analyze the racial underpinnings of welfare retrenchment in the crucial years of 1996 and 1997. For the public at large, and for state policymakers in particular, welfare reform raised new questions about the terms that should govern aid for low-income families. Some states used their new discretion to pursue relatively stringent and punitive program rules; others opted for a more moderate course. Some citizens supported the most restrictive new approaches to public aid; others resisted the call to "get tough" with recipients. Accordingly, our analysis proceeds on two levels. First, we ask how racial factors might help explain why some but not all states chose to impose restrictive welfare policies in the name of reform. Second, we ask how race and racial attitudes shaped public support for such policies.

In what follows, we use multivariate analysis to isolate the impact of race on state policy choices and citizen policy preferences under welfare reform. In doing so, we consider a variety of alternative explanations for state- and individual-level outcomes. Our findings affirm that "get tough" welfare reform has had complex political roots. No factor, however, eclipses the central importance of race. In the period immediately following federal legislation in 1996, the strictest welfare reforms were significantly more likely to be adopted in states where people of color made up a larger proportion of the welfare caseload. Public support for these tough new welfare measures arose from many sources. But support ran stronger among whites than blacks, and within the white population support was significantly enhanced by negative stereotypes of African Americans and Hispanics. The entwining of race and welfare provision has a long and troubled history in the United States. Regrettably, our contemporary experience suggests that the past remains prologue. Much is new in today's welfare politics, but the "problem of the color line" remains.

Welfare Policy Making: A New Division of Labor

When the federal government abolished the AFDC program in 1996, it removed a framework of rules that had structured state-level administration of cash aid since the 1960s. The new block-grant system ended the federal guarantee of matching funds and allowed states to pursue a wider variety of policy innovations without seeking waivers from the federal government (on waivers, see Fording, this volume). Proponents touted the new TANF system as a "devolution revolution" that would liberate the states from stifling federal rules, allowing them to create more effective poverty policies. Such claims contain a grain of truth regarding shifts in the intergovernmental division of labor, but they also mislead by implying that states were given a historically unprecedented degree of liberty.

In the American political system defined by federalism, localism, and a relatively weak and fragmented national government, state-level politics has always played a key role in shaping the amount and form of public aid for the poor (Trattner 1999; Noble 1997; Skocpol 1996). Beginning in 1911 with mothers' pensions, and later in the Aid to Dependent Children program, state administration and interstate variation were defining features of public aid for poor families (Gordon 1994). In the wake of legal activism in the 1960s, the federal government applied a broad set of national standards to administrators (Davis 1993; Melnick 1994). Interstate variation, however, remained a signal characteristic of the AFDC program that distinguished it from the national system of social insurance coverage in the United States (Peterson and Rom 1990).

With welfare reform in 1996, states gained more authority over eligibility rules and administrative procedures than they had enjoyed for three decades (Mettler 2000). At the same time, however, the federal law imposed a variety of new mandates that constrained state lawmakers and bureaucrats (Kincaid 1998). The new law, for example, set strict quotas on the percentage of adult recipients who must participate in "work-related activities" and defined these activities in a narrow manner that left states with little room to maneuver.[2] Likewise, the 1996 law prohibited states from spending TANF funds on nonworking individuals who receive assistance for more than two years or on individuals who receive aid for more than five years in a lifetime.

The system of public aid established in 1996 can be described as one in which the states enjoy increased discretion in choosing *means* so long as they toe the line in meeting federally prescribed *ends*. In principle, this system permits states to make benefits more accessible to poor families and to enable clients to pursue new opportunities. Indeed, a small number of states have emphasized enabling and opportunity-producing policies, and most states have passed at least some policies that fall into this category (Berlin 2000; Massing 2000). Momentum for welfare reform, however, was fueled by perceptions that AFDC was too permissive, and the federal legislation in 1996 reinforced this zeitgeist by creating outcome-based penalties for states that did not act quickly to enforce work and lower caseloads (Bryner 1998). The result is that policy innovation in the states has been skewed in a restrictive direction (Mettler 2000). Many states stuck close to the basic requirements set forth by the federal government. But among those that deviated, the vast majority "used their new authority to limit access to social provision and, most especially, to shift the balance in welfare policy design from rights to obligations, imposing burdensome sanctions on recipients" (Mettler 2000, 26).

Why were some states more likely than others to pursue a welfare strategy based on restrictive and punitive policy choices? In what ways, if at all, should race be singled out as a factor that drove state choices to get tough with welfare recipients? Answers to these questions should matter to anyone who evaluates welfare reform because they tell us something about how welfare devolution functions in practice. Reform rhetoric in the 1990s promised a race-neutral process of policy experimentation; attention to the history of American welfare provision suggests reasons for skepticism about this claim. What is needed is an empirically grounded account that locates race among the variety of forces that actually drove policy choices once states were given the freedom to pursue their own visions of reform.

To develop such an account, we begin by identifying the policy choices that best capture the 1990s movement against welfare "permissiveness." We then develop and test a general model of policy choice at the state level. Finally, we turn to individual-level data to ascertain the sources of public support for get-tough reform. Drawing our state- and individual-level evidence together, we specify how and in which policy areas the roots of reform can be traced to the politics of race.

Policy Choice in the States

In selecting policy choices for analysis, we emphasized two goals: covering the major domains of "get tough" welfare reform and identifying the policy choices that were most salient in public debate and widely considered in the states. Surveying scholarly books and articles, policy reports, legislative materials, and mass media, we found a consistent emphasis on four key areas in which lawmakers sought to end permissiveness.[3]

The first focused on imposing obligations in exchange for assistance, especially the obligation to work. Here, the central policy choice for states was whether to demand work from recipients earlier than the federal requirement of 24 months. The second goal for reformers was to end long-term program usage. In this area, state governments had to decide whether to adopt a lifetime eligibility cutoff shorter than the federal limit of 60 months. The third dimension of reform focused on social behavior, especially the reproductive behaviors of poor women. Here, the most widely debated policy choice was whether to impose a family cap denying additional benefits to children conceived by recipients. Fourth, reformers called for penalties tough enough to force compliance with the new regime of program rules. Toward this end, states could choose a weak, moderate, or strong sanction policy to punish client infractions.

Accordingly, our study focuses on four types of policy choices. First, we analyze the factors that led states to adopt weak, moderate, or strong sanctions.[4] Sanction strength provides direct evidence of a state's willingness to restrict aid for families who are needy but deemed to be out of compliance with new program rules. In addition, states adopting stronger sanctions have experienced significantly larger declines in their welfare caseloads since 1996.[5] Our other three dependent variables are dichotomies that measure whether states adopted a work requirement stricter than the federal mandate of 24 months, a time limit shorter than the federal limit of 60 months, and a family cap denying benefits to children conceived by current recipients.[6] As a group, these program rules define the key terms of participation for citizens who seek aid under the TANF program; they also capture the most fundamental goals of 1990s welfare reform.

In analyzing these program rules, it is important to acknowledge that political forces, including race, may affect different policy choices in different ways. Family caps, time limits, and work requirements are widely viewed as complementary tools for combating "permissiveness," but each is tied to a distinct goal articulated by reformers: deterring childbirth among recipients, enforcing work obligations, and ending long-term dependency. In addition to variation across these three policy areas, we might also expect sanction policies to emerge from a distinctive set of political forces. Unlike the other policies, sanctions are broad punitive tools used to enforce a diversity of program rules that may have very different political constituencies. Because of this greater reach and ambiguity, sanction choices may be subject to a wider range of influences.

With these differences in mind, we pursue separate analyses of each of our four policy choices. These analyses make it possible to directly observe whether a particular political factor, such as race, relates to different dimensions of policy choice in different ways.[7]

Welfare Policy Choices: What Factors Matter? What Role for Race?

Existing welfare scholarship suggests many reasons states may differ in their willingness to adopt stringent welfare policies. We begin by outlining why one might expect a racial basis for state policy choice; we then turn a broader array of forces that seem likely to exert some influence. (See appendix A for all measures, sources, and descriptive statistics.)

Racial Politics

Welfare politics in the United States has always had deep roots in race relations. In debates over the Social Security Act of 1935, southern members of Congress managed to exclude domestic and agricultural workers from social insurance coverage, effectively channeling people of color into public assistance programs controlled at the state level (Lieberman, this volume). Many scholars argue that state administration of these programs continued to be shaped by race from the 1930s to the 1990s, and that programs associated with nonwhite clients are more likely to be saddled with popular hostility and punitive rules (Quadagno 1994).

State-level research on welfare spending and benefit levels provides mixed but suggestive evidence regarding racial effects on the financial dimensions of welfare provision (see chapters by Hero and Johnson, this volume). Larry Orr (1976), for example, found that after controlling for other relevant factors, AFDC benefits were systematically lower in states where black recipients made up a higher percentage of the caseload. In fact, Orr estimated that a state with an all-black caseload would offer AFDC recipients almost $2,000 less per year than would a state with an all-white caseload. Similarly, Gerald Wright (1976) found that all else equal, states with smaller proportions of black residents and more progressive racial policies (as measured by civil rights laws) tended to offer higher AFDC benefits. Christopher Howard (1999) finds that states with larger black populations offered significantly lower AFDC benefits as recently as 1990.

All of this evidence suggests race may have played a key role in shaping the ways states set the terms of public relief after 1996. Most existing research focuses on African Americans as the group most likely to be targeted by antiwelfare sentiment and less generous welfare policies.[8] Some observers, however, have speculated that "as the country's Hispanic population continues to grow, attitudes toward welfare and poverty may become as strongly associated with perceptions of Hispanics as they are now with perceptions of blacks" (Gilens 1999, 71). Consequently, we investigate two variants of our *racial disparity hypothesis*. The first predicts that tougher TANF policies will be adopted in states where African Americans made up a higher percentage of the AFDC caseload in 1996.

The second predicts that tougher TANF policies will be adopted in states where Latinos made up a higher percentage of the AFDC caseload in 1996.

Additional Forces Shaping Policy Choice

The roots of policy choice may be traced in many directions. Thus, to offer a reasonable assessment of any single influence, such as racial effects, one must build an analysis that addresses other plausible explanations. To do so, we turn to a set of contrasting (but not mutually exclusive) images of welfare policy as *(a)* an arena for policy innovation, *(b)* a site of ideological conflict, *(c)* an outcome of electoral politics, *(d)* a mechanism of social control, and *(e)* a forum of moralistic problem-solving.[9]

Many observers have suggested that policy choice under welfare reform might be viewed as a form of problem solving driven by concern over high rates of counternormative behavior (Bryner 1998). Specifically, the *dependency hypothesis* predicts that states with higher caseload-to-population ratios under AFDC in 1996 will adopt more restrictive policies under the TANF system. The *reproductive behavior hypothesis* predicts that more restrictive TANF policies will be adopted by states in which a higher percentage of all 1996 births were to unmarried mothers.

Our next hypotheses suggest that TANF policy choices may reflect relatively durable differences between the welfare orientations of liberal and conservative states (Rom 1999, 357). To begin with, one might expect states that adopted a more liberal approach under the old AFDC system to continue pursuing a more liberal path after 1996; states that worked to keep their caseloads down under AFDC might simply deepen their efforts under TANF. In contrast to the dependency hypothesis, this *continuity hypothesis* predicts that states that had higher caseload-to-population ratios in 1996 will adopt less restrictive policies under the TANF system. Looking beyond these past practices, one might also expect policy choice to be shaped by the ideologies of current elected officials. Specifically, our *government ideology hypothesis* predicts that states with more liberal governments will adopt less restrictive TANF policies.

An alternative perspective on welfare politics suggests that TANF policy choices might reflect each state's general propensity toward policy innovation (Walker 1969, 1971; Gray 1973; Berry and Berry 1990; Skocpol et al. 1993; Soule and Zylan 1997; Lieberman and Shaw 2000). The TANF policies examined here share a get-tough quality, but within a constrained area defined by the federal government, they also represent a form of policy innovation. Accordingly, our *policy innovation hypothesis* suggests that states with a stronger propensity toward welfare policy innovation (as indicated by earlier requests for AFDC waivers) will be more likely to adopt restrictive TANF policies.

It also seems plausible that TANF policy choices might reflect two important features of state electoral systems. To begin with, we might follow V. O. Key's (1949) classic argument that the policy process is more responsive to the needs of the disadvantaged when political parties are more evenly matched and, hence, forced to compete with one another for voters. Accordingly, our *interparty competition hypothesis* predicts that states with more evenly matched two-party systems will adopt less restrictive welfare policies. A second relevant electoral factor may be the degree to which low-income voters go to the polls. All else equal, stronger turnout among this group should push politicians to respond to the needs of the poor and working class (Piven and Cloward 1988; Hill, Leighley, and Hinton-Andersson 1995; Hicks and Swank 1992; Hill and Leighley 1992). Accordingly, our *lower-class mobilization hypothesis* predicts that states with higher turnout among low-income voters will adopt less restrictive welfare policies.

Scholars who analyze welfare systems as mechanisms of social control suggest a final perspective on TANF policy choices. In a well-known argument, Piven and Cloward (1993) contend that when hard economic times combine with civil unrest, relief is readily extended to mollify the poor and maintain legitimacy for the state. Under stronger economic conditions, access to public aid is restricted in order to push potential workers toward available jobs, thereby easing the pressures that tight labor markets exert on employers. Given the strong economy of the late 1990s and the relative scarcity of civil unrest, Piven and Cloward's argument suggests our *labor market hypothesis:* states with lower unemployment rates will adopt more restrictive TANF policies—especially in the area of work requirements.

Social control theory also suggests that TANF policy may reflect general orientations toward the use of formal mechanisms to enforce social order. Societies combat disorder through a mix of informal controls in families, neighborhoods, and communities and formal controls deployed by the state (Rose and Clear 1998). Greater reliance on institutional tools such as incarceration is generally viewed as an indicator of more political will to "crack down" on marginal groups (Hunter 1985; Jacobs and Helms 1996; Rose and Clear 1998). During the 1990s, this is precisely what happened in the United States. State officials throughout the United States passed stiffer penalties for criminal behaviors, increased funding for prison construction and maintenance, and imposed tough new work requirements on prisoners (Parenti 1999; Lafer 1999). Between 1990 and 1996, incarceration rates soared throughout the nation (especially among the poor), but the rate of this increase varied considerably across the states (Lynch and Sabol 1997). Following the view that incarceration rates indicate state dispositions toward tough formal regulatory mechanisms, our *formal control hypothesis* predicts that states with larger increases in incarceration from 1990 to 1996 will make more restrictive TANF policy choices.

Empirical Analysis of State-Level Data

To test these explanations of state policy choice, we conducted separate logit analyses for each of our four policies. The results, shown in table 9.1, suggest that the collection of hypotheses outlined in the preceding section have a significant amount of explanatory power. In each of the four policy domains, we find that stringent policy choices are systematically related to the state-level characteristics included in our model. Considering the four models as a group, we find that nine of our ten independent variables yield statistically significant results in at least one equation. In addition, the results in table 9.1 prove to be robust across a wide range of model specifications.[10]

Turning to our individual hypotheses, we see some striking patterns. In one policy area, work requirements, we find no racial effects at all. Instead, we find a tight cluster of determining factors related to our social control hypotheses. States with larger increases in incarceration from 1990 to 1996 were significantly more likely to adopt strict work requirements, as were states with tighter labor markets. By contrast, family caps and time limits—the two policies most closely related to program usage and reproduction—emerge here as outcomes directly tied to the racial makeup of recipients. All else equal, family caps and strict time limits were significantly more likely in only two kinds of states: those with a higher percentage of African Americans in their AFDC caseloads and those with higher percentages of Latinos in their AFDC caseloads.

Finally, in the results for sanction policy, we find a more complex set of relationships. Strict sanctions were significantly more likely to emerge in states with conservative governments, states with less vigorous party

TABLE 9.1. State Policy Choices under TANF

Dependent Variable	Strength of Sanctions		Stricter Work Requirements		Stricter Time Limits		Family Cap	
	Coeff.	SE	Coeff.	SE	Coeff.	SE	Coeff.	SE
Unmarried Birth Rate	.188*	.109	.040	.124	-.036	.108	-.090	.117
Caseload-to-Population Ratio	-1.319***	.447	.087	.367	-.274	.372	.016	.402
Government Ideology	-.055***	.019	-.022	.017	-.008	.018	-.015	.018
Interparty Competition	-5.441***	2.358	-6.17	2.315	-1.237	2.229	-.314	2.401
Low-Income Voter Turnout	-10.094	9.750	-2.975	10.447	-11.571	9.865	-12.453	10.150
Unemployment Rate	.333	.452	-1.048*	.571	.061	.501	-.854	.655
Change in Incarceration Rate	.010	.017	.051*	.028	.039	.029	-.035	.021
Percent Latino	-.019	.029	-.006	.034	.071**	.034	.087**	.043
Percent African-American	.039*	.018	-.017	.022	.049***	.021	.072***	.025
Welfare Innovation	-.202***	.073	-.078	.067	.070	.068	.023	.071
Intercept 1	-26.026	9.069	11.848	9.003	-2.454	8.200	9.199	8.203
Intercept 2	-22.521	8.788	—		—		—	
Overall model	$LR\ \chi^2 (10\ df) = 39.75$ $p = .001$ $N = 49$ $PRE = .46$		$LR\ \chi^2 (10\ df) = 21.10$ $p = .020$ $N = 49$ $PRE = .63$		$LR\ \chi^2 (10\ df) = 19.23$ $p = .036$ $N = 49$ $PRE = .30$		$LR\ \chi^2 (10\ df) = 20.13$ $p = .028$ $N = 49$ $PRE = .50$	
Method of analysis	Ordered Logit		Binary Logit		Binary Logit		Binary Logit	

Note: The significance test for caseload-to-population ratio is two-tailed; significance tests for all other coefficients are one-tailed. *PRE* (proportional reduction in error) estimates are based on classification of concordant and discordant pairs. All analyses were performed in STATA 6.0.

$*p < .05$ $**p < .025$ $***p < .01$

competition, states with higher unmarried birth rates, states that engaged in policy innovation by making earlier requests for AFDC waivers, and states that maintained smaller AFDC caseloads. But here again, we also see evidence of racial effects. All else equal, states with larger numbers of African Americans in their AFDC caseloads were significantly more likely to adopt stricter sanctions.

As expected, these results affirm that many forces shape state policy choice. Still, it is hard not to be struck by the prominence of race as an explanatory factor. Even after accounting for the effects of other state differences, the racial composition of welfare recipients is a significant predictor of state choices in three of our four policy domains. Racial effects appear in these models more often than do any other kinds of effects; and in two policy areas, racial effects constitute the only significant relationships.

How much impact does the racial composition of recipients have on state choices to implement strict welfare policies? One way to answer this question is to use an interpretive procedure developed by Gary King, Michael Tomz, and Jason Wittenberg (2000). After setting all other variables at their means, we can shift the value of each racial variable from one standard deviation below its mean to one standard deviation above its mean (for ease of style, we refer to these values as *low* and *high*). By calculating the probability of a policy outcome before and after this shift, we can estimate how changes in the racial makeup of recipients would alter the likelihood of a particular policy choice *under the assumption that no other state characteristic changed at all.*[11] Following this procedure, we find that as the black percentage of recipients rises from low to high, the probability of a hypothetically average state adopting strong sanctions increases from .05 to .27. A similar shift raises the probability of a state adopting strict time limits from .14 to .66. Most dramatically, it raises the probability of a family cap from .09 to .75. The estimated effects of having more Latinos on the rolls are similarly large, lifting the probability of strict time limits from .22 to .61 and boosting the probability of a family cap from .19 to .63.

Taken as a whole, then, this part of our analysis suggests that state actions in the wake of welfare devolution were driven by a variety of social and political forces. The racial makeup of the welfare target population mattered greatly, but its role varied considerably across policy domains. In the case of sanction policy, the racial composition of caseloads operated as one factor among many that shaped policy choice. In the case of work requirements, we find no evidence of racial effects at all.

In two policy areas, family cap and time limits, racial factors have a large impact *and* appear to be the only factors systematically related to state policy choices. On balance, these results suggest that policy devolution created new openings for racial distortions in the shape of U.S. welfare policy. In addition, our findings underscore that the extent to which "race matters" for welfare policy choice depends on what kind of policy is under consideration. In the following section, we turn our attention from state legislatures to the public at large.

Race and Public Support for Welfare Reform

Public opinion rarely offers a sufficient explanation for shifts in welfare policy. Institutional arrangements, organized interests, skewed political participation, and a host of other forces all function to refract the popular will (Noble 1997). Equally important, mass support for a public policy is itself a political outcome that hinges, in part, on the ways elites, activists, and mass media frame the issues at hand (Zaller 1992; Gamson 1992). Still, it is hard to imagine that welfare reform in the 1990s could have been achieved without significant public support. The link between mass opinion and public policy varies across issue areas, but majority opinion is generally a good predictor of policy outcomes (Sharp 1999; Stimson, Mackuen, and Erikson 1995; Wright, Erikson, and McIver 1987). In the welfare context, public sentiment tends to be strongly correlated with the ways welfare policies vary over time and across political locales (Wlezien 1995; Jacobs and Shapiro 1994; Wright, Erikson, and McIver 1987). Thus, to adequately assess the racial underpinnings of welfare reform, we must devote some attention to the distribution and nature of public support.

Advocates of conservative welfare reform contend that large majorities of the public support tough behavior-oriented welfare rules; this public support constitutes "the long-run explanation for the shift" toward conservatism in U.S. welfare politics; and the roots of this support do not lie in racial prejudice (Mead 2001, 202–8). Regarding the first of these claims, polls provide compelling evidence of broad public support for reform (Gilens 1999). To discern the meaning of this support, however, we consider it essential to note two points about public opinion on welfare reform.

First, the public as a whole is, in the main, *weakly informed* about what specific welfare policies do and how the 1996 reforms changed existing programs. Polls conducted in 1996, at the height of media coverage of reform, showed that a large majority of Americans supported the new legislation; but when probed, almost half of the public admitted they had not heard about it or did not know enough to have an opinion (Weaver 2000, 338). Thus, while a majority of the public thinks "welfare reform" sounds good, this majority is also unsure about what "welfare" and "reform" mean. Second, in addition to lacking information on welfare reform, the public is also *misinformed*. Research suggests that Americans overestimate the number of families on welfare, the proportion of the budget that goes to welfare, the level of benefits provided to families, and the percentage of recipients who stay on the rolls for long periods of time (Kuklinski and Quirk 2000). In substituting these stereotypes for facts, individuals also tend to exhibit overconfidence in the accuracy of their welfare knowledge and to resist correcting their beliefs when supplied with correct information (Kuklinski and Quirk 2000). Thus, calls to "give the people what they want" must, at the very least, take into account that the public might want different things if it were informed more fully and accurately.

With these points about the weak knowledge base of public support in hand, we can turn to our central concern: the relationship between public support and race. As a first step toward understanding this relationship, it is helpful to compare welfare attitudes among white and black Americans. In the United States, public opinion frequently varies along racial lines. Indeed, compared with other group differences, the racial gap has often loomed so large that some scholars have deemed it "the divide without peer" (Kinder and Sanders 1996). The racial divide, not surprisingly, is widest for policies that bear directly and explicitly on racial matters (Schuman et al. 1997). Nevertheless, the difference between black and white opinion on social welfare policy has tended to be substantial, and the roots of this gap have been traced in part to basic beliefs about the appropriate role of government in American society (Kinder and Winter 2001).

So, how did black and white Americans feel about welfare issues in 1996? The 1996 American National Election Study (ANES) provides a unique opportunity to address this question because it includes good measures of four relevant welfare attitudes: individuals' feelings toward "people on welfare," support for welfare spending, and support for time limits and family caps.[12] Assessing these measures as a group, we find consistent evidence of a racial gap. As measured by a 100-point "feeling thermometer," black respondents held considerably warmer feelings toward welfare recipients than did their white counterparts (a black mean of 62.5 vs. a white mean of 49.5). Similarly, while only a 40 percent minority of whites wanted to maintain or increase current levels of welfare spending, almost a two-thirds majority of African Americans (65 percent) held this position. Turning to the family cap and time limit policies, we find that these reforms drew majority support from both black and white respondents but this support ran stronger among whites. African American support for the family cap stood at 58 percent in 1996, while white support stood at 70 percent. Sixty-four percent of black respondents favored time limits compared to 80 percent of white respondents.

To further clarify the racial divide, it is helpful to use multivariate analyses that control for factors that might obscure or exaggerate racial differences. To do so, we rescaled all four welfare attitudes so that their values ran from 0 to 1 and then ran parallel regression models that assessed racial effects alongside the effects of gender, age, education, income, and region (South).[13] The results yielded several interesting findings. First, in all four cases, black respondents emerged as significantly more liberal than whites in their response to welfare, even after controlling for other demographics. Second, relative to the differences associated with other demographics, the racial divide was comparatively large. It had the third largest effect on family cap support, the second largest effect on support for spending, and the largest effect of any demographic factor on both feelings toward welfare recipients and support for time limits. Third, comparing the racial divide across these four welfare attitudes, we find an increasing order of effects as we move from the family cap through feelings toward recipients, time limits, and (largest of all) welfare spending.

The racial divide on welfare policy is instructive. However, the impact of race on public preferences in 1996 may also be traced to the ways in which racial *attitudes* affected white policy preferences. Contrary to myth, white Americans tend to support most kinds of public aid targeted at poor people; what they tend to support less is "welfare," a program label that has become synonymous with rewarding the *undeserving* poor (Weaver, Shapiro, and Jacobs 1995; Smith 1987a). Suspicions that "people on welfare" are lazy and socially irresponsible fuel a relatively targeted public desire to limit welfare spending and impose restrictive rules on welfare recipients (Gilens 1999, 174–203). To understand the roots of support for get-tough reform, then, we must ask why welfare recipients—virtually alone among the beneficiaries of public social programs—have been perceived in such a negative light.

Here, it is helpful to begin with V. O. Key's (1966, 2–3) famous dictum: "The voice of the people is but an echo. The output of an echo chamber bears an inevitable and invariable relation to the input. . . . Even the most discriminating popular judgment can reflect only ambiguity, uncertainty, or even foolishness if those are the qualities of the input into the echo chamber." What sort of information does the public typically receive regarding poor people and welfare recipients? Martin Gilens (this volume) finds that, from 1965 to 1992, media stories about poverty systematically overemphasized images of black people; moreover, the proportion of black images tended to rise in stories that portrayed the poor in an unsympathetic light and in periods of heavier welfare criticism. With this sort of "input into the echo chamber," it is hardly surprising to find that Americans tend to overestimate the proportion of poor people who are black (Gilens 1999). Moreover, as Avery and Peffley suggest (this volume), individuals who encounter media images of poor black people (as opposed to images of poor white people) tend to have more critical responses to welfare in general.

The critical link here is racial stereotyping. Despite dramatic changes in racial attitudes over the past forty years (Schuman et al. 1997), old stereotypes of black laziness and irresponsibility persist in American media and public perception (Entman and Rojecki 2000). Because Americans tend to believe that most welfare recipients are black, these stereotypes encourage the public to view welfare recipients as morally undeserving (Gilens 1999). The effect on public sentiment toward "welfare" is profound. Analyzing survey data from 1991, Gilens (1999, 96) finds that the perception that blacks are lazy is the second most powerful predictor of opposition to welfare spending. This antiblack stereotype is also the single largest influence on whether individuals believe that welfare recipients are an undeserving group—the most powerful predictor of opposition to welfare spending.

Based on these findings from earlier periods, there are good reasons to suspect that white racial attitudes may have helped fuel public support for tougher program rules in 1996.[14] Popular sentiment toward welfare, however, tends to be complex; its origins lie in a variety of nonracial considerations (Feldman and Zaller 1992; Sniderman and Piazza 1993). Accordingly, support for welfare reform among white Americans must be analyzed with an eye to how racial attitudes operate within the broader web of attitudes that shape public opinion. Our model begins with demographic measures that test whether support for reform was especially intense among particular subgroups of the white citizenry.

Specifically, we include measures of each respondent's *Age, Education, Family Income, Sex,* and *Employment Status.*[15] (See appendix B for measures and descriptive statistics for all individual-level variables.)

To capture the partisan and ideological sources of white opinion, our model includes measures of *Liberal-Conservative Identification* and *Partisan Identification.* In addition, we employ three measures tapping values that figure prominently in welfare policy debates: a *Moralism* index based on support for "traditional" family arrangements, an *Individualism* measure indicating whether respondents believe government should stand back and let individuals get ahead on their own, and an *Egalitarianism* index based on questions that ask about the desirability of equal opportunity and whether equality should be pursued more or less vigorously. Finally, our last variable in this group indicates respondents' preferred approach to reducing crime: punishment versus provision of social services. All else equal, we expect support for family caps and time limits to run heaviest among conservatives, Republicans, strong moralists, strong individualists, weak egalitarians, and people who favor a more punitive approach to crime.

To assess how white racial attitudes affect support for time limits and family caps, we employ separate measures of prejudice toward Hispanics and African Americans. The "prejudice scale" used here is designed to capture both the cognitive and affective components of negative group attitudes.[16] The scale is based on three measures of group stereotyping and one measure of group-based antipathy. The stereotype items indicate the difference between white respondents' ratings of white and black people, or white and Hispanic people, on traits of intelligence, laziness, and trustworthiness. The affective measure is a standard feeling thermometer score indicating how "warm" or "cool" white respondents feel toward black people of Hispanic people. Rather than pit these cognitive and affective elements of group prejudice against one another in a multivariate analysis, we use a single prejudice scale based on a factor score generated by all four items.

Table 9.2 presents the results of our ordered logit analyses of support for time limit and family cap policies among white Americans. Because our black and Hispanic prejudice scales are highly correlated ($r = .73$), we assess their effects in separate equations. Each of the four models shown in table 9.2 offers a significant amount of explanatory power, and each yields support for several of our specific hypotheses. The results for our demographic measures indicate that support for these two policies varied only slightly across social categories that might divide white Americans.

TABLE 9.2. Support for Time Limits and Family Caps among White Americans

Dependent Variable	Support for Family Caps Coeff.	SE	Support for Time Limits Coeff.	SE	Support for Family Caps Coeff.	SE	Support for Time Limits Coeff.	SE
Age	-.005	.004	-.014***	.004	-.004	.004	-.015***	.005
Education	-.017	.051	-.112**	.051	-.031	.052	-.090	.051
Family Income	.026*	.013	.026*	.014	.029*	.014	.016	.014
Woman	.381**	.150	.187	.150	.389***	.153	.163	.151
Unemployed	.061	.374	-.017	.371	.104	.381	-.059	.378
Liberal-Conservative ID	.178**	.073	.214***	.074	.144**	.074	.199***	.075
Partisan ID	.042	.045	.037	.045	.063	.046	.030	.046
Moralism	.035	.023	.018	.023	.040	.023	.022	.023
Individualism	.140***	.054	.115**	.055	.139***	.055	.121**	.056
Egalitarianism	-.060***	.024	-.049*	.025	-.066***	.025	-.049	.025
Punitive Crime Orientation	.165***	.043	.144***	.044	.156***	.044	.136***	.044
Antiblack Prejudice	.022***	.009	.027***	.010	—	—	—	—
Anti-Hispanic Prejudice	—	—	—	—	.027**	.009	.034***	.009
Intercept 1	1.121	1.002	-.025	1.047	1.176	1.001	.083	1.020
Intercept 2	1.957	1.003	.801	1.047	2.027	1.002	.919	1.020
Intercept 3	2.893	1.006	1.965	1.048	3.973	1.005	2.111	1.022
Overall model	LR χ^2(12 df) = 130.8 p = .001 N = 751 PRE = .07		LR χ^2(12 df) = 128.9 p = .001 N = 768 PRE = .07		LR χ^2(12 df) = 134.1 p = .001 N = 733 PRE = .08		LR χ^2(12 df) = 125.8 p = .001 N = 751 PRE = .07	
Method of analysis	Ordered Logit		Ordered Logit		Ordered Logit		Ordered Logit	

Note: Significance tests for demographic variables are two-tailed; significance tests for all other variables are one-tailed. *PRE* (proportional reduction in error) estimates are based on classification of concordant and discordant pairs. All analyses were performed in STATA 6.0.

*p < .05 **p < .025 ***p < .01

Younger respondents were significantly more likely than older ones to support time limits, but this factor had no effect on support for the family cap. Higher education appears to depress support for time limits, but it has no discernible effect on opinion toward the family cap.[17] Women were significantly more likely than men to support the family cap, but no more likely to favor time limits. The effects of family income were a bit broader: wealthier white people were significantly more likely than their poorer counterparts to support family caps and (in one of the two equations) time limits. White Americans who were unemployed in 1996 held preferences for these policies that were indistinguishable from the rest of the white citizenry.

Turning to our attitudinal hypotheses, we find that support for get-tough program rules was in every case stronger among self-identified conservatives, but in no case did support vary significantly across categories of partisan identification. The results for our three value measures are equally clear cut. Strong moralists do not emerge here as a distinctive group. However, individualism and egalitarianism are consistently strong predictors of welfare policy preferences. All else equal, support for each policy was significantly higher among white people who held strong individualist values and/or weak commitments to egalitarian values. Finally, in both policy areas, we find that support for stringent reforms was significantly higher among white Americans who favored a more punitive approach to dealing with crime.

The results in table 9.2 provide consistent evidence of racial effects. Among white Americans, higher levels of antiblack prejudice were associated with significantly stronger support for both the family cap and time limits. Stronger anti-Hispanic prejudice had a parallel effect, producing a significant increase in support for each of the two policies. How much effect did prejudice have? Following the procedures employed earlier for our state-level results, we can use predicted probabilities to clarify the effects of group stereotypes on support for the new welfare policies. Holding all other variables constant at their means, we can estimate the effect that a change in racial prejudice would have on the probability that a white respondent would strongly support each policy. Shifting the antiblack stereotype measure from low to high, we find that the probability of strong support rises from .40 to .74 for the family cap and from .41 to .80 for time limits. An equal shift in the anti-Hispanic stereotype measure raises the probability of strong support from .40 to .78 for the family cap and from .40 to .84 for time limits. To put these probability changes in perspective, it is important to note that *in every model shown in table 9.2, the effect of group prejudice is larger than any other single factor included in our analysis.*[18]

Discussion

Perhaps the most central question raised by welfare reform in the 1990s was "On what terms should government offer aid to low-income families?" In this chapter, we have asked whether racial factors influenced the ways state governments and citizens answered this question. Our findings suggest a qualified but unequivocal answer of "yes." We do not find racial effects in every policy area; and our results underscore that race was only one factor among many that drove public and governmental preferences for tough new policies. In the 1990s, as in earlier eras of welfare politics, racial dynamics played out alongside a variety of other forces that shape state action and public sentiment. Let us consider each of our four policies in turn.

In contrast to policies that deny benefits to particular classes of individuals (e.g., sanctions, family caps, and time limits), work requirements impose a directive and supervisory system of behavioral controls on adults who receive public assistance (Mead 1997). Many discussions of race and welfare politics emphasize antiblack stereotypes surrounding work effort (Gilens 1999). Yet, our state-level analysis of work enforcement policy provides the clearest example of a case in which it would be a mistake to speak of racial effects in global terms. Our results for work requirements show no relationship with the racial makeup of the rolls, but point instead to a tight cluster of predictors centered on the social control thesis. Consistent with the formal control hypothesis, states that took the toughest approaches to incarceration in the 1990s were significantly more likely to pursue strict work requirements under TANF. In addition, we find support for Piven and Cloward's (1993) argument that when labor markets tighten, lawmakers will be more likely to use welfare policy to set the poor to work.

Sanction policy provides our best example of a case in which racial effects intersect with a variety of other forces to shape state policy choice. The imposition of strong sanctions was especially likely in states with large numbers of black welfare recipients. But strong sanctions were also significantly more likely in states with conservative governments, states with less vigorous party competition, states with higher unmarried birth rates, innovative states that made earlier requests for AFDC waivers, and states that maintained smaller AFDC caseloads. Why did so many different forces influence the passage of sanction policies? Here, we think it is possible to offer some reasonable speculation based on the fact that sanctions are not tied to a specific program goal. Punitive sanctions raise the stakes for clients who fail to comply with *any* of a variety of new welfare initiatives. As a result, sanctions may be attractive to proponents of very different reforms or to lawmakers who simply believe that threats are necessary to bring about change. This versatility may make sanction policy an ambiguous political object that is open to an especially broad array of political influences.

Our analyses of time limit and family cap policies focus our attention squarely on race as a central problem for welfare reform. In debates over welfare in the 1990s, the quintessential "welfare queen" was often portrayed as a black woman with a long-term addiction to the dole and a willingness to use childbirth as a way to prolong and increase her welfare check (Fraser and Gordon 1994; Lubiano 1992). Welfare reform raised the possibility of using new tools to combat these problems: time limits provided a way to cut off long-term recipients and the family cap offered a way to end benefit increases for childbirth. Based on evidence drawn from two levels of analysis, we conclude that race played a major role in shaping public and governmental responses to these policy options.

At the individual level, several important conclusions stand out. First, the traditional racial divide in welfare opinion persisted in 1996. Like other Americans, a majority of black people supported key elements of reform, but the level of this support was consistently weaker than what we find among white people. Relative to whites, African Americans in 1996 expressed significantly more positive feelings toward welfare recipients, more support for welfare spending, and less support for family caps and time limits. Second, our analysis of white support for family caps and time limits reveals relatively minor demographic divisions. The results suggest a broad base of support rather than concentrated support in particular subgroups. Third, we find that support for these reforms was driven by a variety of nonracial attitudes. The strongest support came from white people who identified themselves as conservative, embraced individualistic values, rejected egalitarian values, and preferred punitive approaches to crime. Fourth and finally, our results underscore the crucial role that racial and ethnic prejudice played in white support for get-tough welfare reform. Among white Americans, support for reform appears to have been fueled to a significant degree by prejudice against *both* blacks and Hispanics. Such prejudice proved to be a significant influence on white support in all four of our models; and in every case, it emerged as the most powerful predictor of white support for get-tough reform.

In our state-level analysis, we find that adoption of family caps and strict time limits was unrelated to any factor other than the racial composition of the rolls. From this evidence, we can only conclude that the "devolution revolution" has created openings for new forms of racial inequality in the U.S. welfare system. For example, because states with more black recipients have adopted stricter policy regimes, black families are now more likely to participate under the most punitive program conditions. Such policy disparities not only can produce inequalities in the distribution of resources, they also subject citizens from different social groups to systematically different treatment at the hands of government. Thus, a black woman who conceives a child while receiving welfare is now less likely than a white woman to live in a state that offers additional aid for the child. Likewise, a black client who misses a meeting with a caseworker is now disproportionately likely to live in a state where this single infraction results in a termination of benefits for the full family. White clients committing this same infraction are more likely to live in states that respond in a more lenient fashion.[19]

To illustrate the importance of such disparities, it is worth considering a single policy in some detail. In the period after 1996, sanctions emerged as one of the most pivotal TANF measures. Among policy factors, they became the strongest predictor of state caseload decline (Rector and Youssef 1999). From 1997 through 1999, approximately 540,000 families lost their entire TANF check due to a full-family sanction, and these families tended to fare worse (socially and economically) than families that left for other reasons (Goldberg and Schott 2000). Our analysis of state policy choice in 1997 suggests that one might expect a racialized pattern of vulnerability to sanctions to emerge in the ensuing years. An analysis of 1999 caseload data confirms this prediction three years into the life of the TANF program.[20] Among TANF recipients in 1999, 63.7 percent of black families were participating under the threat of a full family sanction, while the same was true for only 53.7 percent of white families. If somehow one could have waved a magic wand of racial justice and made the black percentage equal to the white percentage (53.7 percent), the number of African American families at risk for full-family sanctions in 1999 would have been reduced by about *102,000 families.*

Not surprisingly, state-level studies from this period indicated that TANF exits due to sanctions (rather than income increases) were higher among black families than among white families (Lower-Basch 2000).

Conclusion

For students of welfare politics, policy retrenchment in the 1990s offers unique opportunities for analysis. Citizens and legislators were confronted with fundamental questions about how and when government should extend aid to the poor. In a short span of time, the political process that set the terms of relief for poor families was replicated 50 times over in the states, each time under a slightly different configuration of political forces. Taking advantage of these circumstances, we have asked why some states were more likely than others to get tough on the poor by making restrictive policy choices. At the individual level, we have pursued a complementary analysis designed to illuminate the roots of public support for new welfare policies. Above all, our analysis confirms that, even in the midst of great policy change, race has remained a troubling and complicated political force in welfare politics.

Our individual-level analysis should give pause to those who celebrate welfare reform as a democratic expression of the popular will. In our view, it would be misleading and unwise to simply dismiss white support for welfare reform as an expression of racism. The sources of white support are diverse; and at any rate, ugly attitudinal correlates do not justify a suspension of democratic norms. But at the same time, we would not want to see too little made of the connection between racial prejudice and white support for welfare reform. White Americans' preferences for get-tough welfare rules cannot be adequately understood apart from their racial component. Racial prejudice is, in the aggregate, a significant part of what white support for welfare reform means. In this context, we believe that reflexive calls to "give the people what they want" should be subject to close scrutiny.

The same may be said of claims that welfare devolution will free states to act as rational "laboratories" of policy experimentation. From the era of mothers' pensions up to the welfare rights victories of the late 1960s, public aid for poor families was characterized by virtually "unregulated state discretion over eligibility conditions and the amounts of grants" (Rosenblatt 1982, 266; Patterson 1994). Historians have demonstrated that such discretion was used for a variety of social purposes. Program rules (such as "suitable home" and "man in the house" clauses) were used to control women's sexual and parental behaviors (Abramovitz 1988; Gordon 1994). They were also used to regulate the labor activities of the poor, absorbing them during slow economic times and forcing them to work when more hands were needed in the factories or fields (Piven and Cloward 1993). In addition, states tended to administer benefits in a racially biased manner, imposing tougher conditions for aid on people of color and using program rules to punish those who violated racially biased norms of social conduct (Bell 1965).

Thus, freedom from the federal tether in the first half of the twentieth century did not produce a detached posture of experimentation in state governments; it simply hitched welfare policy to social and political forces that operated at the state level. Today's TANF system exists in a political and legal context that makes it unlikely that the worst of earlier practices could be replicated. Still, an analysis of state policy choices in the 1990s suggests nothing so much as that the past remains prologue. Today in the United States, welfare policy is rooted in a rapidly changing but still-too-familiar politics driven by race and ethnicity, gender and family relations, class and labor market conditions.

New TANF policies include a variety of rules that explicitly target women's sexual and familial behaviors—measures designed to dissuade unmarried women from having sex, deter current recipients from bearing children, and promote two-parent family formation (Mink 1999). Likewise, work enforcement remains critical in the contemporary reform era, and it is being pursued most vigorously in states that have tighter labor markets and stronger tendencies toward incarceration. Finally, and most pointedly, our analysis underscores that race and ethnicity continue to be a major influences on the terms of relief state governments set for poor families.

Looking to the future, we are struck by recent evidence that caseloads in many states are becoming more skewed toward people of color (Schram, this volume). This development does not bode well for racial justice in the U.S. welfare system. At the same time that TANF rules are getting harsher, they are also becoming more detached from the lives of white Americans. People of color are disproportionately likely to remain in the tough new welfare system, and they are especially concentrated in states adopting the strictest policies. In addition, our findings suggest that a shifting of caseloads toward people of color may encourage a deepening of tough-minded reforms in the states. In the coming years, the American welfare system will continue to grapple with the problem of the color line. There are dangers here, but perhaps there are also opportunities to begin speaking with a louder voice about the corrosive effects of racial prejudice, the persistence of racial inequalities, and the ideals of racial justice.

APPENDIX A: STATE-LEVEL SOURCES AND MEASURES

Government Ideology, 1996: Ideological score for each state government in 1996. Range = 1.3 to 93.9, on a 0 to 100 scale, with higher values indicating a more liberal government. Mean = 39.8; standard deviation = 26.4. Source: Berry et al. 1998.

Interparty Competition, 1996: The difference of proportions for seats controlled by each major party (Democrat and Republican) in each state's lower and upper house. Range = .30 to .97, on a 0 to 1.0 scale, with higher values indicating greater party competition. Mean = .74; standard deviation = .18. Source: U.S. Department of Commerce 1998.

Low-Income Voter Turnout, 1996: The proportion of all individuals falling below the Census Bureau's poverty threshold who voted in the 1996 elections. Range = .34 to .62, with higher values indicating a higher proportion of low-income persons voting. Mean = .45; standard deviation = .06. Source: U.S. Department of Commerce 1996.

Per Capita Welfare Caseload, 1996: The average monthly number of AFDC recipients in each state as a percent of the total resident population as of July 1, 1996. Range = 1.9 to 8.2 with higher values indicating a higher per capita caseload. Mean = 3.96; standard deviation = 1.40. Source: U.S. Department of Health and Human Services 1997.

Percentage of Caseload African American, 1996: The proportion of each state's AFDC caseload in 1996 that was classified by the government as African American. Range = .3 to 86.2, with higher values indicating that African Americans made up a higher proportion of the caseload. Mean = 32.07; standard deviation = 26.51. Source: U.S. Department of Health and Human Services 1997.

Percentage of Caseload Latina, 1996: The proportion of each state's AFDC caseload in 1996 that was classified by the government as Hispanic. Range = 0 to 57.4, with higher values indicating that Latino/as made up a higher proportion of the caseload. Mean = 11.00; standard deviation = 14.73. Source: U.S. Department of Health and Human Services 1997.

Unemployment Rate, 1996: Official unemployment rate for each state. Range = 3.1 to 8.1 with higher values indicating a higher percentage of the labor force was unemployed. Mean = 5.19; standard deviation = 1.13. Source: U.S. Bureau of Labor Statistics: Local Area Unemployment 1996.

Unmarried Birth Rate, 1996: Percentage of all births born to unmarried women. Range = 16.0 to 45.0, with higher values indicating that unmarried women accounted for a higher proportion of all births. Mean = 31.30; standard deviation = 5.69. Source: U.S. Department of Commerce 1998.

Policy Innovation: The year of each state's earliest AFDC waiver request. Range = 77 to 97, with higher values indicating a later starting date (97 indicates no waiver requests under the AFDC program through 1996). Mean = 87.5; standard deviation = 7.1. Source: Lieberman and Shaw 2000.

Change in Incarceration Rate, 1990–96: The percentage change in the state prison population from 1990 to 1996. Range = –4.2 percent to 164.5 percent, with higher values indicating larger increases in incarceration. Mean = 44.9; standard deviation = 25.0. Source: U.S. Department of Justice 2000.

Sanction Policy by State, 1997: Range = 1 to 3, where 1 is weak sanctions (delayed and not applied to the entire family's benefit), 2 is moderate sanctions (delayed but applied to the full family), and 3 is strong sanctions (full-family immediate sanctions). The frequency distribution is 31 percent (weak); 42 percent (moderate); and 27 percent (strong). Source: Burke and Gish 1998.

Work Requirement by State, 1997: Range = 0 to 1, where 0 is a policy equivalent to the federal 24-month requirement and 1 is less than 24 months. While 51 percent of the states adopted stricter work requirements, 49 percent did not. Source: American Public Welfare Association 1997.

Time Limit by State, 1997: Range = 0 to 1, on a 0 to 1 scale where 0 is a time limit that is the same as the federal five-year requirement and 1 is less than five years. While 41 percent of the states adopted stricter time limits, 59 percent did not. Source: American Public Welfare Association 1997.

Family Cap by State, 1997: Range = 0 to 1, on a 0 to 1 scale where 0 is no family cap is adopted and 1 is where the family cap is adopted. While 41 percent of the states adopted the family cap, 59 percent did not. Source: American Public Welfare Association 1997.

APPENDIX B: INDIVIDUAL-LEVEL MEASURES

Based on White Respondents from the American National Election Study, 1996

South: Coded 1 for South and 0 for other regions, based on the state of interview (v960109).

Age: R's age in years at the time of the interview (v960605). Range = 18 to 93; mean = 48.1; standard deviation = 17.6.

Education: R's formal educational attainment (v960610). Range = 1 to 7; mean = 4.2; standard deviation = 1.7.

Family Income: R's family income (v960701). Range = 1 to 24; mean = 15.6; standard deviation = 6.0

Woman: R's sex, coded 1 for women and 0 for men (v960066).

Unemployed: R's employment status, coded 1 for not working and not retired, 0 for all others (v960615).

Liberal-Conservative ID: R's liberal/conservative self-identification (v960368). Range = 1 to 7; mean = 4.4; standard deviation = 1.4.

Party Identification: Partisan self-identification, measured on a seven-point scale that ranges from Strong Democrat (0) to Strong Republican (6) (v960420). Range = 0 to 6; Mean = 2.9; SD = 2.1.

Moralism: Additive index base on R's responses to four traditional morality items (v961247, v961248, v961249, v91250). Range = 4 to 20; mean = 14.0; standard deviation = 3.2.

Individualism: R's commitment to individualism, based on a question that asks respondents to place themselves on a scale that runs from "Government should see to it that every person has a job and good standard of living" to "Government should just let each person get ahead on their own" (v960483). Range = 1 to 7; Mean = 4.6; SD = 1.6.

Egalitarianism: An additive index based on six items that ask about the desirability of equal opportunity and whether equality should be pursued more or less vigorously (v961229–v961234). A higher value indicates more egalitarian views. Range = 6 to 30; Mean = 19.7, SD = 3.5.

Punitive Crime Orientation: Whether R favors reducing crime by treating "social problems that cause crime, like bad schools, poverty and joblessness" or by "making sure criminals are caught, convicted, and punished" (v960519). Range = 1 to 7; mean = 4.5; standard deviation = 1.9.

Anti-Hispanic Prejudice: Factor score based on R's feeling thermometer score for Blacks and stereotype items regarding laziness, trustworthiness, and intelligence. Range = 0 to 100; mean = 51.2; standard deviation = 9.9.

Antiblack Prejudice: Factor score based on R's feeling thermometer score for Blacks and stereotype items regarding laziness, trustworthiness, and intelligence. Range = 0 to 100; mean = 54.2; standard deviation = 9.7.

Family Cap Support: "Some people have proposed that a woman on welfare who has another child not be given an increase in her welfare check. Do you favor or oppose this change in welfare policy? [Follow up] Do you favor/oppose this change strongly or not strongly?" (v961321, v961322). Range = 1 to 4; mean = 3.1; standard deviation = 1.1.

Time Limit Support: "Another proposal is to put a two year limit on how long someone can receive welfare benefits. Do you favor or oppose this two year limit? [Follow up] Do you favor/oppose the two year limit strongly or not strongly?" (v961323, v961324). Range = 1 to 4; mean = 3.3; standard deviation = 1.0.

NOTES

1. We would like to extend our thanks to Robert Albritton, Jim Baumohl, Nathan Dietz, Richard Fording, Heather Girvin, Gary Krueger, Claudia Krugovoy, Julia Littell, Justine McNamara, Frances Fox Piven, Ellen Szabo, Greg Caldeira, and the anonymous reviewers for suggestions that helped us improve on earlier versions of this paper. We also thank Gary King, Michael Tomz, and Jason Wittenberg for technical help regarding their Clarify program and Robert Lieberman and Greg Shaw for sharing their data.

2. States were required to have 25 percent of the targeted caseload working 20 hours per week in 1997 and 50 percent of the caseload working 30 hours per week by the year 2002. Moreover, the law's definition of "work-related activities" limited education and training to no more than one year. Subsequent legislation restricted the number of recipients states could have in education and training programs to no more than 20 percent of clients counted in the work quota.

3. For elaboration, see Soss et al. 2001.

4. Our trichotomous measure is based on coding from an analysis by Rector and Youssef (1999). Sixteen states (Alaska, California, Hawaii, Indiana, Kentucky, Maine, Minnesota, Missouri, Montana, New York, North Carolina, Pennsylvania, Rhode Island, Vermont, Washington) adopted weak sanctions that permit welfare agencies to sanction only the adult portion of the TANF check, except in unusual circumstances. Thus, recipients retain the bulk of their family's TANF benefits even if they fail to perform workfare or other required activities. Twenty-one states (Alabama, Arizona, Colorado, Connecticut, Delaware, Illinois, Iowa, Louisiana, Maryland, Massachusetts, Michigan, Nevada, New Hampshire, New Jersey, New Mexico, North Dakota, Oregon, South Dakota, Texas, Utah, West Virginia) adopted moderate sanctions. Nineteen of these states imposed a progressive sequence of penalties, sanctioning the full TANF check only after longer periods of noncompliance or repeated performance infractions. Two adopted policies that sanction the full family check only under specific circumstances. Fourteen states (Arkansas, Florida, Georgia, Idaho, Kansas, Mississippi, Nebraska, Ohio, Oklahoma, South Carolina, Tennessee, Virginia, Wisconsin, Wyoming) adopted strong sanctions that eliminate aid for the full family at the first instance of noncompliance with a program requirement.

5. Examining caseload changes from January 1997 to June 1999, we find that states with stronger sanctions had significantly steeper declines ($F = 7.745$, $p = .001$). On average, the TANF rolls dropped by 31 percent in states with weak sanctions, 41 percent in states with moderate sanctions, and 53 percent in states with strong sanctions. These results are consistent with those reported by Rector and Youssef (1999) for January 1997 to June 1998.

6. Our measures are based on a report published by the American Public Welfare Association (1997). Twenty-six states adopted a work requirement stricter than the federal requirement: Arkansas, Arizona, Connecticut, Florida, Georgia, Iowa, Idaho, Illinois, Massachusetts, Michigan, Minnesota, Montana, North Carolina, North Dakota, New Hampshire, New Mexico, New York, Oklahoma, Oregon, South Dakota, Tennessee, Texas, Utah, Virginia, Washing-

ton, and Wisconsin. Twenty-one states adopted a time limit shorter than the federal requirement: Arkansas, Arizona, Connecticut, Delaware, Florida, Georgia, Idaho, Illinois, Indiana, Louisiana, Massachusetts, North Carolina, Nebraska, New Mexico, Ohio, Oregon, South Carolina, Tennessee, Texas, Utah, and Virginia. Twenty-one states adopted a family cap: Arkansas, Arizona, California, Connecticut, Delaware, Florida, Georgia, Illinois, Indiana, Massachusetts, Maryland, Mississippi, North Carolina, North Dakota, Nebraska, New Jersey, South Carolina, Tennessee, Virginia, Wisconsin, and Wyoming.

7. In an earlier version of this analysis, we adopted a more cautious analytic approach that took no a priori position on whether state policy choices should be treated as separate dimensions of reform or merely as multiple indicators of a single outcome. For evidence that separate policy analyses offer advantages over an analysis that uses a general index of policy severity, see Soss et al. 2001.

8. Consistent with this emphasis, Gilens (1999) reports that when beliefs about black people are compared with beliefs about other ethnic minorities, negative stereotypes of African Americans are far stronger predictors of opposition to welfare.

9. For reasons of space, we present only brief statements of our nonracial hypotheses here. For full discussions of each, see Soss et al. 2001.

10. To test the robustness of our findings, we employed a number of alternative measures for our independent variables and introduced a variety of supplemental controls into our models. For descriptions of alternative specifications and their negligible effects on our results, see Soss et al. 2001.

11. For a more detailed discussion of our procedures and a presentation of first differences with confidence intervals for all significant variables in our models, see Soss et al. 2001.

12. The 1996 ANES did not ask respondents any questions about work requirements or sanction policies.

13. Full regression results are not shown here due to space constraints; interested readers may obtain them from the authors on request.

14. Our expectation here is bolstered, in part, by scholarship that extends Gilens's (1999) research to the mid-1990s. Analyzing stories from 1993 to 1998, Clawson and Trice (2000) find that the public encountered particularly intense media coverage of poverty and welfare issues, and, as in earlier periods, this coverage was marked by racial bias. The authors conclude that newsmagazines painted "a stereotypical and inaccurate picture of poverty." Images of the poor were disproportionately black; welfare recipients tended to be portrayed as undeserving; and black faces predominated in stories that adopted a negative tone or emphasized unsympathetic traits.

15. We also tested a measure for region (South versus non-South). This measure yielded no significant results and did not produce any nontrivial effects on the results reported in table 9.2.

16. Our use of the term *prejudice scale* should not be read as a strict application of Allport's (1954) definition of prejudice as "an antipathy based on a faulty and inflexible generalization." Specifically, our evidence does not indicate whether respondents who score high on this scale hold demonstrably false or inflexible beliefs. Moreover, as Glick and Fiske (2001, 279) have argued, the scope

of prejudice extends beyond pure antipathy (contemptuous prejudice) to ambivalent forms that combine "both hostile and subjectively favorable beliefs about outgroups" (envious prejudice or paternalistic prejudice). We use the term *prejudice* simply to denote a negative evaluative orientation toward a specific social group (and its members) that incorporates negative stereotypes and negative affect. More data would be needed to tell whether respondents' beliefs are demonstrably faulty, resistant to new information, or devoid of positive sentiments.

17. The coefficient for education in the second time limit model falls just shy of statistical significance, $p = .07$.

18. For example, the significant coefficients in the first column of table 9.2 yield the following probability shifts for "strong white support for the family cap" (listed in ascending order of magnitude): Woman (.10), Family Income (.15), Individualism (.21), Punitive Crime Orientation (.24), Egalitarianism (.27), Anti-black Prejudice (.34).

19. For black-white comparisons based on 1997 data, see Soss et al. 2001.

20. The results for 1999 are based on the authors' calculations using caseload data from the Administration for Children and Families and policy data from the State Policy Documentation Project. Results are available on request.

CHAPTER 10

Contemporary Approaches to Enduring Challenges

Using Performance Measures to Promote Racial Equality under TANF

SUSAN TINSLEY GOODEN

The Personal Responsibility and Work Opportunity Reconcilia-tion Act (PRWORA) allows states considerable discretion in developing their Temporary Assistance for Needy Families (TANF) pro-grams. Although national TANF caseloads have decreased dramatically, recent studies suggest racial disparities exist in caseload declines, case management services, and employment outcomes. This chapter first pro-vides a historical context, outlining the importance of race in welfare administration and discussing why this context is an important factor in contemporary welfare policy. In doing so, it highlights the lack of national attention to the role of case management and labor market dis-crimination in explaining differences in employment outcomes among welfare recipients. Second, it identifies five key areas in TANF policy that are important in examining the contemporary relationship between race and welfare. Finally, it discusses the common approach of using perfor-mance measures to identify, assess, and encourage social policy goals. It proposes an extension of the contemporary application of performance measures in welfare services to include specific racial dimensions.

The Historical Importance of Race in Welfare Administration

Around 1910, states began to provide public assistance in categorical programs for particular types of needy people.[1] These programs, called Mother's Pension programs, were intended for children whose fathers were deceased. The mothers who received a Mother's Pension grant were regarded as prestigious. To be judged capable of living up to such standards not only differentiated them from the mass of paupers, but set them apart from the totality of mothers (Bell 1965, 13).

The state and the mother entered into a partnership in which both parties assumed certain responsibilities directed toward ensuring that a small group of needy children would remain in their own homes and be supervised and educated so as to become assets, not liabilities to a democratic society (Bell 1965, 5). The state would grant sufficient financial support to enable mothers to maintain "suitable homes" as determined by welfare administrators in local social service agencies. Home inspections, as well as character evaluations from neighbors, clergy, former employees, and relatives were routine (Bell 1965, 8).

Local discretion was the norm in mothers' pensions programs in all states. State supervision existed only in a small number of states in which there was state financial participation. Each local agency developed its own policies, practices, and mechanisms or programmatic accountability. Opportunities existed for discrimination in the consideration of applications within a state and even within a single county. Local workers infused policy terms with meaning, and in doing so, they tended to restrict the programs to white widows and move separately, but in concert, to protect their young programs from black and/or unmarried mothers who might attract criticism (Bell 1965, 19).

The Department of Labor conducted the only systematic study of the racial composition of mothers' pensions in 1931. This report contained information on approximately half of the aided families across the nation. Of 46,597 families, 96 percent of them were white, 3 percent were black, and 1 percent were of "other racial extraction" (U.S. Department of Labor 1933). African Americans were simply not eligible at the same rates as whites. Almost half of the African American families aided were reported by counties in two states, Ohio and Pennsylvania. The reports by the other states indicated that few, if any blacks received benefits.

In examining race, the Department of Labor noted,

Comparison of the percentage of Negro families in the total population of counties reporting race, with the percentage of the families aided that were Negro, shows that provisions for Negro families was limited in a number of States. The disproportion between probable need and provision is even greater when the lower income level of Negro families is taken into consideration. (U.S. Department of Labor 1933, 13)

Additionally, limited provision for African American families was particularly obvious in areas in which 19 to 45 percent of the families were African American. The most common tactic states employed was to avoid establishing Mother's Aid programs in localities with a large African American population.

The New Deal Era

The structure of the Social Security Act of 1935, which contained the Aid to Dependent Children (ADC) or "welfare" component, changed the dynamics of program administration. It shifted the emphasis from state-local relations to federal-state relations. The act stipulated that states had to provide a single agency to administer public assistance programs and allowed for federal supervision of state programs. But the federal supervision was quite general, allowing states and localities broad discretion in program administration. The guidelines included a broad definition of eligible children, general minimum level for stipends, and minimum qualifications for administrators and investigators (Gordon 1994, 274). Most importantly, the model state law distributed by the Social Security Board encouraged reliance on the "suitable home" requirements encoded in most state mothers' pension statutes. This model state law read, "any dependent child who is living in a suitable family home" will be eligible (Gordon 1994, 274). This subjectivity of recipients to a morals test made ADC a unique federal welfare policy in that state and local discretion were the central determinants of eligibility determination.

Most black people, still trapped during the 1930s at the socioeconomic bottom of the South, were excluded from or severely disadvantaged within America's original social programs (Weir, Orloff, and Skocpol 1988, 20). In order for the New Deal to become a reality, President Franklin D. Roosevelt needed cooperation from the southern coalition, which controlled both the House Ways and Means and the Senate Finance committees in Congress. To accommodate this southern bloc, Roosevelt and northern Democrats agreed to proposals of federal welfare legislation that continued state welfare discretion, especially in regard to eligibility determination (Quadagno 1988, 239). Southern leaders insisted that states retain the right to establish eligibility criteria and to decide who received benefits. They wanted to maintain "local labor conditions," which meant keeping black laborers in low-paying domestic and agricultural jobs. The great leeway left to the states in the legislation of the 1930s ensured that racist interests would control welfare coverage, benefit levels, and methods of administration in large stretches of the nation, and especially in the South, where the vast majority of blacks lived at the time in poverty and political disenfranchisement (Skocpol 1995b, 164). As Gary Delgado (2000, 2) summarizes, "In the 1930s, of course, it didn't occur to anyone that women of *color* might claim a right to welfare benefits. AFDC was intended to support the *deserving* poor (read: white and married) mothers and their children, albeit at a benefit level ensuring that they remained in dire, if genteel, poverty."

Many southern states passed additional eligibility criteria targeted directly at black women. During the late 1930s and 1940s, states created seasonal employment policies that cut ADC recipients off the welfare rolls during cotton-picking season (Quadagno 1998, 117). Southern states typically could "see no reason why the employable Negro mother should not continue her usually sketchy seasonal labor (Gordon 1994, 274). Many southern states required ADC mothers to take jobs whenever available, kicking them off the rolls under the institutional "farm policy."

The accepted rationalization by ADC administrators was that blacks "could get by" with less than whites. This discriminatory administrative interpretation resulted in striking differences in benefit distribution. In the nation's capital city, social workers had two standard budgets for relief benefits, a higher one for whites and a lower one for blacks (Green 1967, 223).

In 1941, there were three times as many families receiving Aid to Dependent Children in the United States as there were in 1933. This fact illuminates the dramatic impact that public assistance had upon state and local welfare agencies (Leahy 1941, 3). With the additional federal resources available to the states, all localities in states with approved plans participated in ADC and other social welfare programs. From October 1939 to January 1940, for example, the total monthly expenditures in the Virginia Program of Aid to Dependent Children expanded by approximately 50 percent (Commonwealth of Virginia 1940, 8).

As state reporting became more systematic, national reports of the 1940s and 50s began to document the disproportionate exclusion of black children. In 1941, the Federal Bureau of Public Assistance reviewed the ADC program in six states. They noted that "these policies were subject to a wide range of interpretation, and despite years of agency experience in dealing with families, 'suitability of the home' and 'fitness' of the parent were still indefinable" (Bell 1965, 40). In reviewing this type of eligibility decision the Bureau concluded that the emphasis was placed according to the importance attached to certain subjective standards by the community, the agency, and the individual worker. With no uniform guidelines in place, states and localities tended to fall back on the "normal" tests of legitimacy: status and color (Bell 1965, 41).

In 1942, the Bureau of Public Assistance studied 16 state programs. The most significant finding was the wide divergence in state attitudes toward assisting nonwhite and illegitimate children. No eligibility condition explicitly excluded them, but where the "suitable home" philosophy prevailed, their exclusion was endemic (Bell 1965, 41). As one such report indicated:

> the number of Negro cases is few due to the unanimous feeling on the part of the staff and board that there are more work opportunities for Negro women and to their intense desire not to interfere with local labor conditions. The attitude that "they have always gotten along," and that "all they'll do is have more children" is definite. (Bell 1965, 34–35)

Finally, the federal government had to provide leadership for its own program. In 1947, the federal government tightened requirements for states. It became mandatory for state agencies to provide that (1) no person would be refused the opportunity to apply for any categorical program, (2) the application process would be carried out promptly and efficiently, (3) each applicant would be assured the right to a determination of his eligibility, and (4) assistance would be paid to each eligible applicant (U.S. Department of Health, Education and Welfare 1947). Federal administrators fell short of forbidding the use of "suitable home" provisions. Instead they merely recommended that states repeal the suitable home eligibility provisions. This kept the discretionary door open to state and local agencies, which allowed discrimination to continue.

Despite the continued use of state and local discriminatory tactics, federal administrative changes began steering states toward more equitable program access. The strides toward a more democratic administration meant that black and illegitimate children were becoming increasingly prominent in the caseload, even in southern states. The states responded by explicitly defining illegitimacy as a "black" problem and by reframing their analysis to question the usefulness of tax-supported welfare programs. States redefined welfare as a set of governmental handouts to barely deserving people who might be trying to avoid honest employment. During the late 1940s and throughout the 1950s, state administrators and politicians began to reframe ADC from a benefit for deserving mothers to a handout for lazy poor people of questionable morals.

The ADC issue became politically compelling in part because opponents of aid to black unwed mothers suggested a direct association between the sexual behavior of these women and the money it cost the (white) taxpaying public (Solinger 1992, 42). As white unwed mothers were portrayed as a threat to the moral integrity of the family, black unwed mothers were often construed as an economic threat to the same white family. The money to pay for the consequences of their sexual behavior came out of the white family's wallet, some politicians argued, and seriously undermined its economic security (Solinger 1992, 42).

The most persistent charge against ADC was that these benefits were incentives for black women to have illegitimate children (Solinger 1992, 42). As "reproductive citizens," black unmarried mothers became the concern of taxpayers, politicians, and social service professionals worried about rising welfare expenditures and their ever-escalating costs (Solinger 1992, 49).

According to some analysts, the causes of illegitimate children among black and white women were very different.

> [W]hite girls were the products of complex, cultural patterns, refined community and gender mores, and traditional family structures. Aberrations within any of these entities, particularly the last, could cause psychiatric problems, such as unwed pregnancies. Black girls, on the other hand, were, according to this view, products of no such higher-order structures. Their behavior, in contrast to whites, was unmediated, natural, biological. (Solinger 1992, 43)

The number of black illegitimate children receiving ADC benefits was actually quite small. Of an estimated 2.5 million surviving children registered as illegitimate at birth from 1940 through 1957, 1 million were white and 1.5 million nonwhite. "It appears that the nonwhite population is supporting and caring for as many as 1.2 million illegitimate children without public assistance funds. On the other hand, [only] 200,000 white illegitimate children apparently are supported from sources other than aid to dependent children (U.S. Department of Health, Education and Welfare 1947, 36). This evidence suggests that illegitimacy rates were indeed higher among black women but that these women did not proportionally receive ADC benefits.

In late 1958, estimates made for 32 states indicated that the percentage of illegitimate children receiving assistance varied from 2 percent to 25 percent. An analysis of southern states is particularly revealing. In these states where per capita income was low, economic differences among races were profound, and a high proportion of the black population was in poverty, very few illegitimate children were receiving ADC benefits.

Defining "suitability of the home" in terms of illegitimate pregnancies was a very useful method of excluding a disproportionate share of black children. One of the primary reasons for the continued low rates of black and illegitimate children receiving ADC benefits was the states' continued use of "suitable" home restrictions. Despite the recommendations of the federal government, the 1950s witnessed an increase in state laws relating to suitable home provisions. Between 1952 and 1960 formal suitable home requirements were strengthened or adopted in Georgia, Mississippi, Virginia, Michigan, Arkansas, Texas, Florida, Tennessee, and Louisiana. The state policies differed substantially in their impact on families, but each in its own way helped to control the growth of the caseload and the increase in public welfare costs. In Virginia, as in many other southern states, ADC could be denied without making alternative arrangements for a needy family (Bell 1965, 178).

Nationally, dramatic changes on the political front began to occur in the late 1950s that paved the way for major policy changes in the 1960s. Racial tensions flared at the surge of the civil rights movement. The Democratic party courted black political participation in the North. Federal courts and welfare rights activists began to think differently about welfare. Civil rights activists claimed that welfare rights were no different from the right to vote or the right to ride public transportation systems. The implementation of ADC as an elitist policy for the few was no longer acceptable. All poor mothers and children deserved equal access to welfare benefits. But black and morally problematic recipients would not be so readily placed in a program designed to provide long-term support. These "new arrivals" to the welfare system meant that welfare was now in crisis and that work expectations would be clearly defined for members in this new conception of public assistance.

Civil Rights and the Great Society

During the 1960s, equal rights in social policies were one of many outcomes desired by integrationists. Government intervention for civil rights meant that the struggle for equal opportunity came to permeate issues of social policy (Quadagno 1994, 195). Especially in southern states, there was a direct relationship between civil rights activism and eligibility for welfare policies. African Americans who engaged in civil rights activities or who tried to register to vote were systematically excluded from welfare. During voter registration campaigns, county officials cut African Americans off the welfare rolls, suspended benefits, and warned that they would restore benefits when blacks "surrendered their uppity ideas about changing the local balance of power" (Quadagno 1994, 129).

Many southern states strengthened their already subjective suitable home provisions. Louisiana enacted a law stating that "no assistance shall be granted to a child living with its mother if the mother has had an illegitimate child after receiving assistance." Louisiana's attorney general ruled that the law was to be retroactive. An analysis of Louisiana's 1960 policy changes indicated that 95 percent of the children affected by their new provisions were black. About 30 percent of these black children were legitimate by any definition of the term (Bell 1965, 138). In less than 1 percent of the cases, financial assistance was discontinued due to evidence of neglect, abuse, or exploitation. Tensions began to mount. Southern states, with steadfast opposition to civil rights at any level, continued to strengthen "suitable home" provisions, even as the civil rights movement gained momentum. The federal government received increasing pressure from civil rights advocates to respond.

On January 17, 1961, the secretary of Health, Education and Welfare, Arthur F. Fleming, issued a statement regarding a new federal "suitable home" ruling to which states must conform if they wished to receive federal matching funds to aid needy children.

> Effective July 1, 1961, a state plan . . . may not impose an eligibility condition that would deny assistance with respect to a needy child on the basis that the home conditions in which the child lives are unsuitable, while the child continues to reside in that home. . . . It is of great importance that state agencies should be concerned about the effects on children of the environment in which they are living and that services be provided which will be directed toward affording the children maximum

protection and strengthening of family life. . . . It is completely inconsistent, however, to declare a home unsuitable for a child to receive assistance and at the same time permit him to remain in the same home exposed to the same environment. (Bell 1965, 147)

The Civil Rights Act of 1964 was designed to have an impact on racial discrimination by state and local agencies. Under Title VI, Section 601, "No person in the United States, shall, on the ground of race, color, or national origin, be excluded from participation in, be denied the benefits of, or be subjected to discrimination under any program or activity receiving Federal financial assistance." Civil rights legislation in general and the Fleming rule, in particular, made it clear that states would have to eliminate a major discriminatory practice in determining benefit eligibility. But the states were slow to comply.

In 1968, the Supreme Court's ruling in *King v. Smith* supported the path outlined by the Fleming rule. *King v. Smith* involved a recipient's challenge to an Alabama regulation that denied AFDC eligibility to any family in which the mother had "frequent or continuing" sexual relations with an "able-bodied" male. The plaintiff was a black mother of four children who earned a weekly salary of $16 as a waitress in Selma, Alabama. Her supplementary welfare benefits were discontinued after it was alleged that she consorted with a man who could provide parental support, thus making her children ineligible. The state accomplished this goal by defining any regular male sexual partner of the mother as a "substitute father" regardless of whether he actually provided any financial support for the family or had any legal obligation to do so. The family would become ineligible for assistance because the children were not deprived of "parental support."

The Court struck down the Alabama regulation and held that the state could not alter the federal statutory definition of parent to include a "substitute father." The Court also rejected the state's attempt to justify the regulation as a legitimate measure to combat the "immorality" of mothers of needy children. The Court held that termination of assistance to a family due to "immorality" was inconsistent with the "paramount" goal of AFDC, the protection of dependent children. The Court found that the Fleming rule prohibited states from combating a mother's immorality in ways that led to the denial of support for needy, dependent children. The Court's decision in *King v. Smith* sent an even stronger message to the states. The decision affected 18 states and the District of Columbia, all of which had some version of the "man in the house" rule.

In policy terms, this meant more black women and illegitimate children would qualify to receive public assistance.

Black women took an active role in confronting the racially embedded institutional structures. They formed the National Welfare Rights Organization (NWRO), a grassroots organization designed to ensure that black welfare recipients received the same benefits as white. Dr. George A. Wiley, who also opened the Poverty/Rights Action Center (PRAC) in Washington, D.C., provided the organizing vehicle for NWRO. Participating groups ranged from Mothers of Watts to Mothers for Adequate Welfare in Boston to Chicago's Welfare Union of the West Side Organization. By 1969, NWRO claimed more than 100,000 dues-paying members in some 350 local groups (Piven and Cloward 1971, 323). In the South, welfare leaders' homes were subject to gunfire and torchings. But the group continued to press for justice. One of their largest demonstrations was mounted in conjunction with the Poor People's Campaign.

On May 12, 1968, George Wiley and Coretta King, widow of Dr. Martin Luther King Jr., led more than 5,000 welfare recipients on a "Mother's Day" march in Washington, D.C. (Piven and Cloward 1971, 323). In 1969, 1,000 recipients and university students took over Wisconsin's legislative chamber to protest a cutback in welfare appropriations (Piven and Cloward 1971, 323). They demanded the same benefit levels and educational opportunities advocated under the Great Society programs.

There is no real way to measure separately the impact of the Fleming rule, the Supreme Court decision, and work by NWRO on access to welfare benefits. Attorneys and welfare rights organizers in the South estimated that tens of thousands of families were denied aid under discriminatory state and locally administered provisions (Piven and Cloward 1971, 309).

With the Great Society programs of the 1960s, the federal government's role in social welfare continued to grow. The main achievements of this period were to expand employment, reduce poverty, and improve opportunities for "nonwhite" citizens. During this time, the Johnson administration recognized that many low-income people might not benefit economically from more equal rights or employment opportunities. Johnson concluded that their skills were too limited to compete in the job market, even if the economy were booming. The new Great Society programming was designed to compensate for those deficiencies. But many of these programs, though passed at the federal level in the 1960s, were not "up and running" at the state and local level until the 1970s.

By the end of the "benefits access" storm of the 1960s, two facts were apparent. First, state discriminatory tactics that kept black and illegitimate children from receiving benefits were largely eliminated. The federal government strongly denounced such practices, and the states had to comply with federal standards in order to continue receiving federal assistance. Racial discrimination in access to benefits had been largely dismantled. Its successor was much more subtle. It revolved around disparities in education, services, and training provided by local agencies.

Second, during this same time, public support for these programs declined. As a result of mass protest, litigation, and new services—all focusing on welfare rights—local welfare agencies were confronted with an unprecedented volume of applications and unprecedented pressures to approve the granting of benefits. This welfare explosion produced "exceptional stories of welfare recipients driving luxury cars and using Food Stamps to purchase filet mignon and of women bearing children solely to obtain added AFDC benefits," stories "gullibly accepted by the public as the norm" (Cottingham and Ellwood 1989, 12). The image invoked by white Mother's Pension programs with mothers needing long-term public support to stay home with their children had been replaced by an image of black, lazy, mothers having more and more illegitimate children to stay at home and avoid personal responsibility. Welfare support was to be tolerated, not advocated.

Contemporary Welfare Policy and Race

The Personal Responsibility and Work Opportunity Reconciliation Act of 1996 eliminated AFDC as an entitlement and created a block grant for states to provide time-limited cash assistance for needy families. These state programs are funded under the Temporary Assistance for Needy Families (TANF) program. States may use their TANF funding in any manner "reasonably calculated to accomplish the purposes of TANF" (U.S. Department of Health and Human Services, TANF legislation). States have broad discretion to determine eligibility, method of assistance, and benefit levels. The discretionary setting of TANF is very different from that of AFDC because (1) the Department of Health and Human Services must determine that a state's plan is legally complete, but does not otherwise have authority to approve or disapprove a plan and (2) it is not clear whether there is any consequence if a state fails to follow its plan (Greenberg and Savner 1996).

Based on the historical relationship between race and welfare in the United States, several areas of TANF policy are particularly relevant and should be systematically evaluated to ascertain racial bias. These areas include:

1. Client diversion
2. Case management including client assessment; access to training, community work experiences, and education; availability of support services such as child care and transportation assistance; and the issuance of sanctions
3. Labor market opportunities and earnings
4. Time limits
5. Lack of uniformity in political subdivisions.

Client Diversion. Before a client can receive services, she must first make it through the front door. A key component of TANF policy is to "divert" potential TANF applicants by identifying their specific needs and assisting through other mechanisms, such as services available through other governmental agencies and community and faith-based organizations. Are minority requests for assistance more likely to be diverted than similar requests from whites?

Client Management. Case management is a key component of any welfare reform plan. An analysis of clients' experiences with their case managers facilitates better understanding of the nature of a program's "treatment" in practice. Case managers become agents of the policymakers and give a program model its concrete meaning. They operationalize their relationship between the client and the program be applying, in specific situation, legislative and regulatory directions about who must participate; in what activities they should participate, and what support services they should receive (Doolittle and Riccio 1992). How case managers complete these tasks will have a great effect on the program outcomes experienced by their clients. In delivering policy, public service workers or "street-level bureaucrats" have substantial discretion in their work. They are entrusted to make decisions about people that affect their life chances (Lipsky 1980). In this case, these chances involve the likelihood of self-sufficiency (Gooden 1998a).

There are four key areas in TANF where examining racial differences in case management is critical. These areas include client assessment;

access to training and education; availability of support services such as child-care and transportation assistance; and the issuance of sanctions. Client assessment is a core function designed to assess a client's skills and identify barriers to self-sufficiency such as developmental delays, domestic violence, and substance abuse. To what extent are minority and white clients assessed similarly and to what extent are they assessed differently? Are assessment tools applied on a race-neutral basis? For example, are African Americans assessed as frequently for domestic violence as whites? Are whites assessed for substance abuse as frequently as African Americans? The identification of barriers should be preceded by examining them with a race-neutral lens.

TANF stresses immediate job placement or "Work First." Especially during the early implementation of TANF, education and training support was very limited. Although it is well documented that earnings are positively correlated with increased education, if TANF caseworkers are implementing the program similarly across racial groups, then all groups should be encouraged to pursue immediate employment. A research study that examined the promotion of education by caseworkers among black and white clients in two Virginia counties found 41 percent of white clients reported their caseworker continued to promote education, compared to none of the black clients (Gooden 1998a, 28).

The same study also examined the degree to which caseworkers provided assistance to clients in securing child-care and transportation assistance—two key factors in a client's attempt to attain employment and job retention. Most respondents in the Virginia study expressed that they needed minimal assistance from social services in finding child-care. Only 12 percent of the white respondents and 14 percent of the black respondents sought such assistance. Among both groups, clients evaluated the caseworkers as helpful in providing a list of child-care providers and child-care options for their children (Gooden 1998a, 28). Over 66 percent of the respondents (68 percent of African Americans and 65 percent of whites) indicated that they had transportation barriers. These barriers included lack of a driver's license, vehicle, or gas resources. Although all of the respondents reported that caseworkers provided them with gas vouchers to assist with transportation, there were differences in the levels of discretionary transportation assistance afforded to each group. Forty-seven percent of the white respondents reported that their caseworker expressed a willingness to provide additional transportation assistance including helping them obtain a driver's license, a vehicle or vehicle repairs. None of the African American respondents reported any offers of transportation assistance aside from the standard issuance of gas vouchers. Clearly, client supports are a key aspect in promoting employment and economic self sufficiency. Do minority and white clients receive similar levels of support?

Under TANF, caseworkers may issue a financial sanction for welfare clients who do not comply with program rules and work activities without good cause. Deciding whether to issue a sanction or to excuse nonparticipation based on good cause is an area of caseworker discretion. A study of five panhandle counties in Florida found blacks were much more likely to be sanctioned for noncompliance than their white counterparts (61 percent versus 48.4 percent) (Clarke, Jarmon, and Langley 1999, 130). Are sanctions and good causes issued in a race-neutral manner?

Labor Market Opportunities and Earnings. The PRWORA does not directly consider the role of labor market discrimination as affecting employment outcomes for minority welfare clients, thus presenting an important welfare policy paradox: A clear expectation of employment for welfare clients coexists with well-documented labor market discrimination against racial minorities.

It is clear from past and contemporary research that the U.S. labor market is discriminatory (Turner, Fix, and Stuyk 1991; Wilson 1996; Fix and Turner 1999) and that racial discrimination is a major cause of poverty among racial minorities, especially African Americans (Blalock 1967; Blauner 1972; Dowdall 1974; Glenn 1966; Jones 1972; Siegel 1965). What is less clear is how this discrimination systematically or uniquely affects minority welfare recipients as they attempt to secure, retain, and advance in their employment. Specifically, how does labor market discrimination impact the ability to meet the employment goals of TANF for minority welfare clients? And how do factors such as geographical location, industry type, percentage of minority-owned businesses, and employer size affect the degree to which labor market discrimination is a barrier to employment?

PRWORA does not consider the role of labor market discrimination in the written guidelines of TANF, despite policy consideration of other labor market conditions. For example, TANF guidelines allow a state to exempt additional clients from participation if the state experiences a high unemployment rate. The reasoning is that high unemployment rates systematically reduce opportunities for employment, thus limiting a state or locality's ability to meet the employment goals of TANF. How is the role of labor market discrimination different? Attempting to minimize the impact of labor market discrimination is an obvious factor that can contribute to whether a minority welfare client achieves employment success, both over the short and long terms. Hence, the noticeable absence of labor market discrimination in the national welfare policy discussion defies logical reasoning.

Even among working former recipients of welfare, racial differences occur. Clarke, Jarmon, and Langley (1999) found a 35 percent differential in postwelfare poverty figures, with white respondents reporting a mean income of $10,403, compared to $6,736 for blacks (122). When examining employer demand for welfare recipients in four urban cities, Holzer and Stoll (2000) found that "relative to their white counterparts, black and Hispanic welfare recipients are less likely to be hired in suburban and/or smaller establishments, and for blacks, in the retail trade industries" (26).

There are a few studies that suggest favorable outcomes for minorities under TANF. Studies in Arizona, Georgia, and Ohio suggest that the percentages of blacks who are employed exceed the percentages of whites who are employed and even report somewhat higher quarterly earnings (Savner 2000). Holzer and Stoll (2000) also report employer demand for all racial groups of welfare recipients is somewhat higher in minority-owned businesses and that contact with the relevant local agencies is associated with substantial increases in demand for white and black recipients when initiated by agencies and especially for Hispanics when initiated by firms (35).

Time Limits.   Under PRWORA, a state is prohibited from using federal TANF funds to provide assistance to a family who has received federal TANF assistance for 60 months. However, states may provide hardship exceptions for up to 20 percent of the average monthly number of families receiving TANF assistance (Greenberg and Savner 1996). States determine the criteria for a hardship exemption. What will be the racial composition of these exempted populations? Will these determinations include a racial bias?

Lack of Uniformity in Political Subdivisions.   Although state plans must include outlines of how the state intends to conduct a program designed to serve all political subdivisions in the state, this plan does not have to operate in a uniform manner. As the devolution of welfare reform moves from the state to the local level, will there be key programmatic differences between those operating in counties with a high minority welfare caseload and counties with mostly white welfare recipients? For example, will there be differences in the promotion of education at the agency level?

Lack of Rigorous Evaluation Requirements. Current evaluation standards of PRWORA do not require evaluation of racial disparities or bias. The Department of Health and Human Services (HHS) conducts research on the benefits, effects, and costs of operating different state programs funded under TANF, including time limits relating to eligibility for assistance. HHS can also assist states in developing their evaluation plans, but these evaluation plans are largely state-directed. Will state evaluation plans examine racial disparities in services and outcomes? Why would a state self-select to hold itself accountable along goals of racial equality and fairness? Are their data systems being developed to support such an analysis?

As with any policy, the values of PRWORA are best learned through the actual language of the legislation. Three years after the passage of PRWORA, the Health and Human Services Office for Civil Rights issued guidance on civil rights laws and welfare reform "to help states and other public entities comply with federal civil rights laws as they implement their welfare reform programs and create new programs" (U.S. Department of Health and Human Services 1999). Federal laws[2] prohibiting discrimination in federally funded programs and activities on the basis of race, color, national origin, sex, disability, and age have applied to the TANF program since its inception (U.S. Department of Health and Human Services 1999). By law, welfare programs may not exclude, deny, or impose different standards or procedures in benefit determination on the basis of race, color, national origin, disability, age, or sex. Moreover, "a welfare office may not refuse to provide translated written materials to applicants when a significant proportion are limited English proficient" (U.S. Department of Health and Human Services 1999, 2). However, a study of the Hmong population in Wisconsin found that 67 percent could not communicate with their caseworkers and 87 percent could not read the welfare program's materials (Moore and Selkowe 1999, ii).

Civil rights legislation is a necessary, but not sufficient, component to promote equality of access to welfare services, supports, and employment opportunities. The U.S. social policy record suggests that achieving such equality will need concerted attention. The implementation of performance measures may offer hope in promoting racial equality at the street level.

The Role of Performance Measures in Welfare Reform

Through measurement, organizations give accountability for their results. Performance measures can consist of an ongoing activity that indicates how well an organization or unit is progressing toward strategic objectives and can impact funding decisions (Berman 1998, 51). Performance measures are routinely used to measure key aspects of a program in quantifiable goals, focus on the achievement of specific program goals, and ensure that federal and state program standards and goals are being met.

Many public, private, and nonprofit welfare service providers operate under contracts that reward the attainment of specific outcomes. A National Governors' Association (1997) survey of 37 states found that 20 were establishing performance standards for their entire workforce development systems. These measures typically include specific criteria for employment at high wages, employment with health benefits, or job retention (Meyer et al. 1997; Gooden 1998a, 1998b). For example, a contract may specify a minimum job-placement hourly wage or issue graduated payments at higher placement wages.

Performance measures are also a beneficial tool in ensuring that welfare clients receive appropriate services in a timely fashion. Under TANF, welfare recipients face time-limited assistance, thereby making it imperative for welfare agencies to use their time efficiently and effectively in servicing welfare clients. Providing specific performance measures provides agencies with financial incentives to secure quality jobs and supportive services for their clients.

Table 10.1 provides an illustration of a common use of performance measures in TANF policies. A set of appropriate performance goals are identified, specific measures are selected to measure the goals, data are collected to measure program performance, and the information is used to evaluate program performance.

The use of performance measures in welfare reform is not limited to state and local agencies. The 1996 PRWORA provisions award $200 million in annual bonuses to high-performing states. The first round of awards rewards states for annual results in four categories: job placement, job success (measured by retention and earnings gains), biggest improvement in job placement, and biggest improvement in job success (U.S. Department of Health and Human Services 2000a, 1). States can also qualify for increased funding base on having demonstrated a net decrease in out-of-wedlock births, without an increase in abortions.

Under many existing TANF performance contracts, targeted populations, such as the "hard to serve" or populations with multiple barriers are identified to avoid creaming (meeting performance goals by placing those who are easier to serve into employment, and underserving the harder cases). I offer a racial extension to the existing targeted approach.

Enhancing Performance Measures to include Racial Equality

Performance measures can be used in a similar fashion to address racial and ethic disparities in employment levels and case management services. The use of specific performance measures offers a concrete way to monitor racial outcomes of the 1996 welfare reform legislation. Section VII B of the TANF regulations specifies that TANF-funded programs are subject to laws relating to nondiscrimination. Such measures can provide an assessment of how the programs' performance goals are being met within various racial/ethnic subgroups of the welfare population. This also encourages welfare service providers to provide active case management and employment promotion for all of their welfare clients, and forces agencies to develop innovative strategies to minimize the impacts of labor market discrimination.

TABLE 10.1.   Example Performance Measures in TANF Programs

Criterion	Minimum Level	Bonus Level
Employment	35% of welfare clients must have obtained a job	40% of welfare clients must have obtained a job
Wages	20% of welfare clients must have obtained a job at $8.50 per hour or above	25% of welfare clients must have obtained a job at $8.50 per hour or above
Health insurance	30% of employed clients have health insurance available through their job	40% of employed clients have health insurance available through their job
Job retention	75% of employed clients are still employed after 30 days; 50% are still employed after 90 days	85% of employed clients are still employed after 30 days; 60% are still employed after 90 days
Educational activities	75% of welfare clients without a high school education are in educational activities	85% of welfare clients without a high school education are in educational activities
Educational advancement	20% of welfare clients without a high school education complete their GED	30% of welfare clients without a high school education complete their GED

Table 10.2 adds a racial component to the earlier example of performance measures. It measures performance outcomes by racial subgroup, thereby providing specific agency attention to minimizing the impact of racial disparities in supportive services and labor market discrimination in employment. Each state or local agency can modify the measures based on their standard performance measures and the racial and ethnic groups represented on their caseload.

The table also yields baseline data on how racial subgroups are faring in their search for employment under time-limited TANF assistance. For each locality, this could assist in identifying racial or ethnic subgroups that are experiencing more difficulty in navigating the labor market, and force service providers to develop innovative strategies to ensure that each welfare client under TANF has an opportunity for employment success.

TABLE 10.2. Racially Enhanced Performance Measures in TANF Programs

Criterion	Minimum Level	Bonus Level
Employment		
African Americans	35% of welfare clients must have obtained a job	40% of welfare clients must have obtained a job
Native American	35% of welfare clients must have obtained a job	40% of welfare clients must have obtained a job
Asians	35% of welfare clients must have obtained a job	40% of welfare clients must have obtained a job
Hispanics	35% of welfare clients must have obtained a job	40% of welfare clients must have obtained a job
Whites	35% of welfare clients must have obtained a job	40% of welfare clients must have obtained a job
Wages		
African Americans	20% of welfare clients must have obtained a job at $8.50 per hour or above	25% of welfare clients must have obtained a job at $8.50 per hour or above
Native American	20% of welfare clients must have obtained a job at $8.50 per hour or above	25% of welfare clients must have obtained a job at $8.50 per hour or above
Asians	20% of welfare clients must have obtained a job at $8.50 per hour or above	25% of welfare clients must have obtained a job at $8.50 per hour or above
Hispanics	20% of welfare clients must have obtained a job at $8.50 per hour or above	25% of welfare clients must have obtained a job at $8.50 per hour or above
Whites	20% of welfare clients must have obtained a job at $8.50 per hour or above	25% of welfare clients must have obtained a job at $8.50 per hour or above

TABLE 10.2. *Continued*

Criterion	Minimum Level	Bonus Level
Health Insurance		
African Americans	30% of employed clients have health insurance available through their job	40% of employed clients have health insurance available through their job
Native American	30% of employed clients have health insurance available through their job	40% of employed clients have health insurance available through their job
Asians	30% of employed clients have health insurance available through their job	40% of employed clients have health insurance available through their job
Hispanics	30% of employed clients have health insurance available through their job	40% of employed clients have health insurance available through their job
Whites	30% of employed clients have health insurance available through their job	40% of employed clients have health insurance available through their job
Job Retention		
African Americans	75% of employed clients are still employed after 30 days; 50% are still employed after 90 days	85% of employed clients are still employed after 30 days; 60% are still employed after 90 days
Native American	75% of employed clients are still employed after 30 days; 50% are still employed after 90 days	85% of employed clients are still employed after 30 days; 60% are still employed after 90 days
Asians	75% of employed clients are still employed after 30 days; 50% are still employed after 90 days	85% of employed clients are still employed after 30 days; 60% are still employed after 90 days
Hispanics	75% of employed clients are still employed after 30 days; 50% are still employed after 90 days	85% of employed clients are still employed after 30 days; 60% are still employed after 90 days
Whites	75% of employed clients are still employed after 30 days; 50% are still employed after 90 days	85% of employed clients are still employed after 30 days; 60% are still employed after 90 days
Educational Activities		
African Americans	75% of welfare clients without a high school education are in educational activities	85% of welfare clients without a high school education are in educational activities
Native American	75% of welfare clients without a high school education are in educational activities	85% of welfare clients without a high school education are in educational activities

(continues)

TABLE 10.2. *Continued*

Criterion	Minimum Level	Bonus Level
Asians	75% of welfare clients without a high school education are in educational activities	85% of welfare clients without a high school education are in educational activities
Hispanics	75% of welfare clients without a high school education are in educational activities	85% of welfare clients without a high school education are in educational activities
Whites	75% of welfare clients without a high school education are in educational activities	85% of welfare clients without a high school education are in educational activities
Educational Advancement		
African Americans	20% of welfare clients without a high school education complete their GED	30% of welfare clients without a high school education complete their GED
Native American	20% of welfare clients without a high school education complete their GED	30% of welfare clients without a high school education complete their GED
Asians	20% of welfare clients without a high school education complete their GED	30% of welfare clients without a high school education complete their GED
Hispanics	20% of welfare clients without a high school education complete their GED	30% of welfare clients without a high school education complete their GED
Whites	20% of welfare clients without a high school education complete their GED	30% of welfare clients without a high school education complete their GED

Fulfilling Work Opportunity

Contemporary welfare reform is built on the premise of work first, with the expectation that employment is the primary vehicle to move a poor family out of poverty. Much research focuses on individual factors contributing to long-term welfare dependency such as teenage pregnancy, intergenerational welfare dependency, family formation, and the lack of minority business development, but the role of institutional racial barriers does not receive similar consideration.

The TANF block grant is the centerpiece of the Personal Responsibility and *Work Opportunity* Reconciliation Act of 1996 (emphasis added). Much attention has been given to the personal responsibility portion, including the requirement of signed client personal responsibility agreements, monitoring of program compliance, documenting client use of services, and issuing financial sanctions for noncompliance. The work opportunity language deserves similar attention, especially for racial and ethnic minority groups who have historically competed, and are presently competing, in a discriminatory labor market.

Early opponents of TANF concede that welfare reform has not produced the detrimental results forecasted. Even in its worst light, it has provided the support for some welfare recipients to move into the labor market and begin the slow process toward economic self-sufficiency. These goals should be consistently advanced for all racial and ethnic subgroups and performance measures may help in achieving this goal.

Performance measures are not without fault. Certain desired outcomes are not quantifiable, data reporting must be carefully monitored, and outcomes must be accurately measured. Yet they can be helpful in identifying, diagnosing, and improving program productivity. In a policy area involving race, employment, and welfare, it is difficult to sort out with a reasonable degree of certainty the impact of individual motivation and work ethic versus the impact of case management and labor market discrimination, especially across multiple local conditions. The scales are typically tilted toward measuring motivation and work ethic. Perhaps it is time to rigorously examine the impact of agency case management practices and labor market discrimination.

NOTES

1. This section of the chapter is adapted from Gooden 1995.

2. Including Title IX of the Education Amendments of 1972, Title VII of the Civil Rights Act of 1964 (Title VII), the Age Discrimination in Employment Act (ADEA), the antidiscrimination provision of the Immigration Reform and Control Act of 1986 (IRCA), and the Equal Pay Act (EPA).

Beyond Welfare Reform

RACE & SOCIAL POLICY IN THE STATES

CHAPTER 11

Race/Ethnicity and Referenda on Redistributive Health Care Policy

CAROLINE J. TOLBERT AND
GERTRUDE A. STEUERNAGEL

As the preceding chapters have shown, racial and ethnic diversity has played a significant role in shaping welfare policy outcomes. Despite the importance of this research, the existing literature is limited in two important ways. First, past research on race and welfare policy has focused almost exclusively on a cash assistance program—Aid to Families with Dependent Children (now Temporary Assistance for Needy Families). Based on the individual-level evidence (Gilens 1999; Peffley and Hurwitz 1998), we might expect whites to view the targets of any redistributive policy—not just cash assistance—as less deserving if they are minority (black or Latino). Thus, we are left to ask if the significance of race in explaining welfare policy outcomes extends to in-kind as well as cash assistance programs.

A second limitation concerns the fact that most of the literature on welfare reform and welfare retrenchment focuses on legislative action or bureaucratic disentitlement. Over the last two decades, however, direct democracy elections (ballot initiatives and referenda) have become increasingly important for social welfare outcomes in the states—especially outcomes that have direct effects on racial and ethnic minorities. To better understand the politics of welfare reform, and possibly what to anticipate in the future in some states, we therefore need to pay attention to how citizens have behaved when presented with opportunities to exercise direct control over social policy.

In this chapter, we address both of these questions. As is well known, there are vast disparities in access to health care in the United States. In addition, access to health care is distributed unequally among rich and poor, and among racial and ethnic groups. Insofar as the beneficiaries of health policy might be perceived as disproportionately minority, we might expect whites to be less supportive of policies that extend health care coverage to the poor. To investigate this question, we examine racial voting patterns on Proposition 186 in California, which would have expanded health care access for the poor by establishing a universal health care system. Section 1 discusses the increasing importance of direct democracy in state policy-making, and their relationship to race/ethnicity and social policy. Section 2 documents the growing trend of placing questions of health care policy and financing on statewide election ballots, describes current inequities in access to health care in the United States, and provides an overview of the arguments for and against a California citizen initiative (Proposition 186, 1994) that would have created a universal health care system for the state. Section 3 provides an empirical analysis of racial voting patterns on the ballot proposition.

Direct Democracy in the States

Twenty-four states provide for the initiative process, allowing groups outside of the legislature to petition to place policy on the statewide election ballot for a popular vote. If adopted by a majority of voters in the election, the initiative changes either statutory or constitutional law (Magleby 1984). In the referenda (popular or legislative), in contrast, voters can only respond to policy formulated by the state legislature. The appendix lists the initiative states by type.

The initiative process, or the threat of a pending or circulating initiative, is often necessary to translate citizen preferences into policy when state legislatures or bureaucratic agencies are unwilling or unable to act. The process has been used to adopt policies resisted by elected officials, corporate or economic interests, and established political parties, but supported by a majority of the public. Thus, it is not surprising that state legislatures under direct legislation threats have been found to be more likely to adopt the proposed legislation (Gerber 1996, 1999).

California historically has been a leader in the use of the initiative process and was the first state in the nation to adopt many new policies at the ballot box. Since California adopted the process in 1911, it ranks second only to Oregon in the number of initiatives placed on the ballot over the past century (Tolbert, Lowenstein, and Donovan 1998). Since 1978, the year California voters adopted tax limitation Proposition 13, use of direct democracy has increased dramatically. More than any other state, California has shifted in favor of direct democracy over other forms of governance. Some of the state's most important decisions—on taxes, education, social policy, immigration, affirmative action, campaign finance reform, environmental protection—have been the subject of statewide referenda votes (Schrag 1998). The expanding role of the initiative process in California is also reflected in initiative spending, which climbed from $9 million in 1976 to $127 million in 1988 to $140 million in 1996 (Gerber 1998).

Most state provisions for the initiative process were adopted during the Progressive Era (Schmidt 1989). Progressive Era policies adopted in some states by initiatives and referenda included the eight-hour workday for women, child labor laws, prohibition, mothers' pensions, women's suffrage, environmental legislation, and regulation of the railroads (Schmidt 1989). In the late twentieth century, the process has been used to adopt progressive policies such as major conservation measures, protection of open space, campaign finance reforms, and the legalization of marijuana for medical purposes, as well as conservative policies such as ending government affirmative action, curtailing reproductive rights, limiting taxation, and enacting term limits. The use of ballot initiatives for health care reform at the turn of the twenty-first century is consistent with early usage of the process during the Progressive Era.

Direct Democracy, Racial and Ethnic Diversity, and Social Policy

Direct democracy elections provide an ideal context for measuring citizen policy preference, as well as racial and ethnic voting. In California, the policy preferences of the dominant white electorate are sometimes at odds with the state's growing racial and ethnic groups. Over the past two decades, initiatives and referenda have shaped California's social policies and governmental structures, some with direct and others with indirect consequences for the state's ethnic populations (Schrag 1998). In 1986, California voters adopted an initiative declaring English as the state's official language. In 1994 California voters adopted Proposition 187, which denied social services, including welfare benefits, to illegal immigrants (primarily Latinos and Asians) and their children. Two years later, voters adopted Proposition 209, which prohibits race- or gender-based affirmative action in public employment, contracting, and education. In 1998, voters adopted Proposition 227, which eliminated bilingual education in public schools. Surveys indicate that a majority of whites supported each policy, while a majority of racial and ethnic minorities opposed them (Tolbert and Hero 2001).

Other California ballot measures overturning the state's fair housing laws that prohibited discrimination by race in rental housing (Proposition 14, 1964), restricting new public housing projects (Proposition 15, 1974), prohibiting school busing on the basis or race/ethnicity (1972), or curbing welfare benefits (Proposition 165, 1992) have direct effects on racial and ethnic minorities, as do initiatives increasing penalties for repeat criminal offenders (Proposition 184, 1994) or gang-related activities (Proposition 21, 2000).

Clearly, direct democracy elections have important policy implications for minority groups. A number of recent studies attempt to estimate the effects of initiatives and referendums on the rights of racial and ethnic minorities. Some scholars (Gamble 1997; Cain 1992) suggest that minorities fare poorly in direct democracy elections, as voters have effectively used the process to undo protections and social policy benefits for minorities passed by state legislatures. Others (Donovan and Bowler 1998; Frey and Goette 1998) conclude that the detrimental effects on minorities are more limited, and that civil rights and policy benefits are more vulnerable in local referenda elections than statewide elections where the scope of conflict is broader.

A whole range of policy issues that are not obviously oriented toward racial and ethnic minorities—including education policy, fiscal policy, criminal justice policy, and of course social welfare policy—nonetheless have important implications for them. California's famous property tax limitation initiative (Proposition 13, 1979) may have had the greatest effect on the well-being of racial and ethnic minorities by dramatically lowering the ability of local jurisdictions to provide a variety of public services (Schrag 1998). Of the six million children in California public schools in 2000, barely two million (35 percent) are white, making education policy a priority for racial and ethnic groups (Baldassare 2000). California ballot initiatives in the 1990s have proposed statewide school vouchers, reductions in class sizes for primary schools, and increased spending for public schools.

Racial cleavages may occur even when ostensibly "race neutral" policies, such as health care, education, and fiscal policy, are at issue. A recent study provides evidence of a racial and ethnic divide concerning a range of public policies decided via ballot propositions in California over the period 1980 through 1998 (Hajnal, Gerber, and Louch 2002). Unlike previous studies examining voting patterns on one or a few highly controversial ballot contests, the research examines outcomes across the entire array of issues addressed through direct democracy (47 propositions) in California since 1980 using 15 different *Los Angeles Times* polls. Hajnal, Gerber, and Louch (2002) explore the probability that racial and ethnic minorities will be on the winning side in initiative and referenda elections. Their analysis provides evidence that Latinos, blacks, and Asian Americans are more likely than whites to be on the losing side on minority-targeted initiatives, but not in initiative elections overall. Latinos, however, are more likely to be on the losing side, even when the subject of ballot propositions cover issues that are most important to them, and even when they vote cohesively.

We have good reason to be interested in how voters respond to health reform ballot initiatives, even those that fail. Recent research suggests voters are capable of making rational decisions in direct democracy elections, even with limited information (Bowler and Donovan 1998). Voters can make decisions consistent with their policy preferences in initiative and referenda elections by relying on simple voter cues—political party, interest group, and media endorsements or opposition (Lupia 1994). Voter pamphlets distributed by the secretary of state providing arguments for and against each ballot measure are the most often cited sources of information. Analyzing voting in referenda elections on real policy questions also avoids many of the limitations of survey data to study racial attitudes (Sniderman and Carmines 1997).

Direct democracy elections thus provide an ideal forum for studying instrumental or self-interested voting among white and nonwhite racial and ethnic groups in the area of redistributive policy. Redistributive policies involve efforts by the government to shift the allocation of wealth, income, property, or rights among broad classes or groups of the population, often involving economic groups such as the haves and have-nots (Lowi 1964). Policies with a redistributive influence include the graduated income tax, health care programs, and welfare programs. High levels of conflict characterize these policies. They confer benefits to narrowly defined groups, with dispersed costs to society (taxes paid by the general population). When redistributive health care policy is the subject of statewide referenda, we might expect cohesive racial and ethnic voting, if the minority is likely to be winner and the majority the loser.

Health Reform Ballot Initiatives

President Clinton's 1994 failed effort at health care reform suggested to some commentators that the public was apathetic on the issue. Nonetheless, 46 million uninsured Americans, widespread discontent with managed care, and the ongoing problems of funding and delivering care under Medicaid and Medicare continue to keep health care reform on the political agenda. A recent CBS poll, for example, found a majority of those surveyed said the "problem of the uninsured" is the "biggest health care problem" facing the nation (Guiden 1999). A *Washington Post* poll in 2000 reported that 72 percent of those surveyed believed the "federal government should work to increase the number of Americans covered by health insurance" (Roper Center Online Poll 2000, Accession number: 0374367, Question number: 045). Indeed the political landscape itself may be changing. Once a chief opponent of national health insurance, seven prestigious physicians' groups, including the American Medical Association, promoted a grassroots campaign to make universal health care coverage a priority in the 2000 presidential elections.

Since health is important to every individual, we might expect a high level of citizen involvement. Ironically, health care policy decision making in this county is more often than not characterized by very little direct citizen participation. The process is quasi corporatist (Leichter 1996) in form, involving information negotiations among key health care stakeholders, such as the insurance industry and physicians groups, and the elected officials dependent on the campaign contributions of these same stakeholders. There are signs, however, that things may be changing. Citizens and professional organizations (health care providers) in several states are using ballot initiatives as a vehicle for placing health care reform on the political agenda. Although largely unsuccessful to date, these initiatives hold the promise of granting the public a larger voice in determining health care policy.

In the 1990s questions of health policy and financing were placed before voters in California, Washington, and Oregon. Although the initiatives involving changes in health care financing were for the most part unsuccessful, some of the other health policy initiatives succeeded, California voters, for example, defeated two citizen initiatives, Proposition 166 in 1992 and Proposition 186 in 1994 (the subject of this chapter), that, had they been adopted, would have created a universal health care system for the state. Then again, in 1999 voters in one hundred communities in Illinois overwhelmingly approved an advisory referendum requiring the state to provide health coverage to all residents. As a result, a state constitutional amendment is pending that would require the state to enact a plan for universal coverage.

High-profile constitutional amendments on the ballot in Oregon in 1996 and 1998 legalized physician-assisted suicide. Ballot measures legalizing the medical use of marijuana have been adopted in a dozen states since California voters first approved of this policy in 1996. Failed ballot propositions in Oregon and Washington (1998) would have allowed individuals direct access not only to medical doctors but also to osteopathic doctors, chiropractors, naturopaths, and nurse practitioners. An Oregon measure (1998) would have mandated comprehensive reform of managed care companies. Two 1996 California propositions sponsored by organized labor and the California Nurses Association would have regulated health maintenance organizations (HMOs). Both propositions were eventually defeated. However, under the threat of these initiatives, the California legislature introduced twenty-seven bills (which were later defeated) regulating HMOs (cf. Gerber 1996). In 2000, Arizona voters approved an initiative to allocate tobacco litigation settlement proceeds to finance specified health care benefits for the poor and elderly. Also in the 2000 elections, Massachusetts voters narrowly—by three percentage points—defeated a citizen initiative, Question 5, that would have created a universal health care system for the state (Tolbert and Steuernagel 2001).

Race, Ethnicity, and Health Care Access

In addition to institutional mechanisms for direct democracy, racial and ethnic context has been shown to be important in shaping public policy at the state level, particularly in the areas of health, education, and welfare (Hero 1998). Empirical analysis based on fifty-state data suggests racial minorities tend to fare poorly in terms of social policy outcomes in bifurcated and homogeneous racial/ethnic contexts, relative to minorities living in heterogeneous contexts, with large white ethnic populations (Hero 1998).

California has been characterized as having a bifurcated social structure with a large minority (primarily Latino) population and a large white (nonethnic) population (Tolbert and Hero 1996). As the nation's most ethnically diverse state, growing racial and ethnic diversity is a defining feature of California politics. In 2000 California become the first 'majority-minority" state, in which racial and ethnic minority groups now outnumber non-Hispanic whites (Baldassare 2000). Projections by the U.S. Census Bureau indicate that by the year 2025 whites will comprise just 30 percent of the state's population (Johnson 1999).

California politics is also characterized by a mismatch between the composition of the voting electorate and the population. While racial and ethnic minorities comprise roughly half of California's population, the electorate is still largely white. In 1996 whites represented only 53 percent of the population but accounted for 88 percent of registered voters. In contrast, the nonwhite registered voters were 11 percent Latino, 5 percent black, and 4 percent Asian (Chavez 1998). In 2000, whites represented less than 50 percent of the state's population, but comprised 68 percent of the electorate, while Latinos represented only 19 percent, and blacks and Asian Americans followed with 6 and 7 percent respectively (Baldassare 2000). The electorate exaggerates the power of white voters, and thus elections (especially initiative elections) may be a critical mechanism for white voters to exert their policy preferences over minority groups in a number of policy areas, including health care (Tolbert and Hero 2001).

Given existing disparities in access to health care, we would expect racial and ethnic minorities to be more supportive of expanded government health care provisions than whites. There are vast disparities in access to health care in the United States by race and ethnicity. Among whites in 1999, 11 percent lacked health insurance, compared to 21 percent of African Americans, 21 percent of Asians, and 33 percent of Hispanics (U.S. Department of Health and Human Services 2000). This translates directly into higher infant mortality, lower life expectancy, and lower immunization rates. The health status outcomes or disease statistics by race/ethnicity in the United States are highly correlated with uninsured rates (U.S. Department of Health and Human Services 2000). In no state are the disparities in access to health care more evident than in California. In 1994–95, 15.5 percent of nonelderly Americans in the United States, or over 40 million people, were without health insurance (Liska, Brennan, and Bruen 1998). In California, a staggering 19.7 percent of the population is uninsured. Overall 5.56 million of California's 28 million people are without health insurance (Liska, Brennan, and Bruen 1998, 111).

There is also a dramatic gap in the health insurance coverage (of nonelderly) by economic class. Of the 84.96 million families in United States living below 200 percent of the poverty line, 26.7 percent, or 23 million, are without health insurance. In contrast, of the 72.62 million U.S. families earning at least 400 percent of the poverty line, only 5 percent, or 3.63 million, are without health insurance. In California, this division is more dramatic. Of the 12 million families living below 200 percent of the poverty line, 29 percent were without health insurance in 1994–95. Of the 9.3 million families earning at least 400 percent of the poverty line, only 7 percent were uninsured (Liska, Brennan, and Bruen 1998, 76–81). Racial and ethnic minorities comprise a disproportionate percent of those living below the poverty line. Given these disparities in access to health care, we would anticipate that racial and ethnic minorities would be more supportive than whites of attempts to create a universal health care system.

California's Universal Health Plan Initiative (Proposition 186)

Proposition 186, the "single-payer initiative" of 1994, provides an important test case of a referendum on universal health insurance. A costly statewide campaign battle provided extensive information to voters, and a number of diverse constituencies were involved.

Proposition 186 would have replaced the current system of private health insurance with a Canadian-style government-run health care system. It would have guaranteed health insurance coverage to all legal residents of the state, including the estimated six million Californians uninsured at the time.[1] It would have given all the state's residents complete health care coverage, including full mental health benefits, full long-term care benefits, prescription drug coverage, and some dental benefits. Citizens would have been permitted to choose their physicians, and physicians, in turn, would have had responsibility for all medical decisions, although the health care system was to be run by an elected health commissioner.

Proposition 186 was a redistributive policy requiring new personal income and business taxes along with a one-dollar-a-pack tax on cigarettes. The nonpartisan State Legislative Council projected that the new taxes would raise $40 billion annually, doubling the state budget. Money raised by the tax increases would be used to dispense more than $100 billion in health benefits annually to more than 30 million Californians (Morain 1999).

Proponents argued that California should lead the nation in reforming health care, and that any increase in taxes for a family would be offset by a reduction in out-of-pocket health care expenditures. Opponents objected to what they characterized as a government takeover of health care by the state bureaucracy and the burden additional taxes would place on employers. They also argued that California's personal income tax would almost double, jobs could be driven from the state, and the overall business climate would be impaired. Despite these claims, the initiative was supported by the California Nurses Association, consumer unions, labor unions, the California branch of the American Association of Retired Persons (AARP), and the California League of Women Voters. The grassroots citizen movement relied on ten thousand volunteers to collect over one million signatures to quality the initiative for the ballot (cf. Leichter 1996). It was opposed by the health insurance industry, business groups, taxpayer groups, and medical executives. Eventually, Proposition 186 was defeated by the electorate, garnering only 26.6 percent of the vote.

Opponents of the single-payer initiative far outspent proponents, in a pattern typical of health care reform initiative campaigns (Tolbert and Steuernagel 2001). Led by the insurance and health care industries, opponents spent more than $9 million in an effort to defeat the initiative, while opponents mounted no media campaign. The Health Insurance Association of America alone poured more than $1.5 million in the effort to defeat Proposition 186. Of the four citizen-generated initiatives on the 1994 ballot, Proposition 186 was the second most expensive, after a tobacco tax initiative. Total spending on the five initiatives was 35 million (Morain 1999), far more than total expenditures on all election campaigns for the state legislature. Research suggests that campaign expenditures by proponents does not increase the chance of successful passage, but negative campaign expenditures by opponents significantly increases the probability of defeating an initiative (Gerber 1999).

Data, Methods, and Findings

What is the role of race and ethnicity in shaping support for universal health care in California as it would have been enacted by Proposition 186? To answer this question, we examine survey data from the Voter

News Service Exit Poll of California voters conducted on November 8, 1994. The dependent variable in our statistical models is a "yes" vote for Proposition 186.

Since minorities represent a disproportionate percent of those without health insurance in the United States, we expect racial and ethnic respondents to be significantly more supportive of Proposition 186 than whites. We measure the race and ethnicity of the respondent (black, Latino, Asian American) with a series of dummy variables, with non-Hispanic whites as the reference group. In addition, women also tend to have higher uninsured rates in terms of private insurance, so gender is also considered.

We also control for personal economic factors, education, political ideology, age, and policy preferences. Personal income is measured as the yearly family income of the respondent. We expect those with lower incomes to have more difficulty paying for needed health care and thus to be more supportive of universal health care. The models also control for changes in personal finances over the past year and perceptions of the state's economy (Bowler and Donovan 1994). Higher values for these variables are associated with negative evaluations of the state economy and personal finances.[2] Conservatives have historically disfavored policies that entail extensive government involvement, while liberals have generally been more favorable of greater government intervention. The variable "liberal" and "conservative" were measured with dummy variables, with moderates as the reference group. The models also control for the number of years of formal education completed and age of the respondent (ordinal level variable with higher values equaling more education).

Descriptive statistics highlight a divide along racial, economic class, and ideological lines in support for health care reform providing universal coverage. While only 30 percent of whites voted for Proposition 186, over 40 percent of all minority groups[3] (blacks, Latinos and Asian Americans) supported the ballot measures (though Asian Americans tend to have a higher socioeconomic status than other minority groups).

Equally interesting is the breakdown of the vote by income. Of those respondents earning under $15,000 annually, almost a majority (45 percent) supported the policy, compared to only 24 percent of those earning $100,000 or above. Of those earning between $15,000 and $29,000, almost 40 percent voted for Proposition 186. This reveals a significant socioeconomic class divide in support for universal health care.

Party affiliation was also a strong predictor of opposition or support for the initiative. Of self-reported Republicans, only 15 percent favored the initiative, compared to 47 percent of Democrats. What is notable is that not even a majority of Democrats voted in favor of this health reform proposal. Thirty-five percent of Independents favored the policy, approximately the mean popular vote. It is not surprising then, that 56 percent of self-reported liberals favored the single-payer initiative, compared with only 18 percent of conservative voters. Surprisingly, gender had no impact of support for the initiative. The same percentage of males and females supported the policy. Do these patterns and relationships remain in a multivariate regression model, when controlling for other factors?

Explaining the Vote for Universal Health Care (Proposition 186)

Since our dependent variable is a binary variable indicating a vote for or against the health care reform, we use logistic regression. In table 11.1 we see that a number of variables have a statistically significant effect on support for Proposition 186. Race/ethnicity appears to be important. Nonwhite voters, self-identified as black, Asian Americans, or Latino, were significantly more likely than whites to support the ballot measure,

TABLE 11.1. Voter Support for Universal Health Care (Proposition 186)

Explanatory Variables	Unstandardized Coefficient (β)	Standard Error	Probability	Odds-Ratio
Nonwhite	*.340*	*.186*	*.069*	*1.404*
Liberal Ideology	*1.00*	*.192*	*.000*	*2.721*
Conservative Ideology	*−.499*	*.195*	*.011*	*.607*
Personal Finances Worse	−.187	.191	.327	.829
Income	*−.189*	*.063*	*.003*	*.828*
Education	.096	.079	.229	1.100
View State Economy Worse	−.172	.129	.183	.842
Age	.045	.038	.235	1.046
Female	−.048	.163	.770	.954
Constant	−.239	.534	.654	
Log/ratio Chi-square	73.69		.000	
Log likelihood	−469.924			
Pseudo R^2	.07			

Source: Voter News Service Exit Poll and phone survey, November 4, 1994.

Note: N = 804. The dependent variable is binary, 1 if voted for Proposition 186 and 0 if voted against it. The coefficients presented are logistic regression coefficients with standard errors in parentheses. Stata logistic regression command code available upon request. Probabilities based on two-tailed test. *Statistically significant variables in bold italic.*

even after controlling for ideology, income, perceptions of the economy, personal finances, education, age, and gender. The odds-ratio indicates that liberal ideology was the single most important factor in shaping support or opposition to the ballot measure, followed by the race/ethnicity of the respondent. This suggests racial minorities (blacks, Latinos, and Asian Americans) and the white majority may vote differently even on general social policies, such as health care, that are not explicitly "minority issues," such as welfare policy. These findings highlight an important racial division in health policy preferences.

The nonwhite population in California is not homogeneous, and specific ethnic groups may have diverse policy preferences. Table 11.2 replicates table 11.1 but includes separate variables for black, Latino, and Asian American respondents with white voters as the reference (comparison) group. The coefficients for black and Latino respondents, like minorities in general, are statistically significant and positively related to support for Proposition 186. Blacks and Latinos were clearly more likely than whites to support this policy. Asian Americans, however, were not more supportive of this policy than whites. The higher socioeconomic status of Asian Americans may dampen their support for "redistributive" policy. In both models, political ideology was an important factor in shaping policy preferences.

TABLE 11.2. Voter Support for Universal Health Care (Proposition 186)

Explanatory Variables	Unstandardized Coefficient (β)	Standard Error	Probability	Odds-Ratio
Asian American	.352	.294	.232	1.421
Latino	.472	.189	.012	1.602
Black	.486	.203	.017	1.626
Liberal Ideology	1.005	.140	.000	2.734
Conservative Ideology	−.653	.144	.000	.521
Personal Finances Worse	−.213	.138	.121	.808
Income	−.241	.047	.000	.786
Education	.147	.059	.012	1.159
Age	.046	.028	.100	1.047
Female	.049	.118	.677	1.051
Constant	−.769	.279	.006	
Log/ratio Chi-square	174.82		.000	
Log likelihood	−880.09915			
Pseudo R^2	.09			

Source: Voter News Service Exit Poll and phone survey, November 4, 1994.
Note: N = 1,530. The dependent variable is binary, 1 if voted for Proposition 186 and 0 if voted against it. The coefficients presented are logistic regression coefficients with standard errors in parentheses. Stata logistic regression command code available upon request. Probabilities are based on two-tailed test. Statistically significant variables in bold italic.

There also appears to be a strong class division in support for universal health care. In both models (tables 11.1 and 11.2) the coefficient for personal income is statistically significant and inversely related to support for Proposition 186. Voters with lower income levels (and more likely to be without health insurance) were more supportive of the policy, even after controlling for other factors. Individuals with higher incomes (and likely to have private health insurance) were more likely to oppose this policy. This is a logical finding that emphasizes again how important redistributive issues are when considering health reform in America. The level of education of the respondent was also clearly important, but only in table 11.2. Voters with higher education were more supportive of universal health care after controlling for other factors. The age or gender of the respondent had no statistical impact when controlling for other factors.

The Significance of the Statistical Models

To facilitate interpretation of the regression coefficients presented in table 11.2, probability simulations were calculated using Clarify Software (King, Tomz, and Wittenberg 2000). This method allows estimates of the expected probability of a yes vote for the Proposition 186 under various scenarios, by varying the race and ethnicity of the respondent, while holding all other variables constant at their mean value. Because gender (female) is a binary variable, it must be set at either 1 or 0 in the simulations. Because variation in this variable is of substantive interest, even if not an important predictor , separate estimates of support for Proposition 186 are reported for males and females. Table 11.3 shows the expected probability of a "yes" vote and associated standard deviation of support for Proposition 186, by varying race, ethnicity, gender, and economic characteristics of voters. All independent variables (personal finances, income, education, perception of state economy, age) were set to their mean value, except ideology, in which the variable "liberal" was set to 1 and "conservative" set to 0.

Table 11.3 reveals a clear pattern of support for universal health care relative to the race, ethnicity and economic status of the respondent. Row 1 suggests that the overall probability of support for the ballot measure in the survey was 31 percent, slightly higher than the actual popular vote (26 percent). Setting all independent variables at their mean value, but varying the race/ethnicity of the respondent from white to minority (black, Latino, or Asian American), increased the probability of support for Proposition 186 by 8 percent for both males and females. Varying the economic status of a respondent from wealthy to poor increased the probability of voting for universal health care by nearly 20 percent for males and females. For example, a minority woman who reported a liberal ideology had a 59 percent chance of supporting the ballot measure, with all other variables set at their mean value. The same woman who was white instead of a racial minority had only a 51 percent chance of voting yes. Similarly, the probability of a minority male supporting the initiative was 60 percent. The probability of a white male voting yes on the initiative was only 52 percent. This is a difference of 8 percent points based on race alone for males and females. Table 11.3 suggests that race/ethnicity and economic class were important determinants of support and opposition to expanded health care, even after controlling for other factors.

TABLE 11.3. Expected Probability of Support for Universal Health Care (Proposition 186)

	Average Vote	Standard Deviation
Overall probability of a yes vote	.31	.02
Minority Women	.59	.06
White Women	.51	.05
difference	8%	
Minority Male	.60	.05
White Male	.52	.04
difference	8%	
Poor White Women	.62	.05
Wealthy White Women	.39	.06
difference	23%	
Poor Minority Women	.69	.06
Wealthy Minority Women	.47	.07
difference	22%	
Poor White Men	.63	.05
Wealthy White Men	.40	.06
difference	23%	

Note: Estimates based on logistic regression model reported in table 11.1. *Minority* = Latino, black, or Asian; *White* = non-Hispanic white respondent. Probabilities calculated using software written by Michael Tomz, Jason Wittenberg, and Gary King (1999): CLARIFY: Software for Interpreting and Presenting Statistical Results, Version 1.2.1 (Cambridge: Harvard University), http://gking.harvard.edu/.

Conclusion

Proposition 186's defeat came only months after President Clinton's national health reform plan failed in Congress in 1994, highlighting the effectiveness of well-financed media campaigns mounted by the health insurance industry to defeat universal health care proposals proposed via state ballot initiatives or U.S. presidents. Health care reform, however, remains a salient problem in the United States (Hackey 1998; Marmor and Mashaw 1996; Leichter 1997; Rich and White 1996; Skocpol 1997; Steinmo and Watts 1995; Weissert and Weissert 1998). Statewide ballot initiatives proposing health care reform will likely remain on the political agenda in the next decade.

Was the defeat of universal health care at the national level and in California also the result of a racial and ethnic divide, in which white voters perceived that the policy would disproportionately benefit minority (particularly black and Latino) groups, as is currently the case with welfare benefits? Does the recipient of government provided health care have a "black or brown" face in the eyes of the majority white electorate? Clearly, access to health care in this country is uneven, particularly for lower-income and minority groups. This research suggests that voters engage in instrumental voting when health care policy is the subject of statewide referenda, casting votes consistent with their self-interest. To date, most health reforms adopted by state legislatures, such as mandating coverage for particular procedures, have benefited middle-class, primarily white citizens who currently have health insurance. When health policy is the subject of statewide referenda, it may benefit a broader segment of the population.

This research suggests that race and ethnicity are important determinants of voter support for universal health care, even after controlling for other factors, such as socioeconomic conditions. California voters overwhelmingly rejected the ballot measure examined here. Rather than a public good, Proposition 186 (universal health care) was framed as a redistributive policy that would have transferred millions of tax dollars from the middle- and upper-middle-class, primarily white population to the poor, largely black and Latino population without health insurance. There was a clear racial divide in support for Proposition 186. Blacks, Latinos, and those with lower incomes were significantly more likely to support a state-run health care system, whereas wealthier whites were more likely to oppose the policy. We find evidence of the same racial and ethnic division in support for redistributive health care policy, as reported by scholars who study referenda on affirmative action and illegal immigration (Tolbert and Hero 1996; Hero 1998) and by scholars who study welfare policy, as reported in other chapters of this volume.

It is clear why people of lower economic classes would support a state-run health care system, as they are generally less able to pay for private health insurance. However, it is less clear why minorities, income notwithstanding, support state-run health care systems. Research suggests Latinos in California have divergent policy preferences than whites. On fiscal issues, such as government taxes and spending, Latinos are more liberal than most Californians. Latinos are more supportive of increased general welfare spending, including health care and education, on the one hand, but morally conservative on the other, showing less support for abortion rights (Baldassare 2000, 187). While most Latinos in California would classify themselves moderate to somewhat conservative, much like whites, what distinguishes Latinos from whites has more to do with their specific policy preferences than their political philosophy (Baldassare 2000, 110–23). Not only are Latinos more likely to vote Democratic, but they have a more positive and less fearful attitude toward government, suggesting their preference for a more active government. Latinos have more liberal attitudes when it comes to taxes and spending on social programs, such as Social Security and health care (58 percent), even if it means higher taxes, than do whites (50 percent) (Baldassare 2000, 122–23). Latinos may want a more active role of government because of their lower socioeconomic status and positive views of government, characteristics often associated with immigrant groups.

Research suggests that a larger and more politically active Latino population in California would swing the state's political pendulum to the left. A major trend is the growth in the Asian and Latino vote. As the new California immigrants have become citizens, they have emerged as the fastest-growing groups of new voters. In the 1990 gubernatorial election, only 4 percent of the electorate were Latino. By the 1998 gubernatorial election, the Latino share had increased to 14 percent based on Voter News Service exit polls (Baldassare 2000, 110–12). It is likely that their participation in elections has been hastened because they have felt threatened by political reaction to their growing presence, as reflected in ballot initiatives directly affecting minority groups (Baldassare 2000). Turnout rates in California elections among Latinos have risen dramatically over the past decade as policies opposed by a majority of Latinos—ending welfare for immigrants, Official English, ending bilingual education, ending affirmative action programs—have been approved in statewide referenda elections. Over time, demographic diversity may change elections and representation, as California faces the conflicting demands of white, black, Asian, and Latino voters. If Latino and black turnout rates increase in the future, as many predict they will, states like California may adopt general social welfare policies, even provisions for universal health insurance coverage.

As the vote on Proposition 186 demonstrates, referenda on redistributive health policy can be racially and ethnically polarizing. Other states will likely follow California's lead and place health policy, and other forms of social policy, directly on the statewide ballot as a coalition of Massachusetts citizens did in the 2000 general elections. The increasing racial and ethnic diversity of the United States combined with the growing importance of direct democracy elections will likely continue to shape social and welfare policy in the states with important implications for substantive and procedural democracy in the next century.

APPENDIX: TYPES OF INITIATIVES IN THE U.S. STATES

	Direct Constitutional	Indirect Constitutional	Direct Statute	Indirect Statute
Alaska			X	
Arizona	X		X	
Arkansas	X		X	
California	X		X	
Colorado	X		X	
Florida	X			
Idaho			X	
Illinois	X		X	
Maine				X
Massachusetts		X		X
Michigan	X			X
Mississippi		X		
Missouri	X		X	
Montana	X		X	
Nebraska	X		X	
Nevada	X		X	X
North Dakota	X		X	
Ohio	X		X	X
Oklahoma	X		X	
Oregon	X		X	
South Dakota	X		X	
Utah			X	X
Washington			X	X
Wyoming				X

Note: Constitutional initiatives amend the state's constitution. Statutory initiatives amend statutory law.

NOTES

1. Detailed information on the ballot initiative process in California is available at the website of the Office of the Secretary of State, http://www.ss.ca.gov.

2. The variables for perceptions of the state economy and perceptions of personal finances are coded 5 (worse), 3 (same), and 0 (better).

3. In the survey, average (or mean) support for the initiative was 31 percent, while in the population (or state) it was 26 percent. This is the difference between the survey sample and the true population.

CHAPTER 12

Racial/Ethnic Diversity
and States' Public Policies

Social Policies as Context
for Welfare Policies

RODNEY E. HERO

The federal structure of the U.S. governmental system is important in numerous and varied ways. One major implication is that state governments are significant policymakers in the United States. Historically, the states have been the primary domestic public policymakers and, despite tremendous changes over time, they remain so (Elazar 1966). By many accounts the importance of state government has grown over the last generation in several policy areas. Therefore, social policy in the United States cannot be understood without considering the implications of the federal system of policy authority as a major institutional feature. By extension, a central question is how to best understand states' policy orientations.

Welfare policy, while of substantial importance and probably the most studied, is but one of several major policy responsibilities of state governments in the United States. The "police power" of the states—that they may legislate regarding the "health, safety, morals, and well-being" of their citizens—provides significant authority and substantial discretion in addressing a host of policy concerns. The policy responsibility of states also permits *varied* policy responses and outcomes. States have shared the responsibility for formulating and administering welfare policy, thus assuring important influence. States share responsibility with the national government, itself a "federal" entity in that state and substate constituencies are woven into the national government's structure, adding to the states' considerable influence. At the same time, states clearly have primary legal authority and responsibility for human capital policies, such as education, and for social regulation, such as criminal justice, and others that tend to be intertwined with and have implications for "welfare" needs and policies. For example, education, criminal justice, and welfare policies can, in part, be thought of as causes and/or consequences of each other. Moreover, if welfare policy may be thought of as "regulating the poor" and minorities (cf. Piven and Cloward 1971), public policies such as education, criminal justice, and other policies might also be viewed in this light because they may constrain, or enable, individual and group conditions. In shaping social and economic opportunity, generally through a variety of curricular and pedagogical decisions and through the regulation of behavior through student suspension and other practices, education affects the social standing, income, and broader well-being of individuals. State education and criminal justice policies and outcomes thus provide a backdrop for, and a window onto, welfare policy (cf. Fording 2001).

The importance of federalism, and state policy authority specifically, is heightened by another reality of U.S. political and social history. Race/ethnicity is and has been a pervasive influence in the political and social system, as numerous scholars and observers have argued (Key 1949; Hero 1998; Smith 1993; Carmines and Stimson 1989). Particularly important here, the various racial/ethnic groups are not distributed equally across the states, as detailed below. This has affected politics and policy in the United States, including—and perhaps especially—state policies (Key 1949; Burnham 1974).

"Welfare reform" legislation should be considered within this broader institutional and policy context, and with due attention to such factors as race/ethnicity that are part of the American social, economic, and political fabric. This chapter contends that states' "social diversity" is a major factor in understanding their public policy. That is, the varied racial/ethnic composition and configurations have a major impact on state policies—even after considering the impact of socioeconomic factors such as states' level of income, education, and urbanization. The effects of social diversity on state policies are shown to be substantial and evident in some form in all states; race thus very much remains an *American* dilemma. The manifestations are different; that is, they have different forms or "faces" in different social context(s). This needs to be fully appreciated and systematically incorporated into theory and research on state social and human policy. If there is evidence of racial factors affecting these various policy areas—as is indicated below—then the connection to and impact of race on welfare policies becomes clearer and more readily understood.

In the mid-1900s, V. O. Key (1949) demonstrated that race was the central characteristic of politics in the southern states, and the significance of racial/ethnic diversity for state politics has been suggested in numerous other works (e.g., Hill 1994; Lieske 1993). Despite considerable attention, however, racial/ethnic diversity has not until recently been developed or extensively incorporated in a general interpretation of state politics and public policy. Racial/ethnic diversity can be seen as an "analytical construct" (Hero 1998; Hero and Tolbert 1996b; Lieberman 1993) for examining U.S. state and national politics, as the present study underscores. These assertions about social diversity are also consistent with Smith's (1993) broader claims that theories of U.S. politics need to better acknowledge the inegalitarian ideologies and institutions that have defined the status of racial and ethnic minorities (Limerick 1987). That is, ideas of ascriptive hierarchy, not only "liberal" and "republican" traditions, are evident in American political thought and practice. The several traditions are directly relevant for understanding state public policy as well. As argued below, the traditions are related to and mediated by particular racial/ethnic contexts; those traditions and contexts seem especially important because of the geographically or territorially "narrower scope" of social and political relationships of state politics.

The social diversity thesis asserts that ethnic/racial contexts significantly affect states' policies, and the implications of racial/ethnic context are more complex than commonly assumed and understood. When state politics and policies are analyzed more closely—when state policy *outcomes* are examined in "relative," not simply in "overall" or aggregate terms, as is commonly done—racial/ethnic factors become more apparent and their substantive implications more important. On the other hand, when the impact of race/ethnicity on policy is examined primarily with expenditure-related, or "input," indicators, the impact is sometimes less clear, although other research has found rather strong relationships (cf., however, Howard 2001; Johnson 2001).

This chapter summarizes the findings of previous research on policy outcomes in both overall and relative dimensions. A frequent finding is that states that "do well" regarding overall or aggregate policies as often as not do "poorly" in the relative patterns, and some states tend to be "in between" on both dimensions. This suggests that there are several "faces" of policy, and policy inequality; and each is substantially affected by racial/ethnic diversity context. Thus, racial/ethnic factors are important in understanding policy in all of the states, not just in one region or set of states nor with respect to only a few, explicitly "redistributive" policy issues (cf. Hero 1998, 139–45).

State Racial/Ethnic (Social) Diversity

A central characteristic of states is their racial and ethnic diversity, or relative lack thereof (Hero 1998). As examined here, states' racial and ethnic diversity includes, significantly, black (African American), Latino/Hispanic, and other minority populations—that is, those groups that have been thought of as "minority groups" or "protected classes," implicitly recognizing unique historical experiences in the United States. The distinctive experiences of blacks, Latinos, and other minorities are recognized at a general level in research on state policies, but most empirical theories of state policy have not fully incorporated that significance. One can also differentiate between northern or western European populations versus non-northern and nonwestern Europeans within states (cf. Jacobson 1998). (For purposes of this chapter, the discussion will focus most directly and extensively on *minority* diversity, however.) To be sure, the historical experience of various minority and other groups are each quite complex in themselves. Here, however, the assumption is that there is sufficient similarity within groups and enough differences across groups as delineated to support the designations and arguments made (cf. Elazar 1966, 1994).

To develop the diversity interpretation and systematically assess evidence on racial/ethnic diversity in the states, census data were drawn on to create two major racial/ethnic categories measures or indicators of social diversity: (1) "minority" (blacks, Latinos, Asians) in relation to white populations are used to create an index of *minority diversity,* and (2) "white ethnics" or "European ethnics" (particularly southern and eastern Europeans) are used to create an index of white ethnic diversity (Hero 1998; cf. Sullivan 1973). The residual conditions for each index, low racial and low white ethnic diversity, are indicative of homogeneity (1990) (see fig. 12.1).

The racial/ethnic group categories follow from the logic of the inter-

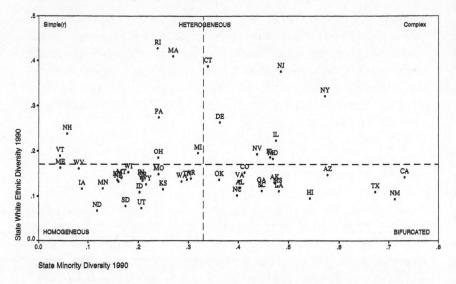

Fig. 12.1.   Distribution of states across different categories of diversity

pretation, and the categories are generally consistent with the scholarship that has considered racial/ethnic group background (Elazar 1966; Wilson and Banfield 1964, 1971). Fundamentally different, however, is the attention to groups as well as the significance attached to racial group context and interrelationships. General state profiles are provided (in fig. 12.1); later I commonly refer to the states with respect to broader patterns or characterizations because the states fall into several groupings relative to their racial/ethnic diversity patterns.

Compared to overall U.S. patterns, some states can be characterized as racially and ethnically *homogeneous*. These states have populations that are primarily "white" or "Anglo," that is, of northern and western European descent; they also have very small minority (black and Latino) populations and relatively few "white ethnics" (i.e., non-northern and nonwestern European whites). In contrast, there are two types of "non-homogeneous" states. Some states have rather large white ethnic populations as well as significant minority populations and moderately large "white" populations; these can be called *heterogeneous*. Finally, some states have *bifurcated* racial/ethnic structures, with large minority populations, primarily black and/or Latino, a large white (nonethnic) population, and a rather small proportion of "white ethnics." The states can be broadly delineated into the several patterns or categories—homogeneous, heterogeneous, and bifurcated—according to the type and degree of racial/ethnic diversity. In the more detailed analysis summarized later, state diversity patterns are measured with "interval" or "continuous" level data, and indicators derived from the data are used throughout the statistical analyses.

Social Diversity and Public Policies

The focus here is on examining public *policies,* an area where diversity has been previously shown to have important impacts (Hero and Tolbert 1996b; Hero 1998; Johnson 2001; Howard 2001). It should also be noted that ethnic/racial diversity has been shown to influence other state political phenomena including various political processes, and "descriptive representation" in governmental institutions (see Hero 1998, chaps. 3 and 4). Several policies or dimensions of policies are examined in this chapter. The policies considered include several that are commonly taken as central state responsibilities such as education, criminal justice, and health (Gray and Jacob 1996). Related issues, having to do with "relative" or "differential" dimensions of the policies, are also considered because social diversity's impact may also be manifested there. The goal, then, is to examine some variety of policies and/or "subpolicies" that are among the major state policy responsibilities and that, like welfare, have central human or social policy (as distinct from "physical") dimensions and implications.

"Public policy is an especially important phenomenon to study because it reflects human agency. . . . Through public policy collective choices are made with significant consequences as to how and whether problems are resolved, how benefits and costs are distributed, how target groups are viewed by themselves and others, and how such groups regard—and participate in—politics." But "public policy is a complex combination of elements, including goals and objectives, agents and implementation structures, targets, tools, rules, and rationales" (Schneider and Ingram 1993, 335–36). Thus, policies, and dimensions of policies, are examined here because of their inherent significance and are considered relative to racial/ethnic diversity, as that is essential to the larger argument.

The policies are selected based on their centrality for state policy, and the "relative" or "disaggregated" indicators focus on the differential policy impact on minority groups (Hero and Tolbert 1996b). The differential policy indicators tend to focus on issues of "equality" of racial/ethnic minorities relative to the general populations of states; indeed, these issues are at the core focus of the discussion. The emphasis tends to be on nonexpenditure measures of policy; considering nonexpenditure indicators should lessen the impact of states' wealth as a factor that influences policy patterns, although the policies are examined with expenditure indicators as well.

The particular reasons and ways race/ethnicity produces the outcomes shown below is not extensively developed here, but has been discussed elsewhere (cf. Hero 1992, 1998; Meier and Stewart 1991; Meier, Stewart, and England 1989; Lipsky 1980, Key 1949; Hill 1994). Briefly stated, the argument is that racial/ethnic inequality and its attitudinal and institutional legacies shaped, and continue to shape, attitudes, public opinion, and public policy formation and implementation as they affect minorities. The impact of ethnic/racial inequality is evident in lesser political participation among racial/ethnic minorities, in political party cleavages and party systems (Hill 1994; Brown 1995; Hero 1998), and in substantial underrepresentation of minorities in the legislative and bureaucratic institutions of state government as well (cf. Hero 1998; Meier and Stewart 1991; Elling 1996, 1999). Moreover, various common practices and "standard operating procedures" in the implementation of government policies often reinforce ethnic/racial policy inequality, contributing to disparate outcomes of the sort delineated below (Meier, Stewart, and England 1989; Meier and Stewart 1991). Disparities are not confined to states with large minority populations. In homogeneous states the disparities in policy outcomes often found for minorities are, I would suggest, attributable to their being too small to have much political impact, or too invisible, or otherwise facing difficulties in convincingly drawing attention to and articulating concerns within the larger sense of community and consensus associated with homogeneity (see Hero 1998, 15–20, 149–51).

Education Policy

Education is a major state policy concern and typically the largest single set of state expenditures, commonly accounting for more than a third of state and local budgets. Education seems especially important to study because there is a strong belief in the United States that education is vital to central concerns such as economic and social equality, societal stability, and the proper functioning of democracy. For individuals, educational achievement is viewed as crucial for upward mobility and as having major impacts on "life chances" in such areas as employment, income, quality of housing, and access to health care (Meier and Stewart 1991). In the tradition of U.S. federalism, the authority for education has rested, historically and presently, primarily with state governments.

State governments are heavily involved in education policy, although it is "locally administered" (Wirt 1990). Like other local governments, local school districts are legally "creatures of the state" and thus subject to a host of structural, financial, procedural, and other formal state influences. The federal government's direct financial role in education is not especially large. State governments bear the major responsibility for education in the United States and state characteristics, such as social diversity, might therefore have major impacts.

Before discussing evidence from the 1990s, it is useful to summarize previous analysis, of mid-1980s data, on education in the states (Hero and Tolbert 1996b). Previous research found that general student educational outcomes, as measured by overall graduation rates, are highest in homogeneous states and lowest in bifurcated states (Wirt 1990; Hero and Tolbert 1996b). Minority diversity was negatively and significantly related to states' overall graduation rates. For example, overall graduation rates tended to be higher in Iowa and other homogeneous states and lowest in the states of the old South. This suggests the impact of race/ethnicity on public policy, which reaffirms expectations, but is not an especially surprising finding.

On the other hand, the previous research found rather distinct patterns regarding the "relative" or "differential" outcomes.[1] The patterns for minorities within states, for the mid-1980s, was considered using two indicators of education outcomes (Hero and Tolbert 1996b). Blacks had substantially lower graduation and significantly higher student suspension ratios across the states, consistent with the diversity interpretation and with the arguments that "two-tiered pluralism" (Hero 1992) and "second generation discrimination" (Meier, Stewart, and England 1989) occur within state policy systems. But an especially notable finding was that minority diversity was actually positively related to graduation ratios—that is, as states have more minority diversity, blacks have higher graduation ratios. Homogeneous states generally have lower black/white graduation ratios than states with large minority populations. Several homogeneous states, including Wisconsin, Minnesota, Washington, and Utah, have substantially lower black graduation ratios than "bifurcated" states such as South Carolina, Alabama, Mississippi, and Texas. However, it should be emphasized that bifurcated states have low overall graduation rates. Racial/ethnic diversity explained (statistically) a considerable portion of the variation in minority/white graduation ratios. This implies that minority diversity is considerably more complicated or "problematic" in the homogeneous environment than generally recognized (Elazar 1966).

A similar pattern was found regarding suspension ratios for blacks. Minority diversity and white ethnic diversity were found to be inversely related to suspension ratios. States with the smallest minority and ethnic populations had the highest suspension ratios for blacks; that is, the disparity in the outcomes for blacks tended to be most pronounced in the most homogeneous states. But aggregate policy indicators mask these findings, and studies that focus only or primarily on general patterns overlook this (Hero and Tolbert 1996b). The education policy findings from the 1980 data, just summarized, can be further examined for a different time frame, the early 1990s.

Assessing education policies, especially with expenditure and/or aggregate measures, requires caution, however. Some states do not spend especially large amounts of money relative to other states, yet have relatively high levels of education as measured by graduation rates and percentage of the population with a high school degree or more. They may spend less because the "need" is not as great Other states spend more, but still have less positive outcomes. These points should be kept in mind as a preface to the following analysis.

Education Expenditures and Effort. First considered are education expenditures and "effort" for the early 1990s: the former is defined as per capita spending on education (including both elementary/secondary and higher education), the latter as state per capita expenditure on education divided by state per capita income. The findings for both measures are similar. Both diversity indicators are significantly related to effort, but not necessarily in the ways that might be expected. Higher minority diversity is related to more education effort, while white ethnic diversity is related to somewhat lower effort. Greater urbanization tends to have a significant negative impact on education spending and effort, while states' (existing) levels of education have a positive impact.

That bifurcation is related to greater "effort" may partly reflect the greater "need" associated with larger minority populations. For example, New Mexico, one of the poorest states, ranked sixth and ninth in per capita spending for "precollege" and "higher" education, respectively

(Wirt 1990). Despite greater "effort," however, the policy outcomes in high minority diversity (bifurcated) contexts tend not to be higher in general terms, as indicated in such measures as overall graduation rates. It is important to examine education outputs and outcomes beyond those associated with expenditures and effort (Schneider and Ingram 1993).

Education Outputs/Outcomes. The question here is, once a state has made a particular level of financial commitment (i.e., expenditures and/or effort) in a policy area, what are the outcomes? Those issues are examined in aggregate, and in relative terms regarding several indicators (using data from the U.S. Department of Education, Office of Civil Rights).

Overall Graduation Rates. One indicator of education policy is overall graduation rates. Analysis indicates that more minority diversity is significantly related to lower overall graduation rates; larger minority population in a state is related to lower overall graduation rates. White ethnic diversity is positively related (but not statistically significant). Thus, minority diversity has a negative impact, or racial homogeneity has a positive impact, on overall graduation rates, as might be expected from conventional wisdom and other perspectives. This impact holds when the impact of socioeconomic variables are considered.

    Minority/Overall Graduation Rates. What is the pattern when a "relative" measure, the graduation rates for minorities compared to overall graduation rates, is examined? First, in all but one or two states, minority graduation ratios are below "parity" (1.0) relative to overall rates, clearly indicating a pattern of "negatively" differential outcomes. In many instances, they are well below parity. Second, larger minority population is actually associated with higher graduation ratios for minorities. Notably, a number of homogeneous states—Wisconsin, Minnesota, Montana, Vermont, and South Dakota, for example—are some of the states with the "worst" minority/overall graduation ratios. And this is consistent with the previous research findings from the 1980s (Hero and Tolbert 1996b). While several homogeneous states do relatively "well," as often as—or more often than—not, homogeneity is associated with lower ratios. White ethnic population is associated with lower minority graduation rates. When the two diversity measures are considered alone, both have a significant effect.

    Minority diversity retains some significant impact when socioeconomic variables are examined; its positive relationship with relative

307

graduation rates remains. When considered along with the socioeconomic factors, the impact of white ethnic diversity continues to have a
negative impact (Hero and Tolbert 1996b). Perhaps this suggests tension
between the "old," that is, "white ethnics," and the "new" ethnics, that
is, blacks and Latinos, in education politics. Interestingly, the socioeconomic indicators themselves have little or no significant impact either.
The patterns suggest that minority diversity interacts with socioeconomic
factors in complicated ways but that diversity retains important
influence. And given that it is more likely that race/ethnicity "explains"
the socioeconomic variables, rather than vice versa, the findings are especially noteworthy.

Minority/Overall Suspension Ratios. Another "relative" dimension to
consider is a "regulatory" policy within schools, that is, suspension
ratios. The highest minority suspension ratios are in six rather homogeneous states—North Dakota, South Dakota, Nebraska, Iowa, Minnesota, Nebraska, and Idaho; these states have suspension ratios for
minorities twice as high as the overall state average. Several of these
states also "stood out" regarding disparate minority/overall graduation
ratios (discussed above). Statistical analyses indicate that minority diversity is negatively and significantly related to minority suspension ratios.
White ethnic diversity is also negatively related to minority/overall suspension ratios. And socioeconomic indicators have no significant impact.
In short, the importance of diversity, particularly minority diversity, for
suspension ratios is strong and consistent. Equally important, the patterns suggest that states with low minority diversity are often appear
among the most "punitive" relatively toward minorities. These are
notable findings, and consistent with past research findings (Hero and
Tolbert 1996b).

Overall, then, social diversity is frequently significantly related to
education policies, with respect to *both* aggregate/overall and
relative/differential indicators. But the direction(s) of those relationships
is equally important to note. For instance, minority diversity is negatively
related to total graduation rates and positively related to minority graduation ratios. Thus, while diversity commonly has an impact, the specific
direction varies somewhat relative to specific policy indicators; it appears
that policy influences the particular politics associated with social diversity (Lowi 1964). While there is a need to better understand the specific
"politics" of the various dimensions of educational policy, one pattern

seems consistent: minority diversity is consistently related to "lower" or "worse" outcomes, in either absolute or relative terms.

Criminal Justice

Criminal justice is a major policy, a social "regulatory" policy, concerning individual behavior, for which states have primary legal authority in the American federal system. It is also an issue where racial/ethnic diversity might be expected to have an impact, based on numerous questions about the fairness of the justice system in the United States. In fact, a leading scholar of criminal justice has claimed that the racial disparities in the imposition of prison sentences and the death penalty are "the most serious—and potentially the most explosive—issue facing the American system of justice" (Skogan 1996). Hence, its importance as a policy, and the states' central role pertaining to it, suggest that it be examined.

Overall Incarceration Rates. Scholars view incarceration rates as a useful indicator of criminal justice policy. Thus, diversity is first examined relative to states' overall incarceration rates. Analysis shows that minority diversity has a significant positive relationship with overall incarceration rates; there are higher incarceration rates overall where there are more minorities, a finding that is not especially surprising (Hero 1998, 105–8).

Black/Overall Incarceration Rates. Another dimension of state criminal justice policy, focused on "relative" outcomes, concerns the situation for minorities in that system. Skogan claims that "one of the greatest challenges to the system of justice in the American states remains the apparent racial disparities in how it operates. African Americans are disproportionately represented at every step in the criminal justice process from arrest to imprisonment." He explains some of the reasons for this, including that "blacks commit (relatively) more crimes" and that "black offenders are even more likely to be arrested" (Skogan 1996). Skogan notes that the patterns "vary from state to state, one obvious reason being the differences in the racial composition of the states," but also claims that patterns may vary considerably between states similar in their racial/ethnic composition. What does the present evidence indicate concerning minority/overall patterns? Only data on blacks were examined because data on Latinos are not provided in the data used (U.S. Department of Justice 1992).

First, black/overall incarceration ratios were found to clearly diverge from, that is, are much higher (worse) than, "parity" across the states. Second, the ratios are actually less disparate, that is, are more similar or equal, where there are larger minority populations. The greatest disparity in incarceration ratios is in Minnesota, followed by Iowa, Connecticut, and Utah. While several racially homogeneous states have low(er) differential ratios, so do some bifurcated states such as South Carolina and Mississippi. Thus, homogeneity is more often than not related to *less* "equitable" relative patterns. On the other hand, more white ethnic diversity is related to higher minority/overall incarceration rates, another notable finding and dimension of ethnic/racial patterns. The patterns, presented in figure 12.2, are broadly similar to the "relative" patterns for several other policy areas, such as student suspension ratios and infant mortality rates (discussed elsewhere in this chapter).

The patterns just described are supported by statistical analyses. Minority diversity has a significant negative relationship to relative incarceration rates. White ethnic diversity has a positive relationship. And more urbanization and higher state education levels are both positively and significantly related, that is, are both associated with greater disparity in incarceration rates for blacks compared to overall rates.

That greater minority diversity is related to less disparity in incarceration ratios is noteworthy. And this is yet another finding not easily accommodated by many interpretations of state politics. White ethnic diversity's positive impact is also notable. That is, larger white populations, whether "white" or "white ethnic," are related to greater disparity of minority incarceration. These statistical relationships hold even when an additional variable, minority versus overall poverty rates, is accounted for. While minority poverty rate itself has a significant relation to relative incarceration ratios, the impact of the ethnic/racial diversity indicators remain when relative poverty rates, and the several socioeconomic variables, are considered. Thus, the findings are not readily attributable to "other" factors.

Health

The states have had an important, but "shared," responsibility with the federal government in the areas of health policy (Albritton 1990). The federal government plays important roles in these areas, more so than in other policy areas such as education. Because the federal government has, in fact, had an important presence in these areas, especially during the

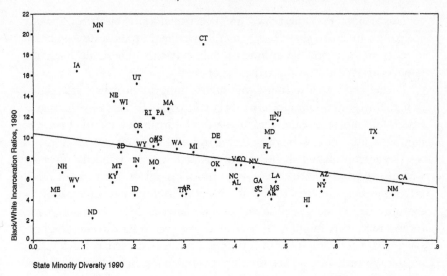

Fig. 12.2. Relationship between state minority diversity and black/white incarceration ratios, 1990

period examined here (early 1990s), it would be anticipated that state-level traits, such as social diversity, might have somewhat less impact in explaining state policy activity.

Medicaid is a major public health policy program in which states share financial and administrative authority with the federal government, and is thus examined here. Infant mortality rates, another important indicator of health policy where state-level factors would be expected to be important, is also considered.

Patterns found in previous research indicate a negative relationship between higher minority diversity and state spending on Medicaid; greater minority diversity is related to lower Medicaid expenditures (Hero and Tolbert 1996b), which is consistent with other research findings. For example, Plotnick and Winters (1985) found a negative relationship between a state's nonwhite population and financial support for Medicaid in their "political/economic" analysis of state income redistribution. Similarly, Grogan (1994) summarizes studies suggesting that "racial prejudice" influences state's social welfare policies; and her own study found that the race of Medicaid recipients is related to at least two dimensions of states' Medicaid policies, financial *eligibility* and benefit coverage (note that these two are not expenditure measures, strictly speaking). In short, there is considerable evidence indicating significant impacts of race on dimensions of public health policy, although the impacts are not always directly on spending.

Earlier research also found that higher minority diversity was related to higher overall infant mortality rates (Hero and Tolbert 1996b). In general, infant mortality rates were highest in bifurcated states and lowest in homogeneous states. On the other hand, black infant mortality ratios were relatively higher in homogeneous states. State minority diversity was inversely related to black infant mortality ratios, the ratio of black infant mortality rates to total state infant mortality rates. Infant mortality rates for blacks in such homogeneous states as Minnesota and Iowa, for instance, were found to be over twice the overall state average (Albritton 1990). Yet in a number of southern, "bifurcated" states, black infant mortality rates were higher than the overall rates, but to a much lesser degree; that is, those states had "better" ratios (Hero and Tolbert 1996b; Albritton 1990). The previous findings regarding homogeneity and infant mortality patterns are neither anticipated nor explained by theories of state policy that do not consider this other face of race/ethnicity (Giles 1977; Elazar 1966). Whether such patterns continue to appear, in data from the early 1990s, is discussed below.

There are a number of number of dimensions one might consider to assess states' Medicaid policy (Grogan 1994); spending is one. Several indicators of Medicaid spending are considered relationship to states' social diversity.

Medicaid Payments per Recipient. When the diversity indicators are examined alone (i.e., in the "bivariate" case) relative to Medicaid payments per recipient, both are significantly related, minority diversity negatively and white ethnic diversity positively. Per capita income is significantly related positively, and urbanization is negatively related when examined without the diversity measures.

Minority diversity continues to be negatively related and approaches, but does not quite achieve, statistical significance, when accounting for socioeconomic variables. White ethnic diversity continues to have a significant positive relationship with Medicaid spending per recipient. Income retains a significant positive relationship. This impact of white ethnic diversity has not been directly identified in most of the previous research (Hero 1998).

Medicaid Spending per Capita. Minority diversity is negatively but not significantly related to per capita Medicaid spending. White ethnic diversity is positively and significantly related. Of the socioeconomic variables, per capita income has a significant positive relationship, and education is significantly negatively related. When all the variables are examined, the multivariate case, only white ethnic diversity has a significant relationship, and it is positive. Minority diversity is negative, but not significant. At the same time, it is notable that none of the several socioeconomic variables are significant either (cf. Erikson, Wright, and McIver 1993).

Medicaid Effort. Medicaid effort is calculated as states' per capita spending on Medicaid divided by per capita income. When the diversity indicators alone are examined relative to this measure of Medicaid policy, both are positive but neither is significant. Education level is negatively and strongly related, but urbanization shows no relationship.

When all the variables are examined, patterns somewhat distinct from those of the bivariate analysis (just discussed) are found. Minority diversity has a positive relationship, but remains nonsignificant. White ethnic diversity retains a positive relationship, but is significant; thus, only when the impact of other variables is accounted for does the importance of white ethnic diversity emerge in this analysis. States' level of education continues to have a strong negative relationship; while urbanization continues not to be significant, its negative impact approaches statistical significance in the multivariate case, though it did not in the bivariate case. Thus, there appear to be interactive effects of white ethnic diversity and urbanization regarding Medicaid effort.[2]

Medicaid Spending and Proportion of "Minority" Recipients. A final way of examining Medicaid spending patterns is considering the proportion of Medicaid recipients who are of "minority" background. As noted earlier, several previous studies have found significant negative relationships between the proportion of minorities as program recipients and policy outputs (Grogan 1994). To pursue such an analysis, the "minority diversity" indicator was removed and another indicator, "minorities as percent of Medicaid recipients," replaced it. Analyses of this and the other variables relative to Medicaid payments per recipient, Medicaid spending per capita, and Medicaid effort were then undertaken.

Minorities as a percentage of Medicaid recipients has a negative but not significant relation to Medicaid payments per recipient. It also has a negative but nonsignificant relationship to per capita Medicaid spending and a positive but nonsignificant relationship with Medicaid effort. Thus, the pattern is for larger percentages of minorities as Medicaid recipients to "lower" Medicaid spending, which is in line with previous findings (Grogan 1994; Hero and Tolbert 1996b). However, the relationships found here tend not to be statistically significant, particularly in the multivariate analyses. Thus, previous studies actually provide stronger support for the social diversity perspective than do these findings.

Infant Mortality Rates

An often-used indicator of states' policies in the health arena is infant mortality rates (Albritton 1990). Both overall and relative indicators of infant mortality rates are examined below.

Overall Infant Mortality Rates. As with the earlier research findings (Hero and Tolbert 1996b), greater minority diversity is associated with significantly higher infant mortality rates, or smaller minority population is related to lower infant mortality rates. White ethnic diversity is negatively but not significantly related. Generally, homogeneity is associated with "better" overall infant mortality conditions, the "typical" expectation. In addition, higher levels of education in a state are related to lower rates.

Minority/Overall Infant Mortality Rates. The patterns for the "relative" outcomes of infant mortality contrast with the aggregate patterns. Minority diversity is negatively related to minority and overall infant mortality rates. As there are more minorities and white ethnics, there are "better" ratios. Infant mortality rates for minorities are, on the whole, worse in homogeneous states. Similar to the 1980s data, the evidence for 1990 indicates that Minnesota and Iowa have minority infant mortality ratios twice that of their overall pattern, and have minority ratios "worse" than a number of southern states, although several homogeneous states do relatively "well." White ethnic diversity also has a strong negative relationship.

These patterns are supported by statistical analyses. Both diversity indicators have negative and significant relationships. These statistical relations occur even after accounting for socioeconomic factors, which themselves also tend to have significant impacts. These findings (re)affirm that homogeneity is related to negatively disparate infant mortality ratios for minorities.

Summary

The evidence suggests that the relationship between social diversity and major public policies is often substantial. Significant relationships are found between minority diversity and several indicators of education policy, including overall graduation rates and minority suspension rates. Statistical relationships tend to be reasonably strong and consistent. The impact of race/ethnicity on incarceration rates, particularly the relative rates, is striking.

Regarding health policy, minority diversity consistently has a negative impact on expenditures, but not as strong as might be expected from previous research findings (Hero and Tolbert 1996b; Grogan 1994). Significant relationships are found between white ethnic diversity and Medicaid expenditure indicators. The impact of race/ethnicity on health policy, and most other policies, is most evident regarding outcome, nonexpenditure indicators.

Another point should be noted. It might be suggested that the "relative" outcomes are attributable to other factors, such as relative poverty rates for whites versus minorities. As indicated earlier, this possibility was examined; a ratio of minority versus overall poverty rates was added to the analysis for various policies. When this was done, the basic findings remained; for several policies, accounting for minority/overall poverty rates does not change the findings. On the other hand, relative poverty rates do have an independent impact on minority and overall infant mortality rates and relative incarceration rates. However, minority diversity itself remains significant. Thus, the several significant "relative" patterns appear related to minority diversity and cannot be explained away by minority poverty rates or other factors, for that matter.

Others might still question, or dismiss, the findings of differential outcomes for minorities in homogeneous settings. It might be argued that minority political "weakness," due to lack of population size or "critical mass," is what explains these findings. That may be so, at least in part. But that is not the argument of such influential interpretations as political culture and the "minority threat hypothesis," or other common interpretations of state politics, to the extent that those other interpretations address these issues at all (Elazar 1966; Hanson 1994).

The threat hypothesis specifies a marked increase in "threat" concerns as minorities' population size increases, resulting in "worse" outcomes for minorities. But the evidence here indicates that where small minority populations are present, minorities often have disparate differential outcomes, and those disparate differential outcomes may actually be relatively higher in more homogeneous settings. Thus, at least two common interpretations seem not to explain some of the findings.

Considering Alternative Interpretations

Social diversity has important impacts on several major state policy areas and dimensions thereof. And socioeconomic variables are important to various degrees and in various ways, although the strength and direction of impact of these variables is not always high nor consistent. While the evidence in support of the social diversity thesis is considerable, do other theories or perspectives help explain the same policies?

A number of alternative interpretations, common in the literature, were considered relative to the various policies examined. On the whole, they do not do as well as diversity in explaining policies. The other alternative interpretations, beyond the socioeconomic (already considered), that were examined are political culture (Elazar 1984), ideology (Erikson, Wright, and McIver 1993), party competition (Holbrook and Van Dunk 1993), legislative professionalism (Squire 1992), and gubernatorial power (Beyle 1990). Variables reflective of each of these interpretations (alone) were analyzed through statistical analyses that also included the two diversity measures and the socioeconomic variables.

In comparing the alternatives with the diversity interpretation I considered whether the alternative interpretations had significant independent explanatory power (itself/themselves) and whether the explanatory power was more than that of diversity. In general, seldom do the alternative interpretations explain the policy indicators "better" than social diversity and (also) achieve statistical significance. In most of the relatively few instances where they do, it is with respect to "overall" rather than "relative" policy indicators. That is, racial/ethnic diversity, rather than other factors, is particularly important in relation to policy *disparities*. The essential substantive findings regarding the alternative interpretations are summarized below.

Political culture is significantly related to, and has a stronger statistical relationship with, overall graduation rates than does social diversity. But for other indicators of education, political culture has little significance, while diversity does. Importantly, political culture shows no relationship to relative policies such as minority/overall suspension rates. Political culture and diversity indicators have about equally strong relationships to Medicaid effort, but political culture shows no impact on minority/total infant mortality rates. Regarding the relative or ethnic/racial equality aspects of the several public policies, political culture provides little explanation, according to the statistical analyses undertaken.

Of the several policy education indicators assessed earlier, states' ideology profiles have a significant impact on only one—minority suspension ratios. More "liberal" ideology is significantly related to lower minority and overall suspension rates; but minority diversity has a stronger impact.[3] While ideology has a significant impact on Medicaid payments per recipient, white ethnic diversity has a stronger impact. State ideology shows no statistical connection to relative infant mortality rates. However, its impact on several welfare expenditure and "effort" indicators is somewhat stronger in some instances than that of diversity. While more liberal ideology might be assumed to lead to greater concern for "equality," or more similar outcomes across racial groups, the evidence examined for several relative policy measures suggests little or no such relationship On the other hand, ethnic/racial diversity clearly does show a relationship to these.

Levels of party competition (Holbrook and Van Dunk 1993) have some impact on per capita education spending and on education effort. However, minority diversity is more strongly related and has more consistently significant impacts. Party competition has no significant impact on the other general education measures or on the relative education indicators; diversity does, especially on the latter. Party competition does have a significant positive relationship to welfare expenditure indicators as well as a significant positive impact on Medicaid effort. However, white ethnic diversity has a stronger impact on these policy indicators. Party competition has no impact on either of the infant mortality rate indicators.

Indicators of the strength of formal government institutions—legislative professionalism and gubernatorial powers—do not have significant relationships with education policies, including the "relative" policy measures. On the other hand, both more professional legislatures and stronger governorships are related to somewhat greater Medicaid spending and effort. But neither has an impact on other relative health indicators, such as minority infant mortality rates.

Conclusion

Social diversity has clear and strong implications for several major state public policies and dimensions thereof. Notably, homogeneous settings are often associated with relatively "worse" policy outcomes concerning minorities, despite "better" absolute or overall patterns. Policies for minorities in homogeneous environments may be less visible because the size of the minority population is (by definition) small(er) in such contexts. But when the differential patterns are examined, the patterns are rather clear; there are larger relative gaps. These findings, for evidence from the early 1990s, corroborate and significantly extend findings from the mid-1980s (Hero and Tolbert 1996b) and from studies of earlier periods (Howard 2001). They also hold even when several socioeconomic variables are considered and controlled. The emphasis in the discussion has been on the importance of *minority* diversity, but white ethnic diversity is also relevant. In short, ethnic/racial diversity is clearly an important factor in understanding several major state public policies. But these findings also show that the importance of ethnic/racial factors in state policy is greater, more widespread, and more complex than any other interpretations have previously suggested, much less understood.

Overall, ethnic/racial diversity appears to have significance for a number of major policies in the states. Its impact on several other policies, especially expenditure policies and those where the national government plays a significant role, appear less strong here. In addition, diversity's impact is commonly at least as important as that of the socioeconomic or other interpretations such as political culture, ideology, party competition, legislative professionalism, or gubernatorial powers. This is especially so for "differential" policy indicators, where the alternative interpretations provide little insight.

The 2000 census indicates the American population is becoming yet more diverse and complex. Particularly notable is the growth of the Latino/Hispanic and the Asian populations. These groups are, to begin with, quite complex in and of themselves. There is considerable evidence that where there are larger Latino populations across and/or within states, legislation that curbs or confronts the policy concerns of Latinos has often been enacted (Tolbert and Hero 2001; Hero 1998, chap. 7; Tolbert and Hero 1996; Hero 1992). And recent evidence on the implementation of the welfare reform legislation of 1996 indicates that larger black population is associated with states adopting stricter policies, as is larger Latino population (Soss et al. 2001). But the patterns are not identical.

Reactions, including policy reactions, to various minority groups may share certain features, but they may also differ due to an array of factors. It may be that responses to blacks are more "subcultural," responses to Latinos more "bicultural" (Hero 1992, 200). Whatever the differences and however they are conceptualized, past evidence suggests that the situation of, and responses to, Latinos will be increasingly important to examine in the future.

Racial disparities are quite common across the states. Significantly disparate policy outcomes, related to social diversity, are often found, but they may be manifested differently. It is not unusual for homogeneous states to have "high" absolute or general outcomes, and "low" relative outcomes. On the other hand, high minority diversity is commonly associated with low aggregate, and high(er) relative, policy outcomes. Again, it appears that diversity is important for many policies, but its effects differ. The American racial/ethnic dilemma is commonly evident across the states—and in states' public policies. The dilemma may appear as often in homogeneous settings as in others; it may just be less visible because aggregate data obscure the evidence and previous analyses have not really "looked for" such evidence. The American federal structure indicates that we should look beyond "national" policies to better understand those policies and the role of race in shaping them.

NOTES

1. There are some differences in data and in states included between the Hero and Tolbert study (1996b) discussed immediately below and the "new" research on "relative" education outcomes presented later. But the differences are not so major as to prohibit comparisons.

2. Albritton argues that Medicaid spending may be especially high in some states, such as New York, where the cost of medical care is, simply, substantially higher than in other states.

3. Erikson, Wright, and McIver (1993) found that ideology had a significant impact on per pupil expenditures. Yet, the measure they used in their study differed from the one used here; this, along with the inclusion of a different group of "control" variables may account for what appear to be inconsistent findings.

Commentary

CHAPTER 13

Why Welfare Is Racist

FRANCES FOX PIVEN

In a racist society, it is inevitable that policies to assist the poor will be designed to shore up racial hierarchy. Thus, where the labor system is organized around racial distinctions, so will assistance programs reflect and reiterate those distinctions. Otherwise the too-generous provision of assistance to racially subordinate groups would create an alternative to the low-wage labor to which they are consigned, thus undermining the racial basis for allocating work and its rewards. And so will political institutions tend to discriminate, privileging those at the top of the racial hierarchy, and muffling the prospects for influence by those at the bottom. Were it otherwise, the disadvantaged would mobilize to pressure government to improve their prospects by intervening in labor arrangements and other social institutions. Thus, the political institutions of the American racial order have always privileged sectional and employer interest groups, while the electoral-representative arrangements that partially offset interest group influence nevertheless systematically underrepresent racial minorities. It follows that American social programs, created and shaped over time in large part by interest group influence and electoral pressure, reflect those institutionalized political inequalities. The broad result in social policy is often commented upon. Blacks and Hispanics are underrepresented in the more generous social insurance programs, and overrepresented in the residual and more niggardly programs we call "welfare." And these residual programs tend to treat minorities more harshly than others of the poor, as the essays in this book demonstrate.

Taken as a whole, the evidence of welfare racism in the United States assembled here seems irrefutable. Robert Lieberman shows how the distinctive American pattern of racial domination within our national boundaries, in contrast to the racial domination of imperial colonies practiced by Britain and France for example, shaped the political coalitions and policy settlements that characterized our history. Michael Brown focuses on the important historical relationship between American fiscal federalism and welfare racism.

In "How the Poor Became Black," Martin Gilens directs our attention to the contemporary role of the mass media in creating public images of the poor as dark-skinned and unsympathetic. James Avery and Mark Peffley amplify the significance of racial media portrayals with data from an experimental survey that randomly varied the race of a (fictitious) welfare mother and child, and found that respondents were decidedly more negative in their evaluations of both welfare and welfare recipients when the race of the recipient was black.

Holloway Sparks shows the multiple ways that minorities, women, and the poor have been excluded from the very discourse of welfare reform, partly as a consequence of biases rooted in the contractual discourse of citizenship, helping to account for the slight influence of the people most affected on the politics of welfare reform. Sanford Schram examines the complexities of talking about race and welfare in an era where the growing majority of recipients are nonwhites.

Several essays make use of the fact that welfare policy has essentially been turned over to the states to search for the race-related factors that account for state variations in racially biased public opinion and the consequences for state policies. Reflecting V. O. Key's well-known racial threat hypothesis, Martin Johnson focuses on the influence of the racial composition of the state's population and of the AFDC rolls in accounting for interstate variations in the scale of reductions in the rolls, and variations in average benefits. Richard Fording uses the prereform period, in which states sought and received waivers from the requirements of the Social Security Act that had governed the old AFDC program, to explore the bearing of a range of independent variables that might influence welfare restrictiveness, and concludes that the racial composition of the caseload is the strongest predictor. Similarly, Joe Soss, Sanford Schram, Thomas Vartanian, and Erin O'Brien ask why some states were more likely than others to adopt restrictive policies after the passage of the Personal Responsibility and Work Opportunity Reconciliation Act of 1996 and show that racial composition of the rolls is the best predictor of "get tough" policies. Susan Gooden points to racial bias in the administration of welfare as reformed. Caroline Tolbert and Gertrude Steuernagel examine the influence of race, ethnicity, and class in a California initiative to promote health care reform.Rodney Hero broadens the inquiry by examining the influence of racial population composition on other public policies that are substantially controlled by the states.

The conclusion that emerges from these different approaches to an examination of American welfare is harsh but indisputable. Welfare policy and practice in the United States is infused with racial biases. Still, that said, there are historical differences that bear both on our understanding of the racism of the new welfare system, and on our ability to think about the contours of genuine reform. There are good empirical grounds for thinking that American welfare is less racist when the role of the federal government enlarges, and when the system is more tightly bound by law and regulation. There are several reasons. One is simply that state and local governments find redistributional policies politically difficult. They are especially susceptible to threats from business and affluent residents to move out of the jurisdiction if taxes are raised to pay for programs that benefit those less well off. As a consequence, employer groups in particular have great influence on subnational governments, and they use that influence to shift the state and local tax burden to the working and middle class who cannot easily threaten to move. Not surprisingly, in a regressive tax system, expenditures that are seen as benefiting the minority poor are more likely to provoke popular resentment.

Another reason that federal policies are at least potentially more benign to minorities was suggested by Grant McConnell (1966) many years ago: "As the most important and influential local interests gain power by being placed in a small sphere, the least influential lose power" (105). Moreover, "The informal structure of the small community will usually be able to suppress a challenge before it becomes overt (107).

Finally, because devolution of responsibility for welfare to subnational governments produces a myriad of particularistic welfare systems, it reduces the power of subordinate minorities to monitor and enforce such rights as they have, thus smoothing the way for more discretionary and arbitrary patterns of welfare administration. Perhaps it is needless to add that minorities have not fared well in American history under local and discretionary rule.

Although welfare as we know it was initiated by national legislation, it was from the start a radically decentralized program, as Lieberman points out, and decentralization clearly had racist consequences (though hardly more so than the earlier mothers' pensions program, from which Blacks were largely excluded [see Bell 1965, 9]). What was to become the main program, initially called Aid to Dependent Children (ADC), and later renamed Aid to Families with Dependent Children (AFDC), was designed as a federal grant-in-aid, which meant that the federal government paid part of the costs but that the program was in the main run by the states and counties. It was the states that set formal benefit levels and elaborated eligibility criteria, for example. Thus, while the national Social Security Act delimited the categories of people whose benefits would be eligible for federal cost sharing—impoverished orphans in the case of ADC—the states were free to set additional limits on who could be aided and how much they could be aided.

The states in turn typically turned the administration of the program over to the counties. Such monitoring as was done by either the federal or state governments was aimed at discovering excessive generosity in the form of ineligibles on the rolls, or overpayments. And to cope with employer pressures and popular animosities, county governments elaborated the distinctive combination of regulatory complexity, intensive bureaucratic oversight, and wide caseworker discretion that characterized the welfare system created in 1935, and has now been resurrected under Temporary Assistance for Needy Families (TANF). The maze of detailed rules, compiled in voluminous and usually secret procedural manuals, in practice gave line workers great discretion in determining eligibility and benefits. At the same time, close bureaucratic supervision of these workers was directed exclusively to scrutiny of decisions to give aid, and not to decisions to withhold aid, inevitably tilting the uses of discretion toward restrictiveness. The vigorous efforts of the states under the current TANF regime to change the "culture" of the welfare office so that aid is withheld whenever possible, by withholding information about benefits, by requiring numerous trips to ascertain eligibility, by subjecting potential applicants to legal and illegal strategies of diversion, or by simply rejecting applicants, is in fact a reconstruction of the welfare "culture" that originally prevailed under AFDC. In the 1960s, the New York City welfare manual moralized that "the withholding of assistance can be as important as the giving of assistance" (Piven and Cloward 1993, 151–56), and this is now the main message of the new TANF regime. Punitive implementation practices did not begin with TANF.

The overwhelming majority of American blacks lived in the South until well after World War II, and so it was the welfare programs of southern states and counties that bore on the life circumstances of blacks.

Southern congressmen had pressed hard and successfully for the elimination from the Social Security Act of any wording that might have been construed as constraining the states from racial discrimination in the administration of welfare. And they used the latitude they had won to run the welfare program in ways consistent with the racial order of their region, as Brown and Gooden detail in the preceding pages. This meant that southern welfare laws and practices were designed to shore up a rigid caste labor system. Blacks were less likely to get aid,[1] and when they did, their benefits were lower than whites so that the welfare check would compare unfavorably with even the miserable earnings of field hands.[2] The average relief payment per person in the southern region was about half the average elsewhere, and black families received less than white families. In rural areas they received much less (Piven and Cloward 1993, 131). And while welfare benefits might be used to sustain some black families at bare subsistence levels when they were not needed in the fields, they were either cut off when seasonal employment became available, or their benefits were reduced. In 1943 Louisiana was the first state to adopt an "employable mothers" rule that instructed local officials to refuse assistance to mothers of school-age children when employment was deemed to be available. Georgia soon followed suit, with a rule that permitted local officials to deny aid to mothers of children over three years of age whenever employment was deemed to be available, that prohibited county departments from supplementing wages even when they fell below welfare grant levels, and that directed welfare officials to deny all applications and to close all cases of mothers deemed able to work when they thought employment was to be had (Piven and Cloward 1993, 134–35).

The South also outdid other regions in inventing moral criteria for welfare eligibility. By 1942 most southern states had enacted "suitable home" laws, under which black mothers who violated sexual norms were denied aid. Myrdal observed that "since all Negroes are believed to be 'immoral,' almost any discrimination can be motivated on such grounds" (1944, 360). The preoccupation of southern welfare departments with the sexual morality of their cases meshed nicely with their preoccupation with enforcing work on even the harshest terms. When the implementation of Florida's suitable home law drove 7,000 families from the rolls in 1959, most of them black, the mothers had no choice but to take whatever work they could get, even work that paid less than Florida's $15 per month per person benefits (Piven and Cloward 1993, 140). Long before the contemporary campaign against welfare, the practices of the South vividly illustrated the intertwining of labor exploitation, racial animosities, and the peculiar sexual obsessions that bedevil American culture.

The culture of the white South was, of course, also deeply racist, so that popular attitudes supported degraded labor arrangements and restrictive welfare laws and practices. But cause and effect are difficult to disentangle here. When a racial group is kept at the bottom of a labor system and excluded from its social and political institutions, the result may be to create, or at least to nourish, the racist popular culture that is then said to be the cause of labor market and political discrimination.

So long as they remained in the rural South, there was little blacks could do to change the racial social order. For one thing, rural blacks were in the grip of the planters on whom they depended for work, for welfare, for credit, and for some protection from the official and unofficial terror that undergirded southern race politics. Moreover, they were without even the recourse of the vote and whatever influence could be wielded by organized voters, for southern electoral systems meshed with southern labor systems by effectively disenfranchising most blacks. The labor system and political system worked together to sustain the racial order. Under these conditions, a state- and county-run welfare system, and the skewed discretion it allowed line workers, produced a deeply racist system of welfare.

The massive migration of blacks from the rural South to the urban North after World War II by itself changed little. The welfare regimes of northern states and counties were not exempt from the American racial order, and in any case used their discretion in ways that were extremely restrictive to poor whites as well as blacks. Indeed, jurisdictions in the North responded to the influx of impoverished black migrants from the South by becoming more restrictive in an effort to ward off the newcomers. A series of political dramas resulted, as politicians fomented scandal after scandal over local welfare liberality. In 1961 and 1962, Senator Harry Byrd, Democrat from West Virginia, launched an investigation of the Washington, D.C., welfare department. His spectacular exposés, well covered by the press, resulted in a sharp drop in the approval of welfare applications, and a sharp rise in terminations. Subsequently, the welfare department's fraud investigators put hundreds of AFDC mothers under parked car surveillance, and concluded that 60 percent of recipients were ineligible, mainly because they appeared to have male visitors. Not surprisingly, in the wake of the exposé, welfare applications fell sharply. Meanwhile, in Newburgh, New York, local officials similarly stirred up welfare scandal, charging massive fraud and illegitimacy. This sort of political theater inevitably affected the exercise of line worker discretion.

Even a New York legislative commission commented on the vague reasons for which families were denied aid. And a national study of terminations conducted in 1961 reported that far more blacks than whites were terminated from the rolls for what were recorded as "other reasons" (Burgess and Price 1963, 55). A few years later, New York City officials explored the options available to them for lowering the welfare rolls, and (premonitions of TANF) suggested longer waiting periods, an intake procedure that would send applicants to an employment agency before they were allowed to complete their application, and the elimination of at least seven offices so that the system would become less physically accessible and backlogs would also build up (Piven and Cloward 1993, 150, 157–58, 160–61, 174).

As Brown and Gooden document, in the course of the 1960s, the welfare system changed dramatically. The federal role enlarged, local discretion was curbed, and something like the rule of law was brought to the system. The agents of this transformation were the protest movements of the period, including protests over civil rights, poverty rights, and welfare rights. The process was not, however, simple and direct.

Underlying the rise of protest and government responses to it were the large-scale changes in American politics spurred by the mechanization of southern agriculture and the ensuing migration of blacks from the rural South to the cities of the South and North. Migration freed blacks from the feudal domination of the rural South, and concentration in the cities lent them at least some resources for collective action. The chain of disturbances that ensued rocked American politics. First, the eruption of civil rights protests and the efforts of national political leaders to appease them helped to precipitate white southern voter defections in Democratic presidential contests, beginning as early 1948. As southern support became more uncertain, the big city base of the Democratic party became more important, especially because urban voters were sometimes able to throw the electoral votes of the big industrial states into one party column or another. Thus, as black numbers, now voting numbers, in the cities grew, they became a critical factor in Democratic presidential calculations. And there was growing evidence that all was not well, as the election of 1956, when the black Democratic vote plummeted by 20 percentage points, showed. Loyal Democrats since 1936, blacks were beginning to defect, a pattern that the spread of protest to the cities was likely to worsen (Cloward and Piven 1974).

National Democratic leaders responded with a series of federal programs targeted to the inner cities where black newcomers were concentrated. The programs, first launched under John F. Kennedy's New Frontier, and then continued and expanded under Lyndon Baines Johnson's Great Society, brought rhetorical encouragement and some resources, including legal resources, to impoverished black communities. And as black discontent escalated, the new federal programs themselves became agents of movement demands, for jobs or housing or education or civilian control of the police or welfare. At least in the short run, the resistance of organized whites whose stakes were being challenged was intense. There was less resistance in welfare. The rolls rose steadily throughout the 1960s and early 1970s and spiraled as protests in the cities escalated after 1965.

The expansion of the welfare rolls in the 1960s has received a good deal of attention, of course. But another aspect of the 1960s transformation was equally important, and until now has received far less attention. Brown and Gooden show that the 1960s curbed administrative discretion and brought something like the rule of law to welfare. With protestors in the streets and sometimes in the welfare offices, more people got aid. The protestors gained some resources and courage from the new federally funded poverty services. Just as important, advocacy services and the litigation that the federal legal services program spearheaded had the effect not only of curbing line worker discretion, but of striking down some of the most egregious rules of the AFDC system. These several developments were cumulative, each encouraging the other. One change was that information about welfare entitlements rapidly became available as the new federal programs, as well as movement organizations, rushed to prepare handbooks on welfare entitlements and regulations, and to distribute these handbooks widely. Another change was that the federally funded neighborhood offices to provide services to the inner-city poor helped people cope with the welfare system. After all, what people typically needed was money, whether to pay the rent or buy food or shoes so the children could go to school, and the better-informed and more confident service center workers could help them get it. Meanwhile, restrictive welfare laws were challenged in suit after suit, with the consequence that the federal courts struck down state residence laws, man-in-the-house rules, "substitute father" rules,[3] and employable-mother rules. In *Goldberg v. Kelly* (1970), the Supreme Court even required that recipients be allowed to challenge welfare decisions through quasi-judicial administrative proceedings. The federal Department of Health, Education and Welfare (later renamed Health and Human Services) also cooperated, issuing new federal regulations that constrained local welfare administration, including a regulation requiring that oral requests for aid be considered formal applications. Of course, racial discrimination in labor markets still disadvantaged blacks, as did discrimination in other spheres where public policies were less responsive to black influence. But the development of a federally influenced rule-bound regime reduced discrimination in welfare.

The essays in this book argue persuasively that the passage of the Personal Responsibility and Work Opportunity Reconciliation Act of 1996 (PRWORA) has meant the restoration of the Old Regime in welfare, and with it, the restoration of welfare racism. The history I have briefly recounted seems to me to explain the structural features of the new system that contribute to the restoration. With the elimination of the AFDC program, many of the legal victories of the 1960s are now moot. The painfully established rule of law in the old welfare system was wiped out with a legislative stroke. At the same time, the new block grant system narrows federal authority over the states to a series of curbs on state generosity. A five-year lifetime limit on aid to any individual is imposed on the use of federal funds, and the states are free to impose more stringent limits. Similarly, the federal law requires that recipients work, but is virtually devoid of safeguards on how the states implement that requirement. And the federal law explicitly asserts that the states have no obligation to provide assistance to any individual or family.

Moreover, as Brown points out, the structure of the block grant itself creates incentives for state restrictiveness, since state governments can simply bank the portion of the block grant that accrues from denying aid or refusing services, or they can spend the money on other programs, or on tax relief.[4] Some of the states have, in turn, replicated this incentive scheme in contracts with private companies who administer parts of the welfare program, allowing them to pocket a portion of whatever they save from decisions to deny or reduce assistance.

The states have used their new authority to move rapidly to restore the distinctive combination of bureaucratic complexity and caseworker discretion that characterized AFDC before the 1960s.[5] Schemes for "diverting" applicants have burgeoned, taking the form of instructing line workers to encourage applicants to get help elsewhere, whether from relatives or soup kitchens, or endlessly elaborating the application process,[6] or withholding information. While line workers have far more discretion, they can also draw on a plethora of new or newly elaborated rules to enforce restrictive decisions, particularly rules governing work requirements. And the rules are coupled with schedules of stiff sanctions for transgressions of the rules, or transgressions of the individual agreements that line workers develop with each recipient in a bizarre ritual pretending to be a "contract" between equals (Schram 2000). In some states, sanctions have been the main device for purging people from the rolls.

The racially discriminatory consequences of the restoration of the Old Regime are documented in these essays. But while I have pointed to features of the new welfare law that open the way for racist practices, I haven't explained the reasons for this broad retreat. After all, American institutions have changed. The old South with its rigid caste system is more or less gone. The victories of the civil rights movement ensured its rapid dismantlement. In particular, the enforcement of minority political rights and the emergence of a significant strata of black politicians, makes a difference, in the South and North alike. Progress has also been made toward opening up jobs and educational opportunities. Even our popular culture has been transformed, with blacks now starring in TV soap operas and detergent commercials. It would seem that the powerful institutional imperatives generated by a caste-based labor system and sustained by social exclusion and political disenfranchisement have at the very least softened.

Of course, the civil rights revolution was incomplete, with telling consequences for the implementation of welfare reform. Racism in labor markets persists, and strong residues of racial bias in adjacent institutions worsen racist patterns in labor markets. Residential segregation confines many blacks to the inner cities where unemployment remains high. Educational deficits make them uncompetitive for many jobs even when employer attitudes are not a problem. The Work First regime of TANF thus feeds people into a labor market deeply rutted with these sorts of barriers, helping to explain why blacks are less likely than whites to leave the rolls, and ensuring that the circumstances of those who do leave are worse relative to whites. The other route off welfare much trumpeted by TANF legislation and practice is through marriage. But the underemployment of black men again underlines the disadvantages of black mothers.

Still, I do not think this is the whole of it. The racism of welfare reform is not simply a reflection of persisting racism in other institutional arenas. A number of the papers in this volume, particularly those by Johnson, Fording, and Soss, Schram, Vartanian, and O'Brien, offer an answer to the political why of welfare racism by proposing that racist attitudes are provoked by the enlarging numbers of blacks in a state and on the welfare rolls. This argument is supported by correlations showing that black numbers are an important determinants of discriminatory welfare practices. The collapse of a rule-bound welfare system and the reconstruction of a discretionary regime obviously means a regime that gives much wider play to public attitudes, including the racist attitudes of line workers, their administrative supervisors, state officials, and the wider publics to whom state officials pander.

Why this strong persisting racism in welfare policy? Part of the answer is probably simply that age-old racist attitudes linger. But the other part of the answer is that these attitudes have been kept alive by the racist appeals of entrepreneurial politicians. Even before the civil rights movement peaked in the 1960s, a roster of Republican politicians were eagerly probing the political possibilities offered by white backlash for building a new conservative majority, a prospect laid out by Kevin Phillips in his 1969 book, *The Emerging Republican Majority*. And for three decades, Republican contenders, especially presidential contenders, have eagerly played the race card by focusing on policies like school busing, or affirmative action, or crime, or welfare, in appealing for political support. In the 1992 campaign, a Democratic contender borrowed the Republican strategy, castigating Jessie Jackson for his ostensible support of Sister Souljah, and campaigning on the slogan, "End welfare as we know it." Four years later he signed a Republican-crafted PRWORA.

So, race-laden political contests have helped keep racist political attitudes alive, and the campaign to reform welfare is a good example of just such an entrepreneurial use of racism. But a racist politics that produces racist policies also has consequences for public attitudes. Earlier I suggested that attitudes are not first conditions, but are shaped and reinforced by experience, including the observation of a socially degraded class of insecure and menial workers whose family life inevitably reflects these insecurities. W. E. B. Du Bois (1996) made this observation about the rise of race prejudice in Philadelphia two centuries ago:

> A curious comment on human nature is this change in public opinion between 1790 and 1837. No one thing explains it—it arose from a combination of circumstances. If, as in 1790, the new freedmen had been given

peace and quiet and abundant work . . . the end would have been different; but a mass of poverty-stricken, ignorant fugitives and ill-trained
freedman . . . swarmed in the vile slums which the rapidly growing city
furnished. (30–31)

I would not conclude, therefore, nor would Du Bois, that the TANF
welfare regime is merely the cipher for a racism originating elsewhere.
Not only does a punitive welfare system shore up a racist economic order
in material terms by denying assistance, but by so doing, it ensures that
many blacks remain impoverished, some of them desperately impoverished, that their family life remains insecure, and that when they do
work, they are consigned to the trap of low-wage work. When racial difference is thus joined to economic and social degradation, race prejudice
flourishes. Moreover, TANF has brought with it a powerful public
rhetoric that treats welfare receipt as an addiction and not a necessity,
and castigates recipients for sexual license. This rhetoric or discourse of
welfare reform is reiterated by the new welfare administrative practices,
by rituals that require people to jump through endless bureaucratic
hoops, and by practices that strip potential recipients of information, of
rights and of power. The implementation of TANF thus creates its own
theater of racial degradation. Du Bois thought that if the freedmen had
been allowed to live differently, then the racism of Philadelphians, and of
Americans generally, would have faded. If the minority poor were
allowed to live differently now, then contemporary racism might also
fade.

NOTES

1. See Myrdal 1944, 359, who documents this discrimination. The most
extreme case he found was Georgia where, in 1940, 38 percent of all children
under 15 were black, but blacks accounted for only 11 to 12 percent of those on
Aid to Dependent Children in 1937–40.
2. The techniques for underbudgeting included assigning high income values
to rent-free shacks in cotton plantations, or counting contributions from relatives
who were not contributing, or assuming utilities were free when they were not,
and so on. See Piven and Cloward 1993, 163–64.
3. In effect these rules made families ineligible when the mother was known
to have a relationship with a man.
4. For a careful examination of the comparative incentives to spend or not
spend, not only with regard to welfare but food stamps and Medicaid as well, see
Chernick and Reschovsky 1999.
5. Brodkin (2001) distinguishes between two waves of work-enforcing wel-

fare reform, one beginning in the 1970s that sought to "eliminate discretion assert greater hierarchical control" and a second wave emphasizing performance standards without regard to how those standards were realized.

6. Diller (2000) reports that New York City now requires applicants to go through at least five separate appointments, "including meetings with a 'financial planner,' an 'employment planner,' and a 'social service planner'" (1156).

References

Abramovitz, Mimi. 1988. *Regulating the Lives of Women: Social Welfare Policy from Colonial Times to the Present.* Boston: South End Press.

Albeda, Randy, and Chris Tilly. 1997. *Glass Ceilings and Bottomless Pits: Women's Work, Women's Poverty.* Boston: South End Press.

Albritton, Robert B. 1990. "Social Services: Welfare and Health." In *Politics in the American States: A Comparative Analysis,* ed. Virginia Gray, Herbert Jacob, and Robert B. Albritton. 5th ed. Glenview, Ill.: Scott, Foresman.

Allport, Gordon W. 1954. *The Nature of Prejudice.* Cambridge, Mass.: Addison-Wesley.

Alvarez, R. Michael, and Tara Butterfield. 2000. "The Resurgence of Nativism in California? The Case of Proposition 187 and Illegal Immigration." *Social Science Quarterly* 81:167–79.

American Public Welfare Association. 1997. "Welfare Reform Management, Service Delivery, and Policy Decisions." *Survey Notes* 1:7–8.

Anderson, Benedict. 1991. *Imagined Communities: Reflections on the Origin and Spread of Nationalism.* Rev. ed. London: Verso.

Ansell, Amy Elizabeth. 1997. *New Right, New Racism: Race and Reaction in the United States and Britain.* New York: New York University Press.

Arendt, Hannah. 1958. *The Human Condition.* Chicago: University of Chicago Press.

———. 1968. *The Origins of Totalitarianism.* New York: Harcourt Brace Jovanovich.

Arnold, R. Douglas. 1990. *The Logic of Congressional Action.* New Haven: Yale University Press.

Asher, Herbert B. 1976. *Causal Modeling.* 2d ed. Sage University Paper series on Quantitative Applications in the Social Sciences Series, 07–003. Beverly Hills, Calif.: Sage.

Ashford, Douglas E. 1991. "Advantages of Complexity: Social Insurance in France." In *The French Welfare State: Surviving Social and Ideological Change,* ed. John S. Ambler. New York: New York University Press.

Baldassare, Mark. 2000. *California in the New Millennium: The Changing Social and Political Landscape.* Berkeley and Los Angeles: University of California Press.

Baldwin, James. 1984. "On Being 'White,' and Other Lies." *Essence,* April, 90–92.

Baldwin, Peter. 1990. *The Politics of Social Solidarity: Class Bases of the European Welfare State, 1875–1975.* Cambridge: Cambridge University Press.

Barber, Benjamin. 1984. *Strong Democracy: Participatory Politics for a New Age.* Berkeley and Los Angeles: University of California Press.

Bartels, Larry. 1991. "Constituency Opinion and Congressional Policy Making: The Reagan Defense Buildup." *American Political Science Review* 85:457–74.

———. 1993. "Messages Received: The Political Impact of Media Exposure." *American Political Science Review* 87:267–85.

Baugher, Elanor, and Leatha Lamison-White. 1996. *Poverty in the United States: 1995.* U.S. Bureau of the Census, Current Population Reports, Series P-60, No. 194. Washington, D.C.: U.S. Government Printing Office.

Baumgart, Winfried. 1982. *Imperialism: The Idea and Reality of British and French Colonial Expansion, 1880–1914.* Oxford: Oxford University Press.

Bell, Derrick. 1992. *Faces at the Bottom of the Well: The Permanence of Racism.* New York: Basic Books.

Bell, Winifred. 1965. *Aid to Families with Dependent Children.* New York: Columbia University Press.

Benhabib, Seyla. 1996. "Toward a Deliberative Model of Democratic Legitimacy." In *Democracy and Difference: Contesting the Boundaries of the Political,* ed. Seyla Benhabib. Princeton: Princeton University Press.

Bensel, Richard Franklin. 1984. *Sectionalism and American Political Development, 1880–1980.* Madison: University of Wisconsin Press.

Berlin, Gordon L. 2000. "Welfare That Works: Lessons from Three Experiments That Fight Dependency and Poverty by Rewarding Work." *American Prospect* 11, no. 15: 68–73.

Berlin, Ira. 1998. *Many Thousands Gone: The First Two Centuries of Slavery in North America.* Cambridge: Harvard University Press.

Berman, Evan M. 1998. *Productivity in Public and Nonprofit Organizations: Strategies and Techniques.* Thousand Oaks, Calif.: Sage.

Berry, Frances Stokes, and William D. Berry. 1990. "State Lottery Adoptions as Policy Innovations: An Event History Analysis." *American Political Science Review* 84:395–415.

Berry, William D., Richard C. Fording, and Russell L. Hanson. 2000. "The Cost of Living in the American States." *Journal of Politics* 62:550–67.

———. 2002. "Reassessing the Race to the Bottom in State Welfare Policy." *Journal of Politics* (forthcoming).

Berry, William D., Evan J. Ringquist, Richard C. Fording, and Russell L. Hanson. 1998. "Measuring Citizen and Government Ideology in the American States, 1960–93." *American Journal of Politics* 42:327–48.

Beyle, Thad L. 1990. "Governors." In *Politics in the American States: A Comparative Analysis,* ed. Virginia Gray, Herbert Jacob, and Robert B. Albritton. 5th ed. Glenview, Ill.: Scott, Foresman.

Bickford, Susan. 1996. *The Dissonance of Democracy: Listening, Conflict, and Citizenship.* Ithaca, N.Y.: Cornell University Press.

Birnbaum, Pierre. 1993. *"La France aux Français": Histoire des haines nationalistes.* Paris: Editions du Seuil.

———. 2000. *Jewish Destinies: Citizenship, State, and Community in Modern France.* Trans. Arthur Goldhammer. New York: Hill and Wang.

Blalock, Hubert M. 1967. *Toward a Theory of Minority-Group Relations.* New York: John Wiley and Sons.

Blank, Rebecca M. 1997. *It Takes a Nation: A New Agenda for Fighting Poverty.* Princeton: Princeton University Press.

Blauner, Bob. 1972. *Racial Oppression in America.* New York: Harper and Row.

Bloch, Marc. 1953. *The Historian's Craft.* New York: Vintage.

Bloom, Jack M. 1987. *Class, Race, and the Civil Rights Movement.* Bloomington: Indiana University Press.

Bobo, Lawrence, James R. Kleugel, and Ryan A. Smith. 1997. "Laissez-Faire Racism: The Crystallization of a Kinder, Gentler, Antiblack Ideology." In *Racial Attitudes in the 1990s: Continuity and Change,* ed. Steven A. Tuch and Jack K. Martin. Westport, Conn.: Praeger.

Bobo, Lawrence, and Ryan A. Smith. 1994. "Antipoverty Policy, Affirmative Action, and Racial Attitudes." In *Confronting Poverty: Prescriptions for Change,* ed. Sheldon H. Danziger, Gary D. Sandefur, and Daniel H. Weinberg. New York: Russell Sage Foundation; Cambridge: Harvard University Press.

Bohman, James. 1996. *Public Deliberation: Pluralism, Complexity, and Democracy.* Cambridge: MIT Press.

Boisjoly, Johanne, Kathleen Mullan Harris, and Greg J. Duncan. 1998. "Trends, Events, and Duration of Initial Welfare Spells." *Social Service Review* 72:466–92.

Bowler, S., and T. Donovan. 1994. "Economic Conditions and Voting on Ballot Propositions." *American Politics Quarterly* 22:27–40.

———. 1998. *Demanding Choices: Opinion, Voting, and Direct Democracy.* Ann Arbor: University of Michigan Press.

Box-Steffensmeier, Janet, and Bradford S. Jones. 1997. "Time Is of the Essence: Event History Models in Political Science." *American Journal of Political Science* 41:1414–62.

Boyne, George. 1985. "Review Article: Theory, Methodology, and Results in Political Science: The Case of Output Studies." *British Journal of Political Science* 15:473–515.

Brace, Paul, Kellie N. Butler, Kevin Arceneaux, and Martin Johnson. 2002. "Measuring Public Opinion in the American States: New Perspectives Using National Survey Data." *American Journal of Political Science* 46:173–99.

Brace, Paul, and Aubrey Jewett. 1995. "The State of State Politics Research." *Political Research Quarterly* 48:643–81.

Branton, Regina P., and Bradford S. Jones. 1999. "Multiculturalism, Diversity, and Prejudice." Paper presented at the Annual Meeting of the Western Political Science Association, Seattle, April 15–18.

References

Brenner, Johanna. 2000. "Organizing around Welfare Reform: Activist Notes." Paper presented at the Work, Welfare, and Politics conference, University of Oregon, February 28–29.

Brodkin, Evelyn Z. 2001. "Reorganizing the Welfare State: New Administrative Models, Old Bureaucratic Problems." Typescript.

Brodkin, Karen. 1998. *How Jews Became White Folks and What That Says about Race in America.* New Brunswick, N.J.: Rutgers University Press.

Brooks, Gary H., and William Claggett. 1981. "Black Electoral Power, White Resistance, and Legislative Behavior." *Political Behavior* 3:49–68.

Brooks, Thomas R. 1974. *Walls Come Tumbling Down: A History of the Civil Rights Movement.* Englewood Cliffs, N.J.: Prentice-Hall.

Brosius, Hans-Bernd, and Anke Bathelt. 1994. "The Utility of Exemplars in Persuasive Communications." *Communication Research* 21 (February): 48–78.

Brown, Michael K. 1999. *Race, Money, and the American Welfare State.* Ithaca: Cornell University Press.

Brown, Robert D. 1995. "Party Cleavages and Welfare Effort in the American States." *American Political Science Review* 89:23–33.

Bryner, Gary. 1998. *Politics and Public Morality: The Great American Welfare Reform Debate.* New York: Norton.

Bullock, Charles S., III. 1981. "Congressional Voting and the Mobilization of a Black Electorate in the South." *Journal of Politics* 43:662–82.

Burgess, M. Elaine, and Daniel O. Price. 1963. *An American Dependency Challenge.* Chicago: American Public Welfare Association.

Burke, Edmund. 1973. *Reflections on the Revolution in France.* Garden City, N.Y.: Anchor Press.

Burke, Vee, and Melinda Gish. 1998. *Welfare Reform: Work Trigger, Time Limits, Exemptions and Sanctions under TANF.* Washington, D.C.: Congressional Research Service, 98–697, EPW.

Burnham, Walter Dean. 1974. "The United States: The Politics of Heterogeneity." In *Electoral Behavior: A Comparative Handbook,* ed. Richard Rose. New York: Free Press.

Bussiere, Elizabeth. 1997. *(Dis)Entitling the Poor: The Warren Court, Welfare Rights, and the American Political Tradition.* University Park: Pennsylvania State University Press.

Button, James W. 1989. *Blacks and Social Change: The Impact of the Civil Rights Movement.* Princeton: Princeton University Press.

Cain, Bruce. 1992. "Voting Rights and Democratic Theory: Toward a Color-Blind Society?" In *Controversies in Minority Voting,* ed. Bernard Grofman and Chandler Davidson. Washington, D.C.: Brookings Institution Press.

Caraley, Demetrios. 1992. "Washington Abandons the Cities." *Political Science Quarterly* 107:1–30.

Carmines, Edward G., and James A. Stimson. 1989. *Issue Evolution: Race and the Transformation of American Politics.* Princeton: Princeton University Press.

Carmines, Edward G., and Richard A. Zeller. 1979. *Reliability and Validity Assessment.* Sage University Paper series on Quantitative Applications in the Social Sciences Series, 07–017. Newbury Park, Calif.: Sage.

Carsey, Thomas M. 1995. "The Contextual Effects of Race on White Behavior: The 1989 New York City Mayoral Election." *Journal of Politics* 57:221–28.

Chapman, Herrick. 1995. "French Democracy and the Welfare State." In *The Social Construction of Democracy, 1870–1990*, ed. George Reid Andrews and Herrick Chapman. New York: New York University Press.

Chavez, Linda. 1998. *The Color Bind: California's Battle to End Affirmative Action*. Berkeley and Los Angeles: University of California Press.

Chernick, Howard, and Andrew Reschovsky. 1999. "State Fiscal Responses to Block Grants." In *The End of Welfare?* ed. M. B. Sawicky. Armonk, N.Y.: M. E. Sharp.

"Chicago Program Aimed at Helping Women Get Off of Welfare." 1995. *CBS This Morning*, February 3.

Citrin, Jack, Beth Reingold, Evelyn Walters, and Donald Green. 1990. "The 'Official English' Movement and the Symbolic Politics of Language in the United States." *Western Political Quarterly* 43:535–60.

Clarke, Leslie L., Brenda Jarmon, and Merlin Langley. 1999. "Qualitative Study of WAGES: People Who Have Left WAGES." Florida Inter-University Welfare Reform Collaborative, fall.

Clarke, Peter. 1996. *Hope and Glory: Britain, 1900–1990*. London: Penguin.

Clawson, Rosalee, and Rakuya Trice. 2000. "Poverty as We Know It: Media Portrayals of the Poor." *Public Opinion Quarterly* 64:53–64.

Cloward, Richard A., and Frances Fox Piven. 1974. *The Politics of Turmoil: Essays on Poverty, Race, and the Urban Crisis*. New York: Pantheon.

Cnudde, Charles C., and Donald J. McCrone. 1969. "Party Competition and Welfare Policies in the American States." *American Political Science Review* 63:858–66.

Cobban, Alfred. 1965. *A History of Modern France*. New York: George Braziller.

Cohen, Bernard. 1963. *The Press and Foreign Policy*. Princeton: Princeton University Press.

Cohen, Joshua. 1989. "Deliberation and Democratic Legitimacy." In *The Good Polity*, ed. Alan Hamlin and Philip Pettit. New York: Blackwell.

Cohn, D'Vera, and Darryl Fears. 2001. "Multiracial Growth Seen in Census Numbers Show Diversity, Complexity of U.S. Count." *Washington Post*, March 13, A1.

Collins, Patricia Hill. 2000. *Black Feminist Thought: Knowledge, Consciousness, and the Politics of Empowerment*. 2d ed. New York: Routledge.

Commonwealth of Virginia. 1940. Local ADC Coverage and Average Grants. Division of Research and Statistics, Department of Public Welfare, vol. 1, no. 6, February.

Congressional Record. 1995. 104th Cong., 1st sess. Vol. 141.

——. 1996. 104th Cong., 2d sess. Vol. 142.

Conlan, T. 1998. *From New Federalism to Devolution: Twenty-Five Years of Intergovernmental Reform*. Washington, D.C.: Brookings Institution Press.

Cook, Fay Lomax, and Edith J. Barrett. 1992. *Support for the American Welfare State*. New York: Columbia University Press.

Cooper, Frederick. 1996. *Decolonization and African Society: The Labor Question in French and British Africa*. Cambridge: Cambridge University Press.

References

Cottingham, Phoebe H., and David T. Ellwood, eds. 1989. *Welfare Policies for the 1990s*. Cambridge: Harvard University Press.

Council of Economic Advisers. 1998. *Economic Report of the President*. Washington, D.C.: U.S. Government Printing Office.

Dahl, Robert A. 1998. *On Democracy*. New Haven: Yale University Press.

Danziger, Sheldon. 2000. "Approaching the Limit: Early Lessons from Welfare Reform." Paper presented at "Rural Dimensions of Welfare Reform," Center for Poverty Research, Northwestern University and University of Chicago.

Darity, William. 1995. "Ethnicity, Race, and Earnings." *Economic Letters* 7:401–8.

Davies, Gareth. 1996. *From Opportunity to Entitlement*. Lawrence: University of Kansas Press.

Davies, Gareth, and Martha Derthick. 1997. "Race and Social Welfare Policy: The Social Security Act of 1935." *Political Science Quarterly* 112:217–35.

Davis, David Brion. 1966. *The Problem of Slavery in Western Culture*. Ithaca, N.Y.: Cornell University Press.

Davis, Martha F. 1993. *Brutal Need: Lawyers and the Welfare Rights Movement, 1960–1973*. New Haven: Yale University Press.

Dawson, Richard E., and James A. Robinson. 1963. "Inter-party Competition, Economic Variables, and Welfare Policies in the American States." *Journal of Politics* 25:265–89.

Day, Phyllis J. 1997. *A New History of Social Welfare*. Needham Heights, Mass.: Allyn and Bacon.

Delgado, Gary. 2000. "Racing the Welfare Debate." *Colorlines* 3, no. 3 (fall). <http://www.arc.org/C_Lines/CLArchive/CL3_3.html>.

Delli Carpini, Michael, and Scott Keeter. 1996. *What Americans Know about Politics and Why It Matters*. New Haven: Yale University Press.

Derthick, Martha. 1979. *Policymaking for Social Security*. Washington, D.C.: Brookings Institution Press.

Diller, Matthew. 2000. "The Revolution in Welfare Administration: Rules, Discretion, and Entrepreneurial Government." *New York University Law Review* 75, no. 5: 1121–1220.

Disch, Lisa Jane. 1994. *Hannah Arendt and the Limits of Philosophy*. Ithaca: Cornell University Press.

Dixit, Avinash, and John Londgegan. 1998. "Fiscal Federalism and Redistributive Politics." *Journal of Public Economics* 68:153–80.

Dommel, Paul R. 1974. *The Politics of Revenue Sharing*. Bloomington: Indiana University Press.

Donovan, Todd, and Shawn Bowler. 1998. "Direct Democracy and Minority Rights: An Extension." *American Journal of Political Science* 42:1020–24.

Doolittle, Fred, and James Riccio. 1992. "Case Management in Welfare Employment Programs." In *Evaluating Welfare and Training Programs*, ed. Charles Manski and Irv Garfinkel. Cambridge: Harvard University Press.

Dowdall, George W. 1974. "White Gains from Black Subordination in 1969 and 1970." *Social Problems* 22 (December): 162–83.

Drucker, Peter F. 1969. "The Sickness of Government." *Public Interest* 14:3–23.

Dryzek, John. 1990. *Discursive Democracy*. Cambridge: Cambridge University Press.

Du Bois, W. E. B. 1986. *The Souls of Black Folk*. New York: Library of America.

———. 1996. *The Philadelphia Negro: A Social Study*. Philadelphia: University of Pennsylvania Press.

Duncan, Greg J., Kathleen Mullan Harris, and Johanne Boisjoly. 2000. "Time Limits and Welfare Reform: New Estimates of the Number and Characteristics of Affected Families." *Social Service Review* 74:55–75.

Duncan, Greg J., and Saul Hoffman. 1995. "The Effect of Incomes, Wages, and AFDC Benefits on Marital Disruption." *Journal of Human Resources* 30:19–42.

Dye, Thomas R. 1966. *Politics Economics and the Public*. Chicago: Rand McNally.

———. 1984. "Party and Policy in the States." *Journal of Politics* 46:1097–1116.

Edelman, Murray. 1983. "Systematic Confusions in the Evaluation of Implementing Decisions." In *Evaluating the Welfare State: Social and Political Perspectives*, ed. Shimon E. Spiro. New York: Academic Press.

Edin, Kathryn, and Kathleen Mullan Harris. 1999. "Getting Off and Staying Off: Racial Differences in the Work Route Off Welfare." In *Latinas and African American Women at Work*, ed. Irene Browne. New York: Russell Sage Foundation.

Edin, Kathryn, and Laura Lein. 1997. *Making Ends Meet: How Single Mothers Survive Welfare and Low-Wage Work*. New York: Russell Sage Foundation.

Ehrenreich, Barbara. 1997. "When Government Gets Mean: Confessions of a Recovering Statist." *Nation*, November 17, 11–16.

Elazar, Daniel J. 1966. *American Federalism: A View from the States*. New York: Crowell.

———. 1994. *The American Mosaic*. Boulder: Westview Press.

Elkins, Stanley M. 1959. *Slavery: A Problem in American Institutional and Intellectual Life*. Chicago: University of Chicago Press.

Elling, Richard C. 1988. "Federalist Tool or Federalist Plot? Michigan Responds to the Reagan Block Grants." In *The Midwest Response to the New Federalism*, ed. Peter K. Eisinger and William Gormley. Madison: University of Wisconsin Press.

———. 1996. "Bureaucracy: Maligned Yet Essential." In *Politics in the American States*, ed. Virginia Gray and Herbert Jacob. Washington, D.C.: Congressional Quarterly Press.

———. 1999. "Administering State Programs: Performance and Politics." In *Politics in the American States*, ed. Virginia Gray and Herbert Jacob. Washington, D.C.: Congressional Quarterly Press.

Ellwood, Deborah A., and Donald J. Boyd. 2000. *Changes in State Spending on Social Services since the Implementation of Welfare Reform*. Preliminary Report. Albany: Nelson A. Rockefeller Institute of Government, State University of New York.

Elwitt, Sanford. 1986. *The Third Republic Defended: Bourgeois Reform in France, 1880–1914*. Baton Rouge: Louisiana State University Press.

References

Entman, Robert M. 1992. "Blacks in the News: Television, Modern Racism, and Cultural Change." *Journalism Quarterly* 69:341–61.

———. 1993. "Framing: Toward Clarification of a Fractured Paradigm." *Journal of Communication* 43:51–58.

———. 1995. "Television, Democratic Theory, and the Visual Construction of Poverty." *Research in Political Sociology* 7:139–59.

Entman, Robert M., and Andrew Rojecki. 2000. *The Black Image in the White Mind: Media and Race in America.* Chicago: University of Chicago Press.

Epstein, Edward Jay. 1973. *News from Nowhere.* New York: Random House.

Erie, Steven P. 1985. "Rainbow's End: From the Old to the New Urban Ethnic Politics." In *Urban Ethnicity in the United States,* ed. Joan Moore and Lionel Maldonado. Urban Affairs Annual Reviews. Beverly Hills: Sage.

Erikson, Robert S., Gerald C. Wright, and John P. McIver. 1993. *Statehouse Democracy.* Cambridge: Cambridge University Press.

Esping-Andersen, Gøsta. 1990. *The Three Worlds of Welfare Capitalism.* Princeton: Princeton University Press.

Favell, Adrian. 1998. *Philosophies of Integration: Immigration and the Idea of Citizenship in France and Britain.* New York: St. Martin's.

Feiock, Richard C. 1991. "The Effects of Economic Development Policy on Local Economic Growth." *American Journal of Political Science* 35:643–55.

Feldman, Stanley, and John Zaller. 1992. "Political Culture and Ambivalence: Ideological Responses and the Welfare State." *American Journal of Political Science* 36:268–307.

Fishkin, James S. 1991. *Democracy and Deliberation.* New Haven: Yale University Press.

Fitzgerald, John, Peter Gottschalk, and Robert Moffitt. 1998. "An Analysis of Sample Attrition in Panel Data." *Journal of Human Resources* 33:251–99.

Fix, Michael, and Margery Austin Turner, eds. 1999. *A National Report Card on Discrimination in America: The Role of Testing.* Washington, D.C.: Urban Institute Press.

"Folio 500: Circulation Figures for the 500 Top U.S. Magazines." 1994. *Folio* 23, no. 12: 52.

Forbes, H. D. 1997. *Ethnic Conflict: Commerce, Culture, and the Contact Hypothesis.* New Haven: Yale University Press.

Fording, Richard C. 1997. "The Conditional Effect of Violence as a Political Tactic: Mass Insurgency, Welfare Generosity, and Electoral Context in the American States." *American Journal of Political Science* 41:1–29.

———. 2001. "The Political Response to Black Insurgency: A Test of Competing Images of the Role of the State." *American Political Science Review* 95:115–30.

Foucault, Michel. 1973. *The Order of Things: An Archeology of Knowledge.* New York: Vintage.

Frankenberg, Ruth. 1993. *White Women, Race Matters: The Social Construction of Whiteness.* Minneapolis: University of Minnesota Press.

Fraser, Nancy. 1989. *Unruly Practices: Power, Discourse, and Gender in Contemporary Social Theory.* Minneapolis: University of Minnesota Press.

———. 1997. *Justice Interruptus: Critical Reflections on the "Postsocialist" Condition.* New York: Routledge.

Fraser, Nancy, and Linda Gordon. 1993. "Contract versus Charity: Why Is There No Social Citizenship in the United States?" *Socialist Review* 22, no. 3: 45–67.

———. 1994. "A Genealogy of *Dependency:* Tracing a Keyword of the U.S. Welfare State." *Signs* 19:309–36.

Fredrickson, George M. 1997. *The Comparative Imagination: On the History of Racism, Nationalism, and Social Movements.* Berkeley: University of California Press.

Freeman, Gary P. 1986. "Migration and the Political Economy of the Welfare State." *Annals of the American Academy of Political and Social Science* 485:51–63.

Frey, Bruno, and Lorenz Goette. 1998. "Does the Popular Vote Destroy Civil Rights?" *American Journal of Political Science* 41:245–69.

"From Welfare to Work." 1996. 4 parts. *Morning Edition,* National Public Radio, April 23, May 7, May 17, May 28.

Fry, Brian R., and Richard F. Winters. 1970. "The Politics of Redistribution." *American Political Science Review* 64:508–22.

Fujiwara, Lynn H. 1999. "Asian Immigrant Communities and the Racial Politics of Welfare Reform." In *Whose Welfare?* ed. Gwendolyn Mink. Ithaca: Cornell University Press.

Gamble, Barbara S. 1997. "Putting Civil Rights to a Popular Vote." *American Journal of Political Science* 91:245–69.

Gamson, William A. 1992. *Talking Politics.* Cambridge: Cambridge University Press.

Gamson, William A., and Kathryn E. Lasch. 1983. "The Political Culture of Social Welfare Policy." In *Evaluating the Welfare State,* ed. Shimon E. Spiro and Ephraim Yuchtman-Yaar. New York: Academic Press.

Gamson, William A., and Andre Modigliani. 1987. "The Changing Culture of Affirmative Action." In *Research in Political Sociology,* ed. Richard D. Braungart, vol. 3. Greenwich, Conn.: JAI Press.

Gans, Herbert. 1995. *The War against the Poor: The Underclass and Antipoverty Policy.* New York: Basic Books.

Gerber, Elisabeth. 1996. "Legislative Response to the Threat of Popular Initiatives." *American Journal of Political Science* 40:99–128.

———. 1998. *Interest Group Influence in the California Initiative Process.* San Francisco: Public Policy Institute of California.

———. 1999. *The Populist Paradox: Interest Group Influence and the Promise of Direct Legislation.* Princeton: Princeton University Press.

Gibson, James L. 1995. "The Political Freedom of African-Americans: A Contextual Analysis of Racial Attitudes, Political Tolerance, and Individual Liberty." *Political Geography* 14:571–99.

Gilens, Martin. 1995. " 'Racial Attitudes and Opposition to Welfare." *Journal of Politics* 90:994–1014.

———. 1996a. "Race and Poverty in America: Public Misperceptions and the News Media." *Public Opinion Quarterly* 60:515–27.

———. 1996b. "'Race Coding' and White Opposition to Welfare." *American Political Science Review* 90:593–604.

———. 1998. "Racial Attitudes and Race-Neutral Social Policies: White Opposition to Welfare and the Politics of Racial Inequality." In *Perception and Prejudice,* ed. Jon Hurwitz and Mark Peffley. New Haven: Yale University Press.

———. 1999. *Why Americans Hate Welfare: Race, Media, and the Politics of Antipoverty Policy.* Chicago: University of Chicago Press.

Giles, Michael W. 1977. "Percent Black and Racial Hostility: An Old Assumption." *Social Science Quarterly* 58:848–65.

Giles, Michael W., and Melanie Buckner. 1993. "David Duke and Black Threat: An Old Hypothesis Revisited." *Journal of Politics* 57:702–13.

Gilkes, Cheryl Townsend. 1989. "Dual Heroisms and Double Burdens: Interpreting Afro-American Women's Experiences and History." *Feminist Studies* 15:573–90.

Gilliam, Franklin D., Jr., and Shanto Iyengar. 2000. "Prime Suspects: The Corrosive Influence of Local Television News on the Viewing Public." *American Journal of Political Science* 44:560–74.

Gilliam, Franklin D., Jr., Shanto Iyengar, Adam Simon, and Oliver Wright. 1996. "Crime in Black and White." *Harvard International Journal of Press/Politics* 1, no. 3: 6–23.

Gillin, John Lewis. 1921. *Poverty and Dependency.* New York: Appleton-Century.

Gilroy, Paul. 2000. *Against Race: Imagining Political Culture beyond the Color Line.* Cambridge: Belknap Press of Harvard University Press.

Gingrich, Newt, et al. 1994. *Contract with America: The Bold Plan.* New York: Time Books.

Glaser, James M. 1994. "Back to the Black Belt: Racial Environment and White Racial Attitudes in the South." *Journal of Politics* 56:21–41.

Glick, Peter, and Susan T. Fiske. 2001. "Ambivalent Stereotypes as Legitimating Ideologies: Differentiating Paternalistic and Envious Prejudice." In *The Psychology of Legitimacy,* ed. John T. Jost and Brenda Major. New York: Cambridge University Press.

Glenn, Norval D. 1966. "White Gains from Negro Subordination." *Social Problems* 14 (fall): 159–78.

Goetz, Edward G. 1996. "The U.S. War on Drugs as Urban Policy." *International Journal of Urban and Regional Research* 20:539–50.

Goldberg, Heidi, and Liz Schott. 2000. *A Compliance-Oriented Approach to Sanctions in State and County TANF Programs.* Washington, D.C.: Center on Budget and Policy Priorities.

Gooden, Susan Tinsley. 1995. "Local Policy and Welfare Policy." *Southern Studies* 6, no. 4: 79–110.

———. 1998a. "All Things Not Being Equal: Difference in Caseworker Support toward Black and White Welfare Clients." *Harvard Journal of African American Public Policy* 4:23–33.

———. 1998b. *Washington Works: Sustaining a Vision of Welfare Reform Based on Personal Change, Work Preparation, and Employer Involvement.* New York: Manpower Demonstration Research Corporation.

———. 1999. "The Hidden Third Party: Welfare Recipients' Experiences with Employers." *Journal of Public Management and Social Policy* 5, no. 1: 69–83.

Goodsell, Charles T. 1981. "The Public Encounter and Its Study." In *The Public Encounter: Where State and Citizen Meet,* ed. C. T. Goodsell. Bloomington: Indiana University Press.

Goodwyn, Lawrence. 1976. *Democratic Promise: The Populist Moment in America.* Oxford: Oxford University Press.

Gordon, Linda. 1988. *Heroes of Their Own Lives: The Politics and History of Family Violence.* New York: Viking Press.

———. 1994. *Pitied but Not Entitled: Single Mothers and the History of Welfare, 1890–1935.* Cambridge: Harvard University Press.

———, ed. 1990. *Women, the State, and Welfare.* Madison: University of Wisconsin Press.

Graber, Doris. 1990. "Seeing Is Remembering: How Visuals Contribute to Learning from Television News." *Journal of Communication* 40:134–55.

———. 1997. "Television News without Pictures?" *Critical Studies in Mass Communication* 4:74–78.

Gray, Virginia. 1973. "Innovation in the States: A Diffusion Study." *American Political Science Review* 67:1174–85.

———. 1994. "Competition, Emulation, and Policy Innovation." In *New Perspectives on American Politics,* ed. Lawrence C. Dodd and Calvin Jillson. Washington, D.C.: Congressional Quarterly Press.

Gray, Virginia, and Herbert Jacob, eds. 1996. *Politics in the American States: A Comparative Analysis.* 6th ed. Washington, D.C.: Congressional Quarterly Press.

Green, Constance McLaughlin. 1967. *The Secret City: A History of Race Relations in the Nation's Capital.* Princeton: Princeton University Press.

Greenberg, Mark, and Steve Savner. 1996. *A Brief Summary of Key Provisions of the Temporary Assistance for Needy Families Block Grant of H.R. 3734.* Center for Law and Social Policy, Washington, D.C., August 13. <http://www.epn.org/clasp/clbskp.html>.

Grieco, Elizabeth M., and Rachel C. Cassidy. 2001. *Overview of Race and Hispanic Origin.* Census 2000 Brief, C2KBR/01-1. Washington, D.C.: U.S. Bureau of the Census. <http://www.census.gov/prod/2001pubs/c2kbr01-1.pdf>.

Grogan, Colleen M. 1994. "Political-Economic Factors Influencing State Medicaid Policy." *Political Research Quarterly* 47:565–88.

Guiden, M. 1999. *The Nation's Flirtation with Universal Health Insurance Coverage Continues.* Denver: National Conference of State Legislatures.

Gujarati, Damodar. 1992. *Essentials of Econometrics.* New York: McGraw-Hill.

Habermas, Jürgen. 1996. *Between Facts and Norms.* Trans. Steven Rendall. Cambridge: MIT Press.

Hacker, Andrew. 1992. *Two Nations: Black and White, Separate, Hostile, Unequal.* New York: Charles Scribner's Sons.

Hackey, Robert B. 1998. *Rethinking Health Care Policy.* Washington, D.C.: Georgetown University Press.

Hajnal, Z., Elisabeth Gerber, and H. Louch. 2002. "Minorities and Direct Legis-

347

lation: Evidence from California Ballot Proposition Elections." *Journal of Politics* 64:154–77.

Hamill, Ruth, Timothy DeCamp Wilson, and Richard E. Nisbett. 1980. "Insensitivity to Sample Bias: Generalizing from Atypical Cases." *Journal of Personality and Social Psychology* 39:578–89.

Hamilton, Dona Cooper, and Charles V. Hamilton. 1997. *The Dual Agenda: Race and Social Welfare Policies of the Civil Rights Organizations.* New York: Columbia University Press.

Handler, Joel F. 1992. "Discretion: Power, Quiescence, and Trust." In *The Uses of Discretion,* ed. Keith Hawkins. Oxford: Clarendon Press.

———. 1995. *The Poverty of Welfare Reform.* New Haven: Yale University Press.

Handler, Joel F., and Yeheskel Hasenfeld. 1991. *The Moral Construction of Poverty: Welfare Reform in America.* Newbury Park, Calif.: Sage.

Hanson, Russell L. 1983. "The 'Content' of Welfare Policy: The States and Aid to Families with Dependent Children." *Journal of Politics* 45:771–83.

———. 1994. "Liberalism and the Course of American Social Welfare Policy." In *The Dynamics of American Politics,* ed. Lawrence C. Dodd and Calvin Jillson. Boulder: Westview Press.

Hanson, Russell L., and Michael T. Heaney. 1997. "The Silent Revolution in Welfare: AFDC Waivers during the Bush and Clinton Administrations." Paper presented at the Annual Meeting of the Midwest Political Science Association, April 10–12, Chicago.

Hapgood, Hutchins. 1902. *Spirit of the Ghetto.* New York: Funk and Wagnalls.

Hartz, Louis. 1955. *The Liberal Tradition in America: An Interpretation of American Political Thought since the Revolution.* New York: Harcourt Brace.

Heclo, Hugh. 1986. "The Political Foundations of Antipoverty Policy." In *Fighting Poverty: What Works and What Doesn't,* ed. Sheldon H. Danziger and Daniel H. Weinberg. Cambridge: Harvard University Press.

Hero, Rodney E. 1992. *Latinos and the U.S. Political System: Two-Tiered Pluralism.* Philadelphia: Temple University Press.

———. 1998. *Faces of Inequality: Social Diversity in American Politics.* Oxford: Oxford University Press.

Hero, Rodney E., and Caroline J. Tolbert. 1996a. "Race/Ethnicity and Direct Democracy: An Analysis of California's Illegal Immigration Initiative." *Journal of Politics* 58:806–18.

———. 1996b. "A Racial/Ethnic Diversity Interpretation of Politics and Policy in the States of the U.S." *American Journal of Political Science* 40:851–71.

Herring, Mary. 1990. "Legislative Responsiveness to Black Constituents in Three Deep South States." *Journal of Politics* 523:740–58.

Hicks, Alexander M., and Duane H. Swank. 1992. "Politics, Institutions, and Welfare Spending in Industrialized Democracies, 1960–82." *American Political Science Review* 86:658–75.

Hill, Kim Quaile. 1994. *Democracy in the Fifty States.* Lincoln: University of Nebraska Press.

Hill, Kim Quaile, and Jan E. Leighley. 1992. "The Policy Consequences of Class Bias in State Electorates." *American Journal of Political Science* 36:351–65.

Hill, Kim Quaile, Jan E. Leighley, and Angela Hinton-Andersson. 1995. "Lower-Class Mobilization and Policy Linkage in the U.S. States." *American Journal of Political Science* 39:75–86.

Hirsch, Arnold R. 1983. *Making the Second Ghetto: Race and Housing in Chicago, 1940–1960*. Cambridge: Cambridge University Press.

Hobsbawm, E. J. 1987. *The Age of Empire, 1875–1914*. New York: Pantheon.

Hochschild, Jennifer. 1984. *The New American Dilemma: Liberal Democracy and School Desegregation*. New Haven: Yale University Press.

———. 1995. *Facing Up to the American Dream*. Princeton: Princeton University Press.

———. 2000. "Lumpers and Splitters, Individuals and Structures." In *Racialized Politics: The Debate about Racism in America*, ed. David O. Sears, Jim Sidanius, and Lawrence Bobo. Chicago: University of Chicago Press.

Hofferbert, Richard I. 1966. "The Relationship between Public Policy and Some Structural and Environmental Variables in the American States." *American Political Science Review* 60:73–82.

Hoffman, Saul D., and Greg J. Duncan. 1991. "Teenage Underclass Behavior and Subsequent Poverty: Have the Rules Changed?" In *The Urban Underclass*, ed. Christopher Jencks and Paul E. Peterson. Washington, D.C.: Brookings Institution Press.

Hoffmann, Stanley. 1963. "Paradoxes of the French Political Community." In Stanley Hoffmann, Charles P. Kindleberger, Laurence Wylie, Jesse R. Pits, Jean-Baptiste Duroselle, and François Goguel, *In Search of France*. Cambridge: Harvard University Press.

Holbrook, Thomas M., and Emily Van Dunk. 1993. "Electoral Competition in the American States." *American Political Science Review* 87:955–62.

Hollander, Jacob. 1914. *Abolition of Poverty*. Boston: Houghton Mifflin.

Holzer, Harry J., and Michael Stoll. 2000. "Employer Demand for Welfare Recipients by Race." Institute for Research on Poverty, Discussion Paper No. 1213-00.

Houppert, Karen. 1999. "You're Not Entitled!" *Nation,* October 25, 11–18.

Howard, Christopher. 1992. "Sowing the Seeds of 'Welfare': The Transformation of Mothers' Pensions, 1900–1940." *Journal of Policy History* 4:188–227.

———. 1999. "Field Essay: American Welfare State or States?" *Political Research Quarterly* 52:421–42.

———. 2001. "Racial Diversity and Social Policy in the American States." Paper presented at the American Politicial Science Association Annual Meeting, August 28–September 2, San Francisco.

Huckfeldt, Robert, and Carol Weitzel Kohfeld. 1989. *Race and the Decline of Class in American Politics*. Urbana: University of Illinois Press.

Hunter, Albert J. 1985. "Private, Parochial, and Public Social Orders: The Problem of Crime and Incivility in Urban Communities." In *The Challenge of Social Control: Citizenship and Institution-Building in Modern Society,* ed. G. D. Suttles and M. N. Zald. Norwood, N.J.: Aldex.

Hunter, Robert. 1904. *Poverty*. New York: Macmillan.

Ignatiev, Noel. 1995. *How the Irish Became White*. New York: Routledge.

References

Inman, Robert P., and Daniel L. Rubinfeld. 1997. "Rethinking Federalism." *Journal of Economic Perspectives* 11, no. 4: 43–64.

Iyengar, Shanto. 1990. "Framing Responsibility for Political Issues: The Case of Poverty." *Political Behavior* 12:19–40.

———. 1991. *Is Anyone Responsible: How Television Frames Political Issues.* Chicago: University of Chicago Press.

Iyengar, Shanto, and Donald Kinder. 1987. *News That Matters: Television and American Opinion.* Chicago: University of Chicago Press.

Jackson, Kenneth T. 1985. *Crabgrass Frontier.* Oxford: Oxford University Press.

Jacobs, David, and Ronald E. Helms. 1996. "Toward a Political Model of Incarceration: A Time-Series Examination of Multiple Explanations for Prison Admission Rates." *American Journal of Sociology* 102:323–57.

Jacobs, Lawrence R., and Robert Y. Shapiro. 1994. "Studying Substantive Democracy." *Political Science and Politics* 27, no. 1: 9–16.

Jacobson, Matthew F. 1998. *Whiteness of a Different Color: European Immigrants and the Alchemy of Race.* Cambridge: Harvard University Press.

James, David R. 1988. "The Transformation of the Southern Racial State: Class and Race Determinants of Local-State Structures." *American Sociological Review* 53:191–208.

Jargowsky, Paul A., and Mary Jo Bane. 1991. "Ghetto Poverty in the United States, 1970–1980." In *The Urban Underclass,* ed. Christopher Jencks and Paul E. Peterson. Washington, D.C.: Brookings Institution Press.

Jaynes, Gerald David, and Robin M. Williams Jr. 1989. *A Common Destiny: Blacks and American Society.* Washington, D.C.: National Academy Press.

Jencks, Christopher. 1992. *Rethinking Social Policy.* Cambridge: Harvard University Press.

Jennings, Edward T. 1979. "Competition, Constituencies, and Welfare Policies in the American States." *American Political Science Review* 73:414–29.

Johnson, Hans. 1999. "How Many Californians? A Review of Population Projections for the State." *California Counts* (Public Policy Institute of California) 1, no. 1.

Johnson, Martin. 2001. "The Impact of Social Diversity and Racial Attitudes on Social Welfare Policy." *State Politics and Policy Quarterly* 1:27–49.

Jones, Bradford S., and Barbara Norrander. 1996. "The Reliability of Aggregated Public Opinion Measures." *American Journal of Political Science* 40:295–309.

Jones, James. 1972. *Prejudice and Racism.* Reading, Mass.: Addison-Wesley.

Katz, Michael B. 1989. *The Undeserving Poor: From the War on Poverty to the War on Welfare.* New York: Pantheon.

———. 1995. *Improving Poor People.* Princeton: Princeton University Press.

———. 1996. *In the Shadow of the Poorhouse: A Social History of Welfare in America.* New York: Basic Books.

———. 2001. *The Price of Citizenship: Redefining the American Welfare State.* New York: Metropolitan Books.

Katznelson, Ira. 1976. *Black Men, White Cities: Race, Politics, and Migration in the United States, 1900–1930, and Britain, 1948–1968.* Chicago: University of Chicago Press.

———. 1981. *City Trenches: Urban Politics and the Patterning of Class in the United States.* New York: Pantheon.

Katznelson, Ira, Kim Geiger, and Daniel Kryder. 1993. "Limiting Liberalism: The Southern Veto in Congress, 1933–1950." *Political Science Quarterly* 108:283–306.

Kaus, Mickey. 1992. *The End of Equality.* New York: Basic Books.

Kazoleas, Dean C. 1993. "A Comparison of the Persuasive Effectiveness of Qualitative versus Quantitative Evidence: A Test of Explanatory Hypotheses." *Communication Quarterly* 41 (winter): 40–50.

Keech, William R. 1968. *The Impact of Negro Voting.* Chicago: Rand McNally.

Kellstedt, Paul M. 1997. "How Race and the New Deal Converged: An Exploration into the Role of Media Portrayals of Poverty and Crime." Paper presented at the Annual Meeting of the Midwest Political Science Association, April 10–12, Chicago.

Kelso, Robert W. 1929. *Poverty.* New York: Longmans, Green.

Kennedy, Paul M. 1976. *The Rise and Fall of British Naval Mastery.* New York: Charles Scribner's Sons.

Kenney, Keith. 1992. "Effects of Still Photographs." *News Photographer* 47 (May): 41–42.

Kerwin, Cornelius M. 1994. *Rulemaking: How Government Agencies Write Law and Make Policy.* Washington, D.C.: Congressional Quarterly Press.

Key, V. O., Jr. 1949. *Southern Politics in State and Nation.* New York: Alfred A. Knopf.

———. 1966. *The Responsible Electorate: Rationality in Presidential Voting.* Cambridge: Harvard University Press.

Kifer, A. F. 1961. "The Negro under the New Deal." Ph.D. diss., University of Wisconsin.

Kincaid, John. 1998. "The Devolution Tortoise and the Centralization Hare." *New England Economic Review* (May): 13–40.

Kinder, Donald R., and Tali Mendelberg. 1995. "Cracks in the American Apartheid: The Political Impact of Prejudice among Desegregated Whites." *Journal of Politics* 57:402–24.

Kinder, Donald R., and Lynn M. Sanders. 1996. *Divided by Color: Racial Politics and Democratic Ideals.* Chicago: University of Chicago Press.

Kinder, Donald R., and Nicholas Winter. 2001. "Exploring the Racial Divide: Blacks, Whites, and Opinion on National Policy." *American Journal of Political Science* 45:439–53.

King, Desmond. 1995. *Actively Seeking Work? The Politics of Unemployment and Welfare Policy in the United States and Great Britain.* Chicago: University of Chicago Press.

King, Gary, Michael Tomz, and Jason Wittenberg. 2000. "Making the Most of Statistical Analyses: Improving Interpretation and Presentation." *American Journal of Political Science* 44:347–61.

Klinkner, Philip A., and Rogers M. Smith. 1999. *The Unsteady March: The Rise and Decline of Racial Equality in America.* Chicago: University of Chicago Press.

Köhler, Peter A., and Hans F. Zacher, eds. 1982. *The Evolution of Social Insur-*

ance, 1881–1981: Studies of Germany, France, Great Britain, Austria, and Switzerland. London: Frances Pinter.

Krosnick, Jon A., and Donald R. Kinder. 1990. "Altering the Foundations of Support for the President through Priming." *American Political Science Review* 84:497–512.

Kuklinski, James H. and Paul J. Quirk. 2000. "Reconsidering the Rational Public: Cognition, Heuristics and Mass Opinion." In *Elements of Reason* ed. Arthur Lupia, Matthew D. McCubbins, and Samuel L. Popkin. New York: Cambridge University Press.

Laclau, Ernesto, and Chantal Mouffe. 1985. *Hegemony and Socialist Strategy: Toward a Radical Democratic Politics*. London: Verso.

Lafer, Gordon. 1999. "Captive Labor: America's Prisoners as Corporate Workforce." *American Prospect* 46, September–October, 66–70.

Langbein, Laura Irwin, and Allan J. Lichtman. 1978. "Ecological Inference." Sage University Paper series on Quantitative Applications in the Social Sciences Series, 07–010. Beverly Hills, Calif.: Sage.

Lara, Maria Pia. 1998. *Moral Textures: Feminist Narratives in the Public Sphere*. Cambridge: Polity Press.

Leahy, Margaret. 1941. "Intake Practices in Local Public Assistance Agencies." *Social Security Bulletin* 4, no. 10: 3–9.

Lebovics, Herman. 1992. *True France: The Wars over Cultural Identity, 1900–1945*. Ithaca, N.Y.: Cornell University Press.

Lee, Joseph. 1902. *Constructive and Preventive Philanthropy*. New York: Macmillan.

Leichter, Howard M. 1996. "State Governments and Their Capacity for Health Care Reform." In *Health Policy, Federalism, and the American States*, ed. Robert F. Rich and William D. White. Washington, D.C.: Urban Institute Press.

———, ed. 1997. *Health Policy Reform in America*. Armonk, N.Y.: M. E. Sharpe.

Lemann, Nicholas. 1991. *The Promised Land: The Great Black Migration and How It Changed America*. New York: Knopf.

Lester, Paul, and Ron Smith. 1990. "African-American Photo Coverage in *Life, Newsweek*, and *Time*, 1937–1988." *Journalism Quarterly* 67:128–36.

Lieberman, Robert C. 1993. "The Structural Politics of Race: Toward a New Approach to the Study of Race and Politics." Paper presented at the Annual Meeting of the American Political Association, Washington, D.C., September 2–5.

———. 1995a. "Race, Institutions, and the Administration of Social Policy." *Social Science History* 19 (winter): 511–42.

———. 1995b. "Race and the Organization of Welfare Policy." In *Classifying by Race*, ed. Paul E. Peterson. Princeton: Princeton University Press.

———. 1997. "Race and Political Institutions: The United States in Comparative-Historical Perspective." Paper presented to the Annual Meeting of the American Political Science Association, Washington, D.C.

———. 1998. *Shifting the Color Line: Race and the American Welfare State*. Cambridge: Harvard University Press.

————. 1999. "Race, State, and Inequality in the United States, Britain, and France." Working Paper No. 149. New York: Russell Sage Foundation.

Lieberman, Robert C., and John S. Lapinski. 2001. "American Federalism, Race, and the Administration of Welfare." *British Journal of Political Science* 31:303–29.

Lieberman Robert C., and Greg M. Shaw. 2000. "Looking Inward, Looking Outward: The Politics of State Welfare Innovation under Devolution." *Political Research Quarterly* 53:215–40.

Lieske, Joel. 1993. "Regional Subcultures of the United States." *Journal of Politics* 55:86–113.

Limerick, Patricia Nelson. 1987. *Legacy of Conquest: The Unbroken Past of the American West*. New York: Norton.

Lindblom, Charles E. 1959. "The Science of Muddling Through." *Public Administration Review* 19:79–88.

Lineberry, Robert L. 1977. *American Public Policy: What Government Does and What Difference It Makes*. New York: Harper and Row.

Lippmann, Walter. 1960. *Public Opinion*. New York: Macmillan.

Lipset, Seymour M., and Stein Rokkan. 1967. "Cleavage Structures, Party Systems, and Voter Alignments: An Introduction." In *Party Systems and Voter Alignments: Cross-National Perspectives,* ed. Seymour M. Lipset and Stein Rokkan. New York: Free Press.

Lipsky, Michael. 1980. *Street-Level Bureaucracy: Dilemmas of the Individual in Public Services*. New York: Russell Sage Foundation.

————. 1984. "Bureaucratic Disentitlement in Social Welfare Programs." *Social Service Review* 58:3–27.

Liska, David, Niall J. Brennan, and Brian K. Bruen. 1998. *State-Level Databook on Health Care Access and Financing*. Washington, D.C.: Urban Institute Press.

Lockard, Duane. 1959. *New England State Politics*. Princeton: Princeton University Press.

Loury, Glenn. 1994. "Self-Censorship and Public Discourse: A Theory of 'Political Correctness' and Related Phenomena." *Rationality and Society* (October): 428–61.

————. 2002. *The Anatomy of Racial Inequality*. Cambridge: Harvard University Press.

Lower-Basch, Elizabeth. 2000. *"Leavers" and Diversion Studies: Preliminary Analysis of Racial Differences in Caseload Trends and Leaver Outcomes*. Washington, D.C.: U.S. Department of Health and Human Services.

Lowi, Theodore. 1964. "American Business Public Policy: Case Studies and Political Theory." *World Politics* 16:677–715.

————. 1995. *The End of the Republican Era*. Norman: University of Oklahoma Press.

Lubiano, Wahneema. 1992. "Black Ladies, Welfare Queens, and State Minstrels: Ideological War by Narrative Means." In *Race-ing Justice, En-gendering Power: Essays on Anita Hill, Clarence Thomas, and the Construction of Social Reality,* ed. Toni Morrison. New York: Pantheon.

Luker, Kristin. 1996. *Dubious Conceptions: The Politics of Teenage Pregnancy.* Cambridge: Harvard University Press.

Lupia, Arthur. 1994. "Shortcuts versus Encyclopedias: Information and Voting Behavior in California Insurance Reform Elections." *American Political Science Review* 88:63–76.

Lurie, Irene. 1997. "Temporary Assistance for Needy Families: A Green Light for the States." *Publius* 27:73–88.

Lynch, James P., and William J. Sabol. 1997. "Did Getting Tougher on Crime Pay?" In *Crime Policy Report.* Washington, D.C.: Urban Institute Press.

Lyndon B. Johnson School of Public Affairs. 1989. *The Social Safety Net Reexamined: FDR to Reagan.* Austin: University of Texas Press.

Magleby, David. 1984. *Direct Legislation: Voting on Ballot Propositions in the United States.* Baltimore: John Hopkins University Press.

de Man, Paul. 1986. *The Resistance to Theory.* Minneapolis: University of Minnesota Press.

Mansbridge, Jane. 1980. *Beyond Adversary Democracy.* Chicago: University of Chicago Press.

———. 1991. "Feminism and Democratic Community." In *Democratic Community,* ed. John W. Chapman and Ian Shapiro. *Nomos* 35. New York: New York University Press.

———. 1992. "A Deliberative Theory of Interest Representation." In *The Politics of Interests,* ed. Mark P. Patracca. Boulder: Westview Press.

———. 1993. "Self-Interest and Political Transformation." In *Reconsidering the Democratic Public,* ed. George E. Marcus and Russell L. Hanson. University Park: Pennsylvania State University Press.

———. 1999. "On the Idea That Participation Makes Better Citizens." In *Citizen Competence and Democratic Institutions,* ed. S. L. Elkin and K. E. Soltan. University Park: Pennsylvania State University Press.

Marcus, George, John Sullivan, Elizabeth Theiss-Morse, and Sandra Wood. 1995. *With Malice toward Some: How People Make Civil Liberties Judgments.* Cambridge: Cambridge University Press.

Marmor, Theodore R., and Jerry L. Mashaw. 1996. "National Health Reform: Where Do We Go from Here?" In *Health Policy, Federalism, and the American States,* ed. Robert F. Rich and William D. White. Washington, D.C.: Urban Institute Press.

Marmor, Theodore R., Jerry L. Mashaw, and Philip L. Harvey. 1990. *America's Misunderstood Welfare State.* New York: Basic Books.

Marshall, T. H. 1964. "Citizenship and Social Class." In *Class, Citizenship, and Social Development.* Garden City, N.Y.: Doubleday.

Marx, Anthony W. 1998. *Making Race and Nation: A Comparison of the United States, South Africa, and Brazil.* Cambridge: Cambridge University Press.

Massey, Douglas A., and Nancy A. Denton. 1993. *American Apartheid: Segregation and the Making of the Underclass.* Cambridge: Harvard University Press.

Massing, Michael. 2000. "Ending Poverty as We Know It." *American Prospect* 11, no. 15: 30–39.

Mayer, William G. 1993. "Poll Trends: Trends in Media Usage." *Public Opinion Quarterly* 57:593–611.

McConnell, Grant. 1966. *Private Power and American Democracy*. New York: Knopf.

Mead, Lawrence M. 1986. *Beyond Entitlement: The Social Obligations of Citizenship*. New York: Free Press.

———. 1992. *The New Politics of Poverty: The Nonworking Poor in America*. New York: Basic Books.

———, ed. 1997. *The New Paternalism: Supervisory Approaches to Poverty*. Washington, D.C.: Brookings Institution Press.

———. 2001. "The Politics of Conservative Welfare Reform." In *The New World of Welfare*, ed. Rebecca M. Blank and Ron Haskins. Washington, D.C.: Brookings Institution Press.

Meier, August, and Elliot Rudwick. 1970. *From Plantation to Ghetto*. Rev. ed. New York: Hill and Wang.

Meier, Kenneth J. 1993. *Politics and the Bureaucracy: Policy Making in the Fourth Branch of Government*. Pacific Grove, Calif.: Brooks/Cole.

Meier, Kenneth J., and Donald Haider-Markel. 1996. "The Politics of Gay and Lesbian Rights: Expanding the Scope of Conflict." *Journal of Politics* 58:332–49.

Meier, Kenneth J., and Joseph Stewart Jr. 1991. *The Politics of Hispanic Education*. Albany: State University of New York Press.

Meier, Kenneth, Joseph Stewart Jr., and Robert England. 1989. *Race, Class, and Education: The Politics of Second Generation Discrimination*. Madison: University of Wisconsin Press.

Melnick, Shep. 1994. *Between the Lines: Interpreting Welfare Rights*. Washington, D.C.: Brookings Institution Press.

Mendelberg, Tali. 1997. "Executing Hortons: Racial Crime in the 1998 Presidential Campaign." *Public Opinion Quarterly* 61:134–58.

Merelman, Richard M. 1994. "Racial Conflict and Cultural Politics in the United States." *Journal of Politics* 56:1–20.

Mettler, Suzanne. 2000. "States' Rights, Women's Obligations: Contemporary Welfare Reform in Historical Perspective." *Women and Politics* 21:1–34.

Meyer, Jack A., N. S. Bagby, and M. Klotz. 1997. *Welfare-to-Work in Indianapolis: A Preliminary Evaluation*. Washington, D.C.: Economic and Social Research Institute.

Miller, Herman P. 1965. "Changes in the Number and Composition of the Poor." In *Poverty in America*, ed. Margaret S. Gordon. Berkeley: University of California Press.

Miller, Warren E., and Donald E. Stokes. 1963. "Constituency Influence in Congress." *American Political Science Review* 57:45–56.

Mink, Gwendolyn. 1994. "Welfare Reform in Historical Perspective." *Connecticut Law Review* 26:879–91.

———. 1998. *Welfare's End*. Ithaca: Cornell University Press.

———, ed. 1999. *Whose Welfare?* Ithaca: Cornell University Press.

Mitchell, W. J. T. 1994. *Picture Theory*. Chicago: University of Chicago Press.

Mizruchi, Ephraim H. 1983. *Regulating Society: Beguines, Bohemians, and Other Marginals*. Chicago: University of Chicago Press.

Moffitt, Robert. 1988. "Has State Redistribution Policy Grown More Conservative?" Working Paper No. 2516. Cambridge, Mass.: National Bureau of Economic Research.

———. 1992. "Incentive Effects in the U.S. Welfare System: A Review." *Journal of Economic Literature* 30 (March): 1–61.

Monroe, Alan D. 1979. "Consistency between Public Preferences and National Policy Decisions." *American Politics Quarterly* 7:3–19.

Monroe, Alan D., and Paul J. Gardner. 1987. "Public Policy Linkages." In *Research in Micropolitics,* ed. Samuel Long. Greenwich, Conn.: JAI Press.

Moore, Barrington, Jr. 1966. *Social Origins of Dictatorship and Democracy: Lord and Peasant in the Making of the Modern World.* Boston: Beacon Press.

Moore, Thomas, and Vicky Selkowe. 1999. "The Impact of Welfare Reform on Wisconsin's Hmong Aid Recipients." Institute for Wisconsin's Future, December.

Morain, Dan. 1999. "Wealth Buys Access to State Politics." *Los Angeles Times,* April 18.

Morgan, Edmund S. 1975. *American Slavery, American Freedom: The Ordeal of Colonial Virginia.* New York: Norton.

Moynihan, Daniel Patrick. 1965. *The Negro Family: The Case for National Action.* Washington, D.C.: Office of Policy Planning and Research, U.S. Department of Labor.

———. 1985. "We Can't Avoid Family Policy Much Longer" (interview). *Challenge,* September–October, 11.

Mueller, Paul D., and Brian S. Krueger. 2001. "Racial Mobilization, Partisan Coalitions, and Public Policy in the American States." *State Politics and Policy Quarterly* 2, no. 1: 167–81.

Murray, Charles. 1984. *Losing Ground: American Social Policy, 1950–80.* New York: Basic Books.

Musgrave, Richard A. 1997. "Devolution, Grants, and Fiscal Competition." *Journal of Economic Perspectives* 11, no. 4: 65–72.

Myers, Robert J. 1985. *Social Security.* 3d ed. Homewood, Ill.: Richard D. Irwin.

Myrdal, Gunnar. 1944. *An American Dilemma: The Negro Problem and Modern Democracy.* New York: Harper and Brothers.

Naples, Nancy. 1997. "The 'New Consensus' on the Gendered Social Contract." *Signs* 22:907–45.

Narayan, Uma. 1997. "Toward a Feminist Vision of Citizenship: Rethinking the Implications of Dignity, Political Participation, and Nationality." In *Reconstructing Political Theory: Feminist Perspectives,* ed. Mary Lyndon Shanley and Uma Narayan. Cambridge: Polity Press.

Nathan, Richard P., and Thomas L. Gais. 1999. *Implementing the Personal Responsibility Act of 1996: A First Look.* Albany: Nelson A. Rockefeller Institute of Government, State University of New York.

National Governors' Association. 1997. *Restructuring and Reinventing State Workforce Development Systems.* Issue Brief. January 15.

Nelson, Barbara J. 1990. The Origins of the Two-Channel Welfare State: Workmen's Compensation and Mothers' Aid." In *Women, the State, and Welfare,* ed. Linda Gordon. Madison: University of Wisconsin Press.

Nelson, Thomas E. 1999. "Group Affect and Attribution in Social Policy Opinion." *Journal of Politics* 16:331–62.

Nelson, Thomas E., and Donald R. Kinder. 1996. "Issue Frames and Group-Centrism in American Public Opinion." *Journal of Politics* 58:1055–78.

Neubeck, Kenneth J., and Noel A. Cazenave. 2001. *Welfare Racism: Playing the Race Card against America's Poor.* New York: Routledge.

Neuman, W. Russell, Marion R. Just, and Ann N. Crigler. 1992. *Common Knowledge: News and the Construction of Political Meaning.* Chicago: University of Chicago Press.

Noble, Charles. 1997. *Welfare as We Knew It: A Political History of the American Welfare State.* Oxford: Oxford University Press.

Nord, Philip. 1995. *The Republican Moment: Struggles for Democracy in Nineteenth-Century France.* Cambridge: Harvard University Press.

Norrander, Barbara. 2000. "The Multi-layered Impact of Public Opinion on Capital Punishment Implementation in the American States." *Political Research Quarterly* 53:771–95.

———. 2001. "Measuring State Public Opinion with the Senate National Election Study." *State Politics and Policy Quarterly* 1:111–25.

O'Connor, Alice. 2001. *Poverty Knowledge: Social Science, Social Policy, and the Poor in Twentieth-Century U.S. History.* Princeton: Princeton University Press.

Ogus, A. I. 1982. "Britain." In *The Evolution of Social Insurance, 1881–1981: Studies of Germany, France, Great Britain, Austria, and Switzerland,* ed. Peter A. Köhler and Hans F. Zacher. London: Frances Pinter.

Oliver, J. Eric, and Tali Mendelberg. 2000. "Reconsidering the Environmental Determinants of White Racial Attitudes." *American Journal of Political Science* 44:574–89.

Omi, Michael, and Howard Winant. 1994. *Racial Formation in the United States: From the 1960s to the 1990s.* 2d ed. New York: Routledge.

Orloff, Ann Shola. 1993. "Gender and the Social Rights of Citizenship: The Comparative Analysis of Gender Relations and Welfare States." *American Sociological Review* 58:303–28.

Orr, Larry L. 1976. "Income Transfers as a Public Good: An Application to AFDC." *American Economic Review* 66, no. 3: 359–71.

Orwell, George. 1954. "Politics and the English Language." In *A Collection of Essays.* Garden City, N.J.: Doubleday-Anchor.

Osofsky, Gilbert. 1963. *Harlem: The Making of a Ghetto—Negro New York, 1890–1930.* Oxford: Oxford University Press.

Page, Benjamin, and Robert Shapiro. 1983. "Effect of Public Opinion on Policy." *American Political Science Review* 77:175–90.

———. 1992. *The Rational Public.* Chicago: University of Chicago Press.

Parenti, Christian. 1999. *Lockdown America: Police and Prisons in the Age of Crisis.* New York: Verso.

Parmalee, Maurice. 1916. *Poverty and Social Progress.* New York: Macmillan.

Pateman, Carole. 1970. *Participation and Democratic Theory.* Cambridge: Cambridge University Press.

Patterson, James T. 1994. *America's Struggle against Poverty, 1900–1994*. Cambridge: Harvard University Press.

Pedersen, Susan. 1993. *Family, Dependence, and the Origins of the Welfare State: Britain and France, 1914–1945*. Cambridge: Cambridge University Press.

Peffley, Mark, and Jon Hurwitz. 1998. "Whites' Stereotypes of Blacks: Sources and Political Consequences." In *Perception and Prejudice: Race and Politics in the United States,* ed. Jon Hurwitz and Mark Peffley. New Haven: Yale University Press.

Peffley, Mark, Jon Hurwitz, and Paul Sniderman. 1997. "Racial Stereotypes and Whites' Political Views of Blacks in the Context of Welfare and Crime." *American Journal of Political Science* 41:30–60.

Peffley, Mark, Todd Shields, and Bruce Williams. 1996. "The Intersection of Race and Crime in Television News: An Experimental Study." *Political Communication* 13:309–27.

"People on Welfare Find It Hard to Get Off Welfare and Get a Job." 1995. *CBS This Morning,* February 1.

Peterson, George E. 1984. "Federalism and the States: An Experiment in Decentralization." In *The Reagan Record,* ed. John L. Palmer and Isabell V. Sawhill. Cambridge, Mass.: Ballinger.

Peterson, Iver, and David M. Halbfinger. 2001. "New Jersey Agrees to Pay $13 Million in Profiling Suit." *New York Times,* February 3, A1.

Peterson, Paul E. 1995. *The Price of Federalism*. Washington, D.C.: Brookings Institution Press.

Peterson, Paul E., and Mark C. Rom. 1989. "American Federalism, Welfare Policy and Residential Choices." *American Political Science Review* 83:711–28.

———. 1990. *Welfare Magnets: A New Case for a National Standard*. Washington, D.C.: Brookings Institution Press.

Phelan, Shane. 1994. *Getting Specific: Postmodern Lesbian Politics*. Minneapolis: University of Minnesota Press.

Phillips, Kevin. 1969. *The Emerging Republican Majority*. New Rochelle, N.Y.: Arlington House.

Pierson, Paul. 2000. "Not Just What, but When: Timing and Sequence in Political Processes." *Studies in American Political Development* 14 (spring): 72–92.

Piven, Frances Fox, and Richard A. Cloward. 1971. *Regulating the Poor: The Functions of Public Welfare*. New York: Vintage.

———. 1982. *The New Class War: Reagan's Attack on the Welfare State and Its Consequences*. New York: Pantheon.

———. 1988. *Why Americans Don't Vote*. New York: Pantheon.

———. 1993. *Regulating the Poor: The Functions of Public Welfare*. Updated ed. New York: Vintage.

Plotnick, Robert D., and Richard F. Winters. 1985. "A Politico-Economic Theory of Income Redistribution." *American Political Science Review* 79:458–73.

Polanyi, Karl. 1944. *The Great Transformation: The Political and Economic Origins of Our Time*. Boston: Beacon Press.

Potter, David M. 1972. *The South and the Concurrent Majority*. Ed. Don E. Fehrenbacher and Carl N. Degler. Baton Rouge: Louisiana State University Press.

Primus, W. 2001. "What Next for Welfare Reform? A Vision for Assisting Families." *Brookings Review* 19 (summer): 17–19.

Prottas, Jeffrey M. 1979. *People-Processing: The Street-Level Bureaucrat in Public Service Bureaucracies.* Lexington, Mass.: Lexington Books.

Quadagno, Jill. 1988. "From Old-Age Assistance to Supplemental Security Income: The Political Economy of Relief in the South." In *The Politics of Social Policy in the U.S.,* ed. Margaret Weir, Ann Orloff, and Theda Skocpol. Princeton: Princeton University Press.

———. 1994. *The Color of Welfare: How Racism Undermined the War on Poverty.* Oxford: Oxford University Press.

Quillian, Lincoln. 1995. "Prejudice as a Response to Perceived Group Threat: Population Composition and Anti-immigrant and Racial Prejudice in Europe." *American Sociological Review* 60:586–611.

Radcliff, Benjamin, and Martin Saiz. 1995. "Race, Turnout, and Public Policy in the American State." *Political Research Quarterly* 48:775–94.

———. 1998. "Labor Organization and Public Policy in the American States." *Journal of Politics* 60 (1): 113–25.

Rank, Mark Robert. 1994. *Living on the Edge: The Realities of Welfare in America.* New York: Columbia University Press.

Rector, Robert, and Janet Youssef. 1999. *The Determinants of Welfare Caseload Decline.* Report No. 99–04. Washington, D.C.: The Heritage Center for Data Analysis, Heritage Foundation.

Reed, Adolph L. 1991. "The Underclass Myth." *Progressive* 55:18–20.

Reed, Adolph Jr. 1999. *Stirring in the Jug: Black Politics in the Post-segregationist Era.* Minneapolis: University of Minnesota Press.

Reed, John Shelton. 1986. *The Enduring South: Subcultural Persistence in Mass Society.* Chapel Hill: University of North Carolina Press.

Reiman, Jeffrey. 1998. *The Rich Get Richer and the Poor Get Prison: Ideology, Class, and Criminal Justice.* Boston: Allyn and Bacon.

Reischauer, Robert. 1986. "Fiscal Federalism in the 1980s: Dismantling or Rationalizing the Great Society." In *The Great Society and Its Legacy,* ed. Marshall Kaplan and Peggy Cuciti. Durham, N.C.: Duke University Press.

Renouvin, Bertrand. 1983. *Charles Maurras, l'Action Française et la question sociale.* Paris: Ars Magna.

Rich, Robert F., and William D. White. 1996. *Health Policy, Federalism, and the American States.* Washington, D.C.: Urban Institute Press.

Ritter, Gerhard. 1983. *Social Welfare in Germany and Britain.* Trans. Kim Traynor. Leamington Spa: Berg.

Roediger, David R. 1991. *The Wages of Whiteness: Race and the Making of the American Working Class.* New York: Verso.

Rogers, Everrett M., and James W. Dearing. 1988. "Agenda Setting Research: Where Had It Been and Where It Is Going?" In *Communication Yearbook,* vol. 11, ed. James A. Anderson. Beverly Hills, Calif.: Sage.

Rogin, Michael. 1996. *Blackface, White Noise: Jewish Immigrants in the Hollywood Melting Pot.* Berkeley and Los Angeles: University of California Press.

Rom, Mark. 1996. "Health and Welfare in the American States: Politics and Policies." In *Politics in the American States: A Comparative Analysis,* ed. Virginia

Gray and Herbert Jacob. 6th ed. Washington, D.C.: Congressional Quarterly Press.

———. 1999. "Transforming State Health and Welfare Programs." In *Politics in the American States: A Comparative Analysis,* ed. Virginia Gray, Russell L. Hanson, and Herbert Jacobs. 7th ed. Washington, D.C.: Congressional Quarterly Press.

Rom, Mark C., Paul E. Peterson, and Kenneth F. Scheve. 1998. "Interstate Competition and Welfare Policy." *Publius* 28, no. 3: 17–37.

Roosevelt, Franklin D. 1938. "Message to the Congress Reviewing the Broad Objectives and Accomplishments of the Administration, June 8, 1934." In *The Public Papers and Addresses of Franklin D. Roosevelt,* ed. Samuel I. Rosenman. New York: Random House.

Rose, Dina, and Todd R. Clear. 1998. "Incarceration, Social Capital, and Crime: Implications for Social Disorganization Theory." *Criminology* 36:441–79.

Rosenblatt, Rand E. 1982. "Legal Entitlement and Welfare Benefits." In *The Politics of Law: A Progressive Critique,* ed. David Kairys. New York: Pantheon.

Rosin, Hanna, and John F. Harris. 1999. "Welfare Reform's Triumph Is Affirmed." *Washington Post,* August 3, p. A1.

Rubinow, I. M. 1934. *The Quest for Security.* New York: H. Holt.

Rueschemeyer, Dietrich, Evelyne Huber Stephens, and John D. Stephens. 1992. *Capitalist Development and Democracy.* Chicago: University of Chicago Press.

Rushefsky, Mark E., and Kant Patel. 1998. *Politics, Power, and Policy Making: The Case of Health Care Reform in the 1990s.* Armonk, N.Y.: M. E. Sharpe.

Ryan, William. 1971. *Blaming the Victim.* New York: Random House.

Saint-Jours, Yves. 1982. "France." In *The Evolution of Social Insurance, 1881–1981: Studies of Germany, France, Great Britain, Austria, and Switzerland,* ed. Peter A. Köhler and Hans F. Zacher. London: Frances Pinter.

Sanders, Heywood T. 1980. "Urban Renewal and the Revitalized City: A Reconsideration of Recent History." In *Urban Revitalization,* ed. Donald B. Rosenthal. Beverly Hills, Calif.: Sage.

Savner, Steve. 2000. "Welfare Reform and Racial/Ethnic Minorities: The Questions to Ask." *Poverty and Race,* 9, no. 4: 3–5.

Schmidt, David D. 1989. *Citizen Lawmakers: The Ballot Initiative Revolution.* Philadelphia: Temple University Press.

Schneider, Anne, and Helen Ingram. 1993. "Social Construction of Target Populations." *American Political Science Review* 87:334–47.

———. 1997. *Policy Design for Democracy.* Lawrence: University of Kansas Press.

Schoeni, Robert F., and Rebecca M. Blank. 2000. "What Has Welfare Reform Accomplished? Impacts on Welfare Participation, Employment, Income, Poverty, and Family Structure." Working Paper No. 7627. Cambridge, Mass.: National Bureau of Economic Research.

Schrag, Peter. 1998. *Paradise Lost: California's Experience, America's Future.* New York: New York Press.

Schram, Sanford F. 1995. *Words of Welfare: The Poverty of Social Science and the Social Science of Poverty.* Minneapolis: University of Minnesota Press.

————. 2000. *After Welfare: The Culture of Postindustrial Social Policy*. New York: New York University Press.

Schram, Sanford F., and Samuel H. Beer, eds. 1999. *Welfare Reform: A Race to the Bottom?* Washington, D.C.: Woodrow Wilson Center Press.

Schram, Sanford F., and Joe Soss. 2001. "Success Stories: Welfare Reform, Policy Discourse, and the Politics of Research." *Annals* 577:49–63.

Schram, Sanford F., and J. Patrick Turbett. 1983. "Civil Disorder and the Welfare Explosion: A Two-Step Process." *American Sociological Review* 48:408–14.

Schuman, Howard, Charlotte Steeh, Lawrence Bobo, and Maria Krysan. 1997. *Racial Attitudes in America: Trends and Interpretations*. Rev. ed. Cambridge: Harvard University Press.

Schumpeter, Joseph A. 1991. "The Crisis of the Tax State." In *Joseph A. Schumpeter: The Economics and Sociology of Capitalism*, ed. Richard Swedberg. Princeton: Princeton University Press.

Sears, David O. 1998. "Racism and Politics in the United States." In *Confronting Racism: The Problem and the Response*, ed. J. Eberhardt and S. T. Fiske. Thousand Oaks, Calif.: Sage.

Sears, David O., Colette van Laar, Mary Carrillo, and Rick Kosterman. 1997. "Is It Really Racism? The Origins of White Americans' Opposition to Race-Targeted Policies." *Public Opinion Quarterly* 61:16–53.

Sears, David O., Jim Sidanius, and Lawrence Bobo, eds. 2000. *Racialized Politics: The Debate about Racism in America*. Chicago: University of Chicago Press.

Semmel, Bernard. 1960. *Imperialism and Social Reform: English Social-Imperial Thought, 1895–1914*. London: George Allen and Unwin.

Shapiro, Ian. 1999. *Democratic Justice*. New Haven: Yale University Press.

Shapiro, Robert Y., and Lawrence R. Jacobs. 1989. "The Relationship between Public Opinion and Public Policy: A Review." *Political Behavior Annual* 2, ed. Samuel Long. Boulder: Westview Press.

Shapiro, Robert Y., and J. T. Young. 1989. "Public Opinion and the Welfare State: The United States in Comparative Perspective." *Political Science Quarterly* 104:59–87.

Sharp, Elaine B. 1999. *The Sometime Connection: Public Opinion and Social Policy*. Albany: State University of New York Press.

Shklar, Judith. 1991. *American Citizenship: The Quest for Inclusion*. Cambridge: Harvard University Press.

Sidanius, Jim, and Felicia Pratto. 1999. *Social Dominance: An Intergroup Theory of Social Hierarchy and Oppression*. Cambridge: Cambridge University Press.

Siegel, Paul M. 1965. "On the Cost of Being a Negro." *Sociological Inquiry* 35 (winter): 41–57.

Sitkoff, Harvard. 1993. *The Struggle for Black Equality*. Rev. ed. New York: Hill and Wang.

Skocpol, Theda. 1988. "The Limits of the New Deal System and the Roots of Contemporary Welfare Dilemmas." In *The Politics of Social Policy in the United States*, ed. Margaret Weir, Ann Shola Orloff, and Theda Skocpol. Princeton: Princeton University Press.

————. 1991. "Targeting within Universalism: Politically Viable Policies to Combat Poverty in the United States." In *The Urban Underclass,* ed. Christopher Jencks and Paul E. Peterson. Washington, D.C.: Brookings Institution Press.

———. 1992. *Protecting Soldiers and Mothers: The Political Origins of Social Policy in the United States.* Cambridge: Harvard University Press.

———. 1995a. "African Americans in U.S. Social Policy." In *Classifying by Race,* ed. Paul E. Peterson. Princeton: Princeton University Press.

———. 1995b. *Social Policy in the United States: Future Possibilities in Historical Perspective.* Princeton: Princeton University Press.

———. 1996. "Welfare: Where Do We Go from Here?" *New Republic,* August 12, 19–22.

———. 1997. *Boomerang: Health Care Reform and the Turn against Government.* New York: Norton.

Skocpol, Theda, Marjorie Abend-Wein, Christopher Howard, and Susan Goodrich Lehmann. 1993. "Women's Associations and the Enactment of Mothers' Pensions." *American Political Science Review* 87:686–701.

Skogan, Wesley G. 1996. "Crime and Punishment." In *Politics in the American States: A Comparative Analysis,* ed. Virginia Gray and Herbert Jacob. 6th ed. Washington, D.C.: Congressional Quarterly Press.

Smith, David Barton. 1999. *Health Care Divided: Race and Healing a Nation.* Ann Arbor: University of Michigan Press.

Smith, Rogers M. 1993. "Beyond Tocqueville, Myrdal, and Hartz: The Multiple Traditions in America." *American Political Science Review* 87:549–66.

———. 1997. *Civic Ideals: Conflicting Visions of Citizenship in U.S. History.* New Haven: Yale University Press.

Smith, Tom W. 1987a. "That Which We Call Welfare by Any Other Name Would Smell Sweeter: An Analysis of the Impact of Question Wording on Response Patterns." *Public Opinion Quarterly* 51:75–83.

———. 1987b. "The Welfare State in Cross-National Perspective." *Public Opinion Quarterly* 51:404–21.

Sniderman, Paul M., and E. G. Carmines. 1997. *Reaching Beyond Race.* Cambridge: Harvard University Press.

Sniderman, Paul M., and Thomas Piazza. 1993. *The Scar of Race.* Cambridge: Harvard University Press.

Sniderman, Paul M., and Philip E. Tetlock. 1986. "Symbolic Racism: Problems of Motive Attribution in Political Analysis." *Journal of Social Issues* 42:129–50.

Solinger, Rickie. 1992. *Wake Up Little Susie: Single Pregnancy and Race before Roe v. Wade.* New York: Routledge.

Soss, Joe. 2000. *Unwanted Claims: The Politics of Participation in the U.S. Welfare System.* Ann Arbor: University of Michigan Press.

Soss, Joe, Sanford F. Schram, Thomas P. Vartanian, and Erin O'Brien. 2001. "Setting the Terms of Relief: Explaining State Policy Choices in the Devolution Revolution." *American Journal of Political Science* 45:378–403.

Soule, Sarah A., and Yvonne Zylan. 1997. "Runaway Train? The Diffusion of State-Level Reform in ADC/AFDC Eligibility Requirements, 1950–1967." *American Journal of Sociology* 103:733–62.

Sparks, Holloway. 1997. "Dissident Citizenship: Democratic Theory, Political Courage, and Activist Women." *Hypatia* 12, no. 4: 74–109.

Squire, Peverill. 1992. "Legislative Professionalization and Membership Diversity in State Legislatures." *Legislative Studies Quarterly* 17, no. 1: 69–80.

Stein, Robert M., Stephanie Shirley Post, and Allison Rinden. 2000. "Reconciling Context and Contact Effects on Racial Attitudes." *Political Research Quarterly* 53:285–303.

Steinmo, Sven, and Jon Watts. 1995. "It's the Institutions, Stupid! Why Comprehensive National Health Insurance Always Fails in America." *Journal of Health Politics, Policy, and Law* 20, no. 2: 329–72.

Sternhell, Zeev. 1986. *Neither Right nor Left: Fascist Ideology in France.* Trans. David Maisel. Berkeley and Los Angeles: University of California Press.

Stimson, James A., Michael B. Mackuen, and Robert S. Erikson. 1995. "Dynamic Representation." *American Political Science Review* 89:543–65.

Stoesz, David. 2000. *A Poverty of Imagination: Bootstrap Capitalism, Sequel to Welfare Reform.* Madison: University of Wisconsin Press.

Sullivan, John L. 1973. "Political Correlates of Social, Economic, and Religious Diversity in the American States." *Journal of Politics* 35:70–84.

Suro, Roberto. 1999. *Strangers Among Us: Latinos' Lives in a Changing America.* New York: Vintage Books.

Suttles, Gerald D., and Mayer N. Zald, eds. 1985. *The Challenge of Social Control: Citizenship and Institution-Building in Modern Society.* Norwood, N.J.: Aldex.

Tannenbaum, Frank. 1946. *Slave and Citizen: The Negro in the Americas.* New York: Alfred A. Knopf.

Taylor, Marylee C. 1998. "The Effect of Racial Composition on Racial Attitudes of Whites." *American Sociological Review* 63:512–35.

Tocqueville, Alexis de. 1958. *Democracy in America.* Ed. Richard D. Heffner. New York: New American Library.

Tolbert, Caroline J., and Rodney E. Hero. 1996. "Race/Ethnicity and Direct Democracy: An Analysis of California's Illegal Immigration Initiative." *Journal of Politics* 58:806–18.

———. 2001. "Facing Diversity: Racial/Ethnic Context and Social Policy Change." *Political Research Quarterly.* 54:571–605.

Tolbert, Caroline J., and Trudy Steuernagel. 2001. "State Ballot Initiatives and Universal Health Care: The Case of Massachusetts." Paper presented at the Annual Meeting of the Midwest Political Science Association, Chicago, April.

Tolbert, Caroline, David Lowenstein, and Todd Donovan. 1998. "Election Law and Rules for Using Initiatives." In *Citizens as Legislators: Direct Democracy in the United States,* ed. Shawn Bolwer, Todd Donovan, and Caroline Tolbert. Columbus: Ohio State University Press.

Tompkins, R. F. 1981. *The Impact of Federal Aid on the City of Cleveland.* Federal Aid Case Studies No. 10. Washington, D.C.: Brookings Institution Press.

Trattner, Walter I. 1999. *From Poor Law to Welfare State: A History of Social Welfare in America.* 6th ed. New York: Free Press.

Tryneski, John. 2001. Executive editor, University of Chicago Press. Interview by Sanford F. Schram, April 20.

Tumulty, Brian. 1994. "Delaware Woman Tells How She Got Off Welfare Rolls." Gannett News Service, January 11.

Turner, Bobie Green. 1993. *Federal/State Aid to Dependent Children Program and Its Benefits to Black Children in America, 1935–1985.* New York: Garland.

Turner, Frederick Jackson. 1894. "Significance of the Frontier in American History." *Annual Report of the American Historical Society, 1893.* Washington, D.C.: U.S. Government Printing Office.

Turner, Margery A., Michael Fix, and Raymond J. Stuyk. 1991. *Opportunities Denied, Opportunities Diminished: Racial Discrimination in Hiring.* Washington, D.C.: Urban Institute Press.

U.S. Department of Commerce, Bureau of the Census. 1961. *Statistical Abstract of the United States, 1960.* Washington, D.C.: U.S. Government Printing Office.

———. 1990. *Current Population Survey, March 1990.* Washington, D.C.: Department of Commerce.

———. 1992. *State Government Employment and Payroll, October 1992.* Washington, D.C.: U.S. Government Printing Office.

———. 1993. *Statistical Abstract of the United Sates: 1993.* Washington, D.C.: U.S. Government Printing Office.

———. 1995. *Statistical Abstract of the United States: 1995.* Washington, D.C.: U.S. Government Printing Office.

———. 1996. *Current Population Survey: Voter Supplement File.* Washington, D.C.: U.S. Government Printing Office.

———. 1998. *Statistical Abstract of the United States.* Washington, D.C.: U.S. Government Printing Office.

———. 1999. *Statistical Abstract of the United States.* Washington, D.C.: U.S. Government Printing Office.

U.S. Department of Health and Human Services. 1994. Office of Planning, Research, and Evaluation. *Characteristics and Financial Circumstances of AFDC Recipients.* Washington, D.C.: U.S. Government Printing Office.

———. 1995. Office of Family Assistance. "Characteristics and Financial Circumstances of AFDC Recipients Report FY1995." <http://www.acf.dhhs.gov/programs/ofa/cont95.htm>.

———. 1996. *Major Provisions of the Personal Responsibility and Work Opportunity Reconciliation Act of 1996 (P.L. 104–193).* Washington, D.C.: U.S. Government Printing Office.

———. 1997. *Indicators of Welfare Dependence: Annual Report to Congress.* Washington, D.C.: U.S. Government Printing Office.

———. 1999. "HHS Office for Civil Rights Issues Guidance on Civil Rights Laws and Welfare Reform." August 27. <http://www.hhs.gov/progorg/ocr.octranfpr.htm>.

———. 2000a. "HHS Awards Welfare High Performance Bonuses: Higher Increases in Job Placements and Earnings Reported." December 16. <http://www.hhs.gov/news/press/2000pres>.

———. 2000b. Administration for Children and Families, Office of Planning, Research and Evaluation. *Characteristics and Financial Circumstances of TANF Recipients: Fiscal Year 1998.* <http://www.acf.dhhs.gov/programs/opre/characteristics/fy98/sum.htm>.

————. 2000c. Administration for Children and Families, Office of Planning, Research and Evaluation. *Characteristics and Financial Circumstances of TANF Recipients: Fiscal Year 1999.* <http://www.acf.dhhs.gov/programs /opre /characteristics/fy99/analysis.htm>.

————. 2000d. Administration for Children and Families, Office of Planning, Research and Evaluation. *Temporary Assistance for Needy Families (TANF) Program.* Third Annual Report to Congress. Washington, D.C.: U.S. Government Printing Office.

U.S. Department of Health, Education and Welfare. 1947. *Handbook of Public Assistance Administration.* Part 4. Item 2300. Washington, D.C., September 3.

U.S. Department of Justice. 1992. Bureau of Justice Statistics.

U.S. Department of Labor. 1933. *Mother's Aid, 1931.* Children's Bureau Publication No. 220. Washington, D.C.

————. 1934. *A Tabular Summary of State Laws Relating to Public Aid to Children in Their Own Homes.* Chart No. 3. Children's Bureau, Washington, D.C., January.

————. 1978. *65th Annual Report: Fiscal Year 1977.* Washington, D.C.: U.S. Government Printing Office.

U.S. General Accounting Office. 1998. *Welfare Reform: Early Fiscal Effects of the TANF Block Grants.* Report to the Chairman, Subcommittee on Human Resources, Committee on Ways and Means, House of Representatives. GAO/AIMD-98-137. Washington, D.C.: U.S. Government Printing Office.

U.S. House of Representatives. 1995a. Committee on Economic and Educational Opportunities. *Contract with America: Hearing on Welfare Reform.* 104th Cong., 1st sess., January 18.

————. 1995b. Committee on Ways and Means, Subcommittee on Human Resources. *Contract with America—Welfare Reform.* 104th Cong., 1st sess. February 2.

————. 1995c. Committee on Ways and Means, Subcommittee on Human Resources. *Welfare Reform Success Stories.* 104th Cong., 1st sess. December 6.

————. 1996a. *Background Material and Data on Programs within the Jurisdiction of the Committee on Ways and Means* (Green Book). Washington, D.C.: U.S. Government Printing Office.

————. 1996b. Committee on Ways and Means, Subcommittee on Human Resources. *Causes of Poverty, with a Focus on Out-of-Wedlock Births.* 104th Cong., 2d sess., March 12.

————. 2000. *Background Material and Data on Programs within the Jurisdiction of the Committee on Ways and Means* (Green Book). Washington, D.C.: U.S. Government Printing Office.

U.S. Senate. 1995a. Committee on Finance. *Broad Policy Goals of Welfare Reform.* 104th Cong. 1st sess., March 9.

————. 1995b. Committee on Finance. "Teen Parents and Welfare Reform." 104th Cong., 1st sess., March 14.

————. 1995c. Committee on Labor and Human Resources. "Impact of Welfare

Reform on Children and Their Families." 104th Cong., 1st sess., February 28–March 1.

U.S. Social Security Board. 1937. *Social Security in America: The Factual Background of the Social Security Act as Summarized from Staff Reports to the Committee on Economic Security.* Social Security Publication No. 20. Washington, D.C.: U.S. Government Printing Office.

Valelly, Richard M. 1995. "National Parties and Racial Disenfranchisement." In *Classifying by Race,* ed. Paul E. Peterson. Princeton: Princeton University Press.

Voss, D. Stephen. 1996. "Beyond Racial Threat: Failure of an Old Hypothesis in the New South." *Journal of Politics* 58:1156–70.

Walker, Jack L. 1969. "The Diffusion of Innovations among the American States." *American Political Science Review* 63:880–99.

———. 1971. "Innovation in State Politics." In *Politics in the American States: A Comparative Analysis,* ed. Herbert Jacob and Kenneth N. Vines. 2d ed. Boston: Little, Brown.

Walton, Hanes. 1985. *Invisible Politics: Black Political Behavior.* Albany: State University of New York Press.

Ward, Deborah Elizabeth. 2000. "Mothers' Pensions: The Institutional Legacy of the American Welfare State." Ph.D. diss., Columbia University.

Warner, Amos. 1894. *American Charities: A Study in Philanthropy and Economics.* New York: T. Y. Crowell and Company.

"Deflecting Welfare Applicants." 1998. *Washington Post,* August 17, A18.

Weaver, R. Kent. 2000. *Ending Welfare as We Know It.* Washington, D.C.: Brookings Institution Press.

Weaver, R. Kent, Robert Shapiro, and Lawrence R. Jacobs. 1995. "The Polls-Trends: Welfare." *Public Opinion Quarterly* 59:606–27.

Weber, Eugen. 1976. *Peasants into Frenchmen: The Modernization of Rural France, 1870–1914.* Stanford: Stanford University Press.

Weintrob, Lori Robin. 1996. "From Fraternity to Solidarity: Mutual Aid, Popular Sociability, and Social Reform in France, 1880–1914." Ph.D. diss., University of California, Los Angeles.

Weir, Margaret. 1999. "Welfare Reform and the Political Geography of Poverty." In *Welfare Reform: A Race to the Bottom?* ed. Sanford F. Schram and Samuel H. Beer. Washington, D.C.: Woodrow Wilson Center Press.

Weir, Margaret, Ann Shola Orloff, and Theda Skocpol, eds. 1988. *The Politics of Social Policy.* Princeton: Princeton University Press.

Weiss, Nancy J. 1983. *Farewell to the Party of Lincoln: Black Politics in the Age of FDR.* Princeton: Princeton University Press.

Weissert, Carol, and William Weissert. 1998. *Governing Health: The Politics of Health Policy.* Baltimore: John Hopkins University Press.

Welfare Law Center. 1996. *Welfare Myths: Fact or Fiction? Exploring the Truth about Welfare.* New York: Welfare Law Center. <http://www.welfarelaw.org/mythtoc.html> (last accessed June 9, 2001).

"Welfare Mom Works Hard to Get Off Handout Treadmill." 1996. *Morning Edition,* National Public Radio, January 3.

White, Steven K. 1997. "Narratives of the Welfare State." *Theory and Event* 1, no. 2. <http://muse.jhn.edu/journals/theory_and_event/001/1.2White.html>.

Wilensky, Harold. 1975. *The Welfare State and Equality: Structural and Ideological Roots of Public Expenditures.* Berkeley and Los Angeles: University of California Press.

Wilhoit, G. Cleveland, and David H. Weaver. 1991. *The American Journalist: A Portrait of U.S. News People and Their Work.* Bloomington: Indiana University Press.

Williams, Linda Faye. 1998. "Race and the Politics of Social Policy." In *The Social Divide: Political Parties and the Future of Activist Government,* ed. Margaret Weir. Washington, D.C.: Brookings Institution; New York: Russell Sage Foundation.

Williams, Linda. 2001. *Playing the Race Card: Melodramas of Black and White from Uncle Tom to O. J. Simpson.* Princeton: Princeton University Press.

Williams, Lucy. 1995. "Race, Rat Bites, and Unfit Mothers: How Media Discourse Informs Welfare Legislation Debate." *Fordham Urban Law Journal* 22:1159–96.

———. 1997. *Decades of Distortion: The Right's Thirty-Year Assault on Welfare.* Boston: Political Research Associates.

Wilson, James Q., and Edward Banfield. 1964. "Public Regardingness as a Value Premise in Voting Behavior." *American Political Science Review* 58:876–87.

———. 1971. "Political Ethos Revisited." *American Political Science Review* 65:1048–62.

Wilson, William Julius. 1987. *The Truly Disadvantaged: The Inner City, the Underclass, and Public Policy.* Chicago: University of Chicago Press.

———. 1996. *When Work Disappears: The World of the New Urban Poor.* New York: Knopf.

Wilson, William Julius, and Katherine M. Neckerman. 1984. "Poverty and Family Structure: The Widening Gap between Evidence and Public Policy Issues." Conference paper, "Poverty and Policy: Retrospect and Prospects," Williamsburg, Va. Institute for Research on Poverty, University of Wisconsin, Madison.

Wirt, Frederick. 1990. "Education." In *Politics in the American States: A Comparative Analysis,* ed. Virginia Gray, Herbert Jacob, and Robert B. Albritton. 5th ed. Glenview, Ill.: Scott, Foresman.

Wlezien, Christopher. 1995. "The Public as Thermometer: Dynamics of Preferences for Public Spending." *American Journal of Political Science* 39:981–1000.

Wolfinger, Raymond. 1974. *The Politics of Progress.* Englewood Cliffs, N.J.: Prentice-Hall.

Woodward, C. Vann. 1974. *The Strange Career of Jim Crow.* 3d ed. New York: .

Wright, Gerald C. 1976. "Racism and Welfare Policy in America." *Social Science Quarterly* 57:718–30.

Wright, Gerald C., Robert S. Erikson, and John P. McIver. 1987. "Public Opinion and Policy Liberalism in the American States." *American Journal of Political Science* 31:980–1001.

References

Wu, Frank H. 2001. *Yellow: Race in America Beyond Black and White*. New York: Basic Books.

Yepsen, David. 1995. "Gramm Proposes Making Dependents Earn Their Keep." *Des Moines Register*, August 7.

Young, Iris Marion. 1993. "Justice and Communicative Democracy." In *Radical Philosophy: Tradition, Counter-tradition, Politics*, ed. Roger S. Gottlieb. Philadelphia: Temple University Press.

———. 1996. "Communication and the Other: Beyond Deliberative Democracy." In *Democracy and Difference: Contesting the Boundaries of the Political*, ed. Seyla Benhabib. Princeton: Princeton University Press.

———. 2000. *Inclusion and Democracy*. Oxford: Oxford University Press.

Young, R. P., and J. S. Burstein. 1995. "Federalism and the Demise of Prescriptive Racism in the United States." *Studies in American Political Development* 9, no. 1: 1–54.

Zaller, John. 1992. *The Nature and Origins of Mass Opinion*. Cambridge: Cambridge University Press.

Zedlewski, Sheila R., and Donald W. Alderson. 2001. "Before and after Reform: How Have Families on Welfare Changed?" Urban Institute. <http://newfederalism.urban.org/html/series_b/b32/b32.html>.

Zelman, Walter A., and Robert A. Berenson. 1998. *The Managed Care Blues and How to Cure Them*. Washington, D.C.: Georgetown University Press.

Ziliak, James P., David N. Figlio, Elizabeth E. Davis, and Laura S. Connolly. 1997. "Accounting for the Decline in AFDC Caseloads: Welfare Reform or Economic Growth?" Institute for Research on Poverty, Discussion Paper No. 1151–97.

Žižek, Slavoj. 1997. "Multiculturalism, or, the Cultural Logic of Multinational Capitalism." *New Left Review* 225 (September–October): 28–29.

Contributors

JAMES M. AVERY is a doctoral candidate in the Department of Political Science at the University of Kentucky. His primary interests are in political behavior, the media, and race.

MICHAEL K. BROWN is Professor of Politics at the University of California at Santa Cruz, where he has taught since 1982. He is the author of *Race, Money, and the American Welfare State* (1999) and *Working the Street: Police Discretion and the Dilemmas of Reform* (1988). He also edited and contributed to *Remaking the Welfare State: Retrenchment and Social Policy in America and Europe* (1988). He is coauthor of *Whitewashing Race: Color-Blind Policies in a Color-Conscious America* (forthcoming).

RICHARD C. FORDING is Associate Professor of Political Science at the University of Kentucky. His primary teaching and research interests include public policy (welfare, criminal justice), state politics, social movements, West European politics, and quantitative methodology. He is the author or coauthor of articles appearing in *American Political Science Review*, *American Journal of Political Science*, *Journal of Politics*, *Social Science Quarterly*, *Comparative Political Studies*, *Political Behavior*, and *European Journal of Political Research*.

MARTIN GILENS is Associate Professor of Political Science and Associate Director of the Institute for Social Science Research at UCLA. He is the author of *Why Americans Hate Welfare: Race, Media, and the Politics of Antipoverty Policy* (1999). He has also published research on media, race, gender, and welfare politics in the *American Political Science Review*, *American Journal of Political Science*, *Journal of Politics*, *British Journal of Political Science*, *Public Opinion Quarterly*, and *Berkeley Journal of Sociology*. He holds a Ph.D. in sociology from the University of California Berkeley and taught at Yale University before joining the faculty at UCLA. His research has been supported by grants from the National Science Foundation and the Social Science Research Council.

SUSAN TINSLEY GOODEN is Associate Professor in the Center for Public Administration and Policy (CPAP) and Director of the Race and Social Policy Research

Center at Virginia Tech. She conducts research in the area of welfare policy with an emphasis on race and welfare; private and non-profit service delivery; and rural welfare policy. Also, she is a consultant to the Manpower Demonstration Research Corporation (MDRC), a non-profit, employment and training research firm based in New York, New York. She is the author or coauthor of articles appearing in the *Public Administration Review, Harvard Journal of African American Public Policy, Journal of Public Management and Social Policy, Review of Public Personnel Administration,* and other journals.

RODNEY E. HERO is Packey J. Dee Professor of American Democracy in the Department of Political Science at the University of Notre Dame. His research and teaching interests are in U.S. democracy and governance, particularly as understood through the analytical lenses of ethnic/racial politics and state-local government/federalism. His major publications include *Faces of Inequality: Social Diversity in American Politics* (1998), and *Latinos and the U.S. Political System: Two-Tiered Pluralism* (1992).

MARTIN JOHNSON is Assistant Professor of Political Science, University of California, Riverside. His interests focus on the influence of social context on public opinion, voting behavior, and public policy. He is author or coauthor of articles appearing in *American Journal of Political Science, Electoral Studies* and *State Politics and Policy Quarterly.* His research on state public opinion has received awards from the National Opinion Research Center and the State Politics and Policy Section of the American Political Science Association.

ROBERT C. LIEBERMAN is Associate Professor of Political Science and Public Affairs at Columbia University. He is the author of *Shifting the Color Line: Race and the American Welfare State* (1998), which won several major book awards, as well as numerous articles about race, welfare policy, and political institutions.

ERIN O'BRIEN is a doctoral candidate in the Department of Government in the School of Public Affairs at American University. She is the coauthor of research appearing in *American Journal of Political Science.*

MARK PEFFLEY is Professor of Political Science at the University of Kentucky. His primary teaching and research interests have focused on public opinion, the mass media, and electoral behavior. His research has appeared in *American Political Science Review, American Journal of Political Science, Journal of Politics, International Studies Quarterly, American Politics Quarterly, Political Behavior, Political Communications,* and *Political Research Quarterly.* He is also coeditor (with Jon Hurwitz) of *Perception and Prejudice: Race and Politics in the U.S.* (1998).

FRANCES FOX PIVEN is Distinguished University Professor at the Graduate School and University Center of the City University of New York. Her many books written with Richard Cloward include *Why Americans Still Don't Vote* (2000), *The Breaking of the American Social Compact* (1997), *Regulating the Poor* (updated 1993), *The New Class War* (1986), and *Poor People's Movements* (1977).

SANFORD F. SCHRAM teaches social theory and policy in the Graduate School of Social Work and Social Research at Bryn Mawr College. He is the author of *Praxis for the Poor: Piven and Cloward and the Future of Social Science in Social Welfare* (2002), *After Welfare: The Culture of Postindustrial Social Policy* (2000) and *Words of Welfare: The Poverty of Social Science and the Social Science of Poverty* (1995) which won the Michael Harrington Award from the American Political Science Association. He has also coedited, with Samuel Beer, *Welfare Reform: A Race to the Bottom?* (1999).

JOE SOSS is Associate Professor of Government in the School of Public Affairs at American University. He is the author of *Unwanted Claims: The Politics of Participation in the U.S. Welfare System* (2000). He is the author or coauthor of articles appearing in *American Political Science Review, American Journal of Political Science, Political Research Quarterly, Politics & Society, Administration & Society, Publius, American Journal of Sociology & Social Welfare, Political Communication,* and *Public Opinion Quarterly.*

HOLLOWAY SPARKS is Assistant Professor of Political Science at Pennsylvania State University. Her research has appeared in *Hypatia: A Journal of Feminist Philosophy* and has been supported by a grant from the Center for American Women and Politics at Rutgers University. She is currently completing a manuscript on the dissident citizenship of women activists in the civil rights and welfare rights movements.

GERTRUDE A. STEUERNAGEL is Professor of Political Science at Kent State University. She is co-author of *Women and Political Participation: Cultural Change in the Political Arena* (1997) and *Women and Public Policy: A Revolution in Progress* (2d ed, 1999).

CAROLINE J. TOLBERT is Assistant Professor of Political Science and Public Policy at Kent State University. She is coeditor of *Citizens as Legislators: Direct Democracy in the United States* (1998) and author of three chapters in that volume. She is author or coauthor of articles appearing in the *American Journal of Political Science, Journal of Politics, Comparative Political Studies, Women and Politics, Political Research Quarterly, American Politics Research,* and *Political Science Quarterly.* She is coauthor of the forthcoming book *Beyond the Digital Divide.*

THOMAS P. VARTANIAN is Associate Professor in the Graduate School of Social Work and Social Research at Bryn Mawr College. He has published numerous articles on poverty and welfare in the *Social Service Review,* the *Journal of Marriage and the Family,* and other journals. He is currently conducting studies on the long-term effects of food and nutrition programs and the delinking of Medicaid and food stamps from cash assistance.

Name Index

Subject Index

ADC (Aid to Dependent Children), 58, 59, 74, 75, 78, 104, 105, 227, 256–60, 326

AFDC (Aid to Families with Dependent Children; *see also* welfare policy), 4, 8, 14, 17, 24, 37, 47–54, 59–61, 63–64, 69, 72, 74, 77, 79–83, 102, 139, 142, 152, 161, 180–81, 184, 189, 191–92, 225–27, 230–33, 264, 279, 326, 328, 331; benefit levels, 82, 157; caseload, 73, 76, 83, 88, 90, 91, 93, 235, 244; dependency, 83, 87; discrimination (*see also* racial bias), 78, 255–64; history of, 74–75, 83, 255–64; racial context, 78–79, 88, 90–91, 104; waivers, 8, 73, 77, 80, 81, 83–94, 235, 243

affirmative action, 127, 135

AFL-CIO (American Federation of Labor and Congress of Industrial Organizations), 107

African Americans (*see also* race), 5, 6, 75, 78, 238; civil rights (*see also* civil rights), 56; criminal justice policy, 308–10; Democratic party, 24; discrimination (*see also* racial bias; racial prejudice; racial subordination; racism), 59, 240, 242, 255–75, 323; disenfranchisement, 33; education policy, 304–9; electoral politics, 24, 286; health care policy, 279–96; media content (*see also* mass media), 9, 11, 101–27, 133, 134;

migration to North, 104–5; mobilization, 24, 83, 260; party politics, 24, 45–46; political coalitions, 24, 43–44; political representation, 88, 93–94; poverty, 49, 101, 198–99, 257; public discourse, 14; residential segregation (*see also* racial segregation), 59; social policy, 23, 24, 34, 58, 298–319; the South (*see also* South, the), 17, 27, 31, 35, 78, 256; stereotypes of (*see also* racial stereotypes), 8, 74, 90, 132; welfare population (*see also* welfare and race), 18, 81, 196–220, 235; women, 47–50, 59, 61, 68–69, 171–93

Alabama, 262, 305

American Association of Retired Persons, 288

American Medical Association, 284

American National Election Study, 237

American political development, 28

Appalachia, 103, 105

Arizona, 268, 285

Arkansas, 260

Asians, 3, 286, 290–91, 295–96

Austria, 35, 39

ballot initiatives. *See* direct democracy; state referenda

Black Belt, the, 27

Black Panthers, 108

black political power, 82, 88, 93